MAL GOODE
REPORTING

UNIVERSITY OF PITTSBURGH PRESS

MAL GOODE

THE LIFE AND WORK OF A
BLACK BROADCAST TRAILBLAZER

LIANN TSOUKAS
AND ROB RUCK

REPORTING

Published by the University of Pittsburgh Press, Pittsburgh, Pa., 15260
This paperback edition, Copyright © 2025, University of Pittsburgh Press
Copyright © 2024, University of Pittsburgh Press
All rights reserved
Manufactured in the United States of America
Printed on acid-free paper
10 9 8 7 6 5 4 3 2 1

Cataloging-in-Publication data is available from the Library of Congress

ISBN 13: 978-0-8229-6745-3
ISBN 10: 0-8229-6745-6

COVER ART: Malvin Russell Goode portrait, the first Black network
news correspondent for ABC television. (Photo by Disney General
Entertainment Content via Getty Images). Photographer/© ABC/Getty
Images.

COVER DESIGN: Alex Wolfe

FOR SCOTT
AND MAGGIE

CONTENTS

AUTHORS' NOTE ON SOURCES AND LANGUAGE

MAL GOODE WAS A STORYTELLER WHO CONVEYED HIS tales on the air, in hundreds of talks and interviews, and in writing. Many versions of those stories are in the Mal Goode Papers at the University of Missouri Archives, Ellis Library, Columbia. Those papers include drafts of chapters for an unfinished memoir, copies of his speeches, interviews, ABC memos and reports, audio and video recordings, and correspondence. When confronted by multiple versions of the same story we selected the language that we thought best captured him. We kept the language he chose to use and capitalized words as he did when he wrote them.

LIST OF ABBREVIATIONS

AAI	African-American Institute
ABC	American BroadcastingCompany
AME	African Methodist Episcopal
CIA	Central Intelligence Agency
COINTEL	Counter-Intelligence Program
CORE	Congress of Racial Equality
FBI	Federal Bureau of Investigation
FROGS	Friendly Rivalry Often Generates Success
HBCU	Historically Black College or University
KKK	Ku Klux Klan
LOPs	lines of progression
MFDP	Mississippi Freedom Democratic Party
MVP	Most Valuable Player (in baseball)
NAACP	National Association for the Advancement of Colored People
NABJ	National Association of Black Journalists
NBC	National Broadcasting Company
NBN	National Black Network
NCAA	National Collegiate Athletic Association
NFL	National Football League
NL	Negro Leagues
NLF	National Liberation Front, South Vietnam
NNN	National Negro Network
NOI	Nation of Islam
OAAU	Organization of Afro-American Unity
OPHR	Olympic Project for Human Rights
PUSH	People United to Save Humanity
R&B	rhythm and blues
RTDNA	Radio-Television Directors News Association

SCLC	Southern Christian Leadership Conference
SNCC	Student Nonviolent Coordinating Committee
UCLA	University of California–Los Angeles
UNIA	Universal Negro Improvement Association
USIA	US Information Agency
USIS	US Information Service
USOC	US Olympic Committee
YMCA	Young Men's Christian Association
YWCA	Young Women's Christian Association

MAL GOODE
REPORTING

INTRODUCTION

ON OCTOBER 28, 1962, AMERICANS WERE STUNNED WHEN broadcasters interrupted scheduled programing to report the unthinkable. The world was careening toward a nuclear confrontation. Just six days before, President John F. Kennedy had addressed the nation, warning that aerial surveillance of Cuba, the Caribbean island just ninety miles from Florida, confirmed the presence of a Soviet nuclear strike capability.[1] The United States, he announced, had issued an ultimatum to the Union of Soviet Socialist Republics to remove those missiles. After days of back-channel talks, UN Security Council sessions, and Cuban anti-aircraft downing a U-2 aircraft, the Cold War confrontation was about to climax.

As US warships raced to intercept Soviet vessels heading for Cuban waters, Americans perched on couches and kitchen chairs, watching the crisis unfold on television and listening to radio updates. Schoolchildren practiced "duck and cover" drills and the nation's armed forces mobilized. When ABC broke into programming with updates on the standoff, there was a new face on the screen and a new voice on the radio. A tall, distinguished-looking African American called Mal Goode calmly delivered one report after another with the United Nations building looming behind him. Never before had the world come so close to nuclear warfare, and never before had a Black man conveyed breaking news for a national network. The threat of war soon faded, but Mal Goode wasn't going anywhere.

Goode made history that day, and the television and radio spots he delivered during the Cuban Missile Crisis were a prologue to his television career, not a one-off. A fixture on ABC News for the next decade, he chipped away at one of media's most stubbornly segregated formats by interpreting the news for a national audience. Goode's sense of mission was clear: to explain the racial currents of a nation in turmoil, inject an African American perspective into the conversation, serve his profession, and address all TV viewers.

But Goode's dramatic career launch was inadvertent. ABC's decision in the summer of 1962 was simply to hire a Black correspondent. Network executives had not thought through what a barrier-breaking national correspondent would do on ABC, much less how and why his presence would matter. The hire was no guarantee that Goode would be on air. His assignment to the United Nations, where most correspondents remained tucked away on what was considered one of least interesting beats for the TV audience, meant that viewers might not catch a glimpse of the historic hire. However, the United Nations was central during the confrontation over Cuba for thirteen harrowing days in October 1962. With tensions rising, ABC news director Jim Hagerty was unable to reach the network's vacationing chief UN correspondent John MacVane. Hagerty did not anticipate that Mal Goode, on the job for less than two months, would easily slide into the role played by MacVane, a legendary foreign correspondent. But Goode did, delivering seventeen on-air reports. He charted the contours of the crisis and the relief of resolution to a weary audience with a calm cool-headed delivery.

ABC, then lagging behind CBS and NBC in the ratings, had gambled that Goode, the grandson of enslaved people, could attract an African American audience without alienating white viewers. His success was all the more extraordinary given his personal saga.

Before Mal Goode's parents met, they came north separately from two different parts of Virginia during the Great Migration. Mal was born in Virginia and the family frequently traveled between there and Pittsburgh, but he had lived in Pittsburgh from the age of eight and worked there until 1962. From a radio studio on the city's Hill District, which Claude McKay had dubbed the crossroads of the world, Goode's basso profundo voice resonated throughout western Pennsylvania. Challenging segregation wherever he saw it and contradicting police accounts of Black men who died in custody, Goode became Black Pittsburgh's paladin. He celebrated the victories of those who broke through by roaring "And the walls came tumbling down!" But Goode chafed at his own inability to break into television until his friend Jackie Robinson dared ABC to give him a chance.

Goode's career, first in Pittsburgh and then with a national network, put him center stage as the civil rights campaign to dismantle segregation reached a tipping point during the 1950s and 1960s. His coverage was tough but fair. Willing to confront the likes of Alabama governor George Wallace and leaders of the American Nazi Party, Goode broke ground in broadcast journalism. He was on the street during the urban rebellions of the 1960s, after Malcolm X's assassination, and during Martin Luther King Jr.'s final campaign. Whether covering African independence struggles, national political conventions, or Atlanta, Georgia, which he profiled in a 1969 documentary as a city "too busy to hate," he brought his take on the struggle for equality to a national audience.

Goode crossed racial divides but also traversed fault lines within Black America. In Homestead, the Monongahela River steel town where he grew up, Goode straddled the rift between Hilltop, an integrated neighborhood where better-off African Americans resided, and the Ward, the crowded, fetid tenements in the shadow of the steel mill that became home to migrants from the Deep South. At Clark Memorial Church, he absorbed the social gospel of racial uplift that many established women and men embraced. But he was just as comfortable in storefront churches in the Ward that ministered to recent migrants from the Black Belt. At ease on the streets of the Hill District he roamed as a juvenile probation officer, he was also sure of himself at the posh Loendi Club or at board meetings at the Centre Avenue YMCA and the city's Housing Authority.

Goode's composure and confidence were shaped by his up-bringing. His educated and commanding mother, Mary, ran a strict and loving home that was intended to imbue the six children with Christian morals and strategies for advancement. His father Bill's admonition: "You're no better than anyone else and no one is any better than you. Now go out and prove it," was his marching order. He took those words to heart, moving easily from ghetto streets to the mayor's office, never turning his back on those who struggled. Deeply empathetic, he gave voice to their grievances and hopes. Mal Goode saw himself as their advocate and stood his ground when they were treated as less than equal. Nor did he quietly accept personal affront.

While regarded as "the dean of African American broadcast journalism," Mal Goode was already fifty-four years old when he made prime time.[2] The half century he lived in Pittsburgh as well as his family's roots in slavery and the Great Migration are critical to his story. They shaped his perspective and demeanor. Goode grew up in the wake of Booker T. Washington and W. E. B. Du Bois. He came of age during the 1920s when the New Negro, the Harlem Renaissance, Black women's club movement, and Marcus Garvey's Universal Negro Improvement Association showcased northern communities in the wake of the migration. He worked at the *Pittsburgh Courier* and on the radio during the late 1940s and 1950s before joining ABC in 1962. Well known in civil rights circles, he assumed a greater profile in the movement as Martin Luther King Jr., Malcolm X, and the Black Panthers roiled the waters. Mal was a familiar face and was trusted by most factions, especially King and Malcolm. First exposed to Africa as a youth attending films and talks at Homestead's Clark Memorial Church, he learned more about the continent while at the *Courier*. Soon after joining ABC, the State Department asked him to conduct seminars for the media in Ethiopia, Tanganyika, and Nigeria. Encountering Pan Africanism and the turmoil of post-independence politics, Goode maintained a focus on Africa during his tenure at

ABC and the United Nations. It's possible that no other African American spoke to more people about Africa than he did during the years he was based at the United Nations. Africa was far from the only part of the world Goode spoke about. In addition to his television and radio work, he addressed a range of audiences almost weekly for forty years. His activism and visibility at ABC prompted the slow integration of network news; it also showcased a presence never before seen or heard on a national network.

Goode's family, church, community, the University of Pittsburgh, and his experience on the job, especially twelve years on night turn at the Homestead Steelworks, molded his character and deepened his commitment to social justice. So did the racial obstacles he faced at school, at work, and in daily life. But adversity did not define or limit him. His upbringing reflected a world that Black Pittsburghers created on their own during segregation. Goode saw their grace and capability at church, in the Negro Leagues where some of his neighbors played, on the pages of the *Pittsburgh Courier,* and at the Crawford Grill, a mecca for jazz. He became a fierce advocate for people otherwise ignored. Part of his personal mandate was to connect them to the larger world, especially Africa.

Goode began working night turns at the Homestead Steelworks during high school and continued to work there while at Pitt. He joined Alpha Phi Alpha, the nation's oldest Black fraternity, and graduated from the university in 1931 as hard times were getting harder. With the economy tanking, he held on to his job at the mill, working a couple of shifts a week until 1936. Goode's plans for law school were shattered by the Depression and so he pivoted. He worked as a juvenile probation officer, mentored youth at the Centre Avenue YMCA, and managed two of the nation's largest integrated public housing projects. In each of these positions, he battled discrimination directed at him personally and on behalf of those he served.

Mal Goode's greatest accomplishment in these early years, by his own testimony, was his marriage to Mary Lavelle. They met when Mal was a student at the University of Pittsburgh. He was instantly smitten but in no position to offer Mary a secure life. Mary was magnetic, wise, and stunning. She attracted multiple suitors—some were his friends—but much to Mal's relief she waited for him. They married in 1936 and shared a devoted and respectful fifty-nine-year partnership that provided the foundation for and gave meaning to Mal's life and work. They had seven children, one who died in infancy. Their marriage was defined by traditional gender roles; Mary took care of the home and children while Mal set out to change the world. He could not have pursued the latter if she were not maintaining the former and serving as a partner in their shared quest for racial justice. Mal made no professional move without Mary's counsel, and his love for her and his family sustained him.

In 1948, Mal Goode joined the *Pittsburgh Courier,* one of the nation's leading Black papers. Its emissary to the South, he boosted circulation in Virginia, Tennessee, Mississippi, and beyond. He met people there who became lifelong friends and sources. When returning to the South as an ABC correspondent to cover the fight for civil rights, these contacts briefed him on the backstory to local protests and made sure he gained access. Though never trained as a broadcaster, Goode initiated a radio broadcast on Pittsburgh's KQV, "The *Courier* Speaks," becoming the only African American on a mainstream Pittsburgh station. By then his sister Mary Dee had crashed radio's gender line to become the nation's first Black female DJ. Mixing gospel with R&B, she blossomed on WHOD, an innovative station in Homestead that appealed to the European immigrants, Black migrants, and their descendants who made up much of greater Pittsburgh. In 1950, Mary Dee and Mal became a brother and sister radio team for WHOD and drove conversations about the city, race, and deindustrialization's early onslaught in the region. Mal's news reports, interviews, and penetrating commentaries attracted a growing audience. African American voices delivering news summaries and editorials were rare. So was what he said and how he said it. Arrested several times after castigating the police for incidents of brutality, he sometimes stashed himself in the trunk of a car to escape harassment as he was driven around the city. But Goode was undeterred. Before long, African Americans applauded Goode for his willingness to fight for them despite the threats he endured.

Goode had a special kinship with athletes. The Veney brothers, who founded the Homestead Grays, lived across the street and worked with his father at the steelworks. Another neighbor, Cumberland Posey Jr., took the Grays to the heights of the Negro Leagues and kept them there for decades. Posey remains the only person inducted into both baseball's and basketball's hall of fame. Mal often brought athletes on to his radio show, including Hall of Famers Jackie Robinson and Henry Aaron, whom he knew from their visits to Pittsburgh when they played in the Negro Leagues and later the major leagues. On one of those visits, he took Aaron to his first meeting of the National Association for the Advancement of Colored People (NAACP), an event that was the genesis of a lifelong commitment to civil rights. Robinson, Aaron, Willie Mays, Roberto Clemente, and almost every ballplayer of color who passed through Pittsburgh wound up at the Goodes' home, feasting on Mary Goode's cooking and seeking Mal's counsel on politics. He channeled their celebrity and dollars into support for the NAACP Legal Defense Fund and bail money for activists arrested during Freedom Summer. When the Milwaukee Braves went to the World Series in 1958, the Black players on the team brought Mal to Milwaukee as their guest.

An indefatigable letter writer, Mal counseled a diverse mix of people who sought his advice on the civil rights movement, politics, and personal quandaries. A shapeshifting speaker, he could preach to congregations with the cadence and fervor of a minister but mellow his delivery when addressing primarily white audiences about "the race question." On the air, he came across with the crisp diction and pointed commentary that correspondents like Edward R. Murrow and Eric Sevareid favored. "As a journalist," veteran broadcaster Bernard Shaw said, "he had the calmness of a church deacon and the probing mind of a Marine drill instructor. This man was a journalistic patriot and an American patriot. His challenge was always to live up to your principles and to your claims."[3]

After ABC hired Goode, the family moved to Teaneck, New Jersey, where they bought the home of New York Yankee star Elston Howard, another friend from the Negro Leagues. In Teaneck, a town lauded as "America's Model Community" for its efforts to integrate, Mal continued to rail against racial inequality as he had in Pittsburgh. He insisted that Teaneck live up to its rhetorical commitments and showed his support to a younger generation of activists who counted on his counsel, experience, and dogged pursuit of racial justice in public and private forums. Goode was a regular attendee at city council meetings, exposing truths while nervous Teaneck leaders quaked. As in Pittsburgh, everyone knew Mal. The Goodes were esteemed members of the community for the three decades they resided in the New Jersey suburb.

Meanwhile, as Goode's ABC stint propelled him to national prominence, he used that platform and spoke to more than a thousand church, school, community, NAACP, and Alpha Phi Alpha audiences. A rare mix of fiery engagement and journalistic gravitas, Goode sustained his activism after he stopped working as a full-time ABC correspondent. He remained at the United Nations as an ABC consultant and joined the National Black Network as a reporter and pundit. His contacts with African nations during the continent's age of independence were exceptional, making him a go-to journalist as colonies on the continent achieved independence. He kept a focus on postcolonial Africa and the struggle against apartheid. His tough talk was often tempered by his favorite ending to his speeches, an impish statement to the audience: "Don't think you're getting out of here without hearing about my kids."[4]

Mal and Mary Goode returned to Pittsburgh in 1993. They both longed to spend their twilight years surrounded by family and in the city that would always be their home. Mal's death in 1995 was mourned by countless people who were inspired, challenged, and chided by him. ABC's *World News Tonight*'s anchor Peter Jennings announced Goode's death at the end of his newscast. Jennings later wrote to Mary: "I am pleased that I was able to say, on the air, and for several print reporters, how warmly I felt about Mal. He was a wonderful guide to me in the early days. He will be remembered with honor."[5] Mary followed Mal in death three years later.

This book is about Mal Goode's path-breaking journey set against the contours and currents of a nation emerging from legalized segregation. It also addresses his role in challenging the cautious leaders of television media to expand the visibility and representation of diverse American voices and people. The timing was propitious, particularly since coverage of the Civil Rights movement was forcing journalism, as a profession, to reconsider its guiding tenets.

In the fall of 1962, Mal was thrust into broadcast television news—a media format that was a work in progress. By then, the ugly realities of racism and white supremacy had challenged journalism's hallowed principle of objectivity. Emmett Till's murder in 1955, the Montgomery Bus Boycott that began a few months later, the struggle to integrate Central High School in Little Rock, Arkansas, in 1957, and the protests, police riots, and murders that came in their wake precipitated a battle between established white journalists and network chiefs over the coverage of civil rights and racial violence. The journalists wanted to report the messy truths of what they were witnessing— maintaining what they believed was their journalistic mission and responsibility. Network chiefs, however, feared the ire of southern affiliates and the loss of advertising. Television news allowed viewers to see events in real time, making them bystanders to history as it unfolded. They were shown and not just told what was happening, a feature that made TV journalism strikingly different from other formats. Mal debuted amid these conflicts between on-the-ground correspondents and network executives that shaped television news as it became a staple in American households.

It was hard enough for an esteemed white journalist such as Howard K. Smith to negotiate this territory. Smith, who earned his credentials as one of the Murrow Boys, the intrepid journalists Edward R. Murrow led during World War II, was fired by CBS president William Paley in 1961 after his controversial and revelatory documentary "Who Speaks for Birmingham?" aired that spring. Smith's reporting exposed the connection between police commissioner Bull Conner and the Ku Klux Klan in the attacks on Freedom Riders and Black people in Birmingham. Smith planned to conclude the documentary by quoting the eighteenth-century British philosopher Edmund

Burke: "The only thing necessary for the triumph of evil is for good men to do nothing."[6] CBS lawyers flagged that as editorializing, a direct violation of Smith's contractual obligation to maintain neutrality. Smith recounts the heated exchange with Paley who accused the correspondent of breaking the cardinal rule of journalism. "The rules are impossible to follow in this case," Smith stated. He was shown the door.[7]

Smith was fired for his beliefs but was in a privileged position, his credentials as a top journalist allowed him to take a principled stand and still find another job. It was more difficult for Black journalists who faced relentless scrutiny and accusations of "advocacy reporting" as civil rights struggles and challenges to white supremacy agitated the country. Network leadership faced unprecedented quandaries. Racial confrontations made for dramatic TV, but who should tell the story and how could it be told without alienating southern affiliates, as had the airing of "Who Speaks for Birmingham?" And how to answer the charges that television was exploiting these upheavals, encouraging flamboyant acts of defiance to boost ratings? How would Goode, an African American, navigate Scylla and Charybdis—between neutrality in covering the civil rights movement and the often violent reaction the movement provoked from those opposed to racial equality, and the moral and democratic imperatives that civil rights demanded.

The Black press and radio had long advocated for the "race" and addressed the struggle for equality in ways that discomforted network bosses and newspaper publishers. Grounded in the Black press and radio, Mal Goode now charted a course on television, an industry that had been off-limits to African Americans. He drew strength from the power and influence of Black media but recognized that integration was damaging the Black press. Black media declined after integration, and there was little effort to bring Black journalists into the mainstream of broadcasting and print journalism.

Leaving his comfort zone in a mostly autonomous, Black-controlled arena, Goode became a lone figure seeking to bring about social change in a strange, new terrain. Although his breakthrough in national network news was celebrated mightily by those who knew him, and countless others were gratified to finally see an African American before the camera, his career did not make him a household name. ABC's apprehension about crossing the color line meant that Goode was often overlooked and the perspective he brought to the network summarily dismissed. Though preternaturally dignified and able to control his displeasure, he scrapped like hell to change how the news was covered, especially the news regarding African Americans.

Fifty-four years old when he arrived at ABC, Mal Goode knew he didn't have much time to fulfill his chosen mandate. While savoring recognition as a barrier-breaker, he embraced the responsibility that came with a national profile. Realizing that he would be held to stiffer standards, he doggedly researched stories and rehearsed his remarks before going on the air. In a departure from how the media had approached the Black community, Goode insisted that not only a few prominent African Americans be heard. He pushed to include the voices of the sharecroppers, steelworkers, and middle-class professionals who were often invisible on national television and radio. He chafed when the networks ignored Martin Luther King Jr., caricatured Malcolm X, or paid attention to Black neighborhoods only when burning. He crafted his own approach, holding Malcolm in high regard and demanding that the network treat King with respect. That became ever more important as his professional and personal relationships with both of them deepened. Goode made sure that his coverage of King's funeral placed the civil rights icon in the river of Black culture and history. So did his coverage of New York City's upheavals in the summer of 1964, the 1967 Black Power Conference in Newark, and his documentary about Atlanta, which showed just how much progress had been made in a city he saw as a model demonstrating both how to bring constructive change and how much was yet to come.

Refusing to be confined to particular stories or to remain silent when coverage was slanted, Goode pressed his bosses and coworkers at ABC to change how they reported on Black America. He contended that they were ignoring stories that merited attention. Instead, he wanted them to focus on efforts to build social capital within Black communities and explain their complex inner workings. Mal Goode's own sense of mission, if not his ABC job description, was to interpret the racial dynamics of a nation reckoning with the realities exposed by the civil rights and Black power movements. He did that from Harlem streets, aboard a mule train from the Mississippi Delta, and on the muddy grounds of Resurrection City during the Poor People's Campaign after King's assassination. As the first African American to fill this role on a network platform, he modeled journalistic integrity while giving voice to African American grievances and expectations. Rather than shy away from difficult stories, he presented Black America in its intricacies, replete with class and internal tensions, rather than as a homogenous monolith. In the vanguard of a small number of Black network correspondents who would be hired in his wake, Goode's success helped solidify an African American presence on media's national stage.

Splitting his time between "the race beat" and the United Nations, Goode established his professional bona fides while pushing ABC to adjust and expand its coverage of civil rights, urban protest, and the internal workings of Black communities. Goode was uncompromising in his belief that network news needed Black voices and perspectives if it were to authentically reflect a diverse country's complexities. Other Black journalists would join Goode in white mainstream media and confront challenges as they circulated among local and national newspapers, magazines, radio, television. Breakthroughs were made in print journalism, but progress was slow and broadcast news as white as a field of snow. A few journalists—Simeon Booker, Dorothy Butler Gilliam, and Nancy Hicks Maynard—had debuted at the *Washington Post* and *New York Times* in the 1950s and 1960s, but they were solitary figures.

As the number of households with television sets exploded during the 1950s, broadcast television newscasts with exclusively white male on-air casts experimented with their approach. Predictably, executives focused on attracting an audience and soliciting advertising dollars. Those in charge understood they were reporting the news on a commercially driven entertainment medium, and that, unlike radio, television could not hide a Black reporter. White people might read a Black journalist's article without knowing the reporter's race, watching a Black reporter deliver a story was different, and television news directors and producers feared the consequences. Mal Goode's story underscored these tensions. He was hired by ABC but stationed at the United Nations where he would remain, many at the network assumed, less noticed by white viewers. ABC had made a bold move to integrate, but executives had no intention of unduly risking the cultural and financial backlash that showcasing a Black reporter might trigger. They had not anticipated the Cuban Missile Crisis, which occurred just weeks after Goode was hired. His posting to the United Nations unexpectedly placed him front and center in ABC's coverage of the crisis.

Black reporters felt that they were repeatedly sent to cover dangerous situations so as to minimize the danger to white reporters, only to have their reporting deemed slanted and biased. They fought with editors to expand coverage of Black communities beyond stories that played into stereotypes about crime, violence, and poverty. Norma Quarles, a television reporter and anchor who debuted on NBC's New York affiliate after Goode joined ABC, told of being assigned a story about women on welfare. After she profiled a white woman, her miffed editor scolded that he assumed she understood that the report should focus on Black women.[8] That was more the norm than the exception. Pigeonholed by ABC and angry about similar assignments, Mal Goode finally dug his heels in and refused to cover another riot.

Producers also denied Black journalists the opportunities to report on major stories that would have given them greater visibility and enhanced their professional status. When Martin Luther King Jr. was assassinated in April 1968, the news director assigning funeral coverage overlooked Goode. He erupted. Confronting the news director and a room full of higher-ups, Goode made clear that he would be in Atlanta at King's funeral with or without ABC credentials. His uncharacteristic ire made the news director realize the foolishness of not sending the reporter closest to King to cover the funeral. When

Mal appeared on the streets outside the funeral service, key figures abandoned white reporters to talk instead with someone they trusted and respected. His reporting gave Martin Luther King Jr. his due and allowed a range of Black voices—from Gordon Parks and Ralph Bunche to Dick Gregory and African American women and men, young and old, standing along the route of the funeral cortege—to honor their fallen leader. Mal hardly endeared himself to ABC's leadership, but they learned something from his defiance. Peter Jennings, ABC *World News Tonight*'s anchor, saw Goode as a mentor and captured his colleague's defiance. "Mal could have very sharp elbows. If he was on a civil rights story and anyone even appeared to give him any grief because he was Black, he made it more than clear that this was now a free country."[9]

Mal Goode's experiences as the first Black reporter on national TV helps unscramble these knotty histories, themes, and tensions. He felt responsible to share his experiences with other journalists who faced similar frustrations and obstacles. He helped those hired after him to expand and deepen their professional network, even while building his own late-breaking career. The National Association of Black Journalists (NABJ) was established in 1975, two years after Goode retired from ABC. It had the potential to be one of most influential Black professional organizations because its members had the skills to influence, enlighten, and move the public into action.[10] Mal Goode was among the first class inducted into its Hall of Fame in 1990, a testament to his role in advancing Black media figures in the mainstream press. Unlike many of their white counterparts, these television reporters fought their battles not just for themselves but for the dignity and welfare of their communities.

There were acts of solidarity as well as episodes of tension and jealousy among African Americans seeking their chance in the industry. Bob Teague, a star college football player who turned down National Football League (NFL) offers to pursue a career in journalism, was hired by NBC in 1963 for what became a thirty-year career. His 1982 autobiography claimed that it was he who broke the color line in the medium when he debuted on the air. Teague acknowledged that

"WABC-TV had put Mal Goode on the air a year or so earlier, but Goode's hair was so straight and his skin was so white that his arrival had been virtually unnoticed." But nobody who listened to Goode and what he had to say could deny his Blackness. Consequently, despite his role as a trailblazer, lifelong activist, mentor, and inspiration, ABC remained ambivalent about showcasing Goode.[11]

After Mal Goode's historic hire, Black reporters slowly began to appear on national network news. But a decade later, there were still very few. In 1971 Goode was inducted as the first Black member of the national Radio-Television News Directors Association. Max Robinson began anchoring ABC News in 1978, and Carole Simpson took the anchor's chair on the NBC evening news in 1988. In 1992 she became the first Black woman to moderate a presidential debate. By then, Charlayne Hunter-Gault had joined PBS's MacNeil/Lehrer report and Ed Bradley was emerging as one of the television's most celebrated journalists, a weekly presence on CBS's *60 Minutes* from 1981 until his sudden death in 2006. And in 2015, after decades at CBS, MSNBC, and NBC, Lester Holt became NBC's evening news anchor. But the growing visibility of Black journalists was not supported by structural change within the industry.

Mal Goode was committed to racial representation, equality, and dignity, and not just in broadcasting. He fought for these goals his entire life, and unsurprisingly, his critique of broadcast journalism sharpened while he was at ABC and even more after his retirement. During the NAACP National Convention in 1983, Goode voiced his frustration with the profession and its lack of inclusion. He lamented that many of the still negligible number of Black reporters and correspondents were "under the illusion that all is well but it's not, because every day something comes up on your job that reminds you that you are Black." Goode detailed the salaries of prominent television journalists, "friends of mine," like Ted Koppel, Harry Reasoner, and Walter Cronkite, who were earning over a million dollars a year. "How many Blacks are earning that kind of money?" he asked. Answering his own question, he speculated that only Max Robinson, Ed Bradley, and Carole Simpson earned above five hundred thousand dollars a year. After pausing, he corrected himself, doubting that Simpson was earning that much.[12] Goode was making an important distinction between Black correspondents' value to the industry and how that industry valued them. Aware that he never made as much as other ABC correspondents, he was tuned into pay disparities across the board. They reflected a stubborn white leadership that allowed African Americans on the air but had yet to acknowledge their worth. This disparity would only be reconciled when Black journalists took their place in the highest ranks of the industry. Only then would network news reflect America's complex truths and diversity.

Mal Goode was the tip of the spear, leading the vanguard of African American correspondents who slowly gained purchase in network news during the 1960s and 1970s. As the first to break the national networks' color line, he showed America, including Black journalists who followed him into the mainstream media, that it could be done. His distinctive rich voice and trademark self-possession contributed to his appeal and served to cover his frustration as he navigated his way through insults, racist attacks, and institutional blindness. A consummate professional, Goode did not hesitate to confront a superior after an indignity, then he calmly returned to work. Quitting was never an option, but the chip he had on his shoulder was a prerequisite to standing up to the pettiness and racism in the industry.

Nearly sixty years after Mal Goode walked into ABC News headquarters at 7 West 66th Street in Manhattan, its president, James Goldston, announced he was stepping down in 2021. During the six decades between Mal Goode's debut and Goldston's departure, African Americans struggled to establish their footing in the industry, savoring each advance but chafing at the roadblocks they encountered. And though television news changed greatly during those years, some of the very issues Mal Goode confronted were still apparent. The networks continued to suffer from a scarcity of Black executive leadership.

The connection between Goode and Goldston was not lost on those fighting for Black representation in broadcast journalism. Ken Lemon, vice president of the NABJ, seized the moment of Goldston's retirement to push the network to put an African American in charge. It would make sense for ABC to break this barrier, he reasoned. "In 1962, ABC hired Mal Goode as the first network news correspondent, and in 1978, NABJ co-founder Max Robinson was named the first Black network evening news anchor." Goode and Robinson had made it possible for African Americans to take the next step and establish a presence in the industry. "While progress has been made in front of the camera," Lemon declared, "it's time for Black advancement in the executive suites."[13] He called for ABC to prove its pluck again and step forward. The network did just that, naming Kimberly Godwin the president of ABC News in April 2021, making her the first African American to run a major broadcast news network. ABC's decision to hire Godwin to head broadcast news made history, as the network had in 1962. ABC made the move, but Goode made the history, playing a leading role in recasting how the news should be covered, and by whom.

This is his story, and that of the family, community, and movement that shaped him.

1

VIRGINIA'S LEGACY

WHEN EIGHT-YEAR-OLD MAL GOODE LEFT VIRGINIA FOR Homestead, Pennsylvania, in 1916, he carried with him the distilled wisdom his family had acquired through two centuries of enslavement and a half century of freedom. Most of all, he brought deeply internalized beliefs about faith, family, and freedom aboard the train from Richmond. He never let go of them; nor did he ever forget his roots in rural Virginia.

Those roots were tangled by the contradictions and complexities of crop, class, and color. The South was more a hodgepodge of local agricultural economies than a unified and homogenous region. But by the turn of the century, the sons and daughters of a people emerging from slavery began streaming northward. Mal's mother, Mary Ellen Hunter, from Folly Farm in Virginia's Shenandoah Valley and his father, William Goode, from the pinewood forests of Southside Virginia, were among them. They and other émigrés were the vanguard of a surge reconfiguring the geography and consciousness of Black America and, ultimately, that of the nation. They were swept up in the Great Migration that witnessed the relocation of six million African Americans from the South to the North and West. Mary Ellen and

William did not know each other in Virginia and experienced vastly different conditions while living in the same state, but their paths finally crossed in Pittsburgh. The Steel City offered them the chance for a better life. Like so many migrants, their journeys were neither linear nor permanent. They frequently returned to Virginia after their family settled in the North.[1]

Mary Hunter brought a commitment to education and uplift with her to Pittsburgh as well as the grit to walk into her children's classrooms and confront their teachers. William Goode hardly knew what the inside of a classroom looked like, but he was well schooled in the field and factory and climbed as high as an African American could at Andrew Carnegie's Homestead Steel Works. Their children were an amalgam of their experiences. So was Black Pittsburgh, where Mal Goode came of age. Its richness and diversity molded him in lifelong ways.

Mal was born on his paternal grandparents' farm in 1908 in White Plains, a tobacco-growing region in Virginia's Piedmont, where he lived sporadically until he was eight years old. "My father's parents were people with devoted and abiding faith in God," he wrote. "They sincerely believed that nobody had freed them from the chains and bonds of slavery but God Himself. They knew their freedom came not by the pen and will of Abraham Lincoln, but by the Almighty's hand of equality."[2]

Mal's grandparents, born in slavery, and his parents, who came of age during the aftermath of Reconstruction, imparted a sense of history that was rooted in their past. "The way of life my family made for me and my brothers and sisters was one deep in the roots of our African heritage," he testified. "My grandparents were privy to the wisdom of their parents who lived in 1820s America and knew that to raise a prosperous and successful family, there must be a viable, close-knit home base. They set out to prove such a dream could come true."[3]

Those African stories and ancestral wisdom were rarely written down, and no family griot can now retrieve them. But that culture was the foundation on which Mal's grandparents built the social capital they needed to find a way forward. Their faith helped them endure the aftermath of African exodus, American bondage, and the collapse of Reconstruction. It would be tested again in the North but never wavered. Mal was a product of their convictions; forging freedom became his life work.

THE SHENANDOAH VALLEY

In much of Virginia, enslaved families were routinely torn asunder by slavery. If their masters calculated that selling surplus labor to plantations in the Deep South was the most profitable way to dispose of them, the bill of sale was written with no regard for the families it destroyed. In northwestern Virginia, coffles of slaves handcuffed to each other by thick links of iron often passed by Folly Farm en route to the Mississippi Delta. Each one of them, an elder in the Brethren Church lamented, had just enough room to walk and lie down to sleep.[4] But in northwestern Virginia's Augusta County, a lucrative hiring out system meant that masters earned greater profit by maintaining ownership of their chattel. Consequently, Mary Hunter's forbears encountered a less familiar form of slavery. Her family remained together at Folly Farm and there's no record of family members condemned to gang labor on distant plantations. For Mary, that meant growing up surrounded by family, immersed in faith, and exposed to education.

When Mary left Folly Farm for Pittsburgh, she carried more than a satchel of clothes. She brought a degree of formal education and sophistication about the world that few African Americans in former slave states then possessed. Mary was literate and relatively well-informed about the world beyond Folly Farm. She and migrants from the Shenandoah Valley brought an unusual level of high culture to Pittsburgh. William, who had arrived in Pittsburgh a decade earlier, was not so worldly or well schooled. He could neither read nor write. The conditions of servitude in Virginia's Southside, where William grew up, hampered the establishment of autonomous Black organizations and offered far less to the generations that bridged the gap between slavery and the Great Migration.

Joseph Smith was a slave master and he, his granddaughter, and her husband loomed large in Mal Goode's life, even though they died before he was born. Smith shrewdly invested in enslaved people, including Mal's maternal ancestors, the Bowles and the Hunters, and built a diversified portfolio of farming, financial, and manufacturing operations by exploiting their labor. Mary Hunter's parents lived in brick cottages near Smith's Folly Farm manor. Each dwelling, measuring twenty by twenty-five feet, had a fireplace and a shared wall. Other enslaved men and women lived at the big house. They tended to fields and livestock, worked in Smith's mills, and were hired out to timber cutters. Unlike many held in enslavement, they were able to build families and shape institutions after emancipation. Mary never fully cut her ties to Folly Farm but did not want to live her life there. As a young single woman she searched for a better life and traveled to McKeesport, Pennsylvania, where she had relatives.

That's where Mary Hunter and William Goode met in 1902. But they returned to Folly Farm to wed. On October 5, 1904, William stood in front of the altar at Bright Hope Church, which Mary's family and neighbors had built in 1891. He was thirty-four years old; she thirty-one. Mary's brother, the Reverend James Hunter, stood alongside William as Mary walked down the aisle and a choir sang from the sanctuary's loft. The pews were filled with Mary's family, Folly Farm neighbors, and William's kin from White Plains, two hundred miles away by train.

Bright Hope Church near Mint Spring overlooks a valley where generations of Hunters worked the land, first as Joseph Smith's property and eventually for themselves. Its weathered sides and tin roof are now covered with a jumble of ivy; tree trunks have melded into its pine planking. Inside, the pews are gone. Instead, the tiny church is cluttered with abandoned farm tools, discarded furnishings, and personal possessions. A worn pair of children's boots dangles from a rusty nail. Nobody has prayed here for over half a century, but this building once reverberated with psalms of joy and lamentations of sorrow. Congregants celebrated life's passages as they faced Reconstruction's broken promises. As W. E. B. Du Bois observed in his 1935 classic, *Black Reconstruction in America*: "The slave went free, stood a brief moment in the sun; then moved back again toward slavery."[5] They cried from happiness and pain at Bright Hope but also engaged in hardheaded, practical debate about how to better their lives. Mary was a toddler when Reconstruction fully collapsed under the pressure of white supremacy. As a girl, she listened to her elders evaluate how freedom would unfold in a hostile nation; as a woman, Mary raised her voice alongside them.

Folly Farm belonged to Joseph Smith, whose estate sat outside Staunton, the Augusta County seat. Stretching diagonally through Virginia for two hundred miles, the Shenandoah Valley spans ten counties. Bounded by the Blue Ridge and Allegheny Mountains and the James and Potomac Rivers, the valley reigned as the wheat kingdom of the South before the Civil War. Slavery shaped the region, but bondage here was different than in Virginia's Tidewater, where tobacco ruled, or on the rice plantations in South Carolina and the cotton fields of the Deep South. The latter were cash crop monocultures where enslaved gangs toiled under the lash of an overseer, churning out ever-greater quantities of tobacco, rice, or cotton for global markets.

Augusta County never fell into the trap of monoculture, blindly chasing the profits offered by a single crop. Nor was it a sleepy rural backwater. Slavery and capitalist modernity were joined at the hip, with planters embracing both un-free labor and the latest means of building wealth. Farmers, quick to diversify, invested in manufacturing. Their enterprise, slave labor, and the felicitous combination of land, water, and weather made the county one of Virginia's most developed and affluent.

Joseph Smith could attest to that. One of thirteen children from a landed family, he arrived in Staunton in the 1790s and bought two mills and land near Mint Spring. His property sat along the Great Wagon Road tying Philadelphia to the Cumberland Gap. A savvy entrepreneur who served in Virginia's House of Delegates, Smith abandoned Staunton to live near his mills, where he built one of the Valley's most impressive homes in 1818. Thomas Jefferson, with whom he had more than a passing acquaintance, influenced its design, particularly a brick serpentine wall, a style Jefferson famously employed two years later at the University of Virginia. The winding wall amused locals, who derided the house as Smith's Folly. Smith, taken with the name, called his estate Folly Farm, and in time, the area became known as Folly Mills. His descendants and those of people he owned still live there.[6]

Wheat drove the Shenandoah Valley's economy and turned up as far away as California, where the forty-niners used it to make sourdough biscuits. Enslaved people grew most of the wheat (the region's cash crop) or corn (a staple for slaves and livestock that could also be made into liquor). Joseph Smith devoured news about crop prices, banking, and manufacturing, alert to the possibilities and perils of an industrializing America. In 1839 his neighbor Cyrus McCormick debuted his reaper on a field of oats Smith owned. But mechanization and innovation only hardened Smith's dependence and that of other farmers on enslaved labor.[7]

Although there were no large plantations, slavery became entrenched after Scots-Irish Presbyterians and Germans descended on the valley in the 1730s. Joseph Smith, with fifty adult slaves and twenty-five hundred acres of land, was one of the largest slaveholders in Augusta County, where most of the eight hundred slaveholders owned just one or two people. His vast holdings put him in a tiny and infamous group. Fewer than 1 percent of whites in slaveholding states owned more than fifty people.[8]

Augusta contrasted sharply with the Southside where Mal's father and grandparents grew up. Virginia's supply of enslaved people had long exceeded demand, and they were routinely sold if deemed surplus. Deep South planters, on the other hand, needed more labor. Unable to purchase slaves legally from abroad after the United States exited the international slave trade in 1808, they turned to Virginia, where profit-seeking slave owners preferred to sell men and women off at high prices rather than pay for their upkeep. By the early 1800s Virginia was exporting more enslaved people to the Deep South than any other state, almost three hundred thousand between 1830 and 1860.[9]

That practice was more common in the Southside, but African Americans in Augusta were not immune from greedy, opportunistic slavers. One speculator advertised weekly in the *Staunton Spectator*: "I wish to purchase one thousand LIKELY NEGROES, of both sexes for the Southern Market, for which I will give the highest cash prices."[10] Despite the number of those sold out of state, Virginia counted a robust population of half a million enslaved African Americans and another fifty thousand living free when the Emancipation Proclamation was declared on New Year's Day, 1863.[11]

Because the Shenandoah Valley's diversified, grain-based economy required less labor than tobacco, rice, and cotton, Joseph Smith didn't need to work his enslaved people in gangs to profit from their labor. White fear of Black insurrection prevailed in slave societies, but since African Americans comprised only one-fifth of Augusta County's population—half of the statewide average—they posed less of a threat to white security. In Brunswick County, Virginia, where Mal's father, William, grew up, African Americans represented almost two-thirds of the population. Enslaved people there were numerous enough to threaten white dominance, and slave patrols, brutality, and the auction block were more common terrors.

Joseph Smith preferred to hire out his surplus human chattel rather than sell them. This was a solid financial move and widespread in the Valley, where farms, mills, distilleries, and iron foundries needed labor.[12] The enslaved men and women of Folly Farm knew the pattern well; prospective leasers would arrive after Christmas each year to negotiate with their owner for their labor, typically setting on a price between $80 and $110 a person for fifty-one weeks. The leasers assured Smith that those people hired out would receive a factory-made blanket, a wool hat, and proper medical care. The enslaved people could generally count on returning to Folly Farm for the Christmas week but otherwise faced a year of sporadic contact with their families and community. But they were not irrevocably parted, and families remained hopeful they would reunite. There was no recourse, however, for any mistreatment unless owners who felt their property had been damaged sought redress, applying the codes that defined slavery.

Smith generally contracted the same people to the same employers each year and pocketed as much as $967 per annum for their labors, which was a sizable sum for the times.[13]

The fragility of nineteenth-century life loomed large for those enslaved at Folly Farm. They watched the Big House intently, knowing changes there inevitably rippled to the slave quarters. Joseph Smith's first wife succumbed giving birth, and their son-in-law died after their daughter conceived a child, Elizabeth Brooke, in 1833. Elizabeth and her mother returned to Folly Farm, where in 1856, Elizabeth married James Cochran, twenty-six, from a prominent Charlottesville family. They lived at Folly Farm, where Cochran helped Smith run the estate and the lucrative practice of hiring out the people he had subjugated. Before long, Cochran was in charge. Smith died in 1863 at the age of seventy-eight, after falling from his mule and breaking a leg. His estate was worth three hundred thousand dollars, an enormous sum in 1863, and was divided between Elizabeth and her sister. His will stipulated that those he had "owned" were to be divided with "regard to family ties existing among them."[14] By then, slavery had entered its death spiral, and the enslaved set their sights on freedom.

Augusta was spared the carnage that savaged Virginia early in the war. But in the summer of 1864, Commander Ulysses Grant ordered Union cavalry to "leave the Valley a barren waste." They overperformed. "I have devastated the Valley from Staunton down to Mount Crawford and will continue," General Philip Sheridan reported. If a crow were to cross the Valley, he chortled, the bird would need to carry his own rations. Anything of value—bridges, rail, and telegraph lines—was demolished.[15] Crops were destroyed, livestock driven off, and Virginia's richest farming county left desolate.[16]

Many in Augusta, including James Cochran, had been conflicted about slavery. Some harbored misgivings on religious grounds. Far more were concerned about their personal security, especially after Nat Turner's 1831 rebellion left hundreds dead less than two hundred miles away from Staunton. Fearing "the bloody monster which threatens us," Augusta women petitioned Virginia's General Assembly to end slavery immediately. They were willing to sacrifice its economic benefits to restore their sense of security.[17] When the countryside settled down, their trepidation faded.

Still, they did not want to secede, and Augusta's twenty-one thousand white residents adamantly opposed secession. In the 1860 election, two-thirds of county voters chose candidates who supported staying in the Union while also maintaining slavery.[18] Consequently, Augusta's delegates to the state convention voted overwhelmingly against secession. But when Lincoln issued a Proclamation of Insurrection after the attack on Fort Sumter and called for seventy-five thousand troops to quash the rebellion, Virginians swiftly reversed course. Augusta County, long a Unionist bastion, voted 3,130 to 10 to secede. In the end, historians William Thomas and Edward Ayers concluded, the county was paradoxically "the last to secede and the most dedicated to the cause."[19]

When war erupted, Augusta whites responded with fervor and six thousand men—almost every male not too young or too old to fight, including James Cochran—rallied to the Confederacy.[20] By the battle of Gettysburg in the summer of 1863, Cochran was a colonel in the Churchville Cavalry, which he led until weeks before Lee surrendered at Appomattox.[21] By then, the number of African Americans in Augusta had dropped by almost 20 percent, with fewer than five thousand remaining. Some fled to Union lines during the fighting and left with Northern troops. A few hired out to timber operators disappeared into West Virginia, which had seceded from Virginia and cast its lot with the Union. But the Hunters, the Bowles, and most people at Folly Farm stayed on.

Augusta rebounded faster than much of the Confederacy, its comeback facilitated by the hiring out system, which provided labor to rebuild. Many resumed working on the same basis as before their liberation.[22] But there were critical differences. Although labor contracts yielded roughly the same money as during slavery, those signing them now pocketed the entire sum. They negotiated directly with employers, without masters profiting from their labor. Landowners and merchants alike tried to exploit these newly freed people, but as the latter gained a better understanding of capital, labor, and market conditions, they navigated freedom with greater assurance.

Mary's parents, William and Martha Bowles, hired themselves out to Thomas Eskridge, an illiterate white farmer living nearby. Eskridge, who often hired out more than half of Smith's enslaved people, cared for his livestock. Their partnership extended beyond business; Smith left an annuity for Eskridge's daughter in his will. He did not, however, bequeath anything to the Hunters, the Bowles, or other families whose labor he had exploited. If not for Smith's daughter and son-in-law, they would have had neither savings, education, nor readily employable skills to tap as they sought security, education, and political power after the war. The last of these would be the hardest to achieve.[23]

When freedom came, regions with African American majorities were particularly volatile. Staunton's freed African Americans worked quickly to establish institutions that signaled their freedom and served as the backbone of their communities. They focused on building schools and churches and turned to the Freedmen's Bureau, a short-lived federal effort, to ease their transition to freedom. The bureau stressed education, which parents wanted for their children. But only a few poorly funded schools were built.[24] African Americans were more successful in creating churches. Abandoning white congregations, most embraced Baptist congregations like Bright Hope, which encouraged demonstrative preaching and a soulful response from the pews. A minister earned his qualifications by responding to a spiritual call to preach, not at any seminary. Bright Hope Baptist might have been a small dwelling, but it was a forum for collective action. The Hunters and the Bowles remained its familial and spiritual core until the 1940s, when it closed. Mary Hunter renewed that Baptist affiliation in Homestead.[25]

Newly freed people's focus on schools and churches was tied to the resistance they faced seeking political power. The specter of upheaval triggered dread in the minds of many whites, who often responded with force. In Augusta, where African Americans were a minority, a poll tax limited the number who could vote. They posed little political threat to the postwar order, which might explain why there was less violence and the Ku Klux Klan did not take hold there. But the specter of violence was ever present. Freedmen's Bureau Supervisor Lt. George Cook observed that Augusta County's African Americans, tolerated "small inconveniences in order to live peaceably [realizing that] shows of impertinence, or independence, in too many instances leads to blows on the part of the whites."[26]

Folly Farm's Black families explored freedom's contours with some help from the Cochrans. While never letting go of his anger over slavery, Mal Goode reckoned that his grandparents' enslavers had some sense of decency. "At the time of the Emancipation Proclamation, they gave their slaves a little more than the stipulated 40 acres and a mule." Although Union General William Tecumseh Sherman issued orders during the Civil War to allot plots of forty acres and a mule to freed families, Andrew Johnson rescinded these provisions after he assumed the presidency following Abraham Lincoln's assassination. Mal believed that the Cochrans had fulfilled this pledge. They gave land to the families once enslaved at Folly Farm and provided funds to purchase seed and plows to till the soil and prepare for independence. Until he could no longer get around, Mal wrote, "Mr. Cochran used to ride out on a dusty, dirt road and visit my grandparents in his horse-drawn buggy." Mal excoriated slavery his entire life but credited the Cochrans for making land and education accessible. His maternal grandparents, the Hunters and the Bowles, remained at Folly Farm, living on their own land in their own home on a street named Hunter Road.[27]

Many African Americans fled during the war, but most at Folly Farm stayed on, building homes on land they came to own. In 1889 they pooled their resources and, for a nominal amount (forty dollars), bought an acre of land from the Cochrans adjoining the land Mary's grandparents had acquired in the 1870s. They built Bright Hope church and a burial yard on it. The church's trustees included members on both sides of Mary's family. Her brother James was Bright Hope's first pastor, her brother Emanuel a deacon, and her sister Martha a congregant. Emanuel and Martha were the congregation's last active members when it closed half a century later.[28]

James and Elizabeth Cochran defied the caricature of slave owners as indolent and mired in the past. Innovative and progressive for the times, they sent their daughter as well as their sons to college. The paternalism and "decency" that Mal noted were evident when they built a classroom in the basement of the Folly manse where the children of formerly enslaved people and their farmworkers did lessons on black-painted oilskins affixed to the walls. Mary Hunter was too old to be a pupil there, but not to be the teacher.[29]

The Hunters had come of age during the backlash to Nat Turner's 1831 rebellion when increasingly punitive slave codes criminalized teaching slaves to read or write. But their daughter Mary, born in 1873, could do more than acquire the rudiments of literacy. "My mother was educated at West Virginia Collegiate Institute (now West Virginia State College) with some of the funds set aside before she was born," Mal explained.[30] Earning a high school education and certification to teach Black children, Mary taught at Folly Farm and then a one-room school in nearby Mt. Sidney, before leaving for McKeesport.

The Commonwealth of Virginia adopted public education in 1870, but the system was segregated and poorly funded, especially for African Americans. Their school year lasted five months while white students attended classes for six. Most Black schools consisted of a single room, with all ages and grades present. That was the sort of education Mary received. While most white schools were soon more than one-room affairs and expanded their curriculum, Mary, who received twenty-one dollars a month in salary during the school year, could only dream of similar circumstances.[31]

Mary was also exposed to Willis Carter, a fiery leader who emboldened the Black community. Carter arrived in Staunton in 1881 after a nomadic quest for education that led him to Wayland Seminary, the Baptist institution for freedmen in Washington, DC, where Booker T. Washington studied. Carter taught in the district encompassing Folly

Farm; it's possible that Mary was his student. She encountered him frequently during his decades as a principal, president of the Augusta County Teachers Association, and editor of the *Staunton Tribune*, the African American newspaper, or at the Colored Teachers Institute training programs he promoted during the summer.[32]

Carter, a Republican Party activist and a robust voice for Black rights, was allied with James Cochran. His advocacy affected Mary, who lived close to town by train. She read Carter's *Staunton Tribune*, whose motto was "Justice for All," and followed its coverage of Lawrence Spiller, a local man hung after a jury took three minutes to convict him of raping and murdering a white girl in 1894. Mary saw Carter back his rhetoric with action, mounting protests after a race riot in Danville led to the death of several African Americans in 1883, campaigning to prevent disenfranchisement, and refusing to let slavery's history be forgotten in the Valley.

Mary first read Booker T. Washington's "Atlanta Compromise" speech in 1896 in the *Staunton Tribune*.[33] Washington implored African Americans to "cast down your buckets where you are" and to emphasize educational, vocational, and entrepreneurial efforts rather than directly confront social segregation and political disenfranchisement in the South.[34] Shaped by Carter and Washington, Mary in turn molded Mal's sense of racial politics. She made sure her children knew about Washington, the Tuskegee Institute president that Mal grew up calling "the leader." But Mal would just as soon joust with authority as cast down his bucket.

African Americans at Folly Farm left no accounts revealing how they felt about their "masters," but there are glimpses of the paternalistic lens that showed how white people thought they felt. The *Staunton Spectator* correspondent at the Cochrans' silver wedding anniversary in 1881 wrote: "A marked feature of the celebration was the presence of all the old servants of the family who had been specially Invited, and also all the colored tenants. . . . They came in great numbers, from all directions and for miles around, and when assembled around the well-ladened table spread in the kitchen, were as happy a lot as could be well imagined." That Blacks attended says something, but the account smacks of condescension. That they were in the kitchen says it all.[35]

Later generations of Cochrans go further. Douglas Cochran, who grew up at Folly Farm decades later, recalled that his neighbors included descendants of those enslaved there. "The families, including my own, were part of a loose farming community that routinely helped each other when needed," he recalled. Whether getting the hay in, repairing a tractor, or pitching in on the farm, the neighbors stuck together. He remembered racial differences as muted and ascribed that sense of community to what the Cochrans fostered after the war.[36]

Joseph Smith's papers reflect attention to medical care and cash gifts to enslaved Black workers at Christmas and harvest, and Cochran family lore casts James as someone who welcomed emancipation and kept in touch with former slaves, helping when he could.[37] That begs the question as to why he did not emancipate them earlier. Running as a Republican (not the easiest path to office in the South at the time), James Cochran was elected to the Virginia Legislature in 1897. As the *Staunton Spectator* observed, this was a case of the office seeking the man, not the man the office. But Cochran did not serve in the legislature. He died suddenly on election day. The *Spectator* remembered him "as free from unreasoning prejudice" and willing to advance "politics which differed from those maintained by a majority of his people." The local citizenry found him down-to-earth with "democratic intuitions . . . accommodating the less favored of fortune . . . without evoking a humiliating dependence."[38] Those who labored for Cochran during slavery and lived on Folly Farm afterward left no record of how they viewed him.

The promise of equality did not materialize for African Americans, particularly after Reconstruction crumbled. Nor was Augusta County, though better off than most of Virginia, immune to the prolonged depression that devastated farmers in the 1870s. When competition with growers at home and abroad slashed commodity prices, few Black farmers had the wherewithal to survive. They embraced populist protest like white farmers but were rejected by many of those white agrarian radicals who could not reconcile making common cause with them.[39]

Making matters worse, African Americans throughout southern states were systematically prevented from voting through a series of laws, policies, and state constitutions after the collapse of Reconstruction. In Virginia, against a backdrop of racial violence, they were purged from the voting rolls after the 1902 convention revised literacy requirements. A Black man needed to satisfy a white official as to his understanding of the new state constitution, something fewer than one-seventh of the state's 147,000 eligible Black voters could do. That was not surprising, given that white officials were the ones deciding their competency to vote. And more than half of the 21,000 who passed the literacy test were disqualified because they could not pay their poll taxes.

At the 1902 convention, a jubilant Carter Glass, an anti-Black delegate who had blasted "negro enfranchisement [as] a crime to begin with," crowed: "This plan will eliminate the *darkey* as a political factor in this State in less than five years." It did just that, and the Black vote remained inconsequential until the 1965 Voting Rights Act.[40] Mary Hunter followed coverage of the state convention, where Willis Carter castigated disenfranchisement and led a last-gasp effort to retain voting rights and equal education. But he could not prevent the storm from breaking. Lynching, disenfranchisement, the Supreme Court's disastrous *Plessy vs. Ferguson*'s "separate but equal" ruling, and Jim Crow made life ever more treacherous.[41] Mary made sure her children knew about those times.

James and Jane Hunter held on at Folly Farm but encouraged their children to explore what the North might offer. In 1902 three of them left for McKeesport, an industrial enclave up the Monongahela River from Pittsburgh where the family had relatives. They weren't the only ones to leave. Augusta's Black population dropped by one-third between 1880 and 1920. Conditions were even worse in Brunswick County, where William Goode, Mal's father, had already joined the migration northward.

THE SOUTHSIDE

Slavery's aftermath was bleaker in the Piedmont than in the Shenandoah Valley. Food shortages and falling tobacco prices after the war hurled freed people and landless whites alike into tenancy, sharecropping, or debt. Night riders swearing allegiance to the Cross Key Blues and the Ku Klux Klan held kangaroo courts, administering terror at the end of a rope. Survival was challenging, acquiring land and education difficult.[42] Mal's mother, Mary, had grown up with some economic security, education, and access to the world beyond Folly Farm, but his father, William, forged ahead with none of those assets.

Mal wrote that his grandparents had been given the land on which he was born in White Plains, Brunswick County, by their "master." If so, Thomas Goode and his wife, Margaret Moore, were not able to hold on to it for long.[43] Both had been born in slavery in Mecklenburg County near the Meherrin River in 1848. They were seventeen years old when freed, twenty-one when wed, and twenty-two when their oldest child, William, was born in 1870. The boundaries of their lives during bondage were likely set by the Goodes of Virginia, a white clan with inescapable power.[44] Those Goodes had benefited from the labor of people like Thomas and Margaret and influenced their destinies long after slavery ended.

Driven from England because of his loyalty to King Charles, who lost the throne and then his head in 1649, John Goode sailed to Barbados. A decade later, he left Barbados for Virginia and established a plantation by the falls of the James River. Amassing considerable wealth and status, he cultivated tobacco with slave labor.[45] Goode's thirteen children begat a sprawling number of offspring, who numbered six thousand families seven generations later. Most were Caucasian, some multiracial. Many, but not all, were slaveholders. Hundreds fought— and more than fifty died—in clashes with the French and Native

Americans, the American Revolution, War of 1812, and the Mexican War. Another seventy-five died fighting for the Confederacy, while two fell defending the Union. The Black Goodes also multiplied, but their stories went unrecorded. Nobody counted how many perished as slaves or stood on the auction block. Neither did the slave-owning Goodes' wealth trickle down to those working their fields.

By the Civil War, African Americans—some of whom were free— comprised two-thirds of the population in Mecklenburg County where Thomas and Margaret were born, and Brunswick, where they settled after emancipation.[46] While most white Goodes were literate and owned property, a greater number of Black Goodes were designated in county deed books as "colored" illiterates with no discernible stake in society. It is likely that Thomas and Margaret were the human property of this white clan, whose territorial footprint covered the Piedmont.[47]

The counties were part of the Southside, an isolated region east of the Blue Ridge Mountains and south of the James River, where conservative cultural ways became entrenched.[48] Its acidic soil—a mix of sandy loam and clay—was not as fertile as that of the Shenandoah Valley, but it was suitable for tobacco. Tobacco, however, has never been particularly good for the soil, those working the fields, or those consuming it. Once its forests were razed, the land lost fertility, and the Southside spiraled downward.

Decline was evident by the 1830s. As agriculture's center of gravity shifted southwest toward the Mississippi Delta, where cotton became king, planters sold off slaves. Some even bred them for sale.[49] Thomas was likely the property of either Elizabeth Goode or John C. Goode, the only Goodes owning plantations near Mecklenburg's border with Brunswick, where Thomas and Margaret were born.[50] Elizabeth owned a small plantation and enslaved thirty people on her property outside White Plains, where Thomas and Margaret later acquired land. She was unable to pay freed people to work for her after the war, and the plantation fell apart. Unmarried and deemed unable to manage her own affairs Elizabeth, aged eighty-one, was declared insane shortly before she died.

John C. Goode fared better. A West Point grad and an attorney who fought in the frontier wars, Goode owned plantations, a ferry, tavern, and more than one hundred people on Flat Creek. During the war, he rose up the Confederate chain of command. Afterward, he represented newly freed people in court. The 1880 census listed Thomas and his family as farm laborers, residing among a group of African Americans near John Goode's property on Flat Creek. Thomas was in jail for a felony at the time but soon regained his freedom.[51]

Goode's plantation, spanning a thousand acres, sat downstream from property belonging to Peter Jefferson, Thomas Jefferson's uncle. Goode's estate, with a library, a smoking room, and live-in servants, was a self-sufficient enclave that included a foundry, a blacksmithing shop, a cooperage, a carpentry workshop, an icehouse, stables, barns, slave quarters, and a racetrack.[52] Enslaved men and women cooked, cleaned, and cared for Goode's children, tended his gardens and livestock, and worked his fields. They made soap, milled grains, preserved fruit, distilled liquor, and butchered animals, smoking and curing the meat.[53]

When Thomas and Margaret were children, their parents received a quart of cornmeal and half a pound of salt pork a day. Children's rations were smaller. They augmented their diets by planting gardens, hunting and fishing, gathering wild fruit and nuts, and eating "chittlins" (pig intestines) and the parts of slaughtered animals that their masters rejected. They made clothes from burlap; if laboring outside in the winter, they received shoes. No family tales described them running away, but if they had, packs of dogs would have chased after them. At night, patrols apprehended those without papers. Masters had considerable leeway to penalize slaves, with little interference from the courts, and overseers used the lash as punishment for insolence or for pilfering food. Enslaved people hardly interacted with masters in Mecklenburg and Brunswick, where African Americans made up two-thirds of the population. Farms were bigger and had more laborers, widening the distance between the white owners and the Black laborers and reinforcing the former's views of the latter as subhuman and stirring their fears of insurrection, knowing they were outnumbered.[54]

The war left 360,000 African Americans in Virginia homeless, mostly in the hard-hit eastern part of the state. Food was scarce, and many had nothing but the clothes they wore. The Freedmen's Bureau offered some relief, but efforts to distribute land—forty acres and a mule—collapsed after Andrew Johnson succeeded Abraham Lincoln as president. With the Southside in turmoil, skirmishes flared over control of property. If African Americans could find unoccupied land and shelter, they moved in. Union troops were inclined to accommodate them, bestowing land to former slaves on abandoned plantations as "freedom dues."[55] When former Confederates tried to remove those squatting on plantation land, some families stood their ground, picking up guns to defend themselves. If Federal troops nearby were led by officers with a radical vision of Reconstruction, they backed the freed men, but when five hundred African Americans near Richmond, "armed and drawn up in line of battle," defied orders to surrender land they had seized, Union troops drove them off and torched their homes.[56]

Whites still held most of the land but were embittered. They felt victimized by Yankee interlopers and worried about retaliation from those they had enslaved. "Defeat brought poverty and Reconstruction brought humiliation," Edith Rathbun Bell and William Lightfoot Heartwell Jr. wrote in the 1950s, a time when the civil rights struggle began placing apologists of the old social order on the defensive. "Conditions in the Old Dominion after the war were worse than in any other Southern state," they claimed, "and in no area of the state was there such misery and poverty as in Brunswick County." Fields were abandoned, plantations reduced to charred rubble. The slaves, they lamented, became "a mass of bewildered and ignorant freedmen, with the doctrine of 'no work' firmly entrenched in the new confusion of their minds." Whites felt abused, and their anger over losing power smoldered. When Union troops withdrew, vigilantes rushed to reassert white rule and avenged their sense of grievance by abusing African Americans.[57]

Mal Goode was horrified by stories of that era. "You need to understand," he declared, "that it was nothing for blacks to be lynched every year, particularly in the South and as far north as Indiana.... If a Negro was charged with something, raping a white woman or breaking into somebody's home, he could be lynched right in the street. And nobody ever went to trial for it. That happened over and over again. It was one of the reasons for the formation of the NAACP—to stop lynching."[58]

Defenders of the Old South portrayed the lynching of Black men as a heroic act of white male chivalry to protect their women from Black sexual predators. Ida B. Wells, who began investigating lynching in 1892, and others debunked this "rape myth." Lynching, they showed, was an arbitrary act designed to terrorize Black communities and shore up white supremacy. The "festival of violence" that often accompanied lynching was a ritualistic and sadistic display intended to suppress African Americans. Thousands of murders stained the collapse of Reconstruction, including about one hundred documented cases in Virginia between 1880 and 1926. News of lynching ripped through Black homes; details of horrific torture were spoken of in hushed and quaking tones as adults impressed on children the dangers of ignoring racial taboos.[59] Mal was haunted by the horror of self-proclaimed vigilantes publicly dismembering and burning African Americans to ash in the wake of a real or imagined offense. That lynchings often were executed in the presence of large audiences of men, women, and children led NAACP field secretary James Weldon Johnson to conclude that "the race question involves the saving of black America's body and white America's soul."[60] Lynching underscored how deeply racist oppression had seeped into every nook of southern society, and Mal Goode never shook off its horrors.

By the time William was born in 1870, his parents were working either as tenants or as sharecroppers on former plantation land.[61] Without land reform, agricultural workers were trapped in a system with dismal prospects. Plantation owners who had reclaimed their land after the war no longer controlled a workforce while African

Americans needed a way to support themselves. As a result, freed people negotiated the terms of their labor, exchanging it for use of land, for which they gave landlords a share of the crop or rental fee. A smaller number hired themselves out.[62] They had minimal leverage, but as historian Leon Litwack observed: "Even as they toiled in the same fields, performed the familiar tasks, and returned at dusk to the same cabins, scores of freemen refused to resign themselves to the permanent status of a landless agricultural working class." They sought to fashion their own lives on their own terms. Many realized that was more likely to happen in the North.[63]

Little is known about the Goodes but that they worked the land, growing tobacco and other crops. Whether they were sharecroppers splitting their crop with a landowner who also profited by advancing them money for seeds, fertilizer, and other essentials, or tenants renting land, or subsistence farmers on their own plot, growing tobacco was backbreaking, financially sketchy, work. Planting and weeding meant repeatedly stooping down to care for thousands of plants. Moreover, tobacco cultivation debilitated the soil. Those with large holdings could leave land fallow to restore its fertility, but for smaller growers such as the Goodes, survival was a losing battle.[64]

The Southside was the epicenter of tobacco production, producing three-quarters of Virginia's forty-million-pound crop in 1860. No other state grew more tobacco. After the war, planters doubled down on its cultivation, which, for most, was a desperate, unsuccessful gamble. Cash-poor farmers, white and Black, borrowed from merchants before the planting season, using anticipated harvests as collateral. But with prices dropping, interest due on loans, and merchants cooking the books when they settled accounts after the harvest, many farmers sank deeper in debt.[65] Tenancy and sharecropping offered at best a way to make it to the next growing season. At worst, it meant falling into debt peonage and despair.

Unable to escape the vicious downward pull of tobacco, Thomas and Margaret tended their fields and borrowed money to make it through each year. They twice hocked livestock to cover debts. In the spring of 1889, the Goodes delivered a cow to J. W. Malone as security for a seventeen-dollar debt. If able to pay Malone by October, they would get their cow back. There is no record they ever did. A year later, the Goodes were indebted to W. S. Purdy for sixty-five dollars and signed over six head of cattle, a horse mule named Charles, and a mule called Rody. This time, they got their cattle, Charles, and Rody back, likely with William's help. He was working in Pittsburgh by then, sending money home. In each transaction, the Goodes made their mark with an X.[66] William, the oldest of eight children, knew work at an early age. Mal Goode reflected:

> My father was a dedicated man, loyal to his wife and children. He was brown skinned, about 5 feet, eleven inches tall, and had no formal school education. My mother taught him how to read and write after they got married in 1904. She taught him so he could read the newspaper and write letters to his folks back in Virginia. There was good reason for my father's lack of education. His mother and father, once free, had to fend for themselves, which was hard for some emancipated slaves, but much easier for those who were tough, smart, and possessed plain common sense. During slavery, many slaves had for the most part run their master's farm for him and knew how to operate the plantation far better than any white owner ever could.[67]

Mal's take on Reconstruction celebrated the Black achievements that flourished when white supremacy was briefly suppressed. "In fact, I would go even further to say that was one reason the so-called 'Southern gentleman' slaveholder fared so badly when the U.S. Army took their cities and farms, looting, pillaging, and burning them to the ground. These slave masters never did a good day's work in their lives; they dished all of the work out to the African American slave. It was only natural when the Confederacy lost the war and the time came to rebuild, the Negro was the only one who could do it."[68]

Most whites, including Pattie Buford, saw matters differently. They bought into the myth of the Lost Cause that took hold after

Reconstruction ended. It depicted the Confederacy as a noble and heroic effort that had little to do with slavery. Although she was compassionate toward African Americans, Buford could not shake off her deeply entrenched assumptions about the proper "place" for African Americans. The granddaughter of a former North Carolina governor and daughter of a well-connected attorney, Buford was born into the Southside's elite. As a girl, she held Sunday school classes for slave children on her father's plantation and later made her own plantation a refuge to educate and care for Black people. She enlisted women from her Episcopal Church to create a school for Black children, opened an asylum for Blacks who had been crippled by infirmity, disease, and poverty, and supported James Solomon Russell's efforts to build the Saint Paul's Normal and Industrial School in Lawrenceville.[69]

For Buford, an entrepreneurial evangelical who saw her endeavors as Christian mission, there were good "colored folks" and irredeemable ones. She was full of praise for former house servants who "idolized their masters and mistresses" and in turn "were loved and cared for by them." These relationships reflected the "poetic, beautiful side" of what she called patriarchal slavery. "Plantation negroes" were another matter. "Left to the tender mercies of an ignorant, often brutal, hired overseer," she wrote, "these creatures were a separate distinct race. Even the house servants looked down on them with ineffable contempt." In her eyes, this forgotten "class of negroes" lived in squalor, diseased with "cancer or some of those fearful scrofulous diseases to which the whole race are peculiarly subject." Helpless, they lacked the capacity to change.[70]

"Alas," she wrote, "The better class of negroes nearly all emigrated," leaving "immense hordes of plantation negroes," who regarded "freedom as immunity from labor" and lived in the backwoods, suffering, stealing, starving, and dying. Making matters worse, in Buford's estimation, a Black majority briefly controlled Brunswick politics after the war. She blamed political tricksters and false prophets for provoking unwarranted bitterness toward former masters.[71]

There was no place in her narrative for the Goodes. Thomas and Margaret were not house servants, could not read or write, and lived in the forest. But they survived in the backwoods, acquired land, and lived without contracting "fearful scrofulous diseases." Disciplined and tenacious, they were healthy, and their children lived considerably longer than most Americans did at the turn of the century. Their son William was almost ninety when he died. But he was a cipher to Buford and white Southsiders.[72]

Work defined Thomas and Margaret's lives and those of their children, in freedom as it had in slavery. The legacy of servitude, coupled with wretched economic and agricultural realities, squelched the development of vital autonomous Black institutions that would foster community strength. Even though William's education ended before it really began, Mal considered his father wise and world-savvy. "I did not realize until well into manhood," Mal told the Conference of Black Mayors when he was eighty, "the power, the influence, the mother-wit and basic intelligence that he had. He did tell me once about his limited education, pointing out that his father felt even at six and seven years of age, that he was too big to be in school. He was needed on the farm, where crops needed tending. Finally, shortly after he reached his eighth year in September 1878, my one-time slave grandmother put her foot down, insisting that 'William has to get some learning.'" Thomas relented but admonished Margaret that William would have to leave school if the harvest got heavy. And just three weeks after William began attending a country school in White Plains, the harvest got heavy, and William's formal education ended. "My grandfather took dad out of school; he needed every available hand he could get," Mal explained.[73] William never returned to the classroom. He was not the only Black child denied the opportunity. In 1885 only half of Brunswick's Black children were enrolled for the five-month term and fewer than one in four came to school each day.[74]

Thomas and Margaret realized that to build lives on their own terms they needed to send William to the North. But until he was twenty, it seemed as if he would never leave the Piedmont. "My father worked ever since he was tall enough to do the job right," Mal declared. For a plow, the Goodes nailed spikes into a heavy beam that a mule dragged through the field to create furrows. William plowed, seeded, hoed, and weeded from sunup to sunset. He was soon country strong, wiry and muscled, and only got stronger laboring in Pittsburgh's mills. When his grandchildren stepped out of line and William grabbed them with one hand, they could not escape what they called his "Indian death grip."[75]

William finally broke free of Brunswick in 1890. By then, plummeting crop prices, pressure from tobacco trusts, floods, and populism's failure to forge cross-racial alliances revealed the handwriting on the wall. There was little chance the Goodes would ever gain land unless a family member sought better-paying work elsewhere and accumulated enough money to buy it. It's possible that William found his first job in a Petersburg tobacco factory, more likely that he went to Richmond to work at the Tredegar Iron Works. Even before the war, Richmond lured Blacks from the countryside. No Southern city had developed its economy more or was better connected by canals, rail lines, and sea to the rest of the South. African Americans worked in its tobacco factories, producing plug and twist that were chewed, not smoked. Others were construction workers, teamsters, or quarrymen. Richmond offered a glimpse of what African Americans would build for themselves. An aura of mystery surrounded its secret societies, so-called because they had kept membership rolls confidential during slavery. These groups, like the Secret Sons of Love and the Rising Daughters of Liberty, underlay a web of mutual aid, trade union, and social organizations.[76]

The Tredegar Iron Works, where one thousand African Americans labored during the war, was probably William's ticket to Pittsburgh. His first job in the city was as a cinder pitman, shoveling waste out of open hearth furnaces at the Black Diamond mill in Lawrenceville, a blue-collar Pittsburgh neighborhood by the Allegheny River. Black Diamond had imported Black workers from Richmond to break a strike a few years before William arrived in 1890. These men had moved up the workplace hierarchy, helping migrants like William secure work and lodging.

William sent money home, enabling his parents to buy land. In January 1899 Thomas and Margaret made their marks on a deed with Dr. W. S. and Annetta Purdy, paying them five hundred dollars for one hundred acres south of the Meherrin River. They had borrowed from the Purdys before and might have been their tenants or sharecroppers. Mal thought highly of Dr. Purdy. "They had no black doctors in Brunswick County then," he explained, and "if somebody got sick in the middle of the night, you got on horseback and rode two miles to Dr. Purdy's and he said, 'All right, I'll be there as soon as I get dressed.'"[77]

Their land was in White Plains, which a century later is an unincorporated stretch of black-topped road with a post office, scattered homes, farmland, and forest. Even with the money William sent home after arriving in Pittsburgh in 1890, Mary and Thomas needed to borrow $230 of the purchase price from the Purdys. But they held on to the property, and five years later, William's brother Ashton bought the adjoining almost seventy-two acres for $900.[78]

William did not return to White Plains to live, but his wife and children did. William and Mary's first two children, James and William, were born in Homestead, Pennsylvania, and Mal was born on the farm in White Plains in 1908.[79] The boys and Mary, who might have been teaching school in White Plains or Lawrenceville, lived there intermittently until 1916. William visited when the Steel Works banked its furnaces and laid men off, which happened most summers.[80]

Mal respected his father and Booker T. Washington, but he came of age during the great migration when the "New Negro," who disdained segregation, made the scene in northern cities. "My father believed blacks had everything to gain and nothing to lose," Mal reflected, "but I disagreed with him. I couldn't follow on this point.... He never admitted how his people, including himself, were being hurt by prejudice and aloofness on the part of our oppressors, all within the guise of so-called democracy. My father knew he was a victim of discrimination, yet he painstakingly rolled with the punches."[81] Growing up when and where he did, William had little choice but to accept racial realities he could not openly confront. He would argue his case years later around the crowded dinner table when his children, especially Mal, challenged his approach.

Thomas and Margaret Goode, as well as James and Jane Hunter, never left the South. But William Goode and Mary Hunter did, along with more than a million African Americans from the 1890s through the 1920s. These men and women changed their lives as they moved into neighborhoods in Chicago, New York, Detroit, Philadelphia, and Pittsburgh. Coming together in "the promised land," they commenced the slow, herky-jerky struggle to transform America. Novelist Richard Wright, born in the same year as Mal, wrote that, while he was leaving the South and flinging himself into the unknown, he "was taking a part of the South to transplant in alien soil, to see if it could grow differently, if it could drink of new and cool rains, bend in strange winds, respond to the warmth of other suns and, perhaps, to bloom." Although Mal was born on his grandparents' farm in White Plains, his future lay in the North. But he, too, brought part of the South with him, and he would always keep a watchful eye on it.[82]

2

HOMESTEAD

WHEN MAL GOODE ARRIVED IN HOMESTEAD IN 1916, HE WAS just eight years old, a slender country boy raised on land not far from where his grandparents once sweated as another man's chattel. But like hundreds of thousands of African Americans, he was swept northward by the tide of humanity that coalesced into the Great Migration. That migration changed his life, just as it did that of the nation. The train ride from Richmond, Virginia, to Homestead, Pennsylvania, took less than a day but offered passage to a bewildering new reality. What Mal saw and heard each day on the streets of the iconic mill town came as revelatory.

Although Mal and his family never cut ties with rural Virginia, they were now at the center of American steelmaking, across the Monongahela River from Pittsburgh. Instead of agricultural rhythms driving family routines, the mighty Homestead Steel Works dictated the pace of their lives. Steel's tempo of long shifts and round-the-clock production punctuated by shutdowns, layoffs, and tense labor struggles was inescapable. Steelmaking fouled the air they breathed; its sounds reverberated through the valley. City folks now, they found planting seasons, harvests, and livestock no longer much mattered.

If steel forged Homestead, the town and the mill shaped the Goodes, reinforcing their core instincts. The Goodes worked hard, stuck together, and kept faith in family, God, and the church. Inspired and encouraged by the promise of the "American Dream," Mary and William Goode anticipated a better future in the North, not only for their children but for their race. "Despite the inequities they experienced," Mal declared, "nothing could break the will of my mother and father." They believed that education was the key to uplift. "Our attending school and church were vital, for both of them believed that one day the discrimination and denial that plagued black Americans would no longer exist." His parents, profoundly affected by hearing Mary McLeod Bethune speak in Pittsburgh, relayed the activist educator's marching orders to the children. "It's better to have a hundred ready and prepared when the door of opportunity opens than to have no one prepared," Bethune implored. The Goode children were trained to charge through that door. Their lives would not, like William's, be consumed by farm and factory. "Our sights were set on higher education," Mal underscored. His parents and Homestead's elders made sure they kept their eyes on that prize.[1]

When Mal settled into Pittsburgh in 1916, the metropolis was just decades removed from James Parton's denunciation that the city was no better than hell with the lid off. The region was home to the nation's largest concentration of steel and manufacturing. No industry hired more men than steel, and no corporation employed more steelworkers than its kingpin, United States Steel, for which William Goode worked. Before long, despite his parent's expectations, so would Mal.

The corporation's voracious appetite for labor had attracted waves of migrants from across Europe. By World War I, Slavs comprised over half of Homestead's steel workforce, with more African Americans arriving daily.[2] The outbreak of war in Europe in August 1914 had pushed Pittsburgh mills and mines to peak production. With demand for labor strong and fewer immigrants escaping Europe's chaos, Black workers were needed. Men boarded trains in Georgia, Mississippi, and Alabama, and got off the next day in Pittsburgh to enter factories where twelve-hour shifts were the norm and where injury and death were daily companions.[3]

The mill was inescapable. Its whistles, sirens, occasional explosions, and the smoke and particulates it belched were constant reminders of what shaped life. Most African Americans flooding into Homestead during World War I took refuge in the Ward along the Monongahela River. There, close to the hulking steelworks, they found shelter in company-built bunkhouses and fetid tenement courtyards. The Ward, already jammed with European families and boarders, became even more of a jumble. Women shopped at butchers and greengrocers nearby on 6th Avenue, patronizing shopkeepers who let them buy on credit; men sought solace at bars and brothels.[4]

The Goodes, however, had options beyond the Ward. Mal's father had arrived in Pittsburgh in 1890, before the Great Migration began remaking Black America. He was part of an earlier wave of Black migrants who crossed the "River Jordan" in hopes of leaving sharecropping, lynching, and Jim Crow behind. Instead of living cheek by jowl with recent migrants, the Goodes looked down upon the Ward from leafier, quieter, streets on Hilltop, where in 1906 they bought a detached wooden house on an integrated block of skilled workers, mechanics, and shopkeepers. For the children of freed people, owning that home on West 12th Avenue was a remarkable achievement. A few Black neighbors moved within the circuit of the fashionable Loendi Club and a social club, the FROGS (where Friendly Rivalry Often Generates Success). Decades later one of their grandchildren, Robert Goode, became a member. Although the North was not the promised land, Hilltop families owned homes and enjoyed job security rarely achieved in the Ward.[5]

Mal had little sense of how special Hilltop was, or how tough circumstances were in the Ward, until he grew older. As a boy he saw Black competence and achievement, as well as respectability and uplift, all around him. The Veney brothers, engineers at the US Steel Works who were also from the Shenandoah Valley, lived across the street. They and their steel working mates formed a ballclub called the Homestead Grays. Captain Cumberland Willis Posey, the son of slaves who became Black Pittsburgh's leading entrepreneur, resided a block above on 13th Street. His son, Cum Posey Jr., would make the Grays, Black baseball's flagship team. Mary Cardwell Dawson, who came to Homestead as a seven-year-old in 1901 and later created the National Negro Opera Company, lived a short walk away. Like Mal's parents, almost three-fifths of African Americans in Pittsburgh and Homestead in 1890 were from Virginia, most from the Shenandoah Valley or Richmond and its environs.[6]

Whether at home, in the pews of Clark Memorial Baptist Church, or on Hilltop, Mal absorbed a code of behavior. The principle that shaped him the most was his father's admonition: "You're no better than anyone else and no one is any better than you. Now go out and prove it."[7] He took those words to heart, moving comfortably between ghetto streets and posh social clubs, never turning his back on those with fewer opportunities. He saw himself as their advocate and stood his ground when they were treated as less than equal. Nor did he quietly accept personal affront.

African Americans from Richmond began working in Pittsburgh over a decade before William arrived. In the 1870s Black workers helped break a strike at the Black Diamond Works in Pittsburgh's Lawrenceville neighborhood and stayed on afterward. Realizing that their long-term interests were best served by allying themselves with white workers, they formed a lodge of the Amalgamated Association of Iron, Steel, and Tin Workers. So did Black workers at Richmond's Tredegar Works, a connection facilitating the northward migration.[8]

After a few years at Black Diamond, William Goode left for Homestead. It's uncertain why he sought work there, other than that the mill was hiring African Americans and returning to Virginia was not promising. The White Plains farm allowed the Goodes to subsist, but little more. Agriculture was steadily losing status, and there hadn't been all that much of it for Black farmers to begin with. Still, owning land meant that the Goodes no longer worked as slaves, tenants, or sharecroppers. "We got our forty acres," Mal said, referring to the Freedmen's Bureau efforts to give former slaves forty acres and a mule after emancipation. Landless sharecroppers, in contrast, often fell deeper into debt no matter how hard they worked. Nor did education offer much of a lift. William, whose boyhood was consumed by labor, knew little of classrooms.

In freedom, as in slavery, Thomas and Margaret Goode never ceased toiling. For their son William, making steel was deadlier than working the land and was just as liable to consume his life. But it offered possibilities that Virginia's soil did not afford. William earned $1.25 his first day on the job. Mal marveled at what he accomplished: "So often my father related the seeming ease with which he saved money on that wage, paying three or four dollars a week for meals and lodgings as a boarder out of a weekly total of less than eight dollars." Like single men and those whose families had not joined them in Pittsburgh, William enjoyed inexpensive lodging, meals, and camaraderie as a boarder. That allowed him to send money home to help his parents acquire land.

William began working in Homestead in the wake of an epic labor confrontation. Prior to 1892, skilled steelworkers at the Homestead Works called the shots on the shop floor. Their knowledge of steelmaking had given them leverage to create what historian David Montgomery called a craftsmen's empire.[9] Their mastery of iron- and steelmaking made them indispensable. Nothing could be produced without them. As a result, they bargained over wages, set limits on how hard they would be pushed at work, and maintained what they considered a manly bearing toward each other and the boss.

But Andrew Carnegie, who bought the Homestead Works in 1883 for $350,000, and Henry Clay Frick, his hardline, union-busting partner, bridled at their power. They sought to revamp production and replace skilled workers with machines and semi-skilled laborers. After turning the mill into an armed camp, the company locked men out on June 30, 1892. If workers would not return to work on management's terms, Carnegie and Frick would bring in men who would.

Although only the mill's seven hundred skilled men were union members, over four times that number—virtually the entire workforce—stayed off the job. They knew working conditions would deteriorate without the union. On July 6, 1892, barges packed with Pinkerton guards came upriver from Pittsburgh intent on resuming production. But when armed workers and their allies met them on the docks, the river ran red with blood, and the Pinkertons were routed in a fight that left a dozen guards and workers dead.

The workers won the battle of Homestead, but Carnegie pushed the Pennsylvania governor, Robert Pattison, to intervene. Beholden to Carnegie, Pattison rushed thousands of state militia to occupy Homestead and safeguard the strikebreakers. Townspeople reviled the militia, spitting Cossack and other epithets at them, but the mill reopened and the company prevailed. Industrial unionism lay dormant until the 1930s. Big Steel's sway extended beyond the works and affected what people were willing to say. "If you want to talk in Homestead," one resident wryly noted fifteen years later, "you must talk to yourself."[10]

There were few Black workers at Homestead in 1892, but more, including William, arrived afterward. Most were not sympathetic to the union. Management, at least, offered them work. The "race question" in Homestead was not about Black migrants but about the new immigrants arriving in unsettling numbers from Austria-Hungary, Tsarist Russia, and Italy. William had more in common with the old guard of skilled white workers from the British Isles, who scorned these émigrés. That was true at work and even more in Hilltop.

William's generation of Black steelworkers benefited from the timing of their hiring—work was steady until the Panic of 1907. That William held a skilled position, which allowed the couple to buy a home, was no anomaly. Homestead's Black steelworkers were better off before World War I than afterward. Although African Americans comprised only 3 percent of the mill's workforce in 1910, almost half of them held skilled or semi-skilled positions. Conditions deteriorated after the war, and most Black workers were relegated to unskilled positions with little chance of promotion. That made William's African

American neighbors on Hilltop a cohort the likes of which would not be seen again. When Mal entered the mill, it was as a cafeteria worker, not as a first helper, his father's position.[11]

William took enormous satisfaction in his work. "His pride was in learning how to make steel and knowing just when a heat was ready for tapping," Mal said. "He learned it well, for despite discrimination so prevalent then, my father managed to reach the top for an Afro-American on the open hearth—a first helper." First helpers led three-man crews and several laborers at one of Homestead's sixty open hearth furnaces. William directed an integrated crew as they melted scraps of iron, ore, and other materials at stunningly high temperatures into steel at Furnace Number 59. When tapped, molten steel poured into ingot molds to cool, later to be reheated and rolled into rails, plates, and beams. A boss melter supervised William and a few other furnaces but did far less strenuous labor, earned more, and usually lived longer.

The US Steel Works ran twenty-four hours a day, with production split into fourteen-hour and ten-hour turns. Men switched shifts every other week. They got Sunday off on alternate weeks but worked a twenty-four-hour shift—the turnabout—the following Sunday. Accidents were frequent on turnabouts as men struggled to stay alert. By the time William tramped up the hill to 12th Avenue after work, his energy and spirits were flagging.

William rarely complained, but when he did, Mal saw the toll it exacted. "I can recall my father coming home after the night turn—a fourteen-hour shift—in time to have breakfast with the children before we left for school." Mal never forgot what his father said to Mary as they sat in the kitchen that morning. "A neighbor, Bud Conroy, who my father taught how to make steel, was promoted the day before to boss melter over him. And though it was many, many years ago, I recall the tears as he related to my mother: 'To think I taught him how to make steel.'"

Conroy had begun as a pull-up boy, raising furnace doors so scrap could be shoveled into the furnace. William had schooled him in the workings of the open hearth, then watched as his neighbor got the job he never would. "He made a decent living, but there was only so far that Black men could go in the mills. My father worked there for thirty-one years, and never became a boss melter. And yet he trained many a fellow who couldn't speak the English language who did."

"Pop," Mal said, "enjoyed relating his knowledge to Andrew Carnegie." By then, the Scottish boy who came to Pittsburgh in the 1840s had become a global titan. "Periodically, Carnegie visited the mill and made it a point to stop by Furnace Number 59. I recall so well my father relating when Carnegie told him, after my father set a record for production on his furnace, 'Billy, it's too bad you're a colored man,' indicating that promotion to boss melter would have been no problem if he had been white." Instead, Carnegie gave William and a Polish coworker a box of cigars to show his appreciation for their record-setting stint.[12]

"Andrew Carnegie owned the plant," Mal fumed. "All he had to do was to say 'make Billy Goode a boss melter,' but Andrew Carnegie didn't have the character to do that. It underscores why many young Negroes lost heart and developed a don't-care kind of attitude. Some of that has come back to haunt us again." Never relinquishing his resentment, Mal acknowledged that: "In all fairness, Carnegie did urge my father, 'Billy, educate your children.'"[13] Carnegie's formal education, like William Goode's, had ended when he was young, but the similarities ended there.

Mal's pride in his father and the ache that he did not attain the position he deserved never dissipated. "That promotion," Mal pointed out, "would have meant earning two or three times the earnings of a first helper. Yet most Afro-American men in those hot open hearths, who worked hard to make that top promotion, had little or no recourse to have even a flicker of hope of gaining a higher position because they were colored." There was, he stressed, no Fair Employment Practices Commission, NAACP, or other means of redress. "And no employer was required to answer to anyone except his own conscience."

William never became a boss melter, but his wages placed him among the top 6 percent of Allegheny County steelworkers when Mal was born in 1908.[14] That was enough to give William's children a leg up on the future. His pay allowed the Goodes to own their own home and their children to seek a college education.

William Goode found not only work in Pittsburgh but love and companionship that endured for half a century. In 1902 he met Mary Hunter in McKeesport, a bustling mill town up the Monongahela River, which flowed northward from West Virginia to the Point in downtown Pittsburgh. "My father was a proud, handsome, brown-skinned man who carried himself well," Mal testified. "That must have been the reason my mother fell in love with him. They met in 1902 and after several years of courtship, chose to make their vow."

Mary taught school in Virginia before leaving for McKeesport, where the Hunters had family. Her siblings—James, Emanuel, and Martha—joined her there.[15] "In McKeesport, Mom worked in a small grocery store owned by a Black man, a rarity for a Negro in 1902. Their chance meeting at the store brought them together; they would never part again. She was a proud, young, Black woman and my father a noble fellow. They had the same philosophy about family, both wanting their future children to do well in every way. When we were born, they set out to see their dreams come true through us."

William, aged thirty-four when they wed in 1904, might have been illiterate when they met, but he was a good catch and Mary, thirty-one, saw his potential. Their prenuptial discussions stressed education: William would learn to read and write and their children would attend college. By the time their first son, James, was born in 1906, William could read the Bible and the newspaper and write letters home to Virginia, where his parents needed someone to read them. Sometimes that was Mary, who along with their sons, occasionally stayed in White Plains while William worked in Pittsburgh.[16]

Two years after they wed, the Goodes bought a lot 30 feet wide and 180 feet deep on 118 West 12th Avenue in Homestead for twenty-five hundred dollars.[17] It was Mary's thirty-third birthday, April 30, 1906. By then, they had two sons—James and William Jr. who were born in Homestead. A third, Mal, was born on the farm in White Plains in

February 1908. William, who like most steelworkers was frequently laid off from work, made trips to Virginia when he could, until the family reunited in 1908. Once in Homestead full-time, Mary juggled running the household with working in small shops that she and William operated. Her brother James clerked at their confectioner's shop in McKeesport the year after they wed; they later ran a fish and poultry store in Homestead. "Dad hoped to found a business that would flourish for the children to take over. This was not to occur as planned. A limited knowledge of business methods and the inclination to grant too much credit to friends led to our selling the store."

The African American presence in Pittsburgh workplaces loomed larger during World War I and had increased fivefold in steel by 1920. Skilled men like William, however, were becoming the exception. As more African Americans flowed into Pittsburgh mills, they lost their relatively privileged position in the plant hierarchy. The number of Black workers at Carnegie Steel mills climbed to more than four thousand in 1917, but they were hired almost exclusively as laborers at the bottom of job ladders. Where a man was assigned when hired had lifelong implications. Each department had job ladders, lines of progression (LOPs). The higher a man rose on an LOP, the more money he made and the more likely he kept his job during layoffs. But African Americans were invariably assigned to LOPs with a limited upside, which vastly reduced their earnings and made them vulnerable during downturns.[18] Whatever aspirations they might have held, skimpy wages and a shaky grip on work made saving to invest in a home difficult. Witnessing these changes, William discouraged his sons from working in steel. "My children will never have to work in the mill like I did," he vowed.[19]

After thirty years in the mill, William's nose and jaw were seared red. "He was singed from standing too close to the hot ovens that melted iron into steel," Mal remembered. Nevertheless, Mal followed his father into the mill. Like William, Mal was fascinated with what it took to make steel and turn it into bridges, railroads, and skyscrapers. Men took pride in that feat. But in 1925 the furnace that William Goode was tending exploded. He survived, but his time at the

Homestead Works was over. William, aged fifty-five, would receive a seventy-nine-dollar disability check from the company every month for the next thirty-five years, until he died three weeks before turning ninety in 1960. "That money came in handy when the depression got bad," his son recalled. His grandchildren still laugh at how long their Pop collected that disability payment. He was one of the five oldest living pensioners at US Steel before he died.

The accident, bad enough to cause William to limp the rest of his life, might have been a blessing. Working at an open hearth was debilitating. Workers endured severe temperature swings, especially when stepping outside during winter. They inhaled dust and particulates and often wound up with pneumonia or lung disease akin to what miners suffered. Moreover, lives were snuffed out with tragic frequency on the shop floor. In one year, from July 1, 1906, to June 30, 1907, 195 men died from accidents in Allegheny County blast furnaces, iron, and steel mills.[20] Despite a limp and a disability check, William Goode did not stop working, an ethic his children absorbed. He still had almost half his life to live.

GROWING UP IN HOMESTEAD

Margaret Byington arrived in Homestead in 1906, soon after the Goodes settled there. The Russell Sage Foundation, a newly launched Progressive Era think tank, had dispatched a team to examine life in Pittsburgh, ground zero for the age of enterprise. Byington's role was to investigate working-class life, especially how women held families together in the shadow of the mill.[21] In her contribution to the Pittsburgh Survey, a multivolume study that sought to rally support for reform, she described Homestead as divided into native-born whites, Slavs, and African Americans. The latter, she learned, held an unusual position.

Greater Homestead—encompassing Homestead, West Homestead, and Munhall—contained about twenty-five thousand residents, mostly mill workers and their families, in 1900. Native-born white Americans comprised 36 percent of the population, while foreign-born whites and their children totaled almost 58 percent, and African Americans 5 percent. Byington listened to the jumble of languages spoken on 6th Avenue—by one count, twenty-six—and saw the foreign-born presence growing larger by the day. The Black community began to grow, too. Its ranks doubled between 1910 and 1920 and doubled again the following decade, boosting Blacks to one-sixth of the town.[22]

Byington spent a year talking with women in their kitchens, learning the tempo of homes that throbbed to the incessant clamor of the steel works. She visited the Ward's courtyards, where one in every three Slavic children died before reaching two years of age, and Hilltop, where infant mortality was substantially lower. She heard stories of corruption, with money passing hands to secure a job. She saw the ravages of disease spread by drinking water fouled by raw sewage and witnessed the wages of work: crushed feet, lacerated hands, amputated limbs, and fatherless families.[23]

A skilled investigator, Byington recognized not only the commonalities of mill town life, but its fracture points. In Homestead, that was nationality, which divided people more than race. "The break between the Slavs and the rest of the community is on the whole more absolute than that between the whites and the Negroes," she concluded. "Neither in lodge nor in church nor with a few exceptions, in school, do the two mingle."[24] The Goodes' life bore that out.

African Americans did not share lodge or church membership with either group but had more in common with native-born whites and immigrants from the British Isles because they spoke the same language and shared more culturally. Byington was struck by how well many African Americans—even those brought in to break strikes—had done in a town where time was measured in terms of how long it had been since the bloody 1892 lockout. Still, Byington wrote, Blacks were often "looked down upon as intruders of alien blood."[25]

Byington could see that Africans Americans like the Goodes aspired to Progressive Era respectability. "I call to mind especially a man who starting as a laborer is now a roller, the highest skilled of the steel workers," she wrote. "These men have in the main come to adopt the same standards as their white neighbors, and are usually treated with genuine respect by the latter." She was not blind to the resentment their success provoked, nor that segregation dictated where Blacks worshipped and which lodges they joined. But, she stressed, "the more prosperous among them are winning respect."[26]

Her co-investigator was Richard R. Wright Jr., the first African American to earn a PhD in sociology, who paid particular attention to Black steelworkers. "Many had neat sitting rooms or parlors containing pianos or organs," he reported. "In nearly all, large crayon portraits and landscape chromos found conspicuous place. Food seemed to be substantial and abundant." Wright watched one day as men arrived to receive their pay. "None came in their working clothes; most had polished their shoes, which were different from the ones worn at work; all were well, even stylishly dressed, and bore nothing about them to indicate their calling."[27] He and Byington could have been sketching William and Mary, at work and at home.

The Ward was another story. "There is a totally different class of colored people," Byington lamented, "who run houses of ill fame and gambling resorts on 6th Avenue; a 'sporty element' which is much in evidence and creates for the race an unpleasant notoriety."[28] The divide between the Ward and Hilltop widened during the Great Migration. The Black population had never been homogenous, and class differences were apparent. Earlier migrants from Virginia, Maryland, Washington, DC, and West Virginia were generally better-off. Often educated, they held better jobs than those from the Deep South who had come during World War I. Many in Homestead were, like Mary Hunter Goode, from the Shenandoah Valley, or William Goode, from the region around Richmond. Historian Laurence Glasco credited these Shenandoah Valley migrants for creating a critical mass of literary societies and reading groups, concert orchestras, chamber music ensembles, and choirs in Pittsburgh. Working-class families like the Goodes sustained these institutions. "Advocates of the self-made man," Glasco argues, "they had great confidence in their abilities and in their own entrepreneurial future."[29]

Although men from the Ward and Hilltop made steel together, they went their separate ways afterward. William Goode did not frequent the Ward, which enjoyed a richly deserved reputation for gambling and prostitution. Mal and his siblings were admonished to stay away from its streets, where single transient men gathered and temptation was ever present. Hustlers of all sorts preyed there, especially on payday.[30]

One-quarter of the white and the Black families that Byington surveyed in 1900 were property owners. Many had purchased homes from the Homestead Realty Company, which sold five-room frame cottages with running water in the kitchen but no bathroom for two thousand dollars, with three hundred dollars down and seventeen-dollar monthly mortgage payments. That was the sort of house the Goodes bought.[31] "It wasn't a fancy home," Mal remembered, "but at least no one ever came to collect the rent. That frame house was our own." They borrowed on it to build a second dwelling out back and to pay college tuition. "By then, the monthly payment was around $40 a month," Mal said. "It may sound like a small sum, but that was a lot of money at that time for anybody, especially for a Negro family in Homestead."

Mal and his siblings had sweat equity in the house. Mary expected her daughters to help with the cleaning, and when her grandchildren moved in for extended stays, they scrubbed and cleaned alongside her. "My brothers and I built the steps leading up from the sidewalk," Mal recounted. "Dad helped build the foundation and we turned and poured the concrete with shovels. Standing atop the highest step, we could see a distance down the street, which was easy since the house was perched on the crest of a small hill." Mary relished sitting with a child or grandchild on the front porch swing, watching the mill light up the evening sky. There was a small front lawn and a backyard, where William planted vegetables.

After the open hearth explosion forced William out of the mill in 1925, he built a second house with three small rooms and a double garage in the backyard. By then, he owned a used Stanley Steamer, a steam-propelled automobile. "A few years later, Dad bought a brand-new Ford Model T flatbed pickup truck to deliver vegetables and fruits when he ran a produce store," Mal recalled. "We started the engine by turning a crank until the engine kicked off. Some folks got broken arms when the cranks kicked back; anything strong enough to start a truck engine was strong enough to break a man's bones."

As much as Mal respected his father, he saw far more each day of his mother, who was just as indomitable as her husband. Mary's aspirations to teach in the North were stifled by the color line. Homestead and Pittsburgh classrooms were integrated, but neither hired African American instructors. Nor did many married women work outside the home in Homestead, where steelmaking skewed employment. Instead, they took in boarders, rising early to prepare breakfast and to pack lunch buckets. Scrubbing the grease out of work clothes without benefit of running water, they closely managed budgets, cooking soups and stews from scratch to hold down costs. Women's domestic labor and frugality allowed families to make it from payday to payday.[32] The Goodes rented the house they built in their backyard to Marshall Johnson, a steelworker, and his wife, Pearl, but Mary never took in boarders. She already had her hands full.

As her family grew to six children, Mary organized the home front, and it ran like her Virginia classroom. She was a model of organization, competency, and accountability to her children, who rarely bucked her, knowing that would trigger William's wrath. The children realized there was only one way to do something—her way. Mary scrutinized their schoolwork and policed their chores, checking to see if shoes were properly shined for Sunday services and household duties performed to her standards. "None of my brothers and sisters ever left the house with dirty clothes on their backs," Mal attested. "The only time we were seen with soiled clothes was during our trip home from work." They internalized Mary's standards and passed them on to their own children. "We all pitched in," Mal stressed. "My parents wouldn't have it any other way. Even if we hadn't wanted to help out, my father would have made us do it."

Each spring, the boys made scaffolds of ladders and boards that reached the ceiling to wash the wallpaper. "We made sure we did the job right because if we halfway did it, my parents would make us do it again and we might get a whipping to boot. Pop was no tyrant and would never have kicked us out, but we knew we had to pull our part of the load."

For African Americans in the 1920s, the Goodes enjoyed unusual security. "My father and mother worked hard to see that we had the best of everything they could afford." And the children knew they had it better than most. Their home had the trappings of middle-class life, something Hilltop's steelworkers prized. "Fine rattan and rag rugs covered wooden floors and carpet in the hallways gave that house flavor and style," Mal recalled. "At least we thought it did and that's all that mattered."

Mal's childhood memories could hardly have been rosier. A coal furnace kept them warm, and an indoor bathroom that replaced their outhouse was cause for celebration. Bathing until then meant heating water on the stove and scrubbing at the kitchen sink or sitting in a tub on the kitchen floor. "But when we got an indoor bathroom, with hot and cold running water, no more boiling water on the stove in pots and pans and buckets. It was terrific."

When the 1920s economy boosted incomes to heights many on Hilltop had never seen before, William and Mary added electricity and another bedroom, which became a haven for their children when they fell on hard times. There was a piano downstairs, as well as a crank-driven Victrola, a four-and-a-half-feet-high record player with a heavy pinpoint needle. Mal remembered gingerly setting the tone arm on the grooves of the record and releasing the catch on the spring to allow the turntable to rotate at 78 rpms, playing mostly gospel music. "I can still hear the popping and hissing sounds the older records made, but it sounded good and kept us amused. We were the only ones on the street to have one of those fancy contraptions and among the first to have a telephone."

Mal, eight, and Bill, a year older, were inseparable. They shared a bed and teamed up at home and on the streets, where they worked on huckster wagons selling produce. "If a housekeeper liked us, they let us fill their order for a basket and deliver to their front door." When their parents ran a fish and poultry business, the boys made deliveries. Their customers included working people and Homestead's most affluent households. Perle Mesta—whose husband, George, owned Mesta Machinery—was a customer. While his sprawling plant along the river made turbines for power plants and equipment for mills, Perle held soirees and mingled with national and global elites. She became the US ambassador to Luxembourg and crossed paths with Mal decades later at the United Nations.

Mal and Bill also worked at a shoeshine stand and took turns at the Blue Goose Barbershop, sweeping the floor and running errands. "Early on Saturday and before Sunday school, Bill or I trekked down to the Blue Goose. That was a most prosperous time for making money. Men would say: 'Boy, shine my shoes. Put a spit shine on 'em before I go home.' 'Shine 'em up, boy, I wanna see my face when I walk down the street.'" Their best customers were men who had spent the night gambling. "Sometimes they'd win $200 or more after a night at a gambling squat, rolling dice or playing skin [a fast-paced card game in which large sums passed hands]. They'd have a roll of bills as big around as my arm and thought nothing about giving up a two-dollar tip. I've gotten as much as five dollars for one shoeshine when the fellow was feeling good or had a good night playing the odds."[33]

William bought the boys shiny Sears and Roebuck wagons for eighteen dollars, which they used for fun and work. With removable side panels and large hard-rubber tires on metal wheels, they could haul three-hundred-pound blocks of ice. Bill and Mal knew about ice. On the farm they had cut and buried ice blocks in the ground each winter, covering them with straw so they would last till summer. In Homestead, they went to the icehouse, picking up three-hundred-pound blocks with seams creased into them that they broke into chunks weighing twenty-five, fifty, and one hundred pounds with their ice picks. A twenty-five-pound of block cost fifteen cents, a fifty-pound block twenty-five cents, and a hundred-pound block fifty cents. By the time the ice melted two days later, the boys were back with new blocks.

"Whenever we went out and made some money, we knew what to do with it." After a morning at the shoeshine stand, Mal gave his earnings to Mary, who returned some for pocket money. That did not always set well with Mal. "I worked hard for that money and sometimes I just wanted to know it was mine, that if I wanted to buy something, I could reach in my breeches' pocket. If I was old enough to work, then I was old enough to spend my money." But he kept those thoughts to himself. "My Christian upbringing taught me what was right and what was selfish. If I didn't like it, that was my problem. I knew what to do with my earnings and if I ever forgot, my father had a sure-fire reminder, a slap across the head, or a strap on my behind."

William Goode was a hard man, but not a harsh one. "My father was strict and never hesitated in taking a strap to our behinds or sending a back-handed slap our way if we got out of line." Boundaries were clear and punishment administered decisively. "Don't think he was a brutal man," Mal implored, "because he wasn't in any way. But he didn't hesitate to knock us down if we talked back to Mother. None of us dared talk back to either one of them without ending up on the floor." And they never walked into the house with their hats on because William would slap it off. That hand to the head was "a reminder that disrespecting an elder or talking back to a parent means pain, and no one in their right mind ever wants pain, not in the Goode family, they didn't."

Mal kept quiet about what he didn't like until he was on his own; from then on, he rarely kept quiet. Sometimes rebellious, he internalized his parents' sense of discipline. In later years, as family disintegration became widespread throughout the country, Mal adopted an old school approach to childhood. "A child has to have discipline," he lectured audiences. "Without the proper paternal and maternal guidance, we would have been wild and ended up in jail or worse, dead." Consequently, Mal said, he and his siblings followed their parents' rules without hesitation. "We never abused what we had as children; neither my mother nor my father would have tolerated such nonsense. We were raised that way from little tykes." Faith and family were intertwined on 12th Avenue. "The belief in God, the Supreme

Being, was strong in my house," Mal explained. "That faith has been with me all of my life and I will believe in God until the day I am no longer able to breathe."

In addition to discipline and faith, their parents offered comforts not widely available, especially when they sat down to eat. Next to giving praise to God, Mal hailed his mother Mary's cooking. "I could never do justice in describing the kinds of foods my mother cooked but I can tell you it was all better than good. There were slabs of thick, hot, steaming cornbread, tomatoes, and lima beans, and we never left the table hungry, not one time. Mom's pork ribs were the best. No one, I mean no one on this earth, ever cooked spareribs the way she would. Whenever I picked up one of her ribs and stuck it in my mouth, the meat just fell right off the bone and melted in my mouth. I ate every slip of meat and never wasted a single drop of the sauce. I would have eaten the bone if I could have chewed it! And Mom made cornbread in the evenings and hot biscuits every morning."

The home on West 12th Street in Homestead long remained the family's gathering spot. Mary and William took out second and third mortgages to help put the children through college and finance their fish and poultry store. "That house was plastered with mortgage," Mal recalled. But in 1942, the six children got together and paid off the last seventeen hundred dollars owed. Friends and members from their congregation joined the celebration on 12th Street the day they retired the mortgage.[34]

On Sunday afternoons, after attending services at Clark Memorial Baptist, the Goodes adjourned to their Hilltop home for dinner. Mary spared no effort, preparing her husband's, children's, and eventually grandchildren's favorites. At times, twenty or more family members crowded into the house. Until they left town in 1962, Mal's family returned to Homestead one Sunday a month for church and dinner. And when Mal suffered a heart attack in 1948, he, Mary, and their children moved back. Mal's sister Mary Dee and her four young children also returned after her divorce, living in the small backyard house.

The Sunday dinner routine was firmly set. William began with a *long* prayer, so long that his grandchildren remember that the food was always cold by the time they were allowed to dig in. But it was still delectable. Baked macaroni and cheese, ham hocks, ox tails, fresh baked rolls, barbecued meats, and saucy beans filled the air, the table, and the bellies of three generations of Goodes. For Mary, the dinner table was hallowed ground. One day, a white insurance man collecting their life insurance premium removed his hat and placed it on the table when Mary left the room to gather the money. She walked in to see the hat on her lace tablecloth and without a word picked it up, took a few steps and threw it out the front door. She gave the money to the stunned insurance man and showed him out. He grasped what her children knew, that this was Mary's home and her dinner table sanctified ground.

William Goode, "Pop" to his grandchildren, presided over the table but hardly monopolized discussion. He set the tone by the prayer and his choice of Bible verse for the day. One of his favorites was "Stand firm then, with the belt of truth buckled around your waist, with the breastplate of righteousness in place" (*Ephesians* 6:14) as if he were warning the younger generations of Goodes of the battles awaiting them. Their grandchildren cherish those meals, both for what was served and what was said during them. At Sunday and holiday dinners, with tables spilling into a second room, there were helpings of politics and debates over "What the Negro Should Do," along with Mary's cooking. Conversations often focused on race. These were lively, far-reaching, and sometimes heated discussions about their hopes and strategies for advancement. They were a chance to vent frustrations, rail against injustice, and challenge each other about what they were doing with their lives. Mary, known as "Nana," brought strength, education, and a firm demeanor to the debates. Her husband sat at the head of the table saying little but presiding with quiet authority. He often warned his impatient son Mal to slow down, fearing white backlash and rage. The family hammered out questions ranging from national issues and NAACP efforts to dismantle segregation to local concerns, including the displacement of

Ward residents when the Homestead Works expanded as it ramped up for World War II, leaving many homeless. Passions flared, tempered by good food and a sense of family.[35]

Mal's brothers gravitated to business. James, the first born, attended Howard University, before leaving for Chicago to set up a real estate business. Mal recalled that he made a go of it financially and that the family never needed to send him money. Moving back to Pittsburgh in 1932, James became one of the city's few Black realtors. Bill, the second born, became a pharmacist with a substantial practice. He and Mal were especially close, living near each other on the Hill and interacting almost daily. Allan, who was four years younger than Mal, was the only one of the children who did not attend college. Instead, he gravitated to the streets and worked in the numbers business. Sharply dressed, with a money roll in his pocket, Allan was short in stature but scrappy and a lady's man before he wed and raised a family. Although well-known at the racetrack and a prolific gambler, Allan had the gift of gab. Car dealerships competed for his services.

Although Mary had schooled her daughters in the domestic sciences, they were spirited young women who did not shy away from the public arena. Mary demanded as much from them as she did from her sons. Mary Dee and Ruth stepped away from traditional women's roles, rejecting gender barriers as well as racial pigeon-holing while fashioning highly successful careers. Mary Dee, as she became known when she took to the airwaves, was four years younger than Mal. Informed and opinionated, she carved out a local, then national, reputation as a pioneering Black radio personality. Ruth, the youngest, was feisty and, to her nephews and nieces, larger than life. Gutsy, boisterous, and sometimes cantankerous, she worked at Bill's pharmacy before plunging into public health work, directing Pittsburgh's sickle cell organization.

"My father believed his children had to have enough to eat," Mal recalled, "just as he believed we ought to have a good education. Those two things were all he ever worried about." Given what a millworker needed to eat to make it through the day, it's no wonder that William's brood ate well. Nor would his children be denied an education. He was illiterate much of his life, but his children were college bound. "When we went to school and got grades of 85, 90, or 95 out of a possible 100, he wanted to know why we fell short of getting a perfect mark of 100. We had to explain why we had failed to make the top grade." When Mal took Russell, his eldest son, to enroll in school, Russell had the same homeroom teacher who taught his father. "He told her," Russell laughed, "'If he misbehaves, whack him.'"[36]

William took the boys on long walks along the river on Sunday afternoons when they had their heart to hearts, but Mary shaped their formal education. She drilled her children on their lessons. "Mom was a frequent visitor to the school," Mal recalled, "not to quarrel, but mainly to assure the principal and our teachers that they could count on cooperation at our home." But if Mary was unhappy with how teachers approached their schooling, she let them know. "'We send you to school learn,' Mom used to say, 'and remember you carry our name and represent this home when you are away from it whether at school, at church, on the playground, or in the street.' This attitude was a fetish with my mother. 'There's nothing like a good name,' she used to say."[37]

The children played in Homestead's nearby Frick Park. Named for Henry Clay Frick, whose heavy-handed tactics provoked the 1892 confrontation with workers, the park was a haven. "Occasionally we went to the picture show at the nickelodeon. It cost a nickel at first and as inflation set in, a dime." *The Birth of a Nation* was playing when Mal first arrived in Homestead. The cutting-edge silent movie celebrated the Klan as the savior of the white Christian South during Reconstruction. Its depiction of history long troubled Mal.

Church was a more frequent destination. "Every Wednesday night, we attended prayer meetings, whether we liked it or not, and on the Sabbath, Sunday school. There was no such a thing as skipping those Bible teachings to go swimming on Sunday morning. But I never disliked studying the Bible because I met my friends there." Religion reinforced the social divide between Hilltop and those who came in the 1890s, and migrants from World War I. Some better-off congregations spurned the recent migrants. Stories still circulate of the brown paper bag test, in which African Americans whose skin color was darker than a brown paper bag were unwelcome at certain churches and clubs. But the Goodes comfortably crossed those lines. "If we didn't go to Clark Memorial, we went to the Second Baptist Church down on 6th Avenue, or Park Place AME Church." They were all, Mal intoned, the Lord's home.[38]

Early émigrés formed Clark Memorial Baptist in the 1890s. Befitting its seniority among Homestead's Black churches and the better jobs its congregants held, Clark Memorial signified status. Its message was in tune with the "New Negro" consciousness coursing through Black neighborhoods in the 1920s, mixing social uplift with gospel. The "race question" was often on the agenda. Clark Memorial functioned smoothly with strict financial accountability. Its ministers, graduates of seminaries and colleges, organized clubs, auxiliaries, educational programs, and a foreign mission. In Sunday school, Mal watched films about African Americans bettering themselves. Upwardly bound role models filled its pews, and Mal absorbed lessons of rectitude and striving.[39] William began worshipping there in the 1890s and was the congregation's oldest member when he died. Mary, who belonged for half a century, was a charter member of the Harmony Club and a stalwart of the Loyalty Club and the Senior Missionary Society.[40]

Second Baptist in the Ward ministered to a different social mix, including newer migrants. Formed in 1905, the church moved among storefronts and frequently changed pastors. Second Baptist could not fund the kinds of activities that Clark Memorial featured, but it stayed faithful to the Ward and provided a rooted, spiritual fellowship for millworkers drawn to its warm embrace. The Goodes felt at home in both churches. Although Mal grew up on Hilltop, he never looked down at the Ward when measuring someone's worth. His father made sure of that.[41]

Religion was more segregated than other parts of life. The streets were often integrated, churches rarely so. Hilltop was a felicitous place to come of age. "The neighbors were good people who worked hard for what they got," Mal emphasized. "Our fathers worked together in the mill; they were almost like brothers, and we grew up with their children." Neighbors celebrated and mourned together, reaching out when there was sickness or death. "That made my neighborhood peaceful and calm."

Hilltop was no racial utopia, and Mal encountered abuse, but he rarely dwelled on childhood insults. "Those bouts of name-calling didn't happen often; it was the good things I remember most." His memories evoke Norman Rockwell's sentimental sketches of mid-twentieth-century America at its best. "We were small children in stature and we looked up to our parents, and held them in high esteem, the way children ought to respect the folks who brought them into the world."

Mal Goode's recollections of childhood grew ever rosier. "Even during the depression, we never once went without the necessities. My father and mother saw to that." His father's disability pension from the mill and earnings as a shopkeeper insulated them from the troubles ravaging Pittsburgh. At its nadir in 1934, Black unemployment and underemployment in Allegheny County totaled 69 percent. By then, Mal was hanging on to a job at the Homestead Works, working only a few days a month and doing what he could to survive.[42]

3
THE EDUCATION OF MALVIN GOODE

MAL COULDN'T GET TO SLEEP. THE OTHER MEN ON HIS NIGHT shift crew were snoring away, but his mind was racing. Punching in at 7:00 that evening, they had worked straight through till 1:00 in the morning before finding a relatively quiet place to stretch out and nap in the cavernous Homestead Steel Works. After an hour of shut-eye, they would finish their ten-hour shifts and trek home or to their day jobs. Mal had worked—and slept—alongside them since entering the mill while in high school.

Mal usually had no problem stealing a bit of sleep, but no matter how hard he tried, he could not stop thinking about what he would face in the morning—his first day of class at the University of Pittsburgh. Unlike his coworkers, who figured they would spend the rest of their working lives at the mill, Mal expected more than a blue-collar job in an industry where racial lines were hardening and the future was murky. And his parents had made it clear that education was his way forward.

Most of his coworkers, like the vast majority of males in 1920s America, had not graduated high school, much less attended college.[1] Entering a factory was the path more often trod. A job at the Homestead mill had been steady enough to allow William and Mary Goode to raise six children in a house they owned on Hilltop overlooking the steelworks. But wanting more for their children, they demanded that their four sons and two daughters pursue education as far as possible. That had been Mary's game plan since she agreed to marry William when he was an illiterate son of former slaves working on a blast furnace. College was a goal that William fully embraced for their children, and Mal, like his older brothers, James and Bill, was about to fulfill it.

"Most parents in the Pittsburgh area fostered only one wish," Mal wrote, "for their boys to grow up and get work in the steel mills. When these kids became 16 or 17 years old, they were, for the most part, destined to work in the mills, some for a lifetime. And don't think for one minute that steel work was a dead-end occupation. Steelworkers were proud people, the money was good, the 24-hour-operation convenient for men who worked two jobs. Steelwork was honest work, and I'm proud to have been a part of the industry."[2] But by the 1920s, the chances of African Americans rising above semiskilled positions had crumbled from what they had been when William Goode became a first helper. That was as high as a Black man could reach at the time, but those times were over. Mal never forgot his father's resentment that he was unable to ascend the mill's job ladder and become a boss melter.

Mal's parents made it clear that their children were ordained for higher callings. That message was reinforced at Clark Memorial Baptist Church and by the *Pittsburgh Courier*. But college cost money, and Mal knew he would have to pay his own tuition. "It wasn't because my father wouldn't pay it," Mal said. "He couldn't pay it and I suppose I felt that I would follow in my Pop's footsteps and make steelworking my life-long career." His parents disagreed about that but knew that the industry offered the best way to acquire the money Mal needed for college. He had few alternatives other than entering Homestead's underground economy to run numbers or bootleg liquor.

Besides, Mal noted, "Because all of the blacks in the mills knew each other well, it was easy for Negroes to get a job." When his friend Louis Fenderson told him of an opening during the summer of 1924, Mal applied. "Soon I was gainfully employed in a job perfectly suiting my needs. I was 16 and worked with Louis in the cafeteria six nights a week for $83 a month and got meals, too. What made it especially good was that I could often sleep awhile, then get up and put ice in coolers and grapefruits and other food out, go home at 5:30 when the shift ended, sleep a couple of hours, and be at high school at 8:30." Even though work curtailed his social life, Mal never missed a shift.

And the money was more than he had ever made before. "There was no income tax or Social Security taken out of our pay, and no Unemployment Compensation to back us up should we lose our jobs. We took our gross salaries home and they paid in cash." Mal gave much of his earnings to his mother, Mary, kept some for pocket money, and banked the rest for college.

Something else attracted Mal to the job. The Homestead Works, which stretched for miles along the Monongahela, was a powerful, mysterious force that dictated the rhythms of the town and the very air he breathed. As a boy, he was in awe of his father and the strength and dexterity required to make steel. Now Mal wandered through the mammoth plant, absorbing its splendor as well as its deadly power. He carried himself with pride because he was a part, no matter how small, of making steel. Mal worked the cafeteria job for a year and a half, juggling school and work, and anticipating someday going to college.

HIGH SCHOOL YEARS

Mal grew up in an integrated neighborhood and attended integrated schools, but belonged to an all-Black crew at the mill. He was able to move easily between the "Old Pittsburgh" Black community that was deeply rooted in the city and more recent migrants from the Black Belt who had few roots there. But he could also handle himself in white arenas. These racial and class dynamics shaped Mal. So did parental stress on education and work. Good grades were nonnegotiable, and his parents insisted that children lucky enough to go to school every day should earn high marks. They internalized the expectations of a father yanked from school after only eight days because his daily labor had more tangible value than the future return on education, and those of a college-educated mother who was uncompromising in her demands that they graduate. It was part of Mary Goode's legacy; her 1956 obituary noted she had "four children in college at the same time."[3]

Her children were also expected to look the part. They did not dare leave the house unless their clothes were cleaned and pressed, ready to pass muster on the street. "These were factors of life ground into us when we were very small," Mal wryly acknowledged, "since father knew what we would run into as black children." The Goodes prepared their children to combat the segregation and bigotry they would encounter, in part by affirming their standard of respectability.

William and Mary, adhering to middle-class values, behavior, and aspirations, stressed balancing schoolwork with gainful labor. Mal's parents prioritized formal education, but he was also schooled on the streets, where he had to determine what was acceptable and what was not for a young Black male. Homestead was a vibrant, diverse community, validating Mal's mantra that "race means nothing to me when a fellow is my friend." He had white pals growing up, but in high school the kids he once had played with no longer acknowledged him. "We lived side by side with white families on 12th Avenue," Mal recalled, "but when you got to be a certain age you weren't running in each other's homes anymore." Although Hilltop's streets were the site of interracial friendships and associations, Mal inevitably confronted the color line in Homestead. Negotiating its racial contradictions was painful.

In one arena, African Americans more than held their own—the ballfield. The Homestead Grays were central to Mal's self-esteem and that of the Black community. African Americans had played ball since the Civil War, but by the 1890s those who made it to the major leagues had disappeared. Given the resurgence of terror in the South after the collapse of Reconstruction, losing that opportunity was hardly

African Americans' most pressing concern. But it mattered because of the role that baseball played in the American psyche.

The nation's pastime, freighted with ideological overtones, had taken on a mythic cast. Many saw sport as a metaphor for American democracy, where a gritty meritocracy trumped class and nationality. Sons of European immigrants proved their merit to become Americans by showing their athletic mettle. African Americans, however, were barred from the major leagues, and most whites thought their absence was because of inherent athletic inferiority. They concluded that Blacks were unable to compete in sport, and by extension, unworthy of citizenship.

On the other side of the racial boundary, however, African Americans created a sporting world of their own. By the 1930s Pittsburgh had become Black baseball's epicenter, in no small measure because of men living on Hilltop. Jerry and John Veney migrated to Pittsburgh from Grottoes, Virginia, and lived across the street from the Goodes. Along with men from work and from the neighborhood, they formed a Black ball club that became legendary—the Homestead Grays. "It meant a lot to see them play," Mal said. "When you're talking about the Homestead Grays, you were talking about one of the prized possessions of the black community."[4]

When the Veneys stepped aside, Cum Posey took over, guiding the Grays' ascent in the sporting firmament. Posey was Pittsburgh's top all-around athlete. His father, Captain Cumberland Willis Posey Sr., had come of age on the river, parlaying his experience on the water into shipbuilding before making the Diamond Coke and Coal Company the city's largest Black-owned operation. President of the genteel Loendi Club, he was a respected and powerful figure.[5]

His son was just as imposing. Born in 1891, Cum Posey led Homestead High to the city basketball championship in 1908, the year Mal was born. "Most black kids worked after school and on weekends to supplement their family's income, but Cum had the time to deal with what was just a hobby and do something with it. He was not only an astute man but a good businessman and made Black baseball profitable." Posey starred at basketball and baseball at Holy Ghost

College (as Duquesne University was then known) where he played as Charles Cumbert, a thinly veiled effort to retain his amateur standing.[6] Though light-skinned, Posey was not trying to pass as white at Holy Ghost Collete, which had no color line. A "have ball—will travel" athlete who dazzled on the diamond and the hard court, he was already making money as an athlete. His alias was a workaround that sportswriters and fans readily accommodated. Sportswriter Wendell Smith considered him the race's outstanding athlete during the 1920s, "perhaps the most colorful figure who has ever raced down the sundown sports trail." Long after his death, Posey was inducted into both baseball's and basketball's halls of fame, the only athlete ever so honored.[7]

Mal often walked up to West Field with his brothers to watch the Grays. "They played the game as good as white ballplayers, if not better," he proclaimed. "These were your neighbors. These were men who worked in the mill just like our dad, in the armor plate department and open hearth. But they could play some ball." Soon the best Black team in the region, under Posey the Grays became Negro League baseball's flagship squad.[8] Baseball inspired Mal, and sport changed his life. But he counted on education to open the doors of opportunity.

Mal sat among the children of industrialists, millworkers, and shopkeepers at a school that touted its academic excellence, superior athletes, and heaps of spirit for the "Blue and Gold." Mal was a member of Homestead's class of "1925 ½," graduating on January 26, 1926, with twenty-three students, seven of whom were African American, which was, he noted, "a lot of us at one commencement." The 1926 yearbook showcased Black students at their best; boys with shiny controlled hair and dark suits, girls sporting crimped bobs, choker necklaces, and crisp white blouses. And though African Americans were rarely featured in the yearbook, Mal's presence was pervasive. His senior picture depicts a young man with big, thoughtful eyes and carefully parted hair, tightly combed to his head. His striped bowtie is perfectly knotted around a white shirt collar beneath a gray houndstooth jacket. Mal looks directly into the camera, a glimmer of a grin lurking beneath a serious expression. He was vice president of the Debating Club, a member of the Dramatic Club, and assistant stage manager for the class play. The inscription beneath his photo in the yearbook read: "If you judged him by his name, You would think him very tame; But little pranks he likes to play, And funny quips he likes to say."⁹

Mal was exposed to global issues early. At Clark Memorial Baptist, sermons and discussions centered on world events; in high school debate, he held forth on the "Philippine Question" and the "Recognition of Russia." These experiences were a prelude to his public advocacy on the airwaves, and his popularity foreshadowed his influence as a leader, speaker, and activist. Mal even authored the class poem.

Mal rose to the top of his class, but school was imperfectly integrated. "The teachers were adequate, I suppose. Rarely did I run into one who was outwardly prejudiced." Mal described how racism intensified as he advanced in school. "Sometimes they would put kids in alphabetical order and the 'Gs' would end up behind the 'Zs' in the back of the class, but I want to make it clear, segregated seating was not the norm in my schools. When you got into high school, that's when segregation began. You couldn't be in the school play; you couldn't sing in the choir."¹⁰ Black students felt they had no choice but to abide with the racial code, so Mal managed the school play but did not appear in it.

He was frustrated that no African Americans taught at Homestead High and would not until 1962, thirty-six years after he graduated. "I never sat under a black teacher in my life, neither in grade school, junior high school or high school, not even at the University of Pittsburgh. The University got its first black professor in the late '40s and Homestead High its first black teacher in 1962. I missed something, never to sit under a black teacher, man or woman." That rankled Mal, who fought for Black educators throughout his life, just as his mother had advocated for her children. Mary Goode did not think twice before showing up unannounced at school and challenging teachers about how they treated her sons and daughters. Even more than her husband, she confronted what she felt was unfair.

Mal juggled work, studies, extracurriculars, church, and family, but he had no time for sports, no matter how much he loved them. Joining a squad meant daily practice, something he could ill afford. Instead, he studied hard and did well, favoring history, civics, and political science classes over math and science. He also had a penchant for languages, for which he credited Miss Sarah Covert, an outstanding Latin teacher. "There was no way then that I could have known what the future had in store for me," he reflected. Mal had dreams, but not ones that transported a young man from Homestead who studied around night shifts to a job with ABC at the United Nations, where a jumble of languages prevailed. Yet his classes, Debate Club, and Miss Covert equipped him with research tools, language skills, and the art of argumentation.

Although only a minority of Homestead's Black youth finished high school, they were an upwardly mobile group sharing Mal's drive. His friend Louis Fenderson, who helped Mal land his job at the works, became the first African American to earn a doctorate in English at the University of Pittsburgh and later taught at Howard University. Edwin Cundiff was Mal's best friend and a member of a prominent Homestead family. After Pitt, Howard University Medical School, and an internship, Dr. Cundiff started a practice in Pittsburg, Kansas, to fill a need for Black doctors. Mal, uneasy with his friend's decision to practice in a mostly white town, drove him to the airport when he departed. He never saw him again. In Kansas City, Eddie mostly tended to Black patients, but he treated just enough white ones to draw notice. Eddie thrived—until he was shot and killed on his porch in August 1935. He was twenty-eight years old. A forty-three-year-old man was arrested for the murder and his motive was allegedly "a frenzied jealousy of his wife and Dr. Cundiff."[11] That man was acquitted, and although the case was never solved, some people in Homestead speculated that white doctors had instigated his murder because he had dared to compete with them. That such suspicions were even voiced reflects how little trust some African Americans had in the rule of law. Forever shaken by Eddie's murder, Mal wrote "I still love him," decades later.

Another friend, Johnny Palmer, avoided confrontation and skipped college, because he preferred to seek immediate financial rewards. Capitalizing on his charm and pluck, Johnny built a newsstand business and set up shop at the stop where workers changed streetcars on the way to work. Soon Johnny was not only selling papers but loaning money to unemployed workers struggling during the Depression. "Young Johnny Palmer," Mal wrote, "a black boy who survived, made more money than his customers ever did!" Mal routinely stopped by Johnny's stand a bit before 7:00 am on his way back from his overnight shift at the mill. Mal was transfixed as his friend negotiated with his debtors. Johnny even loaned money to their former Homestead teachers. Yet Johnny, Mal wrote, was unwilling to settle for a Black man's lot in Homestead and left for Chicago where, according to rumors, he "passed over," abandoning his true identity for the benefits that whiteness afforded. Johnny returned to Homestead for his brother's funeral but never came back again. No matter how remarkable his classmates were, race twisted their futures. Mal was determined to break those barriers wherever and whenever he could.

Mal missed his shift on January 29, 1926, in order to attend his high school graduation, but that rite of passage did not cue an immediate transition to college. The following day, his high school degree on display at home, he was back at work, where academic success counted for little. He left the cafeteria crew for a slightly better paid job in the sanitation department and worked as a janitor, but prospects for promotion were dim. In sanitation, he joined an all-Black crew, mostly grown men with families working ten-hour days and drawing $56.20 every two weeks. It was a decent salary and would pay for Mal's education at Pitt. For that he was grateful. But despite his degree and seniority on the job, his status as a laborer never changed during twelve years at the mill. Mal's resentment deepened as he saw race stifle Black workers' prospects even more than they had for his father's generation. "I had men bossing me who had never been out of high school; one of them finished high school and became my foreman after just three or four years, but it didn't matter that I had been on the job longer than he was."

While Mal had a front row seat to racial realities in the workplace, he enjoyed the camaraderie of the crew as they cleaned offices for sixty hours each week. They worked as a team and devised strategies to get some rest during the shift. "We moved fast until everything was done, starting at 7 p.m, and getting off at 5:30 a.m. Most of the time we worked straight through to 1:00 or 1:30 before we ate lunch. Later we'd catch a nap for two or three hours, and nobody bothered us." Mal internalized the importance of racial solidarity when entering integrated, white-led settings. As his all-Black crew worked together to complete their tasks and get some rest during the overnight shift, an all-white security patrol staffed the mills. "Sometimes an arrogant guard would give us trouble and make it miserable for us, but usually the guards were decent fellows who left us alone." Mal learned who he could count on.

Mal had worked since shining shoes at the Blue Goose Barbershop and riding a huckster's wagon. He fit in easily with his older work-mates, who accepted him as the son of a respected coworker who had gone as far as a Black man could at the mill. Moreover, Mal knew his place on the crew and was eager to learn from his elders. He adjusted to night turns that summer, but when high school classes resumed in September, he was stretched to handle both work and school. His coworkers, proud that he was securing an education they were unable to pursue, covered for him when they could. Those mid-shift naps became indispensable; without them he would have struggled to pay attention in class. Even with them, he fought to stay awake. The year and a half following his high school graduation was easier because he was no longer juggling work and school. But when Mal entered the University of Pittsburgh, the challenges of the previous years were a preview of what he faced as a college student working nights.

Luckily, times were flush and employment steady. With the nation producing a greater share of the world's manufactured goods during the 1920s than ever before, U.S. Steel stock soared in value. But the uber-powerful corporation brooked no challenge from a union on the shop floor. Big Steel had crushed the Amalgamated Association in the 1892 Homestead lockout and triumphed again in the nationwide 1919 steel strike when half a million men walked off the job. Free of unions but sensitive to labor relations and public criticism for its harsh policies, the corporation embraced the American Plan that swept through industry during the 1920s. Rather than simply oppose unions with brute force, the American Plan sought to gain their employees' allegiance with corporate welfare measures.

While stridently anti-union, the American Plan tried to defuse dissent by offering workers a limited voice through company-controlled unions. Personnel managers, believing they could win workers' hearts and minds, introduced company newspapers, lunchrooms, even upgraded restrooms. As a *Time* magazine advertisement for Scott Paper tissue asked: "Is your washroom breeding Bolshevism?"[12] In the vanguard of the American Plan, the Homestead Works offered sports and recreation for workers and the community. U.S. Steel also shortened the workday to eight hours and offered a company stock program. Mal took advantage of both but hardly had the time for company sports.

During the 1920s President Warren Harding's administration joined reformers and the Interchurch World Movement—which had damned steel companies in its *Report on the Steel Strike of 1919*—to push for shorter hours. Steel's iniquitous wages, the report concluded, damaged workers and families. "Americanism is a farce, night schools are worthless, Carnegie libraries on the hill-tops are a jest, churches and welfare institutions are ironic while the steel worker is held to the 12-hour-day. . . . Not only has he no energy left, he has literally no time left . . . not even time for his own family."[13] The Carnegie Library it ridiculed was the one near Mal's home.

A shorter shift was indispensable for Mal, who started Pitt in September 1927. He was on an eight-hour turn, clocking in at 11:00 at night and finishing at 7:00 in the morning. That was a life changer, allowing him to sleep between school and work. Daytime, he sat with a group of well-groomed, upwardly mobile men and women eager to succeed. At night, back in overalls and work boots, he cleaned up after men who hardly gave him a glance. "The pride of it was that you were making a good living," Mal reflected. On top of that, he was able to accumulate savings since he lived at home. Mal also participated in U.S. Steel's employee stock plan, purchasing shares, which soared in value. Once he graduated, he planned to sell his stock and use his profits to attend law school, a career for which those who knew him thought he was destined.

PITT IS IT

Mal's years at the University of Pittsburgh gave him the tools to navigate networks bigger than Homestead or the shop floor. Although Pitt exposed him to a new realm of possibility, racial and class constraints, some of which were evident among African American students, were inescapable. Mal took both literal and figurative notes as he charted his way through school, even though he didn't know when he would be able to put his education to use professionally.

No matter how tired he was, Mal made it to class. By then, he had finished his night shift and hiked up the hill, shed his work clothes, and fallen into bed. Awakening, he transformed himself from worker to student. Dragging himself out of bed well before he was fully rested, he slipped on the loose wool pants and jacket that were typical male student attire and ran to catch a streetcar or headed toward the Homestead bridge to hitch a ride with someone heading across the river toward campus.

His first class started at 11:00 and with public transit uncertain, he was often rushing to get there on time and tired when he arrived. School was stressful, the curriculum demanding, and his professors white. Proportionally, there were even fewer Black students at Pitt than at Homestead High. Mal returned home by 5:00 pm, joined the family supper, and tried to keep up with his studies before napping and reporting to work. That hectic pace eased up when he and Bill bought a car, and he could drive to work and school.

His schedule, unusual for a Pitt student, took a personal and academic toll, but Mal remained grateful. "I was fortunate," he stressed, "to have a job at night that allowed me to get a college education without hardship." That job meant laboring alongside workers trying to make ends meet at night and blending in with better-off students by day. Mal became adept at straddling two worlds, a skill he honed as a correspondent charged with explaining race and politics to diverse audiences.

Pitt was a reasonable goal for Mal, even if a majority of whites and a greater number of African Americans could not dream of attending college in the 1920s. But Mal had watched his brother James enroll at Howard and Bill matriculate to Pitt. They were meeting their parents' expectations, and Mal was determined to follow suit. Still, there were frustrations. Work tethered Mal to Homestead and the mills, limiting his access to what Pitt offered. While he embraced school in the fall of 1927, he was cautious, familiar with the forces at play in white institutions.

After planting roots in 1787 as the Pittsburgh Academy, the institution pulsed with a frontier culture of rebellion. But that frontier spirit had faded, and neither Pittsburgh nor Pitt was free of ethnic and class elitism, much less racial stratification. The institution changed its name, curricula, and location until 1908 when it became the University of Pittsburgh and set its cornerstone on thirty-four acres in the Oakland neighborhood. A few miles east of downtown, Oakland had emerged as Pittsburgh's cultural and educational center. In 1889 Mary Croghan Schenley, the granddaughter and heir to the frontier entrepreneur James O'Hara, donated three hundred acres to the city to create Schenley Park. More land was acquired for Schenley Plaza, where Andrew Carnegie built a library, a museum, a concert hall, and for the Carnegie Institute of Technology in 1895. Sporting, medical, and entertainment venues followed in rapid succession, including Forbes Field, Magee Hospital, the Soldiers and Sailors Memorial Hall, the Syria Mosque, and the Masonic Temple. Oakland—home to a mixed population drawn by the mills along the Monongahela River and the business district downtown—pulsated with the energy of those who worked, studied, and played there. Mal absorbed Oakland's verve as he walked among its grand structures.

Pitt's Black students were a self-selected cohort bonded by a sense of mission. But they were not free of their own class and racial hierarchies. Most African American students brought their connections and social capital with them when they arrived on campus. They were the vanguard of what W. E. B. Du Bois in 1903 had famously dubbed the "Talented Tenth." Arguing that Booker T. Washington's program of industrial education would not properly prepare capable and formidable race leaders, Du Bois stressed that "education must not simply teach work—it must teach life." He touted the liberal arts, because only "intelligence, broad sympathy, knowledge of the world that was and is, and of the relation of men to it" could ready men for the true "manhood" that is the foundation of strength. For Du Bois, advancing the race required access to higher education for its "Talented Tenth."[14] Mal was expected to join their ranks, even as the Goodes upheld the ethic of hard work promulgated by Booker T. Washington.

Mal was well aware of African Americans who had blazed a trail at the university. Pitt's first Black graduate, William Hunter Dammond, had earned a degree in civil engineering in 1893. Dammond's parents had good jobs and worshiped at the Bethel African Methodist Episcopal (AME) Church, a congregation that vociferously advocated for higher education. In 1910 Jean Hamilton Wells became the first Black woman to graduate and the first to earn a doctoral degree. They were outliers. Between 1823 and 1909, an average of just eight African Americans graduated from white colleges in the entire country each year. Between 1890 and 1909, fewer than a dozen African American graduated from University of Pittsburgh.[15]

Robert Vann, the most prominent among them, became a civil rights activist, a lawyer, and finally the editor and publisher of the *Pittsburgh Courier* after graduating from Pitt's law school in 1909. Vann was born and raised in North Carolina by his mother, a cook for a white family. Picking up jobs when he could, Vann graduated as valedictorian from the Waters Training School in Winston, North Carolina, in 1901. He had brief stints at the Wayland Academy and Virginia Union University before winning a scholarship to the Western University of Pennsylvania (which became the University of Pittsburgh) and enrolling as a sophomore in 1903. An anomaly, he notched a major triumph by earning a bachelor's degree despite his race, lack of funds, and age—graduating in 1906, when he was twenty-seven.[16] Continuing to law school, Vann worked as a dining car porter to pay his way, piquing both classmates' and professors' curiosity about the slender, bright student who worked on the rails.

In 1905 his peers selected him as the first Black editor in chief of the university's literary magazine, *The Courant*. One student on the journal's executive board objected, but that, a white classmate recalled, was one of the few instances in which Vann's race was an issue. After passing the bar exam in 1909, Vann became one of five Black lawyers in a city home to more than twenty-five thousand African Americans.[17] Under his leadership, the *Pittsburgh Courier* became arguably the nation's leading Black newspaper. A *Courier* connection was a springboard for many who went on to build national profiles. Knowing Pitt could shape his destiny, Mal paid heed to the experiences of earlier Black students, especially Vann's. Decades later, his path led him to the *Courier*.

For over 140 years, the University of Pittsburgh had responded to the incessant, often precipitous, transformations shaping the city. Despite name changes, relocations, and two fires, by Mal's first year Pitt had defined its role in higher education and its place in the city. The institution promised to integrate Mal and his Black classmates into its mission and that of the nation. It offered a path toward an education and entrée to professions, but the route was fraught with complexities.

The emergence of the New Negro and Harlem Renaissance had showcased Black talent and formidability and celebrated African and African American culture. But at the same time, the Great Migration intensified Black America's class differences. Most days, Mal commuted between Black working people and better-off African Americans whose presence in school displayed their class background. But no African American could rest easy about white supremacy. Lynchings and Ku Klux Klan (KKK) marches were rare in Pittsburgh, but not in the hinterlands surrounding the city. Pennsylvania had upward of 250,000 Klan members with many of its lodges in western Pennsylvania.[18] There had been a KKK march in Homestead when Mal was a boy, and intolerance could surface in a flash.[19]

Seizing the opportunities Pitt offered, Mal set his sights on the Alphas. Alpha Phi Alpha was founded in 1906 at Cornell University, inspiring the formation of other fraternities and sororities. It adopted a dual mission of advancing academic excellence while addressing the injustices African Americans faced.[20] Black Greek letter organizations provided a physical and psychological oasis for Black students navigating a white world and as Black enrollments slowly climbed at Pitt, other intercollegiate Black Greek-letter organizations established branches on campus. Dedicated to public service and civil rights, they provided a sense of community and a vision to students and alumni seeking to advance as individuals and as a community. Fraternities and the "Divine Nine" sororities were critical to Black progress and conferred status and a lifelong affiliation. Mal was a proud Alpha and remained enmeshed in its networks the rest of his life.

Alpha Phi Alpha opened a chapter at Pitt in 1913 by tapping seven of the school's twenty-five Black students. Membership became a badge of distinction worn locally by journalist Frank Bolden, 1934, Olympic medalist John Woodruff, 1939, and National Football League (NFL) Hall of Famer Chris Doleman, 1985. Nationally, Alpha ranks included W. E. B. Du Bois, Charles Hamilton Houston, Martin Luther King Jr., Thurgood Marshall, Jessie Owens, Adam Clayton Powell, and Paul Robeson. The son of a steelworker and a mill worker himself, Mal was an Alpha through and through, eager to fulfill its commitment to service and honor. Affiliation allowed him to mingle with a social elite, including the members of Black sororities. The Iota chapter of Alpha Kappa Alpha, which became Pitt's first Black sorority in 1908, was one of the earliest chapters at a predominantly white institution.[21] These ambitious young men and women strove to assert themselves in the making of a better world.

Mal matriculated to the university during Chancellor John Bowman's reign. Bowman, who inherited a university deep in debt in 1921, sought to usher the university into modern times by capitalizing on the ingenuity and mettle of the city surrounding it. He expected the university to soar to great heights, and he raised ten million dollars to build the Cathedral of Learning, the tallest educational building in the Western Hemisphere, to prove that Pittsburgh was about more than steel and manufacturing.[22] Three years after ground was broken in the fall of 1925, the fully framed steel edifice loomed over Pitt's landscape, a symbol to the students of what could be achieved there. This was the ground Mal walked as he rushed around campus, awed by death-defying workers erecting the Cathedral's steel bones and covering them with Indiana limestone.

Defying expectations, Bowman positioned Pitt as a beacon of spirit, potential, and courage. But he clamped down on radical students and faculty, and despite his rhetorical commitment that the university advance humanity, Black students were marginalized at best and harassed at worst. Nevertheless, African American students made inroads while building their own fraternal networks. A few, including Mal's friends Ken Wibecan and Everett Utterback, ran track and were duly touted by the university for their feats. Otherwise, Black representation was sparse, and African Americans were more tolerated than embraced. But they knew they were academically qualified and were resolved to succeed.

Pitt's Black students were a diverse group. Some came from local communities; others, mostly from financially comfortable families, traveled from afar. Ken Wibecan (1928), son of a prominent Republican civic leader and postal supervisor in Brooklyn, brought class standing and athleticism to Pitt where he was the "Lone Race Lad" to earn a varsity letter in his class. Upon his arrival to Pittsburgh Wibecan was welcomed into the Student Princes and attended fetes with "charmingly gowned pretty girls" dancing to "captivating music," the *Courier* reported. Granville Woodson (class of 1930) was the son of a Washington, DC, structural engineer and grandson of a cofounder of Wilberforce University.[23]

Walter Talbot and Everett Utterback became Mal's closest friends at Pitt. Pittsburgh-born Talbot graduated with majors in math and physics in 1931. Four years later, he became the fourth African American in the nation to earn a PhD in mathematics, also at Pitt, at the age of twenty-four.[24] After his initiation into several prestigious honor societies, the *Chicago Defender* described Talbot as "Pittsburgh's most brilliant young man."[25] Mal was a groomsman in his friend's wedding, and in 1948, while recovering from a heart attack he turned to Talbot and convalesced at his home in Ohio. They remained close friends until Talbot's death in 1977. Mal and Mary Goode's children spoke fondly of family trips to "Uncle Walter's."

Utterback, like Mal, came from a blue-collar background; his father was a bricklayer in Kentucky. Utterback worked for the Pennsylvania Railroad before parleying his athletic abilities into a scholarship. A versatile athlete who competed as a decathlete and in individual events, he won Penn Relay titles and national honors. In 1931 the track and field coach Frank Shea appointed Utterback his squad's captain, making him the first African American to lead a Pitt team. When the university's athletic council objected, Shea stood fast and said he would let the team, composed of twenty-eight white and three Black men, vote for the captaincy. He knew they would chose Utterback, which they did. After earning a law degree, Utterback represented Hall of Famer Satchel Paige, light-heavyweight champion John Henry Lewis, and the Pittsburgh Crawfords owner Gus Greenlee.[26] Utterback and Mal later worked together and were neighbors on the Hill. Like Mal, Talbot and Utterback were unpretentious hardworking men who took little for granted. They interacted with that elite social set but had not been born into it.

As a steelworker Mal's pedigree was blue-collar, and he faced obstacles that more privileged classmates did not encounter. Mal watched the Cathedral of Learning slowly climb above campus on his way to class but the potential of a university education was tempered by nights in the mills and daily commutes. Just as the Cathedral of Learning's construction suffered setbacks, so did Mal. His schedule was rigorous, and several instructors bristled at the concept of Black students earning the same grades as their white counterparts. That, he believed, contributed to his lackluster academic record. Mal struggled and repeated classes; working full-time left little time for study.

"I was majoring in prelaw," he explained. "Obviously, my grades counted a great deal if I wanted to get into law school." In one course, temporary grades were posted after six and twelve weeks, with a final grade at the end of the semester. "We had quizzes every Friday and I never got less than a B on any of them, but the professor gave me a C in the course." Mal went to his office. "I said, 'Doctor, you've given me a C and I would like to know what I can do to improve it. And he looked up to me—I can see him like yesterday—and said, 'Mr. Goode, you don't expect to get what a white student gets, do you?' Do you have any idea what that does to a 20-year-old boy who's working in the steel mills at night in order to get through college? I walked out crying."

Unwilling to let the matter go, he went to see the Political Science Department chair Elmer Graber, a man he admired. "Graber knew I was shook up and after he listened he just said to me that the professor in question 'doesn't understand like some of us do, and I'll go have a talk with him.' Graber made me feel great. That's the good news here—that things can change, that there can be some hope. I mean, suppose he had said essentially the same thing to me: 'Nigger, who do you think you are?' But he didn't. Graber said, 'I'll go have a talk with him.'" But the grade did not change.

"Those times were never easy, Mal remembered. "Make no mistake about it nor for one minute forget it. Yet I enjoyed my classes and stayed happy most of the time." Mal completed his degree in the summer of 1931.

Bill Goode, two years ahead of Mal at Pitt, finished pharmacy school in 1929. "The economy was ripping," Mal recalled, "so we decided to buy an automobile that June and went to the Mutual and Moody Auto Company on Water Street downtown. We had $300 between us, and the white salesman—there were no Black salesmen—wanted to know where we got all that money. He said: 'You boys been shooting craps?' That's not something we would have stood for later on, but we let it slide. Besides, we wanted a car and ordered a blue 1929 Ford Coupe with a rumble seat and Firestone tires." They put $300 down and financed the remaining $444 by paying $40.00 a month for eleven months. "It was no problem paying it off because both of us were working."

"It was as pretty an automobile as I ever saw in my life. We simonized it and painted the Firestones gray. The car had an automatic windshield wiper and could go 60 miles an hour downhill." They shared it, dating girls as far away as Sewickley and Monongahela City. Riding the wave of energy coursing through better-off African American circles, they were confident young men full of Jazz Age exuberance.

Bill had begun focusing on pharmacy in high school, where a chemistry teacher, Lester Fix, had taken a liking to him and convinced him to study pharmacy. He began delivering prescriptions and running the soda fountain at Dr. Crampton's Pharmacy on the Hill, the city's most vibrant Black neighborhood. Becoming a registered pharmacist, he made thirty-five dollars a week, a princely sum at the time. Better yet, he learned the business and got to know just about everybody on the Hill, including those on both sides of the law.

In 1936 a little drugstore up on Wylie Avenue went up for sale. The owner had gambled himself into debt and could no longer replenish his stock. But the man's price of twelve hundred dollars was more than Bill could raise. Nor could the family help because the house was already mortgaged to defray college expenses. But then Teddy Horne walked into Crampton's. Horne, Gus Greenlee, and Woogie Harris had made the numbers game into Black Pittsburgh's biggest business. The numbers were a poor person's lottery, which evolved from West Indian games of chance and exploded in popularity after reaching Pittsburgh in the 1920s. A bettor could wage as little as a penny on a three-digit number based on daily stock transactions or how horses finished in selected races. Although the odds of any randomly drawn three-digit number hitting were 999 to one, the numbers paid winners 600 times the amount wagered. Those odds favored the numbers kings, but even during the Depression, people wagered regularly, figuring they would not miss a few cents each day but cash in if they hit. Some bet their favorite numbers; others selected them from dream books in which particular dreams were paired with numbers.[27]

Horne, like Greenlee, Harris, and Homestead's Sonnyman Jackson, was regarded as a man quick to help when somebody needed a load of coal or cash to pay a doctor. His daughter, Lena Horne, began performing at the Cotton Club in Harlem when she was sixteen, before moving to the Hill to live with her father. The Hill in the 1930s was a mecca for jazz, and Lena learned from native sons Billy Strayhorn and Billy Eckstine. Leaving Pittsburgh before World War II, she became a rare African American crossover star as well as a civil rights activist.

"Mr. Horne had taken a liking to Bill," Mal remembered. "Bill knew all about Teddy Horne's gambling business but he respected him. People didn't look at the numbers as a predatory racket; everybody was playing it and Gus, Woogie, and Teddy kept it free of violence." For many, the numbers kings were the community's bankers, willing to lend money—often never repaid—for tuition, political campaigns, and businesses. "Besides," Mal observed, "it goes back to what we were taught as youngsters, to respect everybody regardless of their station in life. That was the law in our household, and we adhered to it."

Horne asked how much Bill needed, reached for his money roll, counted out twelve hundred dollars, and handed it over. "Buy it, and whatever you need to stock it, I'll give it to you." The family rejoiced. "Just like that, my brother was in business." As his business grew, Bill helped Black pharmacy graduates launch their own careers and hired high school kids to work the soda fountain. After opening a second drugstore, he employed thirty-three people, including Mal's children and their sister Ruth.

Mal took longer to establish himself. That bothered him because he was serious about Mary Lavelle. They courted despite scant time or resources, and a gloomy economy. By then, Mal rued not selling his US Steel stock. "When Bill and I bought the car, we didn't know what was around the corner," Mal recalled. During the 1920s, the stock market was on a rampage. As the economy soared, greed and the ability to buy stock on margin—putting down only a fraction of the cost—pushed stocks upward. Abandoning caution, many who knew little about finances giddily watched their investments appreciate—until October 1929 when fear and panic overcame greed and they lost everything. Mal was caught up in the frenzy but remained smitten with Mary Lavelle. When he intermittently kept a diary in 1929, the first entry was "Received two beautiful ties as present from Mary Lavelle."[28]

"By the crash, I had accumulated 14 shares, which seemed unthinkable at the time." The shares, for which he paid $25 to $30, had risen to $261 a share. "One of my coworkers sold his two shares for $500, paid off his mortgage, and said, 'Mal why don't you sell?' But I said: 'I'm going to keep it so that when I finish school and go to law school, I'll have enough so that I won't have to work.' That would have been in two years, as I expected to graduate in 1931."

The lure of attending law school without having to work was powerful. "I said to myself that if it ever goes to $300 I would sell, which would have meant that I had $4,200—a lot of money in those days." But his plans crashed on the shoals of capitalism's boom-and-bust cycle. Mal's time at Pitt would matter, but not until he labored in the mill for another five years. When U.S. Steel stock plunged after the crash, Mal sold some shares for sixty dollars and the rest for forty-one dollars. "By then parts of the mill were down completely; our department was working two days a week and you were lucky if you got 5 days for a two-week pay. Instead of drawing 57 or 58 dollars, we dropped to between $18 and $22. Fortunately, my father had retired with a pension by then. It was a godsend when the depression struck."

"Many men like myself, who had bought stock, thought they would never be in financial trouble again. Some men couldn't take it; a few jumped off of bridges. There were men in armored plate and departments where it was common to make $20 to $25 a shift. They held jobs a Black man couldn't get, but now they were hardly working. The mill opened a commissary where you could go and get some flour, meat, butter, lard, and cornmeal. They kept a record of what you took and expected you to pay it back when work resumed."

"Some men thought that they would never return to work. During the twenties, the only people not working were crippled, disabled, or bums who didn't want to work. But it got progressively worse after the crash of 1929 and hurt psychologically." In August 1931, Mal borrowed fifty dollars from Joe Twyman, a friend from work, to pay for commencement expenses. Twyman had not had the chance to go to college, but "He and some of the men looked out for me," Mal reflected. "When I was worn out from being in school all day, they sent me to a room where we bailed paper to rest. They covered for me. I could never forget that and felt a responsibility to do something with that education, not just for me and my family, but for them."

COURTSHIP

Mal had fallen for Mary Lavelle, whom the *Courier* called "one of the most attractive members of the younger set."[9] Her parents, the Reverend Franklin Pierce Lavelle and Mary Anderson Lavelle, had settled in Pittsburgh in 1923 where he served as pastor at the Paulson Avenue Church of God following postings in eight other states. The Lavelles and their eight children anticipated settling down in Pittsburgh, but Franklin died suddenly two years later.

His wife used a five-thousand-dollar insurance policy that the church had purchased for her husband to buy a house at 8103 Perchment Street in Homewood. But she struggled to keep her family together, and sixteen-year-old Mary became the primary caregiver when her overwhelmed mother became ill. Buried by cooking, cleaning, and caring for her rambunctious siblings and incapacitated mother, Mary dropped out of school, giving up her stenographer's job and aspirations to become a nurse. She later took night classes and graduated from Peabody High School. Mal and Mary traveled in the same circle of young, ambitious African Americans, but neither had much free time. In addition to the home front, Mary worked at the Darlington Bridal Shop while Mal managed school and work.

Mal's extracurricular life at Pitt revolved around the Alphas. Pitt's "Alpha Men" were a gregarious bunch. Their festive gatherings mingled social pleasures with political purpose. Some Alphas came from Pittsburgh's elite, but the door was open to men from working-class backgrounds, like Mal, with the resolve to crack their ranks. Alphas and their female companions swirled through dances, enjoyed fireworks at porch parties, indulged in late night suppers, played bridge, and navigated Pittsburgh's social scene. For some of them, the Depression was a sideshow. They wore fancy dresses, bought new suits, and kept an eye on style as their lives were chronicled by the *Courier*. Louise Jeffries would become Mary Lavelle's maid of honor and marry Mal's brother James. She was pictured in the paper in 1930. "One of the popular members of the younger set," she exhibited "the trend in dress is definitely toward curls." Her glimmering eyes and warm smile, framed by a bob, au courant at the time, embodied the joy and hope of an upwardly mobile cohort.[30]

Mal's 1931 diploma from Pitt was not a ticket out of the mills, but being an "Alpha man" offered entrée to Black Pittsburgh's upper crust. When a grand surprise party was held in the summer of 1932 for Margaret, the "attractive daughter" of Mr. and Mrs. Lewis McTurner of Monticello Street, the *Courier*'s reporter gushed that Mary Lavelle was among the "beautiful damsels dressed in evening gowns in the varied pastel shades" and Mal one of the "boys in formal warm weather attire." They danced to Clifford Paige's music amid "ferns and greens studded with silver baskets and lovely vases of roses under soft lights . . . while being served fruit punch."[31] This was Mal and Mary's world when they could find time for it. Their families lived in different parts of town and worshiped in different churches, but by the time Mal was a junior at Pitt, he was enamored. Although the Church of God frowned on the social swirl, Mary's brothers gravitated to posher gatherings and sometimes brought her along. Engaging and striking, she became the object of many young men's attentions.

But Mal persisted. He had competition for Mary's affections, even among close friends. "The fellow," he wrote referring to his Homestead friend Louis Fenderson, "can't help it because he likes you so well. In fact, he is not alone in that matter for some other friends of mine crave trips to 8103 Perchment street." Mal was frank: "I have been nice enough to you, yet you understand that a surplus of time is not mine to have. Of course, I intend to do the best I can, nevertheless. Then too, I appreciate how considerate you are."[32]

The Depression foreclosed Mal's options after graduation. Nor was the work at the mill that had sustained him since high school steady or paying what it once had. Mal felt pressured. "We cared a lot for each other, but I wasn't making enough money to promise her anything." Mal saw Mary whenever he could, but he did not feel he was in a position to marry her, even though he wanted nothing more. His situation changed on a Sunday visit to Mary's home in September 1932 when Mary's brother Frank, who sold advertising for the *Courier*, told Mal about an opening for a porter at the Richman Brothers men's clothing store downtown. Mal went to the store but did not reveal he had graduated college, fearing that he would be deemed overqualified. Frank told Mal the pay was ten dollars a week, but the manager only offered eight dollars. Mal questioned that and was told he would be tried out at eight. It took five months for Mal to get ten dollars, on the day that newly inaugurated president Franklin Delano Roosevelt declared a bank holiday and temporarily closed all banks in an effort to prevent more institutions from collapsing.

The steelworking porter with a college degree spent as much time as possible with Mary, somehow maintaining a social life and planning for the future. When the Alphas celebrated Pitt's Omicron chapter's twentieth anniversary, Mal reigned as the toastmaster at a formal dance held at the Elks Lodge. Mal, who dressed his Alpha brothers in good suits at Richman Brothers, kept the "spirits jolly" as he recounted stories of the chapter and Alpha men and led the strikingly attired group in "The Alpha Hymn" and "The Good Old Alpha Spirit." Mary Lavelle was there to witness Mal preside. Hard times might have disrupted their plans, but the "weather is always fair when the Alpha men get together," and even more so when the love of his life was in the room.[33]

"I worked at Richman Brothers for three years and though things were getting a bit better, I finally gave up on law school." Mal came to regret that he had not accepted Sonnyman Jackson's offer to pay his law school tuition. Rufus "Sonnyman" Jackson owned the Skyrocket Lounge on 8th Avenue in Homestead where the ballplayers and the sporting set hung out. "It was a beautiful place—no fights there," Mal recalled. "I've never been a drinker in my life but I felt at home there." A migrant from Georgia, Jackson worked in the mill before entering the numbers game. He supplied Wurlitzer and Seeburg jukeboxes to clubs and bars throughout the Mon Valley and became co-owner of the Homestead Grays. Like many numbers kings, Jackson put money back into the community. "Sonnyman Jackson said 'Register for law school and I'll give you the money.' But I didn't take him up on his offer. He later said 'I thought you were going to law school. What are you doing in the street?' I guess that most everybody thought I was going to law school but the longer I worked, the less it seemed possible."[34] Instead, he worked two jobs and barely supported himself. "I made myself indispensable at Richman Brothers and did everything from cleaning windows and toilets to checking shipments—everything but tailoring. I knew I wasn't being treated fairly but Joe Mulvihill finally gave me the bump to ten dollars."

Soon, he told Mulvihill he was going to quit because the money wasn't good enough. "But Mulvihill was afraid of losing me and raised me to 12 dollars a week right before Easter Sunday, the biggest sales day of the year. When FDR's National Recovery Act passed, he said I would be making $15 a week and asked: 'What are you going to be doing with all that money?' I said 'Mr. Mulvihill, I'm going to buy one more handkerchief.' He didn't like that but couldn't do anything about it because I was indispensable by then."

Mal chafed. Better educated than most of the staff, he was the lowest paid and unable to sell clothes and earn commissions. Still, the Depression meant that many were worse off. By the fall of 1932, the gains that workers had made during the 1920s had evaporated. In 1934 the majority of Black workers in Allegheny County, including Mal, were unemployed or working part-time.[35] But the economy began picking up as FDR's New Deal bolstered people's confidence and introduced a social welfare system.

In December 1934 Richman Brothers feted employees at the William Penn Hotel, distributing checks for a half-week's salary as a bonus. Carl Felder, the general manager, and Charles Richman, the last of the three brothers whose father, Henry, had founded the business in Cleveland in 1879, passed out the checks. Each recipient then thanked them. Mal worked two jobs and often lent to coworkers between pays. They applauded him when he was named.

> But I wanted everyone to understand something, so I said: "I want to thank Richman Brothers for this check, but you ought to know that it's the smallest check being given here. I'm the only Negro here and I do everything but work with Louis Bruno [the tailor]. I hope the day will come when I am paid in accordance with my ability and what I mean to this company—when somebody with the color of skin that I have can sell clothes in the store like Cohen and Fritzie and the salesmen here. Mr. Richman, I'm saying this to you because you own the company and I think you ought to know."

Mal's rebuke echoed his criticism of Andrew Carnegie for praising his father but never eliminating the color line that kept him from becoming a boss melter. After he sat down, there was silence, until Felder and Richman applauded and everybody joined in. The next day, Charles Richman told Mal: "I appreciate what you said last night; it won't always be this way." Mal replied: "I hope it won't, but I don't expect to stay here." A coworker named Kirkpatrick approached Mal later that day. He said, "What in the hell are you doing here?" He told Mal he was too intelligent and educated to be working as a porter. When Mal replied that he was there because of his skin, Kirkpatrick responded: "You're using that as an excuse. You have no right being here as a porter in the store like this—anybody who talks like you did last night." While they might have disagreed about why Mal was there, Mal knew that he was right, that he was capable of much more.

Richman soon allowed Mal to sell clothes to customers who asked for him. That led to Bill Goode, Homer Brown, Everett Utterback, Alpha brothers, and several numbers men showing up to shop. "A lieutenant of Sonnyman Jackson came in one Saturday night. He parked his Cadillac outside the store and when somebody said he might get a ticket, he said that's okay and bought $250 worth of clothes." Those commissions and living at home allowed Mal to save four hundred dollars. He intended to return to school in September 1935, but he never did.

At twenty-eight years old, Mal's prospects were looking up, and he and Mary finally wed. The *Courier* declared their September 1936 ceremony "the prettiest of the season." It was held at the Lavelle home, solving the dilemma of whether to wed at Clark Memorial or the Church of God. The *Courier* described her as "a fairy princess in an exquisite gown of white satin . . . her long veil of lace and tulle was held in place by a high coronet of lace and jewels." Dancing and alcohol were forbidden by the Church of God, but the band leader and jazz singer Billy Eckstine brought a flask that passed among the Alphas, who enjoyed second helpings of cake served by "a most charming" young woman. The "beautiful and sentimental atmosphere," the *Courier* cooed, was energized by the "young love . . . it is s-o-o-o commanding." Mal, trying to ease out of the gathering with his bride and head to their honeymoon at Bedford Springs, discovered his friends had stolen his car and, according to the *Courier*, "done exasperating things to Mary's pretties." The brotherly vandals denied everything.[36]

The newlyweds arrived at their destination well behind schedule, dismayed to see the hotel dark. Mal knocked at the door, and a sleepy manager appeared. Mal apologized for being late and explained that he had secured a room for the night. The manager signaled for him to come in but began to close the door once Mal entered. The groom quickly reached back in the darkness to retrieve his bride and said:, "I have a friend here with me." Mary lost no time in telling him, "A friend? Say I'm your wife . . . for six hours now."[37]

Their partnership would be long, loving, and fruitful, toggling between deep lows and great highs. Determined to tackle the inequities and abuses of a deeply segregated society, Mal had believed that a law degree would have helped him do just that. Many who knew him saw law as his destiny. As a boy, Mal's grandson Randy Wilburn lived with his mother and grandparents. "If my grandfather had been able to go to law school as he wanted, it might have been a whole different world. But he wasn't, and so he had to find a different way."[38] Mal's long deferred dream to attend law school had fizzled and he wasn't sure what to do next.

4

GETTING REAL, 1936-1948

AT LAST A MARRIED MAN, MAL CONFRONTED NEW CHALLENGES. He and Mary needed a place to live and lodging with family in Homewood or Homestead was not what they had in mind. They wanted a home of their own, not a room in a house crowded with in-laws. That meant finding work commensurate with their upwardly mobile aspirations. Working nights as a janitor at the Homestead Steel Works and days as a porter at Richman Brothers for meager wages would never make that possible.

The job—as a juvenile probation officer—came first. It allowed the newlyweds to rent an apartment on the upstairs floor of a modest redbrick home on Anaheim Street in the Hill. Their landlord, *Pittsburgh Courier* circulation manager Leroy Randall, lived downstairs. For Mal, that meant leaving Homestead's Hilltop for the Hill's Sugar Top. For Mary, it was a move from Homewood, an integrated neighborhood in the eastern part of the city.

The Hill was Homestead writ large but with one graphic difference. On the Hill, where African Americans had recently achieved majority status, daily life did not play out in the shadow of the mill—but in both neighborhoods, tensions among African Americans were inescapable. Differences based on place of birth, skin color, occupation, and education had long bedeviled both neighborhoods. In Homestead, the contrast between Hilltop, the agreeable neighborhood where the Goodes lived, and the Ward, where those less well-off crowded into tenements, was easy to see. On the Hill, the separation was between Sugar Top, where the Black middle class congregated, and the lower Hill, where migrants from the Black Belt lived in ramshackle dwellings, squatted in abandoned boxcars, and shared cots in dark, dank rooms. These cleavages had deepened during the Great Migration, just as they had in Black communities across the North.

The differences between the "OPs," the Old Pittsburghers who grew up in the city and benefited from more education and better jobs, and the recent migrants who had journeyed northward to escape sharecropping and Jim Crow were palpable and often vexing. But this divide was not insurmountable, and Mal traversed it daily. No longer a janitor or a porter, he joined a network of African American and white professionals whose work confronted the painful inequities faced by many Black citizens. The three jobs that Mal would hold on the Hill demanded that he address the problems of those less secure than his Sugar Top neighbors. During the first two years after moving to the Hill, he went into the homes of boys who had been tagged as delinquents to fulfill his duties as a juvenile probation officer. He followed that with five years of encouraging young men from all class backgrounds to come to the Centre Avenue YMCA on the Hill so that he could direct their energies in positive directions. Finally, when conflicts between that YMCA and the Metropolitan YMCA's downtown leadership became insurmountable and compromised his prospects for advancement, Mal entered Pittsburgh's maze of recently constructed housing projects, where he became an authority figure and a role model.

The Hill, the historic center of Pittsburgh's Black community, was still reeling from the Great Depression when Mary and Mal settled there in 1936. And conditions did not improve the following year when the economy again dipped precipitously. But even then, circumstances were not as grim as they had been a few years earlier when the Depression plunged to its nadir and a majority of African Americans in the region were jobless or underemployed. Mal, graduating Pitt during the first trough of the Depression in 1931, figured he was fortunate to get a couple days of work a week at the steelworks and a few dollars more at Richman Brothers. But it rankled him to be stuck in those jobs for five years after earning his degree. He chafed at his inability to fulfill the potential he saw in himself.

The election of Franklin Delano Roosevelt in the fall of 1932 and the shift from one-party Republican to one-party Democratic control in Pittsburgh ushered in a local New Deal. Black voters nodded their assent when the *Pittsburgh Courier* publisher Robert L. Vann told them to turn Abraham Lincoln's picture to the wall and vote for Roosevelt in 1932, and they embraced FDR and the Democratic ticket even more tightly in 1936. But the newly empowered Democratic machine did not return their love as fervently. Although more receptive to African Americans than previous administrations had been, the Democrats were far from ready to treat them as equals. A federal safety net meant Works Progress Administration and Civilian Conservation Corps jobs, as well as Social Security, unemployment compensation, and limited welfare measures, but Black Pittsburgh was hurting. That plight was evident on the Hill, and so was the African American community's creativity and resilience.

Black Pittsburgh was a paradox. The city's African American population had almost tripled since 1900, and its share of Pittsburgh's population more than doubled.[1] Although politically weak, disadvantaged at work, and clustered in wards reeling from the highest rates of disease and death in the city, African Americans created an impressive social and cultural infrastructure. They nurtured an entrepreneurial element. African Americans first gravitated to the Hill in the 1800s, living in what was called Little Hayti. Martin Delany, the captivating firebrand often considered the father of Black nationalism, resided there at mid-century. By the early twentieth century, Little Hayti was Black Pittsburgh's central neighborhood, home to the most powerful African Americans in the city. Mixed by class as well as by race, over one-third of Black households had white neighbors in Pittsburgh's most racially integrated neighborhood.[2]

Looming over downtown Pittsburgh from a bluff between the Monongahela and the Allegheny Rivers, the Hill was a magnet for newcomers from Europe and the South. By the time Mary and Mal Goode moved in, southern dialects from the Black Belt mingled with English and half a dozen European languages in its chaotic cosmopolitan streets. While neither majority Black nor home to a majority of African Americans in Pittsburgh until 1930, for many—as Harlem Renaissance writer Claude McKay wrote—the Hill was the crossroads of the Black world.[3] Pittsburgh's Black population was smaller than that of New York City, Philadelphia, or Chicago, but the city sat along critical east–west rail lines, which carried musicians, speakers, and ball clubs who stopped to perform when passing through.[4]

In the wake of the Harlem Renaissance, the Hill hosted an array of local and national talents affirming Black culture. That energy gleamed just a few blocks from the Goodes' second-story apartment on Anaheim Street, where they lived across the street from Homer and Wilhelmina Byrd Brown and next door to Everett and Bernice Utterback. Mal's brother Bill and his wife, Sara, lived nearby. Homer Brown, the son of a Baptist minister who earned a Doctor of Divinity degree, was born in West Virginia. His family joined the migration northward in 1911 when Homer was fifteen. He worked summers in the mills and as a waiter on the Baltimore & Ohio Railroad, before attending Virginia Union University, serving in the army, and graduating Pitt's law school in 1923. The president of Pittsburgh's NAACP chapter from 1924 until 1948, Brown became an influential state representative and Allegheny County's first African American judge. His wife, Wilhelmina Byrd Brown, was the daughter of a North Side preacher who also gravitated to public service. The Browns, Utterbacks, and Goodes shared a commitment to social justice and to each other. They encouraged Mal to take chances, and they were there to help when he faltered. They weren't the only ones.[5]

An even greater catalyst to civil rights and social justice lived nearby on Webster Avenue. After arriving in Pittsburgh in 1909 and marrying restaurateur William Lampkin, Daisy Lampkin was in the vanguard of civil rights activism, locally and nationally, until her death in 1965. Committed to equality for women as well as for Blacks, she plunged into the suffragette movement, led housewives in consumer protests, and became the president of the Negro Women's Equal Franchise Federation (later renamed the Lucy Stone Civic League). Lampkin also became one of the NAACP's most formidable organizers. Renowned for raising money and boosting membership wherever she traveled, Lampkin was the NAACP's national field secretary and on its board of directors. She led a membership campaign that brought two thousand new members to the Pittsburgh chapter in 1929; Mal was likely one of them. She also recruited Thurgood Marshall to become the NAACP's lead counsel. In 1931, the year Mal graduated from Pitt, she brought the NAACP's national convention to Pittsburgh. In a panoramic photograph taken of attendees in front of the Centre Avenue YMCA, she sat in the center, flanked by W. E. B. Du Bois and NAACP president Walter White. Lampkin was also a vice president of the *Pittsburgh Courier* and the confidante of its publisher, Jesse Vann, who became Mal's boss. Perhaps the most dynamic and consequential figure in the city's civil rights history, Lampkin shaped the NAACP, the civil rights organization that became Mal's North Star.[6]

The Hill District neighborhood where Daisy Lampkin and the Goodes lived, formerly called Schenley Heights, was known as Sugar Top. More residential and less crowded than the lower Hill, it was home to Black Pittsburgh's best-off and most influential families as well as many Baptist ministers who resided nearby on "Preacher's Row." Many others, like the Browns, Utterbacks, and Goodes, came from working-class backgrounds. Homes were modest, two-story brick cottages built into the hillsides and close to each other. The narrow streets were filled with children. It was a short walk to Wylie Avenue, a central artery stretching for three miles through the Hill before ending downtown at the Courthouse.

Its epicenter was Wylie and Fullerton Avenues—Claude McKay's crossroads of the world. The Blue Note Café, Stanley's Bar, an Amoco station, and Goode's Pharmacy occupied the intersection's four corners.[7] "If you came to Pittsburgh," Mal proclaimed, "you didn't leave without going to that intersection, and you didn't have to leave the Hill to fulfill your daily needs."[8] He and Mary wandered down the street to watch the Homestead Grays and Pittsburgh Crawfords at Greenlee Field or to listen to Billy Eckstine and Billie Holiday at the Crawford Grill and the Pythian Temple. Duke Ellington and Ella Fitzgerald played the New Granada Theatre and showed up at the Musicians Club, where musicians congregated after hours on the second floor of their union hall. Mal got his hair cut at Woogie Harris's Crystal Barber Shop and caught up on the latest news from the street, including how Woogie's numbers game was faring; Mary patronized nearby hair salons and met her husband at Nesbitt's Pie Shop afterward for a slice of sweet potato pie. They shopped with merchants on Wylie Avenue, got ice cream and filled prescriptions at Bill Goode's pharmacy, and worshiped at neighborhood churches.

The Hill also became the crossroads of Black baseball after numbers baron Gus Greenlee constructed Greenlee Field for the Pittsburgh Crawfords in 1932. The sons of migrants from the Deep South had formed the team in 1925 when they joined a city recreational league and represented the Crawford Bath House, a community center that helped newcomers adjust to city life. Greenlee bought uniforms for the boys and then, after his friend the Steelers owner Art Rooney urged him on, put them on salary. Using profits from the numbers game, Greenlee recruited Satchel Paige, Judy Johnson, Oscar Charleston, and Cool Papa Bell to the squad and built the finest Black-owned ballpark in the country on the Hill. Anchored by homegrown star Josh Gibson, who arrived in a trade with the Grays, the Crawfords became Black baseball's answer to the New York Yankees. Mal, who had grown up watching the Homestead Grays, was now a regular when they played at Greenlee Field.

A few blocks away, the Centre Avenue YMCA hosted a who's who of African American politics and culture. The Goodes listened to Marian Anderson, W. E. B. Du Bois, George Washington Carver, Jacob Lawrence, Alain Locke, Adam Clayton Powell Jr., and Paul Robeson at Black Pittsburgh's cornerstone institution. Mal watched some of the best boxers in the world—Henry Armstrong, Ezzard Charles, John Henry Lewis, and Joe Louis—train there. Downtown was less hospitable, he reflected. "If you saw a black at Gimbel Brothers at that time, he was running an elevator, or he was working in the dining room washing dishes."[9] But on the Hill, lawyers, ministers, shop owners, doctors, tradesmen, and some of the nation's finest ballplayers lived alongside laborers, steelworkers, and domestics.

African Americans were a growing but still subordinate group in Pittsburgh's industrial economy. Many labored in the same occupations that African Americans had held since before the Civil War. A few hundred ran their own businesses, operating barbershops, pool halls, print shops, and pharmacies, or contracted for construction, hauling, and catering work. A far greater number worked as porters, waiters, domestics, and teamsters. The rest were unskilled and semiskilled laborers.[10] But Black Pittsburgh's cultural energy was unquestioned. The University of Pittsburgh had introduced Mal to the Hill. Now he and Mary lived there, in one of the country's most vibrant Black communities.

Black Pittsburgh, as historian Laurence Glasco emphasized in his pioneering study of the community, was shaped not only by racial discrimination but by two additional burdens—bad timing and intractable geography. The region's steel and manufacturing industries plateaued after World War I, not long after many Black migrants arrived. Because Pittsburgh industry lost its competitive advantages and never completely regained them, the bulk of Black migrants came too late to enjoy the occupational and residential security attained by earlier European immigrants. Fathers could not take brothers or sons to their place of work to get them hired as easily as European immigrants did, and frequent layoffs made buying a home and passing it on to children more difficult. As a result, African Americans were more likely to move on than European immigrants. Making matters worse, the city's hills and three rivers divided Black neighborhoods from each other. African Americans never formed one contiguous community. Instead, Blacks settled into several neighborhoods—the Hill, Homewood, Beltzhoover, Manchester, and mill towns along the rivers—undercutting their potential economic and political clout. These burdens made it more difficult for a strong Black middle and professional class to thrive or a viable political movement to coalesce.[11]

The Goodes' roots in the city predated the Great Migration and the decline of steel. Moreover, they had strong ties to the middle class, and if there was a talented tenth or a Black bourgeoisie in Pittsburgh, they were now part of it. On Sugar Top, middle-class African Americans encountered each other on the street, at church, and in their homes. Leroy Randall, whose upstairs rooms they rented, was the *Courier*'s circulation manager and part of that milieu. The influential Black paper already cast a presence that extended beyond Pittsburgh. The largest Black-owned employer in the city, it was located across the street from the Centre Avenue YMCA, where *Courier* writers and editors lunched and played billiards.

These men and women were poised to better themselves and their community. Like Mal and Mary, they had imbibed the gospel of uplift and believed that they were obligated to lead their brethren to better lives. They were not, however, blind to the obstacles African Americans confronted. They saw discrimination on the job, crowded neighborhoods plagued by insufficient services, and the tensions between Pittsburgh-born and southern migrants. These contradictions shaped Mal's career.

Mal was raised to believe that he and the race would eventually triumph:

> As a child, we knew it was going to come. People like my father and mother, and people of their generation, had a deep and abiding faith in God and said it's going to come. My father said "You go to college and get an education. You might not use it right away, but some day you will." And I'm the best example of that in the world. I put down

a scrub bucket and a mop in the mill in 1936 and the next morning
I was a probation officer in the juvenile court of Allegheny County
hired by the late justice Gustav Schramm.

Nineteen men had applied for the position, which paid what Mal described as the fabulous salary of $125 a month and another five cents a mile for the use of his car.[12]

Mal's connection to Judge Gustav Schramm was Everett Utterback, who became a probation officer after graduating Pitt. The former track champion was leaving that position to work at the Kay Boys Club, a recreational center that the Centre Avenue YMCA had opened to complement its work. Utterback's departure created an opening for an African American. "I went to talk with Utterback," Mal recalled, "and he suggested I talk with Judge Schramm, who had taught me political science at the university.[13]

"They said they wanted somebody with a master's degree in Sociology, which I didn't have, but I went over to talk to him anyway. I told Judge Schramm that I was in graduate school and would soon have my degree." Mal had begun taking courses again, in political science and social work, but never finished a graduate degree. Nor had he studied social work or criminal justice; instead, he told Judge Schramm that he taught Sunday school at Clark Memorial Baptist Church. Both Utterback and Jack Peale, the other Black probation officer for Allegheny County, backed him for the position. "I talked him into it," Mal recalled, "and got the job. And it was a very good job for a young black who didn't have a profession."[14]

That was Mal's ticket to the Black middle class. Judge Schramm, who the Pennsylvania Bar Association called a prophet with honor, had broken ground on the judicial bench by seeking to balance the safety of the community with the interests and rights of youth. Rather than treat them as delinquents to be punished for their misdeeds, Schramm wanted to intervene before they turned to crime.[15] As juvenile probation officers, Mal and his colleagues entered Black homes around the city, especially on the Hill. They encountered households with few resources and little education.[16]

The supervision of vulnerable Black youth in Allegheny County was divided along gender lines. Mal and his colleague Jack Peale oversaw boys, and a Black female officer kept watch over girls who landed in the system. For the next two years, Mal supervised about 150 young men. Some, unable to cooperate with authority figures, did not respond well. The most recalcitrant were committed to the Thorn Hill School for Boys or to Morganza, a nearby reform school. But Mal sent few boys there. "We did not have the vicious juvenile crime we have today and there were not so many broken homes," he recalled. "This was the depression, and boys stole food and meat from trucks or were truant from school. I think I had the chance to turn some boys around and talk with some who were discouraged." He found that tremendously fulfilling. Not yet a father, Mal was acting like one.[17]

Mal dealt regularly—and often fought—with principals. "I saw bigotry firsthand, especially in the school system, where they were quick to file petitions against Black boys in juvenile court. I would go in and out of the schools to see boys who had been on probation, but instead of sending them to reform school, I would try to talk with them to set them on the right track of life. I didn't think much of reform schools, they had a way of destroying a boy's dreams."[18]

Mal counted on Judge Schramm's support. "Gus Schramm was a decent man and listened to the case and took the recommendation of the probation officer and his supervisor. Most of them were decent boys and didn't need to be in an institution." He rarely recommended that a boy be committed, but there were some, hardened and unsupervised at home, whom he could not reach. Schramm urged probation officers to stay in touch with the boys, and Mal spent Saturdays playing baseball with them when he could.[19]

Juvenile probation allowed a youth to avoid incarceration and stay at home, with an officer of the court looking over his shoulder, checking whether he was seeking work or attending school. Mal's duty was to help them change their behavior and become productive citizens. He urged them to stop running around and find jobs, a difficult task during the Depression. When moral suasion was not enough, Mal enforced curfews and laid down the law. Most evenings, he walked through the Hill, checking on his wards. Many had dropped out of school and drifted into trouble, making it difficult for them to stabilize their lives. He knew where they gathered and whom he should confront. "He was a tough cookie, fierce with everything he did, but firm and warm," Leon Haley remembered. Haley, one of Mal's Alpha brothers, also worked as a probation officer. "Not an argumentative man, but tough. I expect he was extraordinarily good at this work. He had developed an appreciation that you had to do things right and could transform the lives of young men."[20]

Mary got an early start on the Baby Boom, delivering their first two sons. Malvin Jr., whom they called Russell, and Robert, before World War II began. They would be joined by four siblings, Richard, Roberta, Ronald, and Rosalia, who came to refer to themselves as the "six Rs." Another baby, Walter Emory James, was born in November 1941 but died suddenly on January 1, 1942. He had been named after Mal's friends and Alpha brothers Walter Talbot and Everett Emory Utterback.[21]

Mal thrived at work but his career track as a probation officer was limited by his race and lack of a law degree. He and Mary wanted to do so much for their children, but money was tight. They were heartened when Mal was tapped for a higher profile position in January 1938, after his Alpha brother Pro McCollough left his job as Boys Work Director at the Centre Avenue YMCA for a position with the state. Richard F. Jones, chair of the Boys Work Committee, led the search for a replacement and pushed to expand the incoming director's portfolio. There was stiff competition, but Judge Schramm was in Mal's corner. "He thought that I had the background to do the job and that it would be a good thing if I could head off some of these boys before they ever got to juvenile court." So did Homer Brown and Everett Utterback, who helped him land the job.[22]

Mal and Mary welcomed his new salary—$155 a month and ten cents per mile for use of their car—especially with two little ones at home. At the YMCA, Mal worked with hundreds of boys who competed for its teams, used the pool, gymnasium, and craft rooms, or belonged to Hi-Y Clubs at local high schools. About to turn thirty, Mal was six feet tall and weighed 159 pounds. When the United States entered World War II three years later, many of the boys he had directed at the Y enlisted or were drafted. Mal stayed on the home front, receiving a deferment from the draft because his position was deemed essential to the war effort.

The YMCA gave Mal a platform in the community that allowed him to go beyond working one-on-one with vulnerable youth. He could now develop programs to effect change in the collective behavior and attitudes of African American males. "It was a perfect place for Mal," Leon Haley recalled.[23] "Those five years," Mal reflected, "were the most fruitful of my life. There were rewards which no amount of money could buy." Thirty years later, he pointed with pride at businessmen and professionals he had once supervised at the YMCA and lauded their efforts to give back to the community. His children later encountered men who boasted: "I was one of Mal's boys."[24]

Central to Black life in Pittsburgh, the Centre Avenue YMCA nurtured its emerging middle class. After the YMCA movement began in mid-nineteenth-century London, it crossed the Atlantic, took root, and grudgingly began including African Americans in its endeavor to inculcate Christian values. The "colored" YMCA on the Hill opened in 1893, although the Metropolitan YMCA downtown did not officially recognize it until 1910. Like a score of YMCAs in Black communities, the Centre Avenue YMCA owed thanks to Sears Roebuck magnate Julius Rosenwald, an advocate for Black education.[25] A Rosenwald challenge grant sparked a two-hundred-thousand-dollar fundraising campaign that made it possible to replace the original YMCA on the Hill with a four-story redbrick building at the corner of Centre Avenue and Francis Street in 1923. Leon Haley, who later consulted for the Centre Avenue YMCA and wrote its history, often stopped there for lunch, where he saw Mal at work. The Centre Avenue branch, he observed, did more than offer boys a way to become Christian men. It exposed them to recreation and culture that broadened their vistas.

In the wake of the Great Migration, the Centre Avenue YMCA helped migrants adjust to the realities of city life in the North and connected them to the established Black community. Mal understood the tensions between African Americans who lived on Hilltop in Homestead and worshiped at Clark Memorial and those who lived in the Ward and worked on the lower rungs of the mill's job ladder. Some better-off African Americans feared that less educated, less skilled migrants from the countryside would cast them in a bad light.[26] Mal shared some of their concerns that the migration was undermining the status of African Americans in Pittsburgh, but he did not look down at them. He might have been paternal, but he was never condescending.

Mal was already familiar with the Centre Avenue Y. Because Black students attending Pitt had a hard time finding landlords willing to rent them rooms near campus in Oakland, many joined the fifty or so men rooming at the Y. Rent was reasonable and included access to the dining room and the gym, amenities unmatched elsewhere. Among the men who lived there was the nationally renowned sportswriter Ches Washington, who worked across the street at the *Courier,* and John Woodruff, who won gold at the eight hundred meters in the 1936 Olympics in Berlin when he was a freshman at Pitt. They mingled with the likes of Dizzy Gillespie, Joe Louis, Satchel Paige, Jackie Robinson, and other musicians and athletes booking rooms while performing in town. So did Pullman porters on layovers, as well as lawyers and social workers. No other venue in the city offered comparable community space for African Americans. That made the Y, Haley explained, a "meeting house, recreation center, lyceum, concert hall, schoolhouse, hotel, and on occasion, worship site." Almost every Black civic, fraternal, and professional group in the city used the facility. It connected Black Pittsburghers to each other and national Black networks.[27]

Mal accepted the YMCA's moral imperative that less advantaged youth could become men with Christian values who, as times got better, might share in the nation's bounty. Moreover, he saw the YMCA as an agent for sorely needed change. It built social capital and mobilized people to tackle problems.[28] Mal thrived in that milieu. The Y's leaders were not as ostensibly political as Pittsburgh's NAACP or Urban League, although they helped form both organizations. The Y also showed that African Americans could raise money to build an infrastructure and face social and cultural concerns.

At the Y, Mal helped connect Pittsburgh's Black community to New Deal programs, especially Mary McLeod Bethune's Negro Affairs Division, the National Youth Administration, and their youth initiatives. This work exposed him to national politics and figures, inspiring him to seek new approaches to endemic problems He figured that the YMCA's Hi-Y Clubs that worked with high school students to develop leadership skills and encourage commitment to the community could make a difference for the population of boys he had supervised as a probation office. Acutely aware of the barriers those boys faced, Mal pushed to create a Hi-Y Club at the reform school, the Pennsylvania Training School at Morganza in Canonsburg, southwest of the city. If boys from lower socioeconomic strata interacted with positive role models, Mal hoped, they could expand their sense of what they could achieve and to see education as a way to better themselves. "What better place than Morganza to get black boys back into society?" Leon Haley asked rhetorically.[29]

Mal, like most African American parents, believed in the power of education. Black youth in Pittsburgh were more likely to attend high school than the children of European immigrants, and more than two-fifths of Black students surveyed in 1928 said they wanted to pursue teaching, dentistry, pharmacy, the law, or another profession. Many, however, had difficulty paying for college, and those who did graduate often left town to pursue their chosen professions.[30] Mal did the same to achieve his goals.

Facing resistance from those who feared it was too dangerous to work with boys who had been relegated to reform school, Mal dug in and overcame their concerns. The Centre YMCA's values were ardently middle-class and upwardly mobile, but the youth it served were often among the most vulnerable members of the community. Mal saw himself as their de facto representative and convinced the

Centre Avenue Y's leadership to approve the Morganza Hi-Y, the first one ever organized at a reform school. Its success persuaded other YMCAs to follow suit.

"The fire to desegregate motivated Mal Goode," Haley observed. The YMCA on the Hill, however, was a product of segregation. For many of its leaders, integration was not even on the horizon. While it promoted interracial dialogue and brought youth together to work on projects anticipating a different future, Mal was not satisfied with its agenda.[31] That fire to desegregate led Mal to become part of the battle to integrate the YMCA's Camp Kon-O-Kwee on Connoquenessing Creek outside the city. It also burned within Richard Jones, who led the fight to desegregate the summer camp. Mal looked up to Jones, a Lynchburg, Virginia, native who grew up in Pittsburgh and graduated at the head of his Pitt Law School class, becoming the first African American to be awarded the coveted Order of the Coif. Jones and Homer Brown were law partners, central to city politics and community affairs, but frequently struggled to convince African Americans that they could represent them as well as a white attorney in court. "As we so often said," Mal remarked, "they believed the 'white man's ice was colder.'" But Jones, Mal testified, believed that nobody in the world was better than he was, that race was entirely incidental.[32]

Jones militantly defied racial injustice, and Mal was a ready acolyte. As a school board member, Jones went before a legislative commission that Homer Brown set up after winning election to the state House of Representatives and demanded that Pittsburgh hire Black teachers. It did, but only one, in 1938, the year Jones mobilized to desegregate Camp Kon-O-Kwee. Pittsburgh's white YMCA leadership was slower than YMCAs elsewhere in challenging segregation and resisted the Centre Avenue Y's challenge to long-held discriminatory practices. When it offered the Centre Avenue YMCA fifty thousand dollars to build a "colored camp" instead of allowing Black youth to attend Camp Kon-O-Kwee, Jones retorted: "You can build one for a million dollars, but as long as the Centre Avenue branch is affiliated with the Pittsburgh YMCA, our boys are going to Camp Kon-O-Kwee."[33]

Together, Jones and Mal pressed the Pittsburgh YMCA to desegregate the camp and treat Black members equally at all venues. After
three years of struggle, they won Camp Kon-O-Kwee's integration
in 1941. Byrd Brown—Homer and Wilhelmina Brown's son who had
grown up across the street from Mal and Mary—was among the first
African Americans to attend the camp. By then, Mal's reputation as
a fierce advocate who gave no ground had made him a problematic
figure. The leaders of the YMCA downtown saw him as an irredeemable firebrand and wanted nothing to do with him.

The winds of war in Europe emboldened civil rights advocates
in the United States. In January 1941, A. Philip Randolph and Bayard Rustin proposed a massive march on Washington, DC, seeking
integration of the armed forces and equal access to jobs in the defense industry. The mere threat of the march caused FDR to issue
an executive order prohibiting discrimination in defense work. That
prompted Randolph to suspend the march, but the March on Washington Movement that had built up around it energized the Black
community. When the United States belatedly entered World War
II, that activism inspired the Double V Campaign, which became the
Black battle cry for victory over fascism overseas and for freedom at
home. The *Pittsburgh Courier* popularized the Double V Campaign,
which appropriated British prime minister Winston Churchill's V for
Victory hand gesture, early in 1942. Momentum was building, but
many people were still unwilling to push for integration.

"As rewarding as those five years were," Mal reflected, "I nevertheless found myself constantly at loggerheads with the officials of
the YMCA downtown." They routinely sought to deny his Centre
Avenue boys the chance to participate in citywide conferences and
athletic contests. "But the touchiest situation," he declared, "was the
Y's summer camp." While the downtown YMCA caved on the camp,
they held a grudge against Mal.[34]

Matters came to a head when the Centre Avenue YMCA's executive secretary, Henry Parker, left to take over a branch in Philadelphia.
Richard Jones and the Boys Work Committee pushed hard for Mal to
succeed him. "But there were some elderly men who thought I was too

hot-headed," Mal reflected. He could hardly disagree. "At the month-ly meetings downtown," Mal confessed with pride: "I would get into it with executives from the downtown branch." He fought with di-rectors from white branches who denied Black youth the chance to compete in their athletic tournaments. There was no question of Mal backing down. "I had no fear, no worry, because those seventeen men on the Boys Work Committee were fine men who backed me to the hilt. All I had to do was to complain to them, especially to Dick Jones, and something was done about it."[35]

The leaders at other YMCA branches were not the only ones wit-nessing Mal's defiance. "If any of my boys was discriminated against at Schenley High School, or Peabody, Allegheny, or South Hills," Mal said, "it was war with the school system." But if they could not break Mal, YMCA leaders could block him from becoming the Centre Avenue YMCA's executive secretary, the position he coveted. As Mal realized, "The die was cast for my future with the YMCA. Its officials made it clear I would not be considered."[36]

That rankled. So did the monthly salary of three hundred dollars and the twenty-five cents a mile he would not be making. Mal and Mary already had two children, Russell and Bob, and wanted to have more. Badly wanting the position, which would have increased his annual salary by twelve hundred dollars and elevated his standing in the community, he was upset that it was not to be. "I'll never forget Dick Jones calling me and saying Mal, they're never going to give that to you. They have all kind of excuses and what-not and I don't agree with them, but it's not going to happen."[37]

But Mal did not stay upset for long. Jones, who also served as the Pittsburgh Housing Authority's vice chairman, had not abandoned Mal. He had already secured a landing spot for his protégé and told him to speak with Dr. Brynn Hovde, the housing authority's executive director. "I went to see Dr. Hovde the next day and he said 'You come with fine recommendations, just the recommendation of Mr. Jones is good enough for me. We're going to send you over as an assistant manager at Terrace Village and your salary is going to be $200 a month plus a 5% cost of living adjustment.'" It was less than the YMCA executive secretary's salary, but it was more than Mal was making and a stunning reversal of fortune. "I never dreamed of it," he recalled.[38]

The 1937 Wagner-Steagall Housing Act authorizing federally backed housing projects was one of FDR's last New Deal accomplishments. Pittsburgh quickly took advantage of it to address a chronic shortage of decent affordable housing. Several of the nation's earliest federal projects were constructed in the city, the first three taking shape on the Hill. President Roosevelt visited one of them, Terrace Village, at its dedication in October 1940, shaking hands from the back seat of a convertible.

Terrace Village and Bedford Dwellings, both on the Hill, were integrated projects considered waystations to the respectable working class. African Americans, who comprised a minority of public housing residents during the 1940s, were welcomed but were clustered apart from white tenants. Still, the projects neither warehoused nor marginalized poor people. Instead, they were home to working people anticipating better futures. The projects also accommodated an influx of wartime laborers working in local steel mills and defense factories operating around the clock.

Mal's workplace transition took place overnight. "I left the YMCA on June 30, 1942 and began working at Terrace Village Number Two, right in the heart of the black section of Pittsburgh, on July 1st." Mal felt at home there; he already knew many of the residents, especially some youth he had supervised at the Centre Avenue YMCA a few blocks away. But Mal was not at Terrace Village for long—only six weeks. "Dr. Hovde called me on the morning of August 12, 1942 and said 'Pack up your things, Mal, and get ready to go to Bedford Dwellings. On Monday, you'll be manager of Bedford Dwellings.' When I said, 'Dr. Hovde, you're kidding,' he fired back: 'I wouldn't kid you about something as important as that.'" The housing authority was moving Everett Utterback, who had been managing Bedford Dwellings, to Terrace Village, and Mal would replace him, again following in his friend's occupational footsteps.[39]

Bedford Dwellings, close to the Goodes' apartment on the Hill, had been built on the site where Greenlee Field had once hosted Negro League baseball. In the summer of 1937, the Pittsburgh Crawfords had been torn apart when many of its best players, including Josh Gibson, Satchel Paige, and Cool Papa Bell, jumped to the Dominican Republic to play for dictator Rafael Trujillo's Ciudad Trujillo squad. With Gus Greenlee exiting baseball to concentrate on boxing, Greenlee Field was demolished and Bedford Dwellings rose on the site. Now, instead of watching baseball there, Mal would watch over the lives of hundreds of families seeking to secure their place in an economy that, because of the war and the New Deal, was recovering from the depression.

"My salary was $300 per month," Mal remembered. "You must know how I felt, that in six weeks, to go from $177.50 a month that I was making in June and six weeks later $300 a month. For my growing family, I could see the light of day financially." Mal spent three years at Bedford Dwellings, before returning to manage the larger, 888-family, Terrace Village project. The continuity of his old job at the YMCA and his new one at Bedford Dwellings was apparent as soon as he arrived. "I knew so many people living there already whose boys had gone to the Centre Ave Y under my supervision. It was almost like family as I walked through it. People were shaking my hand and telling me how happy they were that I was there. Many of them were my boys from the Y."[40]

The projects featured low-rise apartments built around courtyards and playgrounds connected by pedestrian paths. Families lived in well-cared-for buildings where the grass was cut, the streets cleaned, and garbage carefully set out for pickup. "People took care of their apartments in those days like it was their own home and they were going to live there forever," Mal enthused. His biggest challenge was collecting the rent when people were short of cash. "But if it was a choice of paying rent or buying food, I told them 'We'll wait for the rent money. You buy the food first.' There were times when I was taken advantage of, but you almost have to expect that. And I was very rough with those who did." He was just as firm with tenants who did not keep their apartments clean. If an apartment was infested, Mal sent a crew to eradicate the problem, even if its tenants resisted. "Thank God for one thing; I recall only taking part in one eviction at Bedford Dwellings and one at Terrace Village." Mal conducted annual reviews with occupants, checking their incomes and adjusting their rents. Families paid relatively little to cover the rent for new four-room apartments and utilities. "And all you had to do was take care of it!" he exclaimed. Mal and residents took pride in their surroundings. "There were many families who kept spotless apartments and saw it as an honor when I showed visitors their homes."[41]

Mal's commitment to the job took its toll. In June 1948 a heart attack forced him to resign from the housing authority. With no income to fall back upon, the family moved to his parents' home in Homestead. There were now four children; Russell, born in 1937, Bob in 1940, Richard in 1943, and Roberta in 1946. The family of six squeezed into a bedroom on the second floor with the three boys sleeping on the floor. Staying there meant living under William and Mary Goode's rules. On Saturday nights, the children lined up on the cellar steps to shine their shoes before taking baths; the next morning, they went to church.[42]

"My doctor urged me not to work for a year," Mal explained, "but this was a virtual impossibility." He convalesced at fellow Alpha Walter Talbot's home in Jefferson City, Missouri, leaving Mary and the children with her in-laws. Talbot, a mathematician and one of Mal's closest friends since Pitt, was on the faculty at Lincoln University. Mal had been a groomsman at Talbot's wedding to Kathleen Almira Mitchell in 1936.[43]

William and Mary demanded a decorum that taxed Mary's ability to control her energetic kids, and when Mal left to convalesce at the Talbots, she and the kids decamped for her mother's home in Homewood, a neighborhood on Pittsburgh's eastside. The boys continued to attend school in Homestead, navigating streetcars as they crossed town on weekdays. In Homewood, Grandmother Lavelle—known as "Mangone" to the grandchildren—oversaw an anarchic, easygoing household. She had gone into a tailspin after the death of her husband and later lost a leg to gangrene. Rebounding, she was perpetually cheerful, whether cooking and baking, hugging her family, or watching her favorite show on TV, *The Guiding Light*. Garbed in starched white dresses, she reveled in the commotion. Their Homestead Nana didn't let the grandchildren get away with anything, Mangone let them get away with everything. Years later, when her house was nearly destroyed by fire, she moved in with the Goodes.

"For four and a half months," Mal remembered, "I wasn't able to do anything." But starting to feel better, and needing a job, he rushed back into the fray, accepting an offer to work under his former landlord and fellow YMCA stalwart Leroy Randall. "I had an opportunity for the career of my life, the opportunity to go with the *Pittsburgh Courier* as an assistant circulation manager. That gave me the opportunity to work for the greatest black newspaper ever published. I was assured that I would not have to exert myself physically," he laughed. Mal, of course, exerted himself mightily; that was his nature. Besides, he believed the position was "a golden opportunity."[44]

5

SPEAKING TRUTH TO POWER

Two men were dead, one a white police officer highly regarded on the Hill, whose streets he had patrolled for fourteen years, the other a former Black heavyweight boxer out on parole with a rap sheet stretching back twenty years. Police reports stated that William Heagy died after Al Spalding shot him in the back during a shootout on Fulton Street in the evening of March 25, 1954. When Spalding was found dead three days later in a cell at the Centre Avenue station, the police said he took his own life. But Mal Goode blanched when reading the police report. Police statements were confusing and contradictory, their evidence implausible. And even if their stories had held together better, when a Black man was found dead in his cell, Mal could not stay silent. He knew too much about lynchings in the South and the deaths of men in custody in the North and had seen too much on the streets that Heagy had walked to uncritically accept police accounts. Mal was anything but naïve about crime and criminals, but he had been waging a war against police beatings and trumped up charges since he began wielding a microphone on the airwaves five years before. A forceful, trusted voice in Black Pittsburgh, he resolved that this time, a Black man's death amid baffling circumstances would not go unquestioned—not as long as Mal was working for the *Pittsburgh Courier* and delivering commentaries on WHOD.

The 1950s were a crossroads for African Americans. After World War II jumpstarted the second wave of the Great Migration, the ranks of northern African Americans swelled in cities like Pittsburgh. The drive for civil rights notched victories but lost momentum with the onset of the Cold War. The 1954 victory in *Brown v. Board of Education* was widely celebrated, but integration proved to be a mixed blessing. Although allowing new opportunities, it triggered a backlash and damaged Black institutions. Roy Wilkins of the NAACP later reflected that the immediate "sense of euphoria" was misplaced. "I failed to anticipate the ferocity of the resistance that quickly grew up in the Deep South," he said. That resistance penetrated the entire nation.[1]

Meanwhile, the Black press was in decline. The Red Scare and a growing reliance on advertising led some papers to tamp down the militancy they had long championed. They also lost several of their strongest journalists to mainstream pressrooms that were willing to integrate. Television posed an even greater threat. By 1960 most American homes featured television sets, changing the way people received—and viewed—the news. As television ramped up, the networks bailed from radio. Desperately searching for new markets, some stations sought Black listeners. African Americans owned few stations, but they were hungry for Black voices and programming tailored to their interests. That was auspicious for Mal. Radio was a medium for which he was uncommonly well-suited, and he soon became one of the voices that turned radio into a political force.

Mal was at the confluence of these shifting dynamics—a civil rights movement again at the crossroads, the decline of the Black press, and the emergence of African Americans on the airwaves. That became clear when he went on air in late March 1954, just days after Heagy and Spalding died. His blistering commentaries resonated in Pittsburgh and beyond. Mal was becoming, as one woman on the Hill called him, the "mouth almighty."[2]

The *Courier* called Heagy "an unusual, even extraordinary, police officer" who had served with extreme self-sacrifice and courage.[3] An outlier on the force, the bespectacled, forty-nine-year-old opponent of the death penalty had recently disputed the prosecutor in a murder case, taking the Black defendant's side. *Courier* columnist Ralph Koger described him as someone who "gave life but never took it," who believed in giving everybody a break, even criminals and newspapermen. "He was absolutely fearless of physical danger or of a verbal battle in which he might be frowned upon because he spoke up for an unpopular cause." That fearlessness got him killed.[4]

Bill Heagy knew Al Spalding, the man accused of his murder, because they both frequented local fight clubs. Heagy had befriended Spalding, who sparred with heavyweight champ Joe Louis and light-heavyweight champ John Henry Lewis but never found much success in the ring. Damaged by repeated blows to the head while fighting, Spalding survived on society's fringes. He had been arrested in half a dozen states since his first detention in 1934. The press reported Spalding's age as somewhere between twenty-eight and thirty-eight. Just one month earlier, in February, he had been released on parole from the county workhouse after serving part of a six-to-twelve-month sentence for assault with intent to kill.[5] He wasn't free for long.

On the night of Thursday, March 25, 1954, Bill Heagy responded to a call that a man had fired shots on a Hill District street and fled. Arriving at the scene, Heagy learned the man cornered inside a building was Spalding. He quickly intervened so that Spalding could surrender without harm. But as he approached Spalding, shots were fired, and Heagy was hit once in the back. He died not long afterward. Spalding, unscathed despite a fusillade of police fire, escaped. Running across rooftops, he hid in the bathroom of a nearby apartment where he was soon discovered. Surrounded, Spalding surrendered without additional gunfire and was taken to the station house on the Hill. Three nights later, he was found dead with a chain that held up his cell's bunkbed wrapped around his neck. The police said it was suicide.

"I didn't hear about the Spalding incident until that Monday morning when I got to the radio station and read the news wire," Mal recalled. "It happened at the #1 Police Station, but for a man to hang himself with a 12-inch chain just didn't sound possible to me." Mal studied police accounts and talked to *Courier* reporters covering the story. He soon heard enough and raised his voice—one amplified by WHOD's growing sway in the Black community and his ties to the *Courier*—to question the police force's version of the truth:

> I went on the air and announced a local news item about the Al Spalding death while in police custody. "You can believe this story if you want to, but I don't believe a word! But we're going to find out about it." I was determined to get to the bottom of such a senseless murder. For over an hour after I got off the air, the phones rang off the hook. "What are you calling me for?" I asked. Call the *Courier*, Dick Jones, or the NAACP. But I knew why they were calling me, they expected me do something about what had happened.[6]

It took Mal awhile to rebound after his heart attack in June 1948. When he did, he came out roaring. Long before returning to the fray, Mal had initiated a life-long conversation with Black folk. As a child, he listened and asked questions. As a young man, he learned from coworkers at the steelworks. His education continued at Pitt and as he worked the streets as a probation officer, directed boys at the Centre Avenue YMCA, and managed housing projects on the Hill. In those venues, Mal witnessed how people coped and learned firsthand about the agencies and courts intervening in their lives. It was no surprise that Mal formed opinions, strong ones, about race and politics. And he knew the players—a cast of rogues and reverends, hardworking people and no-account grifters, the educated and the unwashed.

In late 1948 Mal began working at the *Courier*, ready to join the fight. But it's not what Mal wrote while at the *Courier* that mattered. It was what he learned while crisscrossing the country for the paper and what he said as its on-air spokesperson. Mal's commentaries reverberated through the Black community and caused city fathers and the police to listen closely.

The *Courier* was at its zenith when Mal joined up. First distributed in 1907 as a two-page nickel-a-copy broadside, the paper graduated to city and national editions with a circulation already approaching fifty-five thousand by the late 1920s. Pullman porters carried bundles of the paper with them as they traveled throughout the South and Midwest, bringing African Americans far from Pittsburgh into a national conversation. The newspaper survived the Depression and prospered during the war. Its contingent of foreign war correspondents and the Double V campaign—victory over fascism in Europe and racism at home—solidified the paper's role as Black America's tribune. Given the dearth of elected Black leadership, the *Courier* played a guiding role, building cohesion among African Americans after the northward migrations and bolstering civil rights.

By the late 1940s the *Courier* had branch offices in New Orleans, Washington, Philadelphia, Los Angeles, Chicago, and Atlanta, employing thousands of newsboys, including the Goode boys. At its Centre Avenue offices, Mal learned about journalism from William Nunn Sr., George Schuyler, and P. L. Prattis, whom he considered the finest Black newsmen in the country.[7] But its circulation, like that of other Black papers, went into free fall in the late 1940s when metropolitan papers expanded coverage of race to gain African American readers. Black-owned businesses and colleges built on segregation suffered as white rivals with deeper pockets competed for their customers or students. Even the Homestead Grays were damaged. Fans deserted the Negro League teams for major league play, where they applauded Jackie Robinson and those who followed in his wake. But independent Black baseball collapsed. "After Jackie," Hall of Famer Buck Leonard lamented, "we couldn't draw flies."[8]

Mal was brought on to the staff to boost circulation, especially outside Pittsburgh. He had grown up reading the paper, subscribing to the tenets inscribed on its masthead: "Work, Integrity, Tact, Temperance, Prudence, Courage, Faith." That creed, historian Laurence Glasco noted, was a progressive, Black, middle-class version of the American dream.[9] Pledging to "abolish every vestige of Jim Crowism in Pittsburgh," the *Courier* crusaded for racial equality, especially in federal agencies and the armed forces.[10] Decrying mistreatment of Black citizens by the police and courts, the paper galvanized anti-lynching campaigns. The paper critiqued problems and proposed solutions, an approach that Mal had embraced as a high school debater. He once hoped to go to law school and work with Robert Vann, who became the fifth Black attorney to practice in Pittsburgh before becoming the *Courier*'s publisher. But instead of joining Vann's law office, Mal went to work for the paper that Vann had made a national organ. It was the second time he worked for a Black-owned and operated institution.[11]

Mal came of age believing in the *Courier*'s mission and fought to preserve it. Circulation peaked at 357,212 in May 1947—right before Mal arrived—but had plunged to 280,000 by September 1950. The paper could not stanch the bleeding. By 1954 when Mal blasted the police over Heagy's and Spalding's deaths, circulation was down by 70 percent. By 1960 only one hundred thousand readers were left. With white papers finally covering the civil rights beat and African Americans in sport, Black weeklies everywhere lost ground.

Mal took the job in part because he was told it would not be physically taxing and allow him to fully recover from his heart attack. It was anything but that, and Mal was soon traversing the country on the paper's behalf. Traveling to strengthen circulation, he visited Chicago, Memphis, Nashville, Roanoke, and beyond. In the fall of 1960, on a swing through the South, he lived out of a suitcase for eleven weeks, meeting with mayors, governors, and Black leaders. Their reception, he wrote, underscored "the great respect the *Courier* commanded even from whites in the South, who hated the publication because of its policy of demanding equality for Negroes." Southern mayors, editors, attorneys, and police chiefs resented a northern Black paper meddling in their cities, but they treated Mal carefully. Some offered their phone numbers and beseeched him to give their cities good press.[12]

Others were wary that he would cause trouble. In Memphis, police trailed him when he drove around the city. Mal saw the racism and violence facing southern Blacks. He spoke with sharecroppers whose jobs were disappearing because harvesting cotton had been mechanized and who faced retaliation when trying to register to vote, as did those who championed their cause. Crossing into Mississippi, Mal spoke with Aaron Henry just days after the NAACP leader's home was torched. Frequently hassled and arrested, Henry was once chained to the back of a garbage truck and paraded to the Clarksdale jail. Mal had nothing but respect for Henry and other NAACP stalwarts in the South, knowing he had greater latitude to defy harassment in western Pennsylvania than they had in Mississippi.

When campaigns to gain the vote and other rights triggered vigilante violence, authorities rarely intervened. Still, Mal rarely reduced whites to cardboard stereotypes and knew that racial realities were nuanced. In the *Courier*'s tradition, he sought to interpret conditions in a measured, logical manner. Nor was he blind to the paradoxical ways race played out. Not all African Americans in the South were comfortable with integration. Educators and businessmen "who felt it was wrong to advocate equality" frustrated him. Addressing students at Booker T. Washington High School in Memphis, he said that someday he wanted to return when they were attending integrated schools. When a teacher demanded: "What about our jobs?" Mal answered bluntly. "Individually, you really don't count in the scheme of things." For Mal, integration, even at a cost, was worth it. At another school he visited, only three hundred of twelve hundred students were in class. "The others were picking cotton that October, along with their parents. Later, I stood at the bridge and watched truckload after truckload of Negroes, parents and children, with water barrels attached to the rear of the trucks." He thought of his father being pulled from school after eight days when the harvest got heavy.[13]

"But the real break came for me in 1949 when television started to come in," Mal reflected. The media was in turmoil as television upended the advertising market. "Many stations were for sale and advertisers were transferring ads to television." That led KQV radio to ask the *Courier* to fill two fifteen-minute spots in an effort to broaden its audience. Robert L. Vann had died in 1940, but his widow, Jesse

Vann, had taken over as its publisher. She and editors William G. Nunn Sr. and P. L. Prattis realized a radio presence might boost circulation and provide free advertising. After the reporter assigned the commentaries showed little enthusiasm for the task, Vann asked Mal to take it over. It was a challenge, but one he embraced. Mal would do fifteen-minute editorials Tuesday and Wednesday nights from 10:00 to 10:15 on what was called *The Courier Speaks*. Mal always had a voice, but now he had an audience.[14]

A few Black performers could be heard on the radio after the Great Migration carried several hundred thousand African Americans northward. But they were marginalized until the 1940s. Music written and performed by African Americans might be played, but Black technicians and actors rarely found work. White actors often played Black characters, pandering to racial prejudice. Stereotypes prevailed: the "coon" from minstrel shows, usually a scheming clown who murdered the language; the "Tom" who deferred to whites and acquiesced to racism; and the "Mammy," a loving mother figure happy in her subjugation who came across as an easily frightened earth mother. Mal, on the other hand, was an Alpha—not a member of the Mystic Knights of the Sea, to which Amos 'n' Andy, whose radio characters were performed by whites, belonged. Only a sliver of airtime seriously addressed Black life or featured African Americans. They were not the only ones poorly portrayed; immigrants faced similarly debasing treatment before the war.

Mal was stepping into an important tradition of authentic Black radio initiated by Jack Cooper in the 1920s. Like Mal, Cooper's career was wide-ranging and tied to the Black press. Unlike Mal, he started in vaudeville before moving on to journalism and radio. His position as the assistant theater editor for the *Chicago Defender* and his weekly column "Coop's Chatter" allowed him to combine entertainment and journalism. A successful writer and performer, Cooper began appearing on a white-owned station. But frustrated with white employers' demands for dialect humor and minstrelsy, he was determined to establish programming for a Black audience. *The All-Negro Hour* debuted in 1929 and featured Black entertainers unconstrained by white prejudice and included gospel segments, comic strips, and a disc-jockey format.[15]

Cooper and other Black radio personalities emerged as civic and community leaders who were especially consequential during volatile times. Detroit DJ Martha Jean "The Queen" Steinberg stayed on the air for forty-eight hours during the riots of 1967 to keep listeners calm and informed. As she said: "We were the mayors back then. . . . We were the people that got the information out to the Black community about what was happening."[16] That was Mal's intention.

Activist actor Paul Robeson and a cohort of radical performers confronted radio's racial practices as World War II came to a close. The mobilization of African Americans during the war and the democratic rhetoric infusing the home front reinforced their efforts. Nor did they let up when the Allies triumphed. In 1946, W. H. Tymous, secretary of the Washington Veterans' Congress, blasted stations denigrating African Americans. "This is not the democratic way of life for which so many of our fallen comrades paid so dearly with their lives. This is the Hitler pattern. This is American fascism."[17]

Businesses catering to white consumers were leery of losing their patronage and stations feared chasing advertisers away, especially in southern markets. Those anxieties were widespread. Major league baseball owners had objected when the Brooklyn Dodgers signed Jackie Robinson in the fall of 1945 for that reason, fearing that Black players would attract Black fans and cause whites to stay home. Robinson's feats on the field, however, were royally rewarded at the box office. As Wendell Smith quipped in the *Courier*, "Jackie's nimble, Jackie's quick, Jackie makes the turnstiles click."[18] Brooklyn set attendance records during Robinson's 1947 debut season, and his appeal soon transcended race. A New York City station hired him to host a show in 1948, and within a year ABC featured the *"Jackie Robinson Show"* in its lineup. A decade later, Robinson's media ties redounded to Mal's benefit.

A few stations in markets with sizable Black audiences were programming news and cultural shows targeting African Americans by the late 1940s. In 1943, only four stations carried programs geared to Black listeners. That number ballooned to 260 within a decade.[19] Some took up a cudgel against racial injustice, but the Cold War's anti-communist headwinds smothered these efforts. McCarthyism had stilled progressive voices, and the language of racial solidarity was under attack. But as northern Black populations and incomes surged during the war, advertisers recognized that Black consumers would boost sales and shore up radio audiences that were shrinking because of television. African Americans were an untapped market, and the radio industry estimated Black purchasing power in 1954 at fifteen billion dollars—a sum too large to ignore. Responding to the new market, *The Negro World*, *The Walter White Show*, and *The Editors Speak* put new voices and concerns on the air.

African Americans had been the least likely citizens to own radios before World War II. The 1930 census estimated that over half of native-born whites and almost half of foreign-born whites in cities owned radios, but only one-seventh of urban African Americans, and there were even fewer radios in rural Black homes. But during the 1950s, Black radio ownership grew. The popularity of rhythm and blues (R&B) persuaded more stations to enter the Black market. Minister Al Benson, who popularized the R&B format in Chicago, became known as the "Godfather of Black Radio." That helped Mary Dee, and she boosted her brother.[20]

Mal was an immediate hit on Pittsburgh radio. After six months at KQV, he had built a loyal following attracted to thoughtful, resonant delivery and insight into listeners' concerns. Mal was already a much sought-after speaker and had internalized the *Courier*'s journalistic standards. Speaking precisely and using his voice to great effect, Mal delivered fact-driven narratives. His analysis was measured, but he often could not conceal his fury, making him even more effective. He was a singular voice in Pittsburgh. After six months, when KQV asked the paper to start paying for airtime, Jesse Vann replied: "Nothing doing." She figured that KQV benefited from Mal's commentaries and believed he could easily find a home elsewhere. Without missing a beat, Mal took his *Courier* segment to WHOD, known as "the Station of Nations."[21]

WHOD debuted on August 1, 1948, an underfunded station with just 250 watts of power and a novel vision of what it wanted to become. After the war, navy veteran Roy Ferree persuaded backers to invest in a studio on the Monongahela River near the Homestead steelworks. Promoting racial and ethnic democracy, WHOD saw itself as a platform for blue-collar Americans, aging immigrants, and their descendants.[22] When Mal's sister Mary heard about the station launching, just blocks from her home, she asked Ferree whether his commitment to democracy included Blacks. A recent graduate of the Mann School for Radio Announcers downtown, Mary Dee, as she was known thereafter, was hired with the proviso that she secure three sponsors. Her brothers James, who was a realtor, and Bill, a pharmacist, joined a florist in buying time. Mary Dee was soon WHOD's most popular host. Her daily show, *Moving Around with Mary Dee*, was fifteen minutes long and featured gospel music. Within six months, she had an hour's airtime; within two years, she was on for two hours a day with an expanded playlist. The nation's first Black female disc jockey, Mary Dee was profiled in *Ebony*, and her celebrity eclipsed that of her brother.[23]

Mary Dee and Mal caught the wave that brought Black voices to the fore on radio. A dozen Black DJs (all male) had shows in 1947. Mary Dee joined them in 1948, They played gospel, blues, jazz, and R&B—what was called race music.[24] But not everyone was happy hearing race music and Black voices on Pittsburgh airwaves. Nativists loathed the accents, inflections, and music infused with southern or eastern European heritage or with that of the Black South. WHOD weathered a barrage of vituperative letters and phone calls from listeners whom the *Courier* called "bigoted people with diseased, racist minds." Unmoved, the station soon averaged two hundred to three hundred letters daily, almost all expressing enthusiastic support or posing questions to WHOD's on-air crew. After five years, its audience rivaled that of stations that had been around for decades, and Mary Dee and Porky Chedwick were celebrities.[25] Chedwick—aka Pork the Tork, the Platter-Pushing Poppa—became a broker between white youth and Black music. Other hosts addressed Greek, Italian, Polish, German, and Jewish audiences and acquired steadfast listeners. Mary Dee geared her show for African Americans but developed a following among white youth attracted to her music and vivacity.

Although not as driven by the bottom line as bigger stations, WHOD needed to break even and relied on Mary Dee's appeal to African Americans. "The foreign born and his descendants want help in being orientated to an adopted land," the *Courier* observed. "The Negro listener is loyal to those who lend him a helping hand, and he interprets the program designed for his listening as . . . that kind of helping hand." DJs such as Mary Dee relentlessly promoted products, and shoppers began asking for "that Mary Dee corn meal" or "some Mary Dee hair lotion."[26]

In 1956 Albert Abarbanel and Alex Haley wrote in *Harper's Magazine* that the nation's sixteen million Black citizens' combined annual earnings of a billion dollars exceeded Canada's national income. African Americans, they declared, were "peculiarly susceptible to a specific appeal for their trade," something most advertisers had never attempted. They identified with stations who respected them and with sponsors who sought racial progress. "In city after city, as poll after poll has shown, 50 to 90 per cent of the Negro population listen to the radio station which seems most aware of Negro interests." WHOD thrived because of that bond.[27]

So did Mal. After he had gained confidence in writing and delivering news and commentary on KQV, his transition to WHOD was seamless. Like his sister, Mal's airtime kept expanding, to two fifteen-minute news shows and a ten-minute sport segment daily. By late 1951, he was WHOD's news director, on air five times daily. Mary Dee became so popular that WHOD built Studio Dee at the corner of Centre and Herron Avenue on the Hill. She sat behind a window so fans could see her and request favorite tunes. Teenagers, white and

Black, gathered to listen on outside speakers. Studio Dee soon moved to the *Courier* building, featuring celebrities like Sarah Vaughan and Cab Calloway and the athletes Mal brought on her show.

Mal rapidly built a following among people thirsting for a take on the news that made them central to the story. Listeners trusted him. They took his words personally. "Newscaster Mal Goode's war against police beatings, discrimination in public places, poor housing, and political candidates who have been vicious in their anti-Negro rantings," the *Courier* wrote, "have resulted in listeners phoning him at all hours to tell him of some mistreatment in a township 25 or 30 miles outside of Pittsburgh."[28] If possible, Mal investigated their concerns and addressed them.

By 1960, Black radio rivaled the *Courier's* significance to Pittsburgh. WHOD's success made other stations realize they were missing out on an audience, and some hired African Americans and expanded playlists. But none of them had Mary Dee and Mal.[29] Mal was the only African American on local airwaves offering serious commentary. His remarks reflected a commitment to integration, an appreciation of Black achievement and resilience, and an abiding faith in family and religion. His language and demeanor reflected these sensibilities and drew on Black culture and scripture. But he delivered his newscasts and commentaries at a steady clip and with verbal precision. What mattered the most, he pointed out, was that: "We were dealing primarily with the news of black folk."[30] Nobody else was. And Mal wanted to report on more than Pittsburgh. Although WHOD was a small station with a limited market, he interviewed Senator Estes Kefauver, Filipino statesman Carlos Romulo, future Hall of Famers, Pittsburgh Mayor Dave Lawrence, and Branch Rickey. Nevertheless, he chafed at not being able to gain a foothold in television or reach a national audience.

Frustration turned into anger during the 1950s when expectations for change went unfulfilled. The Heagy-Spalding affair brought that fury to the surface. A seemingly innocuous incident triggered their deaths.

When Al Spalding went into a bar to relieve himself on a March evening in 1954, a man sweeping the floor struck his shoes with a broom. To "the superstitious Spalding," *Courier* reporter Frank Bolden wrote, contact with the broom meant bad luck would befall him. Spalding shoved the man to the floor and rushed outside, where he urinated against a fence. When Willie Hamilton—whom the *Courier* referred to as "a Hill District habitué known as 'Crazy Bill'"—saw that, he scolded Spalding, who glared at him, pulled a gun, and threatened to shoot him. A woman witnessing the exchange from her apartment window called the police and let Spalding know what she had done. Incensed, he fired twice in her direction and ran.[31]

Officer Heagy was among the first to arrive at the building where Spalding had fled. When Spalding did not budge from hiding, police called for reinforcements with riot guns. Heagy was well known on the Hill, and a woman in the crowd gathered nearby told him that the man inside the building was his friend Spalding. Pushing past other officers, Heagy entered the house, yelling: "It's Heagy, Al. Drop your gun and come out. Give that gun up! You can't get away with it."[32]

According to the police, Heagy came face-to-face with Spalding, who pointed a gun at him. When officers persuaded Heagy to scram before Spalding fired, he turned to leave. Heagy was shot in the back before he exited the building. Unleashing a barrage of fire, officers retrieved their wounded comrade and rushed him to a hospital. It was too late; he died on the operating table three hours later. Spalding, unscathed, escaped across several rooftops, only to be trapped in a second-floor bathroom blocks away. He surrendered without firing. That evening, a police inspector reported that officers had fired more than thirty shots at the scene and offered various accounts of how many times Spalding fired his .38 Smith & Wesson revolver.

As word of Heagy's death spread, officers made wholesale arrests on the Hill, taking 125 "suspicious persons" into custody and searching them for weapons. Magistrate Robert "Pappy" Williams—one of the city's few Black justices of the peace—released them all because none had a gun or a knife when apprehended. Spalding was taken to the station house on the Hill, where, according to men in adjoining cells, two officers entered his cell and beat him with blackjacks. Spalding, whose behavior was described as erratic, was found dead three nights later. Officers said he had snapped a chain loose from the bunk bed attached to the wall, wrapped it around his neck, and asphyxiated himself. He was found sprawled on the edge of the bunk, his feet on the ground.

Mal went on the air the next morning. He did not attempt to conceal his disbelief concerning the police claim of suicide. He had spoken with Frank Bolden, George Barbour, John Clark, and other *Courier* journalists covering the story and began raising questions about police conduct. Mal directed his first salvo at Mayor David Lawrence and Police Superintendent James Slusser. "Our city today is carrying a black eye, gentlemen. A black eye because of the shady circumstances under which a man died last night at Central police station and I think you ought to know, gentlemen, that the decent people of Pittsburgh don't like it, not because it was Spalding, but because they now fear that the same thing might happen to one of their loved ones." Mal challenged the authorities: "Can you give us the answers, gentlemen, and we beg of you, can you offer us the protection of the law that's sworn to protect us or shall we continue to tremble lest every time one of these sadistic heathens goes on a rampage, it might include one of us? . . . I await your reply, gentlemen. That's the news and that's my view, thank you and good afternoon."[33] When Mal signed off, WHOD's phones began ringing.

The next few weeks, Mal concentrated on the story in his news wrap-ups and commentaries, challenging the police force's evolving explanation. One commentary spoke directly to the police, stressing that citizens they had sworn to defend were angry and suspicious about Spalding's death. "They are seriously grieved, too, about the death of Patrolman Heagy, a real friend to hundreds of people during his 15 years on the force." But Mal reminded them that "Regardless of who fired the bullet that killed him, it has been a common truism since the days of Adam that no two wrongs ever made a right." Mal realized that what happened in Spalding's cell might never be established. But he was hearing from people who wrote, called, and stopped him on the street, eager to blow the whistle on the police. They saw Mal as a conduit for their stories. Some might have been police officers, but he never burned a source. "We have a letter," he said, "from one who professes to know that many things happened to this human being by way of brutality and punishment before he closed his eyes in death. This no one can prove, but suffice it to say, gentlemen, that brutality does exist. . . . Fellow officers of yours have been known to say 'Yeh, we not only send them to the hospital, we send them to the morgue, too.'" Many of those listening uttered amen, urging Mal on.[34]

Arguing that most officers were decent and just men who upheld their oaths, Mal appealed to them. "Won't you talk with those who work with you, those who are noted for their brutality, those who you have watched as they split skulls and knocked out teeth and beat men into unconsciousness—the sadistic officer who embarrasses not only you, but the Mayor, your fine Superintendent Jim Slusser and the city of Pittsburgh?" Imploring the righteous to monitor their own ranks, he also spoke to those whose behavior he condemned. "To the very limited few on the force, the brutes, the sadistic, inhuman animalistic men, and you know who they are, may I urge that tomorrow you get out to church, see your minister, your priest, bow on your knees and ask forgiveness of GOD Almighty for your viciousness in the past, and ever keep the vision of Al Spalding foremost in your minds and remember that you are not the judge, nor the jury and Spalding should have been allowed to stand trial." If it happened again, he said, "the suicide theory just might not work. That's the news for the week, that's the news for today, and that's my view," he said as he wrapped his commentary. "But tomorrow's Sunday, friends, so get out to church . . . and keep the words of Genesis in mind 'Who so sheddeth man's blood, by man shall his blood be shed.'" The following week, he reported that "there was not the usual head battering and unnecessary abuse of those who were arrested" over the weekend and saluted those who had held abuse in check.[35]

The *Courier* published a skeptical, sobering front page editorial on April 1, 1954. "Pittsburgh's Negro community (and many whites, we

have reason to believe) is shocked" by the puzzling circumstances surrounding the deaths. "Shocked is probably too mild a term. Horrified
is better." Many asked how, if almost all of the shots fired came from
the guns of policemen standing behind Heagy, while Spalding fired
only once and was in front of him, could they be certain that it was
not a police bullet that killed Heagy? "This does not prove that [the
police] accidentally shot Heagy," the *Courier* stressed. "But it does
raise a question of doubt as to who did shoot him."[36]

Mal scrutinized police reports. The policeman who seized Spalding's revolver claimed that two shots had been fired by the gun and
four remained in its six chambers. A police inspector confirmed his
tally of the shots. Those two shots would have been the ones Spalding fired at the woman who called the police. If those were the only
two shots he fired, a bullet from his gun could not have killed Heagy.
Realizing these reports suggested that Heagy might have been killed
by friendly fire, Assistant Police Superintendent Lawrence Maloney
later said that three shots had been fired from Spalding's gun and
three bullets remained chambered. That third bullet could have been
the fatal shot. If the police fired thirty times and Spalding just once,
the police were truly the gang that couldn't shoot straight. But then a
third police report stated that Spalding had fired seven times—twice
at the woman who called the police and five times during the shoot-
out, including the shot that killed Heagy. There was no evidence that
Spalding reloaded, which made that scenario implausible, because
his revolver only had six chambers. If the initial police report un-
intentionally exonerated Spalding of Heagy's death, later accounts
were unsubstantiated. As a result, two days after the shooting, the
Post-Gazette reported that "late last night police were checking the
possibility that the bullet came from a police gun during the brief but
furious gunfire." That line of inquiry was quickly dropped.[37]

African Americans, Mal declared, believed neither the police
version of Heagy's death nor that of Spalding's suicide. "One of the
reasons for the public's doubt," the *Courier* wrote, "is its well-known
acquaintance with police practice. There are too many people who
know what happens to an unfortunate citizen who runs afoul of

the law, finds himself in the custody of the police and is given a 'going-over.'" Mal had covered such beatings. "Prisoners ARE battered in police station cells," the *Courier* added, emphasizing that Spalding had been severely beaten before he was placed in a cell and beaten again while in custody. "The man in the street (and not all of them are Negroes) thinks one of two things: (1) that Spalding was killed by hands other than his own, or (2) constant beating by the police forced Spalding to decide to take his own life. . . . The public is upset. . . . It should be given some satisfaction."[38]

Mal was under no illusions about Spalding; working probation had rid him of any naiveté he might have had about people with long rap sheets. But police accounts were hardly convincing. "I hold no brief for Spalding," he told listeners. "If he committed a crime, he should be punished, and if he took a life, the chair would have been too good for him. But that's the job of judges and juries in our democracy. Mr. Mayor, I heard you say last Friday night that bigotry and discrimination in America represented the most serious problem of our democracy. Could it then be, Mr. Mayor, that our city is one of the sores in this national malady to the point that a handful of vicious police officers can be permitted to embarrass us all?" Mal asked if Mayor Lawrence or his officers would want their nephews, brothers, or sons to be afforded the same justice Spalding received. "Spalding is dead, but he was a human being. Wrong as he might have been, the founders of this nation, when they wrote the canons of law, decreed that every man was entitled to due process of law . . . we all deserve rights of life, liberty and the pursuit of happiness."[39]

Mal had been around enough boxers to agree with the *Courier* that "Spalding had seen much better days." Boxing had taken a toll. "As a prizefighter (against John Henry Lewis and Joe Louis), he must have absorbed a lot of beating. Those who know him contend that in his last days he was subject to behavior like that of a man out of his mind. He babbled and blurted." The *Courier* reasoned that his deteriorating mental condition might have triggered his actions. But, "if what happened to Spalding had occurred in Georgia, it would have been dubbed a 'legal lynching.'"[40]

Mal brooked no lynchings, "legal" or otherwise. He was by then a savvy radio veteran, delivering commentary while wearing a crisp white shirt and tie and speaking with the cadence and style that radio journalists like Edward R. Murrow and Eric Severeid favored. His basso profundo, full of gravitas and authority, underscored his analysis, which resonated with listeners disinclined to accept police accounts.

Hop Kendrick was one of many whose views changed after listening to Mal. Encountering Mal at the YMCA, he fell under his spell during confabs at the Crawford Grill. Most weekdays, a cluster of Black Pittsburgh's leading figures gathered in the "Corner" at the Grill after work. Hop was the youngest at the table. "I don't recall ever seeing Mal drink," Hop chuckled, "but I was mesmerized when I heard him speak. "He was one of the most gifted orators I ever met in my life." Hop listened to Mal at the Grill, on WHOD, and at rallies. "I saw him live; when he spoke, you could hear in his voice that he cared. He wasn't just an orator; he had a sense of compassion, a sense of concern, and always had time for people."[41]

The more he listened to Mal, the more Hop believed that the police killed Heagy in a barrage of gunfire. "At first, I thought that Spalding had killed him, but as stories came out, everybody began to say that there's something wrong with this picture. And when they said Spalding committed suicide, we were 'Ooooooooh no! No, no, no, no, oh no!' After Mal got through, I believed that Heagy was killed by police and Spalding, too. Mal was absolutely convinced of that. And after I got a little older and began to understand how the police department worked, there was no question in my mind that they killed him."

Hop knew the insides of the Hill's station house. He had been arrested on charges that had no substance and were dismissed. "The police," he recalled, "were inhumane in those days. They call them bad now but in those days they were terrible. When we went into the station, our name was Sambo, Slick, Sapphire, Caledonia." Respect was a long time coming, something Hop saw firsthand when he helped create the Allegheny County narcotics force in 1966.

Hop Kendrick wasn't the only one influenced by Mal's crusade. "I would hear Mal speak about it and the crowd just roared." He estimated that 90 percent of the people paying attention agreed. Many feared that Mal's campaign confronting police brutality put him at risk. "I remember guys telling me one night that 'They're gonna kill Mal.' I said 'What do you mean, kill him?' They said the police were so angry that they put up blockades and stopped cars to see if he was in one of them." And Mal was indeed in one of them, concealed in the trunk. "I heard people say: 'Man, he's got them so upset.' It was one of the first times that I recognized the power of speech. I know for a fact that the police never forgave him."

If the police never forgave Mal, his thirteen-year-old son Bob never forgot that spring. "It was the most terrible moment of my young life. I worried about what was going to happen to my dad. The police were stopping him on the road, following him from Belmar Gardens where we lived through Schenley Park all the way over to Homestead." Sometimes, they pulled Mal over, claiming he had committed an infraction. But Mal forced the police to back off. Bob worked after school at his uncle Bill's pharmacy. "Then at dusk, I walked home, up that steep hill, frightened in my gut and my heart, for myself and my father." He worried about somebody making good on the threats they received. "Somebody called the house; once Roberta answered, the other time Richie, and they heard a man say 'We're going to kill your nigger father if he doesn't shut his mouth.'" When they told their mother, her answer was: "Don't answer the phone anymore." Mary Goode never seemed frightened. She later said, "I always felt safe with your dad." Not Bob. "It was lonely walking up the hill at night when the Heagy and Spalding deaths were in the air. And I didn't know enough to go to my mom and tell her I was frightened." Years later, Bob, then a vice president of a bank, met his father for lunch in Manhattan. Bob asked: "Weren't you afraid when the police followed you? He said 'Nah, they wouldn't hurt me. I worked for the *Courier.*'" He often called the *Courier* "one of my life's richest experiences."[42]

"I was the target of the Pittsburgh Police Department," Mal said. "I had WHOD license plates on my car and whenever I was on the streets, they knew where I was. But I never let up on them." After WHOD bought libel insurance for Mal, he went after the police even harder. "I told everybody that if they got beaten at a police station, to come on over to WHOD and tell me on the air where it happened. I had the power to put people on the air just like that, and I used it to the fullest."[43]

Mal recounted being pulled over for alleged violations in and around Pittsburgh. When that happened in New Kensington, Mal said he needed to make a phone call. When the policeman demanded "Who you gonna call, nig . . . ?" Mal retorted: "Ray Guardlock," the mayor. At that, the policeman said: "We gonna let you go this time. Don't let it happen again." Some white politicians feared his wrath damaging their standing with Black constituents. "All of a sudden," Mal said, "I realized that I was a special Negro. But what about my brothers—what about the little fellow who wasn't well known? If I had not been 'special,' there's no telling what would have happened. And that's when I really went after those bigots." In Aliquippa, when a policeman taunted: "Nigger, what you doing speeding down here on the Boulevard?" Mal answered: "Who're you talking to?" When the officer said: "I'm talking to you," Mal responded: "You're not talking to me because I *ain't* no nigger.'" The policeman threatened to lock Mal up. "I'll throw your ass in jail." Mal smiled; he knew Aliquippa's burgess (as the mayor was called). "The year before, classmates from Pitt—I knew them like brothers—asked me to campaign for the man, who was a candidate." Mal agreed after the man pledged to hire Black teachers. "That's all I wanted. And I didn't take a nickel even when offered 'something for my troubles.'"[44]

The burgess was in the squad room talking with the desk sergeant when Mal arrived. "Mal," he said. "How're you doing?" Mal answered: "I don't know" and nodded toward the officer. "Ask him." When the officer said Mal was speeding, Mal said: "Tell the burgess what you called me." When the officer denied calling him anything, Mal said: "You give the burgess your gun and blackjack and you come on back out into the street and tell me I'm a liar because that's what you're calling me." At that, the burgess intervened and told the officer to apologize. Mal later wrote that he had been arrested a total of nine times. That he avoided conviction, Mal stressed, showed that voting rights mattered. "I'm talking about power—political power and civil power. That's the power we have got to use, especially during tough times."[45]

Mal's commentaries and the *Courier*'s prodding were well received in the community, if not by the police. Mal addressed a meeting at Bethel AME Church on Tuesday, April 6, 1954, at which the NAACP, the Greater Pittsburgh Improvement League, the Business and Professional Men's Association, the Baptist Ministerial Association, the Civil Rights Committee of the Elks, and the *Courier* demanded an investigation "of the suspicions and distrust of the police department that underlies the unrest over the circumstances of the death of Aloysius Spalding."[46] More than two thousand people attended, intent on letting Mayor Lawrence and Superintendent of Police Slusser know how they felt.

"People refused to let them speak," Mal remembered. "They just wanted me to have my say." Mal, however, berated the audience for not listening to Lawrence. "I got up and I chewed them out. I told them not to act like that. After all of the letters and calls I received, I was shocked at the way such level-headed people were acting up." He then addressed police behavior. "They've got to stop beating black people to death like they did to Al Spalding," he roared. Mal's rhetoric and two thousand irate constituents persuaded Mayor Lawrence to ask the Civic Unity Council to probe complaints of police brutality.[47] "If there is police brutality to any citizen," Lawrence stated, "we want it stopped. . . . If there is a campaign of misstatement and suspicion being waged against the police, we want that stopped, too."[48]

A week later, Lawrence requested that Mal come to see him. "When I walked in, he told me to sit down. 'I'm too busy to sit down, Mayor. What do you want?' 'That's why I called you in, Mal. What do YOU want?' he said. 'I don't want a thing from you, Mayor. You've got to stop your Cossacks from splitting Negroes' heads open every Saturday night at the #2, #4, and #6, police stations. . . . You can stop it because you're the boss of this town." Frank Bolden, his colleague at the *Courier*, later said: "He took on Dave Lawrence like you would beat a rented mule in Missouri."[49]

Three weeks later, a coroner's inquest convened. Richard Jones, Mal's mentor at the YMCA, cross-examined witnesses on the behalf of the NAACP, the Black community, and Spalding's reputation. The police were adamant that Spalding shot Heagy and denied that Spalding had been beaten or coerced to confess. But three men in adjoining cells that night claimed the opposite—that the police verbally and physically abused him. Jones hammered away at police testimony. He demanded to know what caused the blood stains on Spalding's clothing and whether the marks and wounds on his neck that had *not* been caused by the chain had something to do with his death. When asked if Spalding's death could have caused by somebody other than Spalding, county pathologist Dr. Theodore Helmbold answered, "Yes, I think that it could."[30]

During the inquest, the prosecution stunned the audience by producing a witness who swore he saw Spalding shoot Heagy in the back. Willie Hamilton, now described as a Hill District character rather than as Crazy Bill, testified that Spalding had abducted him when fleeing the scene outside the tavern. He claimed he was in the apartment where Spalding was hiding when the police arrived. "When they kicked in the door, I saw [Spalding] fire a shot. Then I saw a man in blue lying on the ground." Given the officers' description of the scene—a dim hallway in a building besieged by the police—that seemed unlikely. So was Hamilton's never before reported tale of abduction across the rooftops.

The hearing, which lasted seven hours, was the longest inquest in Allegheny County in thirteen years. The six-man coroner's jury, which included two African Americans, deliberated for just twenty-three minutes before ruling that Spalding had killed Heagy and subsequently committed suicide. A month later, the Civic Unity Council concluded that the charges leveled against the police could not be "satisfactorily resolved."[31]

Both the *Courier* and WHOD were praised for their coverage. So was Mal, whose commentaries triggered hundreds of telegrams and letters. Commending his demeanor and clarity, some showered God's blessings upon him. One called his reporting "the finest I have ever heard, direct from the heart and to the point." Another applauded "his fearless speech. . . . I wish we had more Negroes like you." Some were angry, others poetic. "The stage is set, the drama has begun, we have just gotten our repulsive cue, although we have stage fright, this is no time to disperse . . . now is the time to unite." Many feared the police would seek retribution on Mal. Do not, a letter implored, let Mal Goode and a few others "fight this drastic problem alone." The letter writer beseeched people to back Mal, even if that meant leaving their easy chairs and forming a civilized vigilante group to defend him. "Don't put it off, do it now! I'm with you all the way Mel." Like many, he misspelled either Mal's first or last name.[52]

"I have listened to your broadcasting for a long time," a woman wrote. "But Monday it was superb, I don't know when I've heard anything that was so outstanding. . . . I praise you to the highest, May God Bless You. Mr. Goode if there was really more colored men like you, things would certainly change. . . . I'll always remember that you, Mal Goode, tried." Another said: "If we had more red-blooded men like you Pittsburgh would be a safe place for Negroes. Many a mother lie awake at night wondering if the policemen have grabbed her husband or son and whisked him to some deserted spot. . . . May the lord strengthen you and keep you, as a great champion of human rights." A man said: "Let me say in plain words I like your guts. . . . I like your grit." A steady listener wrote: "I thank God for a man like you. One who is able to stand on his own two feet and fights for the right and injustices that have been inflicted on the unfortunates." Even the Universal Negro Improvement Association (UNIA), the Black nationalist group Marcus Garvey formed in 1914, praised Mal's courage, exhorting him to carry on. "And to you, I say keep the people true to the Constitution of the United States of America."[53]

That spring, the Victory Charity Club Tea celebrated Mal for his relentless defense of Black citizens at the Centre Avenue Young Women's Christian Association (YWCA) while the Civil Liberties Department of the Greater Pittsburgh Elks Lodge 115 honored him at the Fort Pitt Hotel. "Scores of city dignitaries, *Courier* and WHOD heads and notables attended the gala affair, lauding the dynamic young crusader of human rights," the *Courier*'s Toki Schalk Johnson gushed. Robert Carter, who assisted Thurgood Marshall in arguing the historic *Brown v. the Board of Education* Supreme Court case, keynoted the testimonial. The court's unanimous ruling desegregating public education just issued had energized Black America. When it was his turn, Mal "electrified the assemblage with a rededication of his life to the cause of civil rights."[54]

"Mal," Hop Kendrick exclaimed, "was the voice I heard in the 1950s. He was THE voice. Mal was considered upper middle class, but we always saw him as a guy on the street. He cared about people." Other voices came along in the 1960s, Hop recalled, "but I would tell people who said: 'You only became interested [in civil rights] when King came on scene' that I heard Mal long before I even knew who King was."[55] Black Pittsburghers agreed. Goode's 1987 obituary on the front of the *Courier* began with the words: "Before Martin, before Malcolm, there was Mal Goode."[56]

Leveraging his bully pulpit, Mal trumpeted racial progress, believing that African Americans needed confidence that they could effect change. His tagline, "And the walls keep tumbling down!" became a familiar refrain. "I used it when black ballplayers were signed where they had never been able to play, or any time a Negro got a good job." When Mal walked into the Crawford Grill, somebody often shouted: "Here he is, and the walls keep tumbling down!" Barriers were crumbling. "The walls then were tumbling down so rapidly. I say rapidly because so many walls had been closed for so long and they began to tumble a little there and a little here; a black man elected to council in Aliquippa, to the school board in Clairton, or in little towns in the Mon Valley. The walls keep tumbling."[57]

Mal saw those walls falling fast in sport where, by the late 1940s, segregation was under assault at swimming pools and community centers as well as in collegiate and pro leagues. "My dad, [the] Reverend Leroy Patrick of Bethesda Presbyterian, and Wendell Freeland led a group of us to Highland Park pool to desegregate the pool," Bob Goode explained. "We couldn't swim and neither could they, but they're in the pool saying 'come on in, kids.' They knew that the white lifeguards were not going to save us so they recruited some black cops to be there to do that."[58] When athletes played in Pittsburgh, they often appeared on Mal's show. Mal became close to Henry Aaron, Billy Bruton, and Wes Covington and when their Milwaukee Braves squad went to the World Series in 1958, the players brought him to the games as their guest.

But nothing was more stirring for Mal than Jackie Robinson's leap across the color line. He was in the stands at Forbes Field when Robinson first played in Pittsburgh in May 1947. "When Jackie came to bat," Mal recalled, "a man sitting nearby screamed: 'Stick that nigger in his ear!'" Mal restrained his friend Charley Johnson, who was about to jump out of his seat and accost the fan. "I said: 'Charley, don't say anything.'" Branch Rickey, ministers, and the *Courier* had cautioned African Americans to stay calm lest fights at the ballpark jeopardize integration. Mal agreed with Rickey that Robinson, by performing to the best of his abilities and not falling for the bait, would optimize outcomes on and off the field.[59]

Later that season, Pirate pitcher Fritz Ostermueller narrowly missed beaning Robinson, who threw up his arm at the last moment and absorbed the baseball's impact with his left elbow. It was one of six times Jackie was hit by a pitch in the first half of the season, more than any player the entire previous season. When the Dodgers returned to Pittsburgh, Ostermueller was back on the mound. Robinson, who had battered Ostermueller's pitching since the near-skulling, got on base and was dancing off third. Distracting Ostermueller, who went into a full wind-up, Robinson dashed for the plate, stealing home for the first—but far from the last—time during his major league career.

"When Jackie stole home on Ostermueller, I was in the stands on the third base side," Mal recalled gleefully. So was the fan who almost provoked a fight at an earlier game. "This same one fellow said: 'Niggers should have been in big leagues long ago!' In broken English, he said that! . . . I'm saying that there must have been thousands of incidents around the country where white businessmen sat and never hired a black to do anything except to mop or to sweep who said 'What's wrong with it? Let's try it, an experiment.'" Those who witnessed Brooklyn's experiment, Mal argued, replicated it in myriad ways, translating it from the baseball field to the corridors of banks, businesses, and corporations. He reckoned that integrating the majors eased the path toward the Supreme Court's *Brown v. the Board of Education* decision seven years later.[60]

Mal saw sport as a catalyst to racial change. "We had a chance to build a tremendously interesting program on WHOD," Mal said. "White ballplayers friendly with the black players, men like Robin Roberts, Stan Musial, Ted Kluszewski, would come on." Future Hall of Famer Roberts, who pitched the Phillies' "Whiz Kids" to a pennant in 1950, made a strong impression. "I picked him up at the hotel and thanked him for coming. He said, 'I'm tickled to death to do it. When I was coming up in the National League, someone said to me, 'Kid, remember how you treat people when you're on your way up because you might meet the same people on your way down.'"[61] Nor did Mal encounter resistance entering locker rooms to conduct interviews. Sports were in the vanguard of racial change. "No other area of life—governmental, business, or even the church—has done more to bring about equality than the world of sport."[62]

Mal's interaction with athletes went beyond the studio. In 1954, the Goodes became homeowners, moving into newly opened Belmar Gardens. After World War II Americans migrated en masse to the suburbs, but restrictive covenants excluded African Americans from those glossy, new neighborhoods. In response, several *Courier* executives sponsored a residential development for middle-income families who were blocked from the suburbs. Belmar Gardens became the first Black-owned cooperative with federally insured mortgages in the United States.[63] The Goodes lived on a hill overlooking a bit of history. Woogie Harris's Queen Anne–style house on Apple Street sat in splendor below them. It was where Homestead's Mary Cardwell Dawson had housed the Negro National Opera Company and where Roberto Clemente once lived.

Visiting ballplayers made a beeline to the Goodes' house for dinner. Segregation in Pittsburgh restaurants was giving way, but Black players were still uncomfortable dining out. "They got tired eating in restaurants and we were proud to have them over," Mal remembered. "I went to Mary and Mal's home," Hank Aaron recalled, "just about all the times we played in Pittsburgh. Most of the Black players did. She was a tremendous lady and a tremendous cook. I don't know anything that she cooked that I walked away from! We didn't have many places to go, and we hung on to them. Me, Jackie, Junior Gilliam, Newc, Willie . . . we all did."[64] They savored Mary's cooking and chewed over what Mal had to say about the state of the nation and the role they could play. During the 1950s and early 1960s, almost every African American and Latin ballplayer passing through Pittsburgh came to dinner at the Goodes' house. In a 1955 photo, Willie Mays, wearing a white shirt and checkered tie, holds a beaming three-year-old Rosalia atop a car in front of their house.

They came for Mary's cooking but left with something to think about. "We went there with the idea of eating, not to talk baseball, but we ended up eating and talking baseball." And not just baseball, but race and civil rights. The ballplayers recognized the breadth of Mal's knowledge and respected his judgment. "He was a mentor to all of us; no question about that," Aaron affirmed. "He had a lot more sense than I had and knew a lot about everything. I thought a lot of him, always have, always will. I thought he was the greatest person in the world. Anytime I wanted to know something I could call Mal. He was aware of everything going on and he knew everybody."[65]

Mal usually telephoned Mary to let her know that he was bringing Aaron or another player to dinner but was often hazy about how many extra plates to set. "Dad would call from the ballpark and say, 'Mary, I'm bringing a couple of the players home for dinner,'" Bob Goode laughed. "She would say: 'Oh Mal, how many?' because it might end up being three to five. If he said four, it could be six or more." Sometimes there were twice as many.[66] "My biggest memory is him calling once and telling our mother he was bringing Willie [Mays] home for dinner," his sister Rosalia recalled. Her father did not mention anyone else. "He let her know that she should make red beans, rice, and corn bread because Willie liked them. And then he showed up with practically all of the San Francisco Giants and some Pirates too! I'm not kidding; there must've been at least a dozen guys. She was frying chicken all afternoon." Mal had to go to the store to buy more food to feed everybody. "She was hopping mad!" Rosalia laughed. The Giants had more African American and Latin ballplayers than any other club at the time. "At one point, Daddy said he had to get Mays back to the hotel and left us there with all these guys who didn't speak English!"[67]

"I have a vivid picture in my mind of Willie Mays and Roberto [Clemente] sitting and eating Mommy's beans with their heads literally in their plates, saying 'These sure are good, Mrs. Goode,'" her sister Roberta related. "Daddy told them to put their heads up because there is plenty more where that came from. They loved her lima beans with cornbread." The daughters were enthralled by their guests and delighted in seeing them so happy and relaxed. "I had huge crushes on Willie Mays, Roberto, Jackie, and Hank Aaron," Roberta smiled, "and those crushes remain!" Her father was huddled in the corner with Jackie, talking in serious tones one night. "Don't fret," her mother remarked. "They're just talking about the race problem." Roberta saw the same intense conversations with Aaron. "Hank and Jackie seemed more mature and interested in race, politics, and other current events," she recalled. "Jackie was one of the few who had been to college," Rosalia said. "And he was a U.S. Army officer, broad-shouldered, serious, and so handsome." But they made sure that each player was welcome. "The younger players were so happy to be eating home cooking," Rosalia recalled. "They just loved Mom."[68]

"While my mother was slaving away in the kitchen fixing dinner," she recalled, the players sat in a semi-circle in the front yard on lawn chairs borrowed from neighbors. "The kids in the neighborhood would go nuts when they saw them and run and tell everyone they were there. Daddy used to buy paddle balls [wooden paddles with small rubber balls attached] for the kids in Belmar Gardens and the ball players would autograph them." Her father savored those evenings, remarking: "It was great for us and great for the community, and certainly a great thing for my kids."[69]

Richard Goode was listening to the Pirates play the Giants one evening with classmates at West Virginia University. When Willie Mays hit a home run, Richard said that Mays often came to his house. Another student laughed and replied: "So has Napoleon." Not long afterward, Richard brought him home for the weekend, where photographs of Mays relaxing in the house were on the mantle.[70] "It meant something more than my wife giving them a good home-cooked meal," Mal said. "It let them know that people were proud of them. You could see it on their faces. For Jim Brown, who played for the Cleveland Browns, it was a matter of pride to come to our house for a meal. You should see what he wrote in our guest book the first time he came for a meal!" Mal had fought to integrate sport, but he had no way of knowing how those victories would change his own life.[71]

Mal and Mary rarely strayed from the traditional gender lanes. Mal didn't worry about the children, his home, or their status at church. Mary took care of that while he focused on providing for the family and his role in the struggle for equality. Their grandson, Randy Wilburn, remembered Mal as the rock pounding away at racial indignities, while Mary—strong, smart, and capable—was the glue.[72] She did the lion's share of family labor, caring for the children and readying meals with little warning when Mal brought guests home.

Mal cherished the time he shared with the children, but he worked nights and was often out of town. The boys eagerly waited when Mal hinted he might come home early enough to take them on an outing. They stopped by Stagno's bakery for day-old bread and did the rounds of green grocers and merchants until they walked in the door with overstuffed bags. Mary was amiably disapproving, chiding Mal that every time she sent him for one item he burst in with giggling boys and budget-busting purchases. He accepted her criticism with a grin, having no intention of changing his ways. Money was tight and a sense of financial vulnerability lingered from the Depression, but Mal never wanted the children to feel they were lacking. As his grandson Randy Wilburn put it, "they never had a ton, but made a ton with what they had."[73]

As Mal threw himself into the civil rights fray, demands on his time grew. Before Belmar Gardens, they rented an apartment in Penn Township. Mary was thrilled to be in her own bright new space. Mal, on the other hand, began voicing their neighbors' concerns. Service in Black sections were substandard, and Mal attended a council meeting with a jar of sewer water that ran down their street. Decrying their second-class status, he climaxed his remarks by threatening to pour the sewer water on the commissioners' table if they didn't fix the problem.[74]

The *Courier* described him as the "veteran Civil Rights campaigner" who helped lead the fight to hire African American teachers in Homestead in 1958. When accused of stirring up trouble, Mal retorted: "We intend to keep it stirred up until Negro teachers are employed in Homestead as they are in Clairton, Monessen, Aliquippa, and Pittsburgh."[75] When the McKeesport NAACP chapter and the Third Ward Boosters Club organized a banquet to honor the town's Little Tigers after the midget football team won the National Milk Bowl championship for the fifth year in a row, Mal keynoted. He applauded the Little Tigers' impact: "You taught adults a real lesson when all of you, both white and Negro, went down to Houston, and made 18,000 Texans stand up and cheer when you whipped their team real bad." He singled out the coaches for refusing to leave Black players at home when playing in the South.[76]

Mary recognized that activism was Mal's calling, but his absences burdened her. When Mal returned home with keys to a city or a plaque of appreciation from an organization, a tired Mary sometimes said, "Mal, don't those people know we can't eat plaques?" Mal soothed her as best he could. "Oh, Mary," he smiled, "there you are complaining with a loaf of bread under each arm." They understood that this was the life he had chosen and which she had accepted. Mal, Mary said, had three wives: herself, the Alphas, and the NAACP.[77]

By 1953, Mal was WHOD's news director and belonged to the National Association of Radio-TV News Directors. Its first Black member, he attended the convention in Cleveland. Eleven years later he discovered that, after he received his credentials, three men challenged his right to be there. If Mal stayed, they would leave. The board of directors called their bluff. Mal stayed, and so did the dissidents. Soon, he began looking beyond Pittsburgh.

Meanwhile, WHOD's success prompted other Pittsburgh stations to adopt all-Black formats. WILY went on the air in 1954, appealing to an audience with rural southern roots. WILY's vernacular approach to language—"Dishing it out Southern style"—upset some African Americans and rekindled Black Pittsburgh's historic class tensions, but it became one of the nation's highest-rated Black stations. Unable to match WILY's powerful signal, WHOD lost its grip on the market. In 1956, WHOD's owners sold the station to a new entity, WAMO, whose name was derived from the first letter of Pittsburgh's three rivers, the Allegheny, Monongahela, and Ohio. WAMO adopted a country and western format and fired Mal, Mary Dee, and other on-air personnel. Mary Dee left for Baltimore.[78] Mal, still with the *Courier*, started broadcasting at WMCK in McKeesport but quit because of friction with the station manager who feared that Mal was after his job. "I started banging on the doors of Pittsburgh's major radio and television stations, always getting the same answer, 'Keep in touch,' or 'Don't call me, I'll call you.'"[79]

But when WILY abandoned Black programming in 1957, WAMO ditched country and western to re-focus on African Americans and Mal returned as news director. "WAMO, Laurence Glasco argued, "became the voice of Black Pittsburgh during the civil rights movement, both because of its dedication and because it filled a growing void." Mal was often that voice when it came to civil rights. The void, Glasco reflected, was largely due to the decline of the *Courier*, which no longer provided comprehensive coverage of the Black community.[80] Mal, an NAACP stalwart since college, began covering civil rights after joining the *Courier*. Holding forth on WHOD and then WAMO, he gained recognition throughout the region as an activist and commentator. By the early 1960s, hard-won victories and appalling backlash prompted Mal to offer a national as well as a local perspective on the air. He grieved when fourteen-year-old Emmett Till was murdered in Mississippi in August 1955 and rejoiced when the Montgomery Bus Boycott came to a triumphant conclusion in December 1956.

Montgomery brought the twenty-seven-year-old Martin Luther King Jr. and his strategy of achieving change through nonviolent protest to his attention. The bus boycott, although sparked by Rosa Park's refusal to give up her seat in December 1955, was the result of sustained grassroots action in Montgomery. King and Ralph Abernathy, a young Baptist minister, became the boycott's most visible leaders. They garnered national attention, but the boycott was organized and maintained by activists from the Women's Political Council, the local chapter of the Brotherhood of Sleeping Car Porters, and a network of Black churches. When the boycott's outcome was uncertain and Black Montgomery's solidarity frayed, women and men like Juanita Abernathy and Brotherhood of Sleeping Car Porters activist E. D. Nixon held the community together. Their grassroots mobilization and King's charismatic leadership led to a signal triumph.

Mal was eager to tell these stories, but his coverage was skewed because his contacts were mostly men, often Alphas and members of the Talented Tenth. He listened to working-class and poorer African Americans and was not blind to the role that women like Daisy Lampkin, Rosa Parks, Jo Ann Robinson, and Juanita Abernathy played in Pittsburgh and Montgomery by holding the movement together, but he rarely sought them out. Nor did he challenge Black middle-class adherence to traditional gender roles; Black men were to lead the race.

The bus boycott required daily sacrifices, and women were instrumental in persuading people to make them. Rosa Parks, the secretary of the NAACP chapter, had sparked the boycott and risked her freedom; Jo Ann Robinson, who taught at Alabama State College, mobilized support for it through the Women's Political Council; and Juanita Abernathy, who used her Royal typewriter and carbon paper to turn out fliers, eight at a time, organized a network that sustained it for over a year. Juanita Abernathy's husband, the Reverend Ralph Abernathy, and Dr. King delivered weekly speeches, but it was Juanita who begged and borrowed vehicles to set up carpools providing alternative transportation. Much of that work took place during meals she served organizers at her dining room table. Without those carpools, Montgomery's domestic workers would have lost their livelihood and the boycott would have fizzled. Those opposing the boycott understood her importance and bombed her home, nearly killing Juanita, who was pregnant, and her daughter. Mal saw Juanita Abernathy on the front lines along with Coretta Scott King, Ralph Abernathy, and Martin Luther King Jr., but never interviewed her.[81] King was another matter. Six months into the boycott, he visited Pittsburgh and Mal began tracking him.

After 381 days of Black citizens surrendering daily convenience and jobs, they won their fight. It was a turning point in the civil rights struggle and underscored that peaceful protest by a Black community could prevail. For years, the Klan had driven through Black neighborhoods in Montgomery, terrorizing families. But when the Klan rode those streets after the boycott ended in December 1956, African Americans stood their ground and laughed at the hooded fanatics.

A few months later, activists created the Southern Christian Leadership Conference. Its first president, King preached that the nation's soul could be redeemed through nonviolent resistance.[82] Eloquent and preternaturally mature, he returned to Pittsburgh to preach at Central Baptist Church on the Hill two years later. He keynoted the Freedom Jubilees that Mal's close friend the Reverend Cornell Talley had organized to jolt the local civil rights effort into action and tie it to what was happening elsewhere. By the time King visited Pittsburgh for a third and fourth time, in the summers of 1960 and 1961, Mal believed that he was leading the movement to new heights.

So were students introducing a more confrontational, but still nonviolent, style to the movement. After victory in Montgomery and the desegregation of Central High School in Little Rock, Arkansas, in February 1960, the following year, four North Carolina AT&T freshmen sat down at a lunch counter in Greensboro, North Carolina, and asked to be served. Though abused and threatened, they sat there, unserved, until closing. Another nineteen students joined them the next day; one hundred were there by day four. By the summer, thousands of demonstrators had been arrested across the country for sitting in at lunch counters, in theatres and ballparks, even at church Sunday mornings.[83]

Several of the students were center stage at the Freedom Jubilees held at Forbes Field that summer. In the weeks leading up to the first Sunday afternoon affair in June 1960, African Americans in outlying towns organized buses and carpools to attend. "There is an expectant buzz in the air around Pittsburgh," the *Courier*'s Phyl Garland wrote. "It is the collective voice of the people rising from the crowded street corners, where the endless informal symposium on Hill life rages through the restless day and fitful nights, the beauty shops, the churches, the barbecue heavens, back yards and everyplace where men and women of color gather. They all know that something BIG is coming." They wanted to hear King, whom Garland called "the South's bronze disciple of Gandhi," as well as Jackie Robinson, Branch Rickey, and students who had risked their lives in the South.[84]

Already the happiest place in Pittsburgh that summer as the Pittsburgh Pirates unexpectedly contended for the National League pennant, Forbes Field rocked at the Jubilee. It was the largest civil rights rally yet held in the city. Joined by Mahalia Jackson, the Queen of Gospel, and Harry Belafonte, the activist actor whose popularity crossed the color line, King called for nonviolent struggle against segregation and argued that "If America is to survive," it must destroy segregation. "It will not be long before black and white, Jews and Gentiles, Catholics and Protestants will say we're free at last."[85]

Mal never forgot that speech and interviewed him afterward. "Dr. King talked for 55 minutes out there in the hot sun and never used a single note. I had never heard a man talk like that before in my life." Mal was gratified that his friends Jackie Robinson and Branch Rickey, United Steelworkers of America president David J. McDonald, and local politicians were on the podium. His spirits were lifted by the choir of five hundred men and women backing Mahalia Jackson. King returned for a second Freedom Jubilee in July 1961 and confronted those who were hesitant to act.[86]

By then, seven Black and six white "Freedom Riders" had left Washington, DC, on a Greyhound bus headed for New Orleans, intent on

challenging southern states that had defied the Supreme Court's declaration that segregated public busing was unconstitutional. The farther
they got into the South, the more violence they faced. They wanted to
arrive May 17, 1954, to celebrate the seventh anniversary of the Supreme
Court's *Brown v. Board of Education* decision. But when they reached
South Carolina, the Freedom Riders, including future Congressman
John Lewis, were attacked as they entered a whites-only waiting room.
In Alabama, mobs firebombed the bus and savagely beat them as they
fled the inferno. While Attorney General Robert F. Kennedy intervened, sending federal marshalls to protect the Freedom Riders, white
supremacists in the South were undeterred. But the Freedom Riders
encouraged others to take a stand. Mob violence showcased their courage, and many watching the action on TV were viscerally affected by
what they saw and read about the Freedom Rides.

King seized on their courage when he spoke again at Forbes Field.
"Gradualism is no more than do-nothingism, which ends up in stand-
still-ism," he thundered to a crowd that roared at his call to action.
"There is a new determination to be free. The student movement has
taken our yearnings for freedom and fashioned them into a creative
protest. The Freedom Riders have come to prove to the nation that
Negroes are willing to suffer in order to win that special something
called freedom." Pointing to the 140 cities that had desegregated public
facilities in recent years, King declared: "This is nothing more than
revolutionary. The Negro can now ride through the South without
facing humiliation." He applauded the activism making that possible
but challenged his audience not to declare victory prematurely. "These
movements reveal that the Negro is eternally through with segregation!" But only 7 percent of southern schools had desegregated since
the Supreme Court decision in 1954. "At this rate it will take 93 more
years before we are free, and we WILL not wait that long. Segregation
is slavery covered with the niceties of complexity."[87]

These fights were only a prelude. "Some say, I've been down so long
that down don't bother me. Others rise up in hatred." King's rhetoric
reached a crescendo. "We cannot cool off. We love America too much
to slow up. We must free her of this dilemma. Racism and colonialism

must go! The clock of destiny is ticking out. If America is to remain a first-class nation, she can no longer have second-class citizens. And in the words of the movement's theme song, 'We shall overcome!'"[88]

King, speaking with Mal on WHOD, called for an end to poll taxes and literacy tests, two common voter suppression methods targeting Black voters. "I don't mind being a troublemaker if it's creative trouble I'm bringing about," he told the press. "I think it's necessary to bring about tension so long as there is non-violence." He didn't mind making people uncomfortable. "I feel there is a small minority in the South that really fights integration, but the silence of those who do not wish to make a stand or who are indifferent is appalling."[89] The second Freedom Jubilee came after John K. Kennedy's inauguration in January 1961. African Americans had been pivotal to his narrow victory the previous November. Kennedy won their support in good measure because he pledged to press for civil rights legislation, enforce laws that were routinely ignored, and end discrimination in federally aided housing with the stroke of a pen. During the campaign, JFK and his brother Bobby had interceded when Martin Luther King Jr. was sentenced to hard labor in a Georgia prison camp. When King was released, Kennedy's standing with African Americans soared.[90]

But in office, Kennedy did little to press for civil rights. The biggest obstacle to passing legislation was the grip that conservative southerners held on congressional committees. Afraid of jeopardizing his entire agenda, Kennedy neither proposed new laws nor used his bully pulpit to advance civil rights. His administration reacted only when federal authority was challenged. His brother Bobby, now the attorney general, was more apt to take action, but many activists felt that JFK had let them down. Matters came to a head in Birmingham, Alabama, in 1963. By then, Mal had left Pittsburgh.

During the early 1960s, Mal frequently appeared on Pittsburgh's three commercial channels but could not land a steady gig. On good terms with news directors, Mal pressed them to integrate their programs and give him a chance. But he only got freelance work, which at least gave him production experience. His favorite assignment was interviewing heavyweight champ Floyd Patterson in Miami Beach before Patterson's third bout with Sweden's Ingemar Johansson in March 1961. Patterson, who lost the title to Johansson, became the first man to reclaim the championship when he won the rematch. He was now giving Johansson a chance to win it back. Mal's ten-minute segment ran over the two nights preceding Patterson's sixth-round knockout in the rubber match.

"But," Mal confessed, "the road became rocky," and he chafed at his inability to break television's color line. When Mal filled in for KDKA's Bob Prince—who announced Pirate games—on a Saturday night in 1958, he knew he had done a first-rate job. Mal stuck around the station for more than an hour taking calls from well-wishers. Some were from delighted Black listeners; others were whites for whom his sporting legitimacy was all that mattered. Mal came into the station Monday to discuss his performance with the general manager and press for a steady gig. They both knew how well Mal had done, but the station had received a call from a viewer demanding to know: "Was that a nigger you had on there in Bob Prince's place?" Instead of anticipating the audience Mal could attract, the general manager feared those he would drive away. "If there was one who felt that way," he told Mal, "there might be a thousand. I know you can do it, but the time isn't right."[91] Mal was crushed, but he had seen this play out before.

Mal, now in his fifties, felt that time was running out. He didn't want to leave Pittsburgh, but his age was an obstacle. "My children were growing. I had two youngsters out of college and four more to go. I was discouraged, disillusioned, and frustrated because of the 'closed-door' policy of local stations, and finally I decided to go to the top. In 1961, I visited Leroy Collins, then president of the National Association of Broadcasters, when he was in Pittsburgh on assignment. He suggested that I go to New York to talk with top network people. I did but found it almost impossible to see them."[92] Then, in March 1962, Jackie Robinson came to Pittsburgh to speak to a B'nai B'rith lodge. Jackie listened to Mal pour out his frustrations and thought hard about what his friend said. And then he did something about it.

FIGURE 1 (ABOVE). Mal Goode, center, graduated from the integrated Homestead High School in the class of "1925 ½." Vice president of the Debating Club, Mal wrote the class poem and was known for his quick wit. From "The Blue and Gold" Homestead High School Yearbook 1925. Photographer unknown. Courtesy of the Goode Family.

FIGURE 2 (RIGHT). Mary Lavelle in her youth. Her parents, Reverend Franklin Pierce Lavelle and Mary Anderson Lavelle, settled in Pittsburgh with their eight children in 1923. The family was left in shock when Franklin died suddenly in 1925. Photographer unknown. Courtesy of the Goode Family.

FIGURE 3 (ABOVE). Mal's early association with Alpha Phi Alpha was captured in this photograph of the Pittsburgh chapter. A lifelong Alpha, Mal might have addressed every chapter in the country. He is standing at the far right in the second row. Photographer unknown. Courtesy of the Goode Family.

FIGURE 4 (RIGHT). Mary Lavelle's high school portrait. Family obligations and caring for younger siblings interrupted her education, yet she graduated from Peabody High School in 1931. Photographer unknown. Courtesy of the Goode Family.

FIGURE 5. Mal Goode and Mary Lavelle during their courtship years. Work and distance made socializing and seeing each other difficult. They traveled in the same circles and stole visits whenever they could. Photographer unknown. Courtesy of the Goode Family.

FIGURE 6. Mary Lavelle, pictured on their wedding day in 1936. Their families' different church affiliations, Mal to Clark Memorial and Mary to the Church of God, led to a compromise. The ceremony was held at the Lavelle home in Homewood. Photographer unknown. Courtesy of the Goode Family.

FIGURE 7. Mary Dee, year unknown. Mal's younger sister Mary Dee was the nation's first Black female disc jockey. She collaborated with Mal on her popular show Moving Around with Mary Dee on WHOD in Pittsburgh. Photographer unknown. Courtesy of the Goode Family.

FIGURE 8. Mal Goode behind the WHOD microphone. On the air five times a day and serving as the news director in 1951, Mal delivered news and commentary, often challenging police and politicians. Photographer unknown. Courtesy of the Goode Family.

FIGURE 9. Mal Goode speaking to Melrose High School students in Memphis, Tennessee. His dynamism and tough, honest talk captivated diverse audiences across the country for more than sixty years. Photo by Hooks Brothers. Courtesy of the Goode Family.

FIGURE 10 (ABOVE). Mal Goode and three sons pictured at a father-son Alpha Phi Alpha event in Pittsburgh in the mid-fifties. Mal's membership in the fraternity led to lifelong connections and friendships. Mal, next to last row in middle. To the left, his son Russell, and behind Russell to the left, his son Robert. Youngest son Ronald smiles in the front row, third from right. Photo by Johnson Studio. Courtesy of the Goode Family.

FIGURE 11 (RIGHT). Hall of Famer Willie Mays holds three-year-old Rosalia Goode on the hood of a car outside their home in Pittsburgh. Black players often came for dinner, relishing Mary's cooking and their conversations with Mal. "We didn't have many places to go," Henry Aaron recalled, "and we hung on to them. Me, Jackie [Robinson], Junior Gilliam, Newk [Don Newcombe], Willie [Mays] . . . we all did." Photographer unknown. Courtesy of the Goode Family.

FIGURE 12. Mary and Mal Goode photographed with the "6 Rs" celebrating around the time of Mal's hiring at ABC. From left to right: Robert, Roberta, Mary, Mal, Rosalia, Ronald, Russell, and Richard. Photo by Teenie Harris. Courtesy of the Goode Family.

6

OCTOBER 1962

MAL GOODE MIGHT WELL HAVE PAUSED AND SAVORED THE enormity of the moment on October 28, 1962. He was about to make his national television debut. But as defining as the next minute would be for him personally, the backdrop, a predicament unlike any the globe had faced, overshadowed his elation. That Manhattan morning was achingly beautiful, as only a sunny, crisp, fall day could be, but storm clouds gathered overhead. If they broke, the United States and the Union of Soviet Socialist Republics would unleash a barrage of missiles, devastating life on earth.

The crisis over Soviet missiles in Cuba and the US ultimatum to remove them was climaxing and Mal, standing in the plaza at the United Nations, was at its epicenter. The fifty-four-year-old had paid his dues to be there that Sunday morning—perhaps more than any television correspondent ever had to reach that point. But like those listening as ABC broke into scheduled programming, Mal was preoccupied by the superpower showdown and humbled to update the largest audience he had ever addressed as it unfolded.

Mal had scant television experience; almost all his airtime had been on radio, a medium well suited for his deep distinctive voice and precise delivery. The few television stories he had done in Pittsburgh had been edited and produced before airing. This time he was on his own. "I'll never forget the thirty-five or forty seconds of the report," he recalled. "I had no writer, and no producer as would happen today. It was just from the shoulder." Minutes before he went on the air, Mal had encountered UN Secretary General U Thant on his way into the UN building. "I asked him about developments and he indicated it was 'not good.'"[1] When Mal entered ABC's tiny cubbyhole, the phone was ringing. Jim Hagerty, who ran the network's news and public affairs, was on the line, frantic for an update. When Mal told him he had spoken with U Thant, Hagerty instructed him to find the ABC crew waiting in front of the UN building so that he could report what he had heard—immediately. Mal quickly set up outside and considered what he had learned from U Thant. When the camera rolled, viewers saw a tall, well-dressed, brown-skinned man with a microphone in his hand as the flags of nations from around the world snapped behind him in the breeze. Many were struck by Mal's composure, which they found reassuring. Little did they sense the emotions coursing through him.

"It's a beautiful October Sabbath here in New York," Mal began, "but I cannot tell you what will happen in this crisis. The Secretary General will be meeting with the principals within the hour and we will keep you posted on developments. This is Mal Goode, ABC News, United Nations."[2] It was over in seconds, but for Mal it had been a long time coming, and it was the first of many appearances that day.

Mal had no experience on television, let alone on a national broadcast. But he believed in himself and had been waiting years for his "Jackie Robinson" moment. He was too seasoned to choke because of nerves. The man who sang and twirled around the bedroom doing a passable Cab Calloway imitation, whom one woman on the Hill in Pittsburgh called the "Mouth Almighty," was about to have that moment. Its meaning to African Americans, for one of their own to guide them through the crisis, or how white Americans would react, would be understood later.

But his reporting reverberated, especially among African Americans. Although ABC's audience, regardless of race, was focused on whether the United States and the Soviet Union would resolve their differences short of war, many realized they were witnessing a break-through that could help normalize integration. Those watching Mal's Sunday morning cut-in saw an African American delivering news on national television for the first time. Those who stayed tuned in to ABC television and radio that day would hear or see him another sixteen times. Over the next decade, those appearances numbered in the thousands. But October 28, 1962, was special.

Just one year earlier, Mal was desperate. Every effort he had made to break into Pittsburgh television had failed dismally. Now in his fifties, at a time when sixty-five was the expected age of retirement, he feared he would never get a chance. And then Jackie Robinson did for Mal what the Black press had done for Black athletes as they challenged segregation. He confronted those with the power to do something to overcome injustice. Robinson had the connections to get to the right people, and the timing was optimal to push ABC to hire an African American correspondent. A bold gesture like that would brand ABC as a pioneer, the first to break network television's color line, rather than the industry's laggard.

Mal and Jackie's friendship began when Robinson jumped major league baseball's color line in 1947. It was personal as well as politi-cal. When *The Jackie Robinson Story* premiered in Pittsburgh, Mal introduced Jackie to the audience. Like Monte Irvin, Willie Mays, Roy Campanella, Henry Aaron, and the other Negro Leaguers who followed in his wake, Jackie knew that Mal was in his corner, ready to provide a home-cooked meal or speak out in his defense. These men trusted Mal, valued his counsel, and were happy to do what they could for him when given the chance.

In 1956 Jackie wrote to convey condolences after Mal's mother died. He then pivoted to their common struggle. "I am sure you know I'll do all I can in our fight," Jackie wrote. He regarded Mal as a coura-geous advocate for equality and measured himself in comparison. "I am only sorry that I haven't been able to do more," Jackie confessed.

"We have a great opportunity to better things for our youngsters but we won't get there by waiting. I wish I had the facility to make a stronger fight. It's too bad there aren't more of us that are willing to put our fight first and the individual second."[3]

Jackie was in the midst of one of those fights, and his letter was a call to action for Mal. While some parts of the South were edging toward integration, progress had stalled elsewhere in the backlash to the Supreme Court's 1954 *Brown v. Board of Education* decision. In Louisiana, after Governor Earl Long signed a bill banning interracial athletics in July 1956, the *Times Picayune* sportswriter Bill Keefe ranted about an imagined African American bogeyman, decrying: "The thickness of his skull, his ape-like arms and characteristic odor by mating with the white race." He singled out Robinson as "the most harmful influence the Negro race has suffered" in sport. Robinson, Keefe grumbled, was insolent, antagonistic, and a troublemaker. What had set Keefe off was Robinson's comment that he would not be satisfied until hotels in the South accepted African Americans. That was unthinkable to Keefe. Robinson, he complained, should have been "muzzled long ago."[4]

Jackie discussed his response with Mal and resolved to write a letter that would be made public. "I do hope you can get the *Courier* to use it."[5] Mal assured him that he would. Robinson's rejoinder was measured and published on the front page of the *Courier* alongside Keefe's column. Ignoring Keefe's more vituperative comments, Jackie tried to reach people who might be persuaded to support civil rights. He emphasized the common ground immigrants shared. With a nod to Keefe's Irish ancestry, he wrote: "I have been told that as recently as fifty years ago, want ads in newspapers carried the biased lie, 'Irish and Italians need not apply' in certain sections of our country." Remarking that Keefe called him "insolent," he wrote: "I'll admit that I have not been subservient, but would you use the same adjective to describe a white ballplayer—say Ted Williams?" He closed with irony: "I am happy for you, that you were born white. It would have been extremely difficult for you had it been otherwise."[6]

Jackie reassured Mal: "Don't worry about me—you know our

fight is my fight and I'll always be in there." Mal had to grin when he saw that Jackie was writing on stationery from The Chase Hotel in St. Louis. When Jackie debuted with the Dodgers in 1947, the hotel refused to let him stay there with his teammates. But Jackie pushed to integrate The Chase Hotel and was staying there when he wrote Mal in what became his last major league season.[7]

Six years later, it was Jackie's turn to help Mal. He found his opening through Howard Cosell, the blustery, frank, and loquacious lawyer-turned-sports-reporter who had joined ABC TV in 1961. Cosell delivered thoughtful commentary with a uniquely truculent style, and Jackie frequently appeared on his show. He asked Cosell to broker a meeting between him and James Hagerty, newly hired by ABC to build a news program that could take on NBC and CBS.

That was a tall order. ABC News, with fewer affiliates, had always been a distant third in viewership. ABC's ratings were lagging far behind CBS and NBC, so much so that the network was dismissed as "fourth among the top three networks." The 1961–1962 season saw only six ABC shows ranked in the top thirty for the season, with no presence in the top ten. But it was willing to gamble in ways that CBS and NBC would not, including hiring Pauline Frederick, the first female radio correspondent not restricted to women's news.[8] In 1961 the network bet heavily on sport and introduced *The Wide World of Sports*. It also beefed up its sports radio programming under sport broadcasting pioneer and the president of ABC Sports Roone Arledge. His instincts were right. Cosell's acerbic, over-the-top, yet erudite commentary on ABC's *Monday Night Football* broadcasts would lead to ratings success. One of the longest-running and most highly rated shows in network history, *Monday Night Football* made Cosell a household name.[9]

As vice president of news, special events, and public affairs, Jim Hagerty needed to make ABC relevant and expand its feeble presence. His credentials were exceptional. After covering politics for the *New York Times*, Hagerty began practicing politics when he caught New York governor Thomas Dewey's attention. Hired as Dewey's press secretary, he became indispensable during the governor's failed effort to defeat incumbent Harry Truman in 1948. In 1952 when Dwight Eisenhower, commander of the Allied Expeditionary Forces in Europe, sought to end twenty years of Democratic rule at the presidential level, Dewey "loaned" Hagerty to him for the campaign. After Eisenhower beat Adlai Stevenson, he made Hagerty his press secretary. The quick-witted, mercurial Irish Catholic thrived in the hothouse of politics. An innovator who brought television cameras into presidential news conferences, Hagerty got along well with reporters while earning the trust of the occasionally volatile yet avuncular Eisenhower. The president's closest day-to-day adviser, Hagerty was the only press secretary to ever last two presidential terms. As somebody who had a seat in the smokey rooms where decisions were made, Hagerty became one of the strongest civil rights advocates close to Eisenhower. He had grit, expertise, and a vision. "You don't scare easily do you?" the president observed early on. "No sir," said Mr. Hagerty, a stocky bespectacled man. "I don't."[10] When Eisenhower left office in January 1961, Hagerty returned to journalism, but this time with the daunting task of building a viable news division at ABC. He moved quickly to bring top print journalists into the fold, believing he could transform them into television correspondents.

In November 1961 Hagerty stopped by the studio to meet Robinson, an American icon about to become the first African American elected to baseball's Hall of Fame. He came expecting to chat, not to be on the receiving end of Robinson's grievances. "Jackie told him it was wrong not to have Afro-American people employed there," Mal explained. "I recall his complaint to Hagerty: 'I've been here several times for Cosell and I've only seen two people of color . . . a maid and a building guard.' Without missing a beat, Hagerty responded: 'We're going to do something about it.'" That didn't stop Robinson from pressing his case. "Jackie emphasized that he had been interviewed by Negro newsmen in Philadelphia, St Louis, and Chicago, and that I had interviewed him many times at WHOD."[11] Challenged by Robinson and swayed by his argument, Hagerty initiated a search.

Robinson soon returned to Pittsburgh to speak in McKeesport on "Jackie Robinson Day." He had visited the city a few months earlier when Mal sought his support after leaping to the defense of the McKeesport Little Tigers and their star running back, thirteen-year-old Gerald "Puddin'" Grayson. The Little Tigers were the best midget football team in the nation and Puddin' Grayson their best player. The squad had won sixty-seven games in a row, attracting bigger crowds than the high school team. Traveling to Texas, Florida, and Mexico, they defeated nationally touted opponents in the Milk Bowl and the Ice Cream Bowl. The 118-pound Puddin' was virtually unstoppable as he broke tackles and juked his way into end zones and the limelight. When the Little Tigers beat a Texas squad in the Milk Bowl that year, KDKA broadcast the game and Bob Prince did the play-by-play. Not to be outdone, WIIC televised a replay of the game two days later.[12]

But that celebrity annoyed some in the Monongahela River Valley steel town. At a banquet honoring the team hosted by the McKeesport NAACP and the Third Ward Booster Club in January 1962, Bill Lickert, the Teamsters leader who coached them, protested: "Some people are trying to make it pretty tough for us to continue our program." He was told that the team could no longer use the high school field and that he should not be coaching because he lacked a college degree. What most upset Lickert was how Puddin' Grayson had been treated at school where a physical education teacher had paddled him for forgetting his gym bag. The teacher had a photo taken of the punishment and threatened to have it published on the front page of a newspaper with the caption "The great American flop." The backlash to the Little Tigers had come after Grayson's picture appeared in *Sports Illustrated*, which called him one of the greatest young athletes in the country. Lickert and most of the audience at the January 1962 banquet believed that the attacks were motivated by jealousy tinged by race.[13]

Most people in McKeesport backed the Little Tigers, twelve- and thirteen-year-olds who reflected McKeesport's interracial mix, and hailed Puddin' as their native son. The high school's senior class had elected an African American as its president that year, but no African American had ever taught there and resistance to racial change was still strong.[14]

"I didn't understand why they were going after me," Grayson recalled. "But the NAACP, with Mal Goode leading the charge, came to our defense. Mr. Goode said: 'You're not going to treat this young man like that. He's a good kid; you can't do that!'" Mal not only used his radio platform to rally support, he called on Robinson to join him in McKeesport. "I really didn't know who Jackie was and what he meant till Mal brought him to a Little Tigers Banquet," Grayson explained decades later. "Mal told me, above all, to be humble and to think before you act. He said: 'Be quick to listen . . . and especially to listen to what Jackie Robinson has to say.' Mal was outspoken and taught me how to do the right thing; how to be a good person. I saw him on TV and we stayed in touch. I'll never forget how he stood up for us—for the Little Tigers, our coach Bill Lickert, and for me." For Mal, this was a fight worth taking on.[15]

Mal picked his friend up at the airport when he returned to Pittsburgh to attend "Jackie Robinson Day" in McKeesport. After he brought Jackie home so that Mary could fix them breakfast, they headed to McKeesport to speak to B'nai Brith, a Jewish service organization. On the way back to the airport that evening, Mal vented his frustrations that television had shut him out. Jackie listened, and then he told Mal about his conversation with Hagerty and urged him to seek an interview with ABC.

Mal was on it. He knew that this would be his best and possibly last chance to crack television. He drafted a letter touting his experience and stressing his desire to fill the job. It was cathartic. "For more than eight years," he wrote Hagerty, "I have been knocking at doors of television stations in the local area, armed with credentials and experience in the field that went back to 1949, but with no success. For some reason, (it might just be incidental that I am a Negro), the local stations have found it impossible to place me." Noting that each of Pittsburgh's three stations had bypassed him when filling vacancies, Mal stressed: "I have long since learned not to carry my feelings on my shoulder in matters of this kind; however, my naivete is not so pronounced that I cannot fathom the reasons for this bypassing. I would count it an opportunity to come to New York to talk with you about the position my friend Jackie Robinson talked with me about last Sunday while he was in the city."[16]

Mal literally prayed that his letter to Hagerty, who was poised to write a new chapter in television history, might make what had been impossible for him to achieve in Pittsburgh a reality on a national level. He relentlessly pursued the position, serving as his own advocate and marshaling broad backing from Pittsburghers who could reach Hagerty. In his letter, Mal wrote that: "Newscasting is loaded with mediocre talent, particularly at the local level and it just seems almost criminal to deny qualified persons an opportunity just because of some racial difference. . . . I would only want an opportunity to display what talents I have in this direction. If the tests are made by 'blind' persons—blind to the color of my skin, and sufficient opportunity is given to adjust to methods used in the field, I'll match any man in America doing this kind of job."[17]

Mal touted his political, media, and sports connections and offered evidence regarding how well his shows on Pittsburgh radio had fared in competition with more powerful stations. Given how much was riding on the letter, Mal showed restraint, keeping it under two single-spaced pages. Hagerty responded quickly, inviting Mal to New York to talk that April. When they met, Mal realized that Hagerty knew quite a bit about him. Branch Rickey, Jackie Robinson, Jesse Vann, Pirates GM Joe Brown, and other friends had already vouched for him with Hagerty. "It was a short meeting." Hagerty told Mal to call back in a month after he interviewed other applicants. When he called in May, no decisions had been made. Finally, in July, ABC whittled its list of thirty candidates to eight men. On July 31, 1962, Hagerty's secretary called to schedule an audition.[18]

The *Courier* sent him off to the audition with a front-page editorial: "We're With You, Mal. . . . People of Pittsburgh and vicinity, we are sure, share our conviction that Mr. Goode has unusual qualifications. He's articulate, forceful, outspoken, experienced . . . and an advocate of full citizenship rights for all Americans. He comes from a dynamic family of people who worked to get ahead. He's the father of a group of children who would make any parent's heart beat with pride." The *Courier* concluded that: "The color of his skin is a birthright which we, as Negroes, wear with pride. Today, it's a symbol of accomplishment through sacrifice. Do your best, Mal . . . we're with you!"[19]

Arriving in New York City on a Monday evening in early August, Mal stayed at the Manhattan Hotel and showed up at ABC early the next day. When Hagerty told him that they had prepared a few news stories for him to deliver, Mal responded: "I'd rather put my own program together." Given a desk, a typewriter, and access to their news teletype machines, he put together a five-minute segment that was placed on a teleprompter. With fourteen executives watching from a booth overlooking the studio, Mal delivered his segment. Then he returned to Pittsburgh and waited.[20]

A few weeks later, he got the call he thought would never come. On Saturday morning August 25, 1962, Mal, Mary, Richard, and Roberta were at home when the telephone rang. Richard, who was about to return to West Virginia University for his sophomore year, answered. Stunned, he cupped the phone in his hand, said: "Dad, it's 'ABC calling for Mal Goode,'" and handed the receiver to his father. Hagerty was to the point. "Mal, the job is yours if you want it." Emotion filled Mal's face but not his voice. In a measured tone, he said: "Mr. Hagerty, I am the grandson of slaves. I never thought I'd see this day."[21]

Roberta was upstairs when she heard the ruckus erupting in the kitchen. "What's going on?" she yelled as she raced down the stairs to find Richard and her parents crying, laughing, and praying. "Your father got the job at ABC!" Mary screamed. This would mean moving to New York, away from Pittsburgh and family, into a new home, and for the three youngest children, entering new schools. The position came with a sizeable salary, thirteen thousand dollars, and the security of a three-year contract, which was especially welcome to Mal and Mary, with six children in college or college bound. Most of all, Mal would be considered the Jackie Robinson of network television, a comparison that came with honor as well as considerable responsibility. "It was like I was coming out of a compound I'd been in all my life," Mal remembered.[22]

Negotiations went smoothly and a contract was signed on September 10th.[23] Later on, Mal remarked: "They looked from November 1961 until August 1962 to find one black man—not too dark, not too light, not too smart, or somebody who would fail. . . . They wanted to . . . make sure they got the right Negro. And they did."[24]

In Pittsburgh, a city that had long frustrated Mal, a celebratory whirlwind swept over the family. The *Courier* published a photo of Mal and Jim Hagerty on the front page with the caption "Television At Long Last Becomes American" and reported that the announcement had precipitated a flood of congratulatory letters, telegrams, and testimonials.[25] They were from public officials, business and civic leaders, sport figures, clergy, friends, even Mal's former elementary school teacher. They spoke of their respect for his tenacity and grit, as well as his compassion and commitment to family and community.

Mrs. A. M. Gibbs Sharp was exuberant: "Malvin, I couldn't be more proud of you if you belonged to me. I'm so sorry your mother and father couldn't have lived long enough to have shared the good fortune with you. Be just as you always have been—honest and upright and God fearing—keep your eyes, as you always have, up, and on the goal ahead, but keep your feet firmly on the ground." She underlined "on the ground." "If you don't, you will hear from one who has always been proud to say: 'Of course I know Malvin Goode. I was his teacher for two years and more than once I made him stand in a corner.'"[26] She was right about his parents, who would have been over the moon. They had admonished him to live up to Mary McLeod Bethune's challenge that: "It's better to have a hundred ready and prepared when the door of opportunity opens than to have no one prepared." That door had opened and Mal was ready to charge through it.[27]

"We are especially happy with this appointment," Herb Wilkerson, executive secretary of the Pittsburgh NAACP, wrote, "because it was awarded to a man who never bites his tongue on what he really believes. . . . This is not only important to us locally, but important to Negroes nationally, and important to freedom fighters of color the world over."[28]

Even those with whom Mal had jousted on the airwaves weighed in. Always willing to disagree, Mal was not disagreeable. "If Mr. K [Soviet premier Nikita Khrushchev] comes to America, I have one word of advice for him—don't try to debate with you," Pitt's athletics publicity director Beano Cook wrote.[29] Cook was referring to a fiery televised debate regarding Pitt's abysmal record recruiting Black student athletes. Beano, known as the Cardinal of College Football, was one of the few who could go toe to toe with Mal. When Mal had challenged Pitt for largely ignoring African American athletes, Cook took umbrage. The school had integrated its teams during the 1950s, but the agonizingly slow pace of that process troubled Mal, who contended that it hurt Pitt's image with Black students. Nor had the university fielded a Black football player since Bobby Grier graduated in 1956. Mal campaigned for Pitt to do more. Cook, also a Pitt graduate, defended the school by stressing the strides Pitt athletics were making, but Mal didn't back down. The image is bad, he said. "In the last ten years a host of great Negro high school basketball and football athletes have come out in Western PA and found it necessary to go to other schools because Pitt never made a positive approach to get them . . . why would a youngster who is a star in high school—if he has a chance to go to Northwestern, Notre Dame, Indiana, or Minnesota—select my school, the University of Pittsburgh, where over the years the record has been so bad?"[30]

Mal heard from Congressman William Moorhead, steel executives, and their union counterparts. Folks he had never met but who had listened to him on the radio or at church weighed in. The Jacksons from Brownsville, a Monongahela River mill town, reprised Mal's own words as they wrote: "Congratulations, Mr. Bridge Builder, . . . the walls are falling down." Another said: "*Trust* in *God*—and *Keep* on *Keeping* on." Judge Samuel Weiss wrote, "Always be 'Mal Goode' and you can't lose."[31]

Nobody cheered Mal's hire more than the sports community. Black athletes across the nation saw him as their paladin while many of their white counterparts respected and liked him. Bob Prince spread word of his hiring during Pirates broadcasts, and Mal heard from Steelers owner Art Rooney, the Pirates General Manager Joe Brown, and local sportswriters. Former Homestead Grays second baseman Clarence Bruce told Mal that "You have made history and my family and I want you to know that we are so proud of you." The *Post-Gazette's* veteran scribe Harry Keck wrote: "You have no idea how happy I was to read about your audition victory for the big ABC job. . . . First there was Jackie Robinson. He's in the Hall of Fame. Now Mal Goode. He'll make it, too."[32]

Mal savored each response. "I've been in the clouds since August 25th when Jim Hagerty of ABC phoned to offer me this job," he confided, "and now my good friends won't let me come down to earth." He was feted at his church and the Loendi Club, and deluged by letters, telegrams, and calls from around the nation. "It's too wonderful to believe," he wrote. "I'm everlastingly grateful to all of you, too, in my hometown."[33]

By October, Mal had been at the United Nations for a month and was settling into new routines. He took the subway early each morning from Harlem, where he roomed at the YMCA. On weekends, he returned to Pittsburgh. Before long, he moved to Henry Kempton Craft's apartment at 270 Convent Avenue in Harlem. Mal knew Craft, who had led the Centre Avenue YMCA before taking the helm at the YMCA in Harlem. He was also friends with Craft's son-in-law Josh Rose, an Alpha brother from Pitt. Family and friends often stayed in Craft's capacious, well-appointed apartment in Harlem's Hamilton Heights. Alexander Hamilton and later Madame Stephanie St. Clair, Harlem's numbers queen, had once lived across the street.[34]

The kids stayed in school in Pittsburgh while Mal began his job. Finding a home in or around New York City could wait. But Mal went home on Fridays, returning Sunday evenings. His first weekend back in Pittsburgh, while the phone was still ringing with congratulations, the family celebrated Russell's marriage to Antje Pilz. Russell, the oldest son, had been stationed in Germany with the Air Force and had returned home accompanied by his German fiancée. The wedding took place in their home in Belmar Gardens with family and close friends. The bride's sole attendant was her friend Dorothy Grier, whose husband, Bobby Grier (a former Pitt football star) had served with Russell in Germany.[35]

Mal had championed Grier when the young man became a cause célèbre for the integration of college sport. On January 2, 1956, just months after Emmett Till's murder and weeks into the Montgomery Bus Boycott, Pitt was slated to play Georgia Tech in the Sugar Bowl. Although Grier was the only African American player on the squad, that was one too many for Georgia's segregationist governor, Marvin Griffin, and some Georgia Tech alumni. They pressured the school to refuse to play rather than be party to integrating the Sugar Bowl. "The South stands at Armageddon," Griffin warned ominously. Pitt was resolute that it would not leave Grier at home. He will "travel, eat, live, practice, and play with the team," a Pitt spokesman said. "Heck, he intercepted the pass (against Penn State) that put us in the Sugar Bowl."[36] That Pitt stuck by Grier was not too surprising. What was unusual was that so did Georgia Tech's players, students, and administrators. A school spokesman said: "Our boys voted to play in the Sugar Bowl and we will not break our contract, especially since Georgia and Tech have played against Negroes before and there has been no criticism." Students went further and took to the streets, carrying torches as they marched on the governor's mansion. Joined by their counterparts at Emory, Mercer, and the University of Georgia, they burned the governor in effigy.[37]

Grier played, although he was forced to stay at a Black hotel apart from his teammates and was barred from the Sugar Bowl's after-game party. Those insults mattered much less to Grier than a pass interference penalty called against him that led to Georgia Tech's sole touchdown in its 7–0 victory. Even the referee who threw the flag, who was from Pittsburgh, after watching film of the play admitted that he had made the wrong call. Mal, for whom sport had always been part of the struggle, covered the story with characteristic fervor.

Sport and politics were muted during Russell and Antje's wedding, which Mary organized, even though she was in the midst of the maelstrom sparked by Mal's hiring. Afterward, Mal returned to Harlem; a few days later Russell departed for his New England base while Antje stayed with the Goodes until base housing was secured.

The UN posting put Mal at the intersection of two critical but often conflicting forces reshaping the postwar world. The first was the Cold War, the nearly half-century-long clash pitting two superpowers in a three-dimensional chess game that often turned deadly. The second, decolonization, was the culmination of struggles by Africans and Asians to free themselves from Western powers. These dramas played out in Moscow and Washington, DC, and from the Mekong Delta to the Congo. Each facet of the rivalry surfaced at the United Nations. Like most Americans, Mal was a Cold Warrior, but not without reservations about American foreign policy, especially when it came to the colonial world. Africa had been on his mind since he attended films and lectures about the continent as a boy at Clark Memorial Baptist Church. He was sympathetic to liberation struggles that most of his countrymen knew little about. And he believed that what some saw as the Cold War was instead part of the fight for independence in the Third World.

An earlier attempt to create a peacekeeping organization emerged after World War I, but US unwillingness to join dealt the League of Nations a blow from which it never recovered. It was unable to contain the tensions in Europe and Asia during the 1920s and 1930s. The United Nations was a different story, with greater buy-in by the world's most powerful nations. The carnage of World War II lent a sense of urgency to the project to form a global body that could foster collective security and defuse conflicts. Representatives from fifty nations met in San Francisco in June 1945 to write the UN Charter. Several nations proposed placing it in Europe, but the continent was digging out from its most destructive war ever and organizers sought a fresh start across the Atlantic. UN headquarters, designed by a team of visionary architects led by France's Le Corbusier and Brazil's Oscar Niemeyer, had opened a decade before Mal arrived. He was dazzled by the gleaming complex of buildings looming over the East River in Turtle Bay, built on land where slaughterhouses and tenement buildings had once stood. Energized by the United Nations and the city, he was captivated by the dramas unfolding inside its chambers and corridors, where he worked among men and women whose attire ranged from three-piece suits to sarongs and dashikis.

Africa was all but absent when the United Nations formed. Only three of the fifty nations that signed its charter in 1945 were African: Liberia, Ethiopia, and South Africa. Liberia had been formed by African Americans sent by the American Colonization Society in the 1820s; Ethiopia, led by Haile Selassie, was the only independent African nation before the war; and the Union of South Africa, ruled by the descendants of Dutch and British settlers, was about to embrace apartheid. By the time Mal arrived, however, European colonialism's grip on Africa was slipping.

Only a few African Americans attended the 1945 meetings, notably Mary McLeod Bethune, Ralph Bunche, Dr. W. E. B. Du Bois, and Walter White. African representation was considerably higher by the early 1960s as colonies on the continent were gaining independence. "If nothing else," Mal reflected, "the forum showed African Americans they were not alone in their battle against oppression. Others, thousands of miles away, fought for the same thing they had fought for when their ancestors were brought by force to this continent. Negroes now knew that they were not the only ones fighting for freedom." Mal considered the United Nations an arena for the entire world to behold. "It remains the final hope in the fight for human rights," he later affirmed.[38]

Once at the United Nations, Mal saw the United States and the Soviet Union continually clashing as they jockeyed to influence as much of the world as possible. The Soviets spotlighted Jim Crow—America's apartheid—and played up racial controversy, especially in the South, to undercut US rhetoric about freedom and democracy. Meanwhile, scores of newly independent nations now sat in the General Assembly. Jim Hagerty anticipated that Mal would be able to gain their confidence.

Mal did not need to be told to do that. He wanted to understand and communicate their voices to ABC's audience and eagerly sought them out. By covering the moment when the Cold War almost blazed white hot—the ten days in October 1962 that became known as the Cuban Missile Crisis—Mal gained credibility. The missile crisis catapulted Mal onto the national stage, and he used that exposure to become a voice for the Third World, especially Africa, for the rest of his life.

During his first few weeks at the United Nations, Mal focused on ABC's production protocols and introduced himself to ambassadors and their staffs. The sole African American correspondent at the United Nations, he quickly established himself by doing interviews for ABC radio. Tall, impeccably dressed, and carrying himself with the gravitas of a veteran newsman, he introduced himself to Secretary General U Thant and African diplomats, who found him simpatico as well as an anomaly.

U Thant, a few months younger than Mal, was emerging as a planetary leader. A trusted advisor to the Burmese government after the British colony achieved independence in 1948, the seasoned diplomat assumed the secretary generalship after his predecessor, Dag Hammarskjöld, died in a mysterious plane crash en route to Congo in 1961. When the United States and the Soviet Union vetoed each other's suggested replacements, nations from the non-aligned bloc proposed U Thant as acting secretary-general. The acting designation was then dropped as U Thant gained the confidence of a broad spectrum of nations. Mal, impressed by his demeanor and steadfast faith in Buddhism, knew that access to U Thant was critical to fulfilling his ABC duties. So did Perle Mesta, the "hostess with the mostest" and former ambassador to Luxembourg, who met Mal when he was a boy on a huckster's wagon in Homestead. Perle spent time in the mill town because of her husband's Mesta Machinery, which abutted the steelworks where Mal and his father worked. When Mal remained seated on the wagon while speaking to her during a delivery, she rebuked him for his poor manners. Mal told his mother, who called Perle and snapped: "You buy my chickens, I'll raise my children!" At a UN reception, Perle introduced Mal to U Thant and happily recounted the story to him.[39]

As wildly exciting as Mal found New York City, the first seven weeks on the job were uneventful. His first interview, with the Iran ambassador, Dr. Mehdi Vakil, was nerve-racking but a one-off. Cuba was altogether another matter. The island, just ninety miles from Key West, had been the focus of US longings since Secretary of State John Quincy Adams in 1823 called it "an object of transcendent importance to . . . our Union."[40] The belief that the United States was preordained to become a continental power had propelled the young republic westward and into the Caribbean. Efforts to annex Cuba faltered, but the island became the United States' winter playground and one of its largest foreign markets in the early twentieth century.

That changed abruptly after Fidel Castro's band of guerilla fighters and urban rebels seized power on New Year's Day, 1959. Relations floundered as Cuba forsook dependence on the United States and aligned with the Soviet Union. When Cuba nationalized US corporate holdings, the United States embargoed the island and cut off diplomatic relations. Taking the presidential oath of office in January 1961, John F. Kennedy inherited a messy relationship with Cuba and then made it worse. Informed of CIA plans to oust Castro by landing an invading force at Playa Giron, he green-lighted the attack. The poorly planned invasion backfired. The Cuban exile community was notoriously indiscreet, and the Cuban military knew it was coming. More than one hundred anti-Castro Cubans died and another twelve hundred were captured soon after landing in April 1961.

Kennedy, settling into his presidency, rued the embarrassing defeat and admonished himself for not realizing it was doomed from the start. But Castro, understandably alarmed by efforts to topple his regime, implored the Soviets for aid to prevent another attack. On July 26, 1962, the warship *Maria Ulyanov* arrived in Cuba to do just that. It was the anniversary of Castro's attack on the Fort Moncada barracks in Santiago de Cuba in 1953. That assault was an utter failure and Fidel and his comrades had been captured on the spot, but the Moncada assault launched the rebellion. Nine years later, Castro welcomed the *Maria Ulyanov* and another one hundred Soviet vessels that followed in her wake. By late August, there were between four thousand and six thousand Soviet troops on the island, offering insurance against another US foray.

During the 1960 campaign, Kennedy had exploited Castro's seizure of power to project a vigorous foreign policy stance. He attacked Republican candidate Richard Nixon—the vice president when the rebels entered Havana—for losing Cuba to the Communists and argued that the United States had fallen behind in the arms race. After Playa Giron, it was Kennedy who appeared weak.

Kennedy was mistaken that the United States lagged behind the Soviet Union militarily; the CIA later confessed that its estimates of Soviet missile capabilities were wildly inflated. He also underestimated Cuban support for Castro. Nikita Khrushchev, more realistic about the balance of power, prized the Soviet alliance with his newfound Caribbean comrade and increased aid to solidify Fidel's grip on the island. Chastened by Playa Giron, the United States supplemented surveillance of Cuba with photo intelligence from aircraft flying at sixty thousand feet. The reconnaissance flights tracked a growing Soviet troop buildup that August, but intelligence analysts assured JFK that they would know if there was a nuclear component. Meanwhile, Republicans pounded Kennedy for the Bay of Pigs debacle as the 1962 congressional elections loomed. JFK lashed back in a September 13, 1962, speech, asserting that the United States would draw the line on Cuba and do whatever was necessary to prevent a Soviet buildup there from endangering US security. The first Soviet missiles arrived in Cuba two days later, but it took a month before US intelligence realized they were there.

Kennedy was alone in his office, reading the paper on Tuesday morning, October 16, 1962, when National Security Advisor McGeorge Bundy startled him by announcing that aerial recon photos analyzed late the previous evening confirmed Soviet missiles. Bundy had waited until morning to tell Kennedy rather than awaken him in the middle of the night. He realized that Kennedy would get little sleep once he knew. A select group of advisors quickly convened. Most of them urged blockading Cuba or launching air strikes.[41] Adlai Stevenson, the US ambassador to the United Nations, argued instead for diplomatic engagement. He suggested the United States remove its Jupiter missiles in Turkey in exchange for the Soviets taking their missiles from Cuba. Precise information was sketchy. The presence of nuclear warheads could not be confirmed, but intelligence analysts believed that missiles on the island were capable of reaching 90 percent of the US population once launch sites were operational. Unwilling to commit to an airstrike and actions he could not walk back, Kennedy rebuffed a hasty military response.[42]

Keeping up appearances, he headed to Chicago afterward for a campaign swing. But his travel was cut short by a call from his brother Bobby, the attorney general. On Air Force One, Press Secretary Pierre Salinger told the press that his boss had a cold. When Salinger had a chance to ask JFK what was going on, the president replied: "When you find out, you'll grab your balls."[43]

On October 20, Kennedy instructed the military to quarantine Cuba, reserving air strikes or an invasion as fallback options. He also asked the networks for prime time to address the nation on the October 22 and sent a copy of his remarks to Khrushchev, who feared a US attack was underway. US troops began moving into position as bombers went on alert and ships steamed toward Cuba to enforce the quarantine. The families of US servicemen were evacuated from Guantanamo, the base on Cuba that was a holdover from the 1898 conflict in which Cuba gained independence from Spain.

Mal's sons Russ and Bob were in the service. While they and other military personnel sensed that something significant was happening, they didn't know it involved Cuba until Kennedy spoke to the nation. Nor did Mal. He was aware of Cuba's contentious relationship with the United States, but it was only one of many issues he was scrambling to understand.

Mal had not yet met the Cuban delegation, but the island abruptly changed his life, which became evident as soon as Kennedy spoke on

October 22. The president revealed that US surveillance had detected a Soviet buildup whose purpose "can be none other than to provide a nuclear strike capability against the Western Hemisphere." The United States, he declared, could not tolerate that and would prevent Soviet military material from reaching the island. Moreover, any missile attack from Cuba would be seen as an attack from the Soviet Union and would result in swift retaliation. Rather than initiate a unilateral military response, Kennedy asked the UN Security Council to "take action against this latest Soviet threat to world peace."[44] He concluded ominously: "My fellow citizens, let no one doubt that this is a difficult and dangerous effort on which we have set out. No one can foresee precisely what course it will take or what costs or casualties will be incurred.... the cost of freedom is always high—but Americans have always paid it. And one path we shall never choose, and that is the path of surrender or submission."[45]

Kennedy's ultimatum was heard around the world. Panicked shoppers cleared supermarket shelves and Khrushchev raged at his commanders for their inability to conceal the missiles. Cubans, anticipating an invasion, mobilized to defend their homeland. Their leaders, schooled in guerrilla struggle and steeled with revolutionary ardor, were resigned to a US attack, but unwilling to back down.

Mal, in the thick of it at the United Nations, tried to find out something—anything—worth reporting. But his contacts knew next to nothing about what was happening. The day after Kennedy's address, the UN Security Council met in special session to address his demand for action against Soviet escalation. The Security Council, which consisted of fifteen members, was the United Nations' most powerful decision-making body. But it was not easy to gain approval for a resolution. Any one of its five permanent members—the United States, Soviet Union, United Kingdom, France, or China—could veto a resolution, undercutting its ability to act decisively if the United States and the Soviet Union were at loggerheads.

Adlai Stevenson, the former Illinois senator and two-time Democratic Party presidential candidate, represented the United States at the Security Council session. Condemning the missile deployment, he called Cuba "an accomplice in the communist enterprise of world domination." His Soviet counterpart, Ambassador Valerian Zorin, largely clueless about the missiles in Cuba, stonewalled. He denied there were Soviet missiles in Cuba and refused to answer many of the questions posed to him.[46]

Faced with his biggest crisis since becoming the secretary general, U Thant sent a proposal to Kennedy and Khrushchev the next day, asking them to stand down and resolve matters peacefully. The Soviets should suspend arms shipment and United States lift its quarantine. Khrushchev agreed, unwilling to risk confrontation by breaking the blockade.[47] When the United States began the blockade at 10:00 that morning, Soviet ships stopped before encountering US vessels. One slipped through but was diverted to a port that could neither unload nor store nuclear weapons, thus allaying US alarms. For the time being, overt hostilities had been avoided.

While negotiations went on in public and through back channels, attention focused on an emergency Security Council meeting on Thursday afternoon, October 25, 1962. Soviet Ambassador Zorin, when pressed, did not back down, denying that the Soviet Union had sent missiles to Cuba. "Falsity is what the United States has in its hands, false evidence," he proclaimed. Manufactured US threats, he said, could have "catastrophic consequences for the whole world."[48]

Stevenson listened intently, then pounced. "I want to say to you, Mr. Zorin, that I do not have your talent for obfuscation, for distortion, for confusing language, and for doubletalk. And I must confess to you that I am glad that I do not!" Mocking his counterpart's protestations, Stevenson said: "All right, sir, let me ask you one simple question: Do you, Ambassador Zorin, deny that the USSR has placed and is placing medium and intermediate range missiles and sites in Cuba? Yes or no—don't wait for the translation—yes or no!" When Zorin did not respond, Stevenson continued: "I am prepared to wait for my answer until hell freezes over, if that's your decision. And I am also prepared to present the evidence in this room."[49]

Mal, thirty feet away in ABC's media booth, watched as Stevenson's aides displayed black-and-white photos of Soviet missiles on Cuban soil. He saw Zorin's consternation as a global television audience absorbed the aerial reconnaissance photographs.[50] The theatrics were so dramatic that Mal had to remember he was working the story and not just watching history unfold.

U Thant, intervening before their showdown spun out of control, addressed the council: "Today the United Nations faces a moment of grave responsibility. What is at stake is not just the interests of the parties directly involved, nor just the interests of all the Member States, but the very fate of mankind. If today the United Nations should prove itself ineffective, it may have proved itself so for all time."[51] He continued to negotiate with Zorin and Stevenson in private while 150 US ships cordoned Cuba off, prepared to intercept Soviet ships en route.

Abruptly, many of them stopped or turned back. The next day, Stevenson attended meetings in Washington and argued that the United States withdraw its Jupiter missiles from Turkey in exchange for the Soviet Union removing its missiles in Cuba. Hardliners objected, but Kennedy was discussing that very proposal with close advisors. Meanwhile, Mal's colleague, ABC correspondent John Scali, was asked to approach the KGB's Washington bureau chief to float a proposal. In exchange for a Soviet withdrawal, the United States would end the blockade and promise not to invade while U Thant would supervise the weapons' removal and monitor compliance.[52]

While back-channel negotiations continued, Castro balked at the deal. By then, there were upward of forty-two thousand Soviet troops in Cuba. Poor lines of communication with the Kremlin meant that, if hostilities began, troops on the ground in Cuba would decide whether to respond on their own. Unsure of what would happen next, the US strategic command raised the level of alert for US forces to Defcon 2. Defcon 1 meant war.

The impasse came to a head that weekend. On Friday, October 26, the USS *Joseph Kennedy*, named for John Kennedy's older brother whose airplane went down in World War II, stopped a Lebanese vessel chartered to the Soviets. The United States knew the ship was not carrying offensive weaponry, but stopping it showed US resolve without forcing an escalation. The same day, ABC's John Scali brought a message from the Soviets. Khrushchev was willing to remove the missiles with UN verification in return for a public US pledge not to invade. Meanwhile in Cuba, Soviet officers asked for permission to shoot at US recon flights, and Castro, believing an invasion was imminent, gave his commanders the go-ahead to fire at any US plane in Cuban airspace.[53] Castro, excluded from these negotiations, was not inclined to compromise. Nor would he necessarily follow Khrushchev's lead, and on Saturday, Cuban anti-aircraft shot down a U-2 plane, ratcheting up the pressure on Kennedy to invade. The pilot was Major Rudolph Anderson Jr. who had taken the October 14 photos revealing Soviet missiles; he did not survive.

The United States moved its nuclear missiles to launch sites, and some military personnel said goodbye to each other. Fidel spent Saturday night at the Soviet embassy in Havana, while in Washington, Kennedy began receiving a jumbled four-part cable from Khrushchev that arrived out of order. In it, the Soviet leader asked the United States to remove its Jupiter missiles from Turkey as part of the deal. Although the Jupiters were relatively worthless military assets, Kennedy wanted neither to make a deal with what he saw as a gun to his head nor to go to war over matters that might be resolved peacefully. ABC's Peter Jennings later said that Kennedy believed that invading Cuba would have been like the D Day invasion in terms of its costs, something he was desperate to avoid.[54]

Neither side felt certain about the situation. The United States didn't know if Moscow had sanctioned downing the U-2 plane on October 27, while Khrushchev wasn't convinced his own generals would obey him. His son later said that his father was alarmed that some fool might start a war. Both Khrushchev and Kennedy, under pressure from advisors, feared disaster if the hawks had their way. Walking through the White House Rose Garden during a break on Saturday night, McGeorge Bundy told Secretary of Defense Robert McNamara that the sky reminded him of a painting by Georgia O'Keefe in which a rose penetrated a skull. McNamara said he thought: "I might not live to see another Saturday night." Kennedy told his press secretary

Pierre Salinger: "If I make a mistake in this process 200 million people will die."[55]

Mal did not return to Pittsburgh that weekend, as he had most weeks since arriving in New York. Instead, he spent Saturday at the United Nations, hardly leaving the building, and returned early Sunday morning. In Washington, DC, the CIA reported that several missile sites were now fully operational and Cuban mobilization accelerating. Meanwhile, a Soviet ship was nearing the interception zone. Robert Kennedy later wrote that "there was the feeling that the noose was tightening on all of us, on Americans, on mankind, and that the bridges to escape were crumbling."[56]

Since beginning at ABC, Mal had done radio spots but not made his television debut. That weekend, however, ABC's UN bureau chief John MacVane was away on a long-planned hunting trip with his sons, leaving Mal in charge. MacVane was a legendary correspondent. He had covered German air raids of Britain from London rooftops alongside Edward R. Murrow early in World War II and accompanied Allied forces during the North African campaign. The first correspondent to hit Omaha Beach on D-Day, he delivered the earliest eyewitness accounts of the invasion. After opening NBC's UN bureau in 1946 and a stint as an advisor to the US mission, he became ABC's UN bureau chief in 1953.[57] The missile crisis would have been his story but he was out of town and unreachable.

And Mal seized the chance. "Sunday, Oct 28, 1962 was the critical day, the most important day in my ABC career. For some reasons I decided to go to the UN early, if wearily, that day." The past week had been high stakes, high drama journalism with little sleep for all involved. Mal had approached diplomats and staff seeking scraps of information, but hardly anyone was talking, and those that were often knew little. But when Mal got to the UN complex that morning, he encountered Secretary General U Thant on his way in. "I asked him about developments and he indicated it was 'not good.'" U Thant's weariness and demeanor underscored his frank appraisal. Mal recognized the boundaries limiting what U Thant could reveal and appreciated that the secretary general added that he would soon meet with Ambassador Stevenson, Deputy Ambassador Charles Yost, and Ambassador Zorin. Before excusing himself, U Thant said he would talk with reporters afterward.[58]

When Mal reached the tiny ABC cubbyhole, the phone was ringing. "It was Jim Hagerty and he was excited because he had been trying to reach someone who could follow up on developments in this world crisis." Hagerty was so worked up he was almost screaming. An ABC television crew on the grounds was ready to go live, and Hagerty was upset that none of his correspondents had anything to say on a morning that might witness the outbreak of war. "When Hagerty learned I had just talked with U Thant, he told me to do a bulletin." Not feeling as if he had learned anything substantive, Mal asked, "About what, Jim?" Hagerty replied: "Just what U Thant told you."[59]

Mal had little time to absorb the enormity of the moment for him personally. He was about to make his ABC television debut by breaking into a morning show. And though he had often arrived at WHOD minutes before airtime, pulling long sheets of yellow paper from the ticker tape machine, wrapping them around his shoulder, and extemporaneously reporting what he gleaned from them, this was different.[60]

Quickly finding the crew, he set up outside the building and awaited the signal that he was on air. "It's a beautiful October Sabbath here in New York," Mal began, "but I cannot tell you what will happen in this crisis. The Secretary General will be meeting with the principals within the hour and we will keep you posted on developments. This is Mal Goode, ABC News United Nations."[61]

Many who watched were seeing an African American on a national television network for the first time. And if they stayed tuned to ABC television and radio that day, they would have heard Mal another sixteen times.[62] Some, so fixated on what he was saying, hardly noticed the color of his skin. "We learned that President Kennedy had warned Khrushchev if the missiles were not removed they would be bombed out," Mal reflected. That would have led to war and that's what mattered the most to those watching, not the race of the man reporting the news.[63]

As the crisis's resolution unfolded that Sunday, Mal kept ABC's audience abreast of developments. By day's end, his face and his voice were familiar, even reassuring, to millions who had never known of his existence before. And when Khrushchev dictated a message that was read on Moscow radio to an audience including the White House, the world exhaled. A deal had been consummated: Soviet missiles would be removed while the United States promised not to invade Cuba. Kennedy demanded that the decision to remove the Jupiters be kept secret.[64] Fidel Castro was furious but unable to block Khrushchev's decision.[65] As the superpowers stepped back from the brink of war, they took steps to prevent another crisis. Within the year, they signed their first nuclear atmospheric test ban. JFK's domestic popularity reached new heights, as did European confidence that the United States could deal with world problems.[66]

By day's end, Mal was thoroughly drained, but also elated, and he basked in the congratulations coming his way. Phones began ringing in Pittsburgh as soon as he went on the air. In a city with few degrees of separation, many quickly learned that Mal was on television, covering the most momentous story since the end of World War II. Word spread as people called friends to tell them that Goode, a familiar figure from the NAACP, Alpha Phi Alpha, the *Courier*, and WHOD, was on ABC. "That is the first time my family saw me on TV," Mal said. "My sister saw it, and some other people saw it, getting ready to go to church. They started calling across the country and calling my family, and when they went to church, they were talking about it. And then people were just glued to their sets."[67]

Russ and Bob Goode were unable to watch because they were on duty. Russ was on alert at the Boston Air Defense Sector at Stewart Air Force Base in New York. "We controlled all of the military air activity in the northeast quadrant of the U.S.," he explained. "That weekend, I was busy directing tankers to their wartime stations so that they could refuel the B52 bombers that President Kennedy ordered to their wartime launch positions." Although concerned about a possible war, he was exhilarated when he heard about his father. His younger brother Bob was in boot camp at Parris Island, South Carolina, with the Marines. He was the last family member to hear about his father' debut, but scores of people described the day to him. "I've told the story so often and with such color that I forget that I didn't see it firsthand!"[68]

For years to come, Mal met people who saw or listened to him that day. A woman in South Carolina wrote the network: "Although I am white, I want to thank that colored man who eased my fears. I want to congratulate him and ABC." Mal was especially heartened when white people crossed the racial divide. "The people who run television were afraid white viewers wouldn't watch a Black person give the news," he told a *San Diego Tribune* writer in 1985. "But if that person does a good job, it doesn't matter." The hostility he encountered was not from viewers but a few coworkers. "Some people felt I had no right to be there, but the authority came from the top and there was nothing they could do about it. But many whites went out of their way to help because they wanted to see me make it." Years later, downplaying his own role, Mal chuckled: "They had to put me on the air. I was the only one working."[69]

His race did matter. For some of those anxiously awaiting to find out whether life as they knew it was about to end, an African American reporter was shocking. But for many Americans—Black and white—who had never dreamed the day would come for such a visible racial breakthrough, it was a harbinger of change.

7

AFRICA, 1963

CUBA MADE MAL'S BONES. NOT WITH MAFIOSI SUCH AS
Sam Giancana and Santos Trafficante whom the CIA enlisted to
assassinate Fidel Castro, in exchange for helping them reclaim their
lucrative operations on the island, but with the networks. Mal could
not have imagined a more dramatic debut. But it postponed his reckoning with an existential question—how to carve out a role on the
civil rights beat. Along with faith and family, that movement had
defined his life. He now found himself in a delicate position with few
precedents. The networks were unaccustomed to African American
journalists, much less one covering civil rights. Mal had to project
impeccable objectivity while reporting lest he reinforce those who
believed African Americans incapable of doing the job. But civil rights
were core principles, and he was not about to forsake them.

Nor was he shielded from racially inspired affronts and obstacles
that left him fuming. He respected and valued most coworkers at ABC,
but there were exceptions. Some assignment editors ignored him, a few
technicians sabotaged his interviews, and others were prone to casting
slurs. Mal's default take on life was upbeat and optimistic, but he bristled at the slightest sign of disrespect and carried an enormous chip

on his shoulder. He kept his temper in check, something he might not have been able to do when he was younger, at least for the time being.

During the 1960s Mal carved out a role that few African American or minority journalists had ever attempted to play. He became a Black voice and a face on the networks that monopolized the airwaves. That made him one of the only African Americans on the national news, where he was determined to remain an advocate for social change. A few other Black correspondents could be seen on local stations. Breaking the networks' color line inspired others to follow in his footsteps, and Mal's success made it easier for the industry to bring other African Americans aboard. But there was a deeper subtext—a Black man achieving visibility made other African Americans believe that they, too, were a part of the nation's fabric. It made them feel more American.

Mal won most of the skirmishes he fought with those standing in his way. His younger colleague David Snell recalled an ABC news director known for his temper and volatility calling Mal into his office to chide him. When Mal returned to his desk, he said he had told the director: "I've got children, and if they knew I allowed you to talk to me that way they'd be embarrassed for me, and I'm not going to allow that. So I'm going to walk away. If you want to talk to me in a civil way, I'll be happy to hear you. But I'm not going to listen to this type of talk." That director was notorious for dressing down reporters, but Snell said, "Mal wouldn't take it. He was a gentleman and not subservient to anybody."[1]

Mal not only gained his colleagues' respect, but he forced hard-line segregationists such as George Wallace to swallow their contempt for African Americans when they dealt with him. In time he won acclaim within the industry. But it was not easy gaining the freedom at ABC to cover civil rights and race as he thought best. Nor was it inevitable that the civil rights movement would bring lasting changes to a nation mired in segregation and inequality.

Mal was cautiously optimistic as the year 1963 began. After witnessing both breakthroughs and horrible setbacks over the previous decade, he felt the movement was gathering strength. In the aftermath of the

Montgomery Bus Boycott, the integration of Central High School in Little Rock, the sit-ins, and the Freedom Rides, efforts to achieve equality were surging. The crusade for freedom rippled through the rural South and found new allies in Congress, northern cities, and college towns.

But these campaigns provoked an ever greater and more violent backlash. They collided in Alabama in 1963. As he delivered his inaugural address that January, Governor George Wallace scorned efforts to integrate, vowing that in Alabama the watchword was "segregation now, segregation tomorrow, segregation forever!"[2] Mal bristled at Wallace's intransigence but was hardly surprised. Neither he nor other activists were deterred by the governor's demagogy, but it instilled a sense of foreboding in the Kennedy White House. JFK had hesitated to push a civil rights agenda despite campaigning to do so if elected. His trepidations about losing the Democratic Party's base in the South prevented him from doing the right thing. But as the backlash became ever more horrific, Kennedy had little choice but to act.

His UN bona fides securely established after Cuba, Mal hungered to head south where Birmingham had become ground zero in the battle for integration. Iron and steel made Birmingham the South's principal industrial center and Alabama's biggest city. Although nearly 40 percent of its residents were African American, Jim Crow was deeply entrenched, and the city was known for its racial intransigence. In April 1963, Birmingham's Black leaders launched Operation Confrontation, a head-on assault on segregation. They were led by the cofounder of the Southern Christian Leadership Conference (SCLC), the minister Fred Shuttlesworth, who asked Martin Luther King Jr. to come and there and lend visibility to the campaign. King's presence in Birmingham attracted photographers and journalists, who hunkered down to chronicle six long weeks of protests, beatings, arrests, and ultimate victory.[3]

By springtime 1963, efforts to desegregate a city some called America's Johannesburg had reached critical mass. Others called it Bombingham because of the eighteen bombs that had been detonated at Black homes and institutions.[4] Sitting in at lunch counters, boycotting merchants, and marching on City Hall, demonstrators fought to integrate public facilities and accommodations and to win better jobs for African Americans. Many were arrested, including King, who was jailed on Good Friday, April 12, 1963, for defying a blanket injunction against protesting. He remained there for eight days until JFK, under pressure, sought his release. During his incarceration, he wrote a "Letter from Birmingham Jail." By mid-May, the violent backlash to Operation Confrontation was reverberating around the world. In its lead story, *Time* magazine pulled no punches:

> The scenes in Birmingham were unforgettable. There was the Negro youth, sprawled on his back and spinning across the pavement, while firemen battered him with streams of water so powerful that they could strip the bark off trees. There was the Negro woman, pinned to the ground by cops, one of them with his knee dug into her throat. There was the white man who watched hymn-singing Negroes burst from a sweltering church and growled: "We ought to shoot every damned one of them." And there was the little Negro girl, splendid in a newly starched dress, who marched out of a church, looked toward a massed line of pistol-packing cops, and called to a laggard friend: "Hurry up, Lucille. If you stay behind, you won't get arrested with our group."[5]

Mal felt that he needed to be there, for both professional and personal reasons, but was unable to persuade his bosses to send him to Birmingham for the duration of the campaign. He did wrangle brief assignments, where he spent time with King and watched the protests unfold. Mal attested:

> Dr. King was out there on the front line when there were eruptions. He wasn't off hiding somewhere in negotiations as some so-called "civil rights leaders" did. I was there when the police turned high powered fire hoses on King and those crowded around him, washing men, women, and children along the curbstone like rats. Dr. King was resolute when that happened. He never ran from any of the

strife. When they put him in jail in Birmingham, Martin wrote *A Letter from the Birmingham Jail* on toilet paper and scraps of paper and smuggled it out when his wife Coretta came to visit him.[6]

In his letter, King rebuked critics, including clergy, who said he and the movement should avoid confrontation and seek to upend racism in the courts instead.

Mal did not suffer those who urged King to tone down his rhetoric and refrain from pushing so hard. "Many people, including some white folks close to him, had told him to ease off. A group of white ministers in Birmingham told him he was upsetting the country. They told him equality with whites would come 'in time.'" That criticism rankled Mal. "Many white folks told me the same thing they told Martin. 'Mal, it's going to come after awhile.' They would say 'Mal, look how well you're doing.' But King thought the time had already come when all men, black and white, should receive the rights that the constitution guaranteed."[7]

Mal first met King's confidant, Andrew Young, during Operation Confrontation. "I was the one bringing him to Dr. King," Young recalled. "There would be press conferences where everybody was there, but we'd always try to sneak him into Dr. King's room. They'd talk. It was more than an interview; there was a friendship there." By then, Mal had established ties with King's closest aides and associates, many of whom he had met in the 1950s. "Mal and Dora McDonald, Martin's secretary, were good friends," Young said. "She was the only one who had total access to Dr. King." That connection with Dora meant that Mal could always reach King. ABC brass had not realized the value of Mal's connections, and it was unclear if they ever would, but civil rights leaders did. They trusted him and knew that he held a mighty big megaphone.[8]

When demonstrations fizzled in April, youth stepped into the breach. Thousands, ranging in age from seven to eighteen, headed to the front lines to democratize one of the country's most racially divided cities. The youth, dubbed the Children's Crusade, walked out of school and into the streets on May 2, 1963. Six hundred of them were arrested for parading without a permit, but they were undeterred. Frustrated and unable to stop the demonstrators by arresting them, Bull Conner, Birmingham's notorious commissioner of public safety, instructed officers to set their dogs loose on the children and to blast them from the streets with high-pressure water cannons. His heavy-handed tactics backfired.

The graphic violence, captured on camera, circulated globally. The *New York Times* on May 4 published a photo, above the fold, of snarling police dogs attacking a seventeen-year-old protestor for violating an "anti-parade" ordinance.[9] Those scenes of dogs terrorizing children, police mauling them, and water cannons batting girls and boys around like ragdolls galvanized sentiment across the country. In northern cities, hundreds of thousands marched to support the young crusaders. Their protests were the tipping point in Birmingham and a catalyst to national action. Civic leaders were embarrassed, fearful of damaging the city's image, while merchants felt the sting of the boycott. Kennedy later said that those horrific scenes were "more eloquently reported by the news camera than by any number of explanatory words."[10]

Birmingham triggered such a visceral response because television brought it into people's living rooms. With revulsion over police violence driving people into the streets across the North, Kennedy could no longer ignore Birmingham. After militant segregationists set off explosives close to where King was staying and bombed his brother's house, JFK sent three thousand troops to the area and indicated he would federalize the Alabama National Guard.[11]

The president instructed his brother the attorney general to force the release of the children. Meanwhile, the administration began working on a major civil rights bill to prohibit racial discrimination and to end segregation in schools, employment, and public areas. In Birmingham, a compromise was reached on May 10. Bathrooms, water fountains, and lunch counters were desegregated, signs proclaiming "Whites Only" and "Blacks Only" were removed, a jobs plan was drawn up, and demonstrators were released from jail on bond. A biracial committee focused on upgrading African Americans on the job and monitored the truce.

Birmingham was a turning point for both John Kennedy and George Wallace. On June 11, 1963, Wallace stood at the door of Foster Auditorium on the University of Alabama campus in Tuscaloosa to prevent two African Americans who had been admitted to the school from entering and completing their registration. Kennedy responded by federalizing the Alabama National Guard and commanding them to remove Wallace so that Vivian Malone and James Hood could enroll. The rabble-rousing governor was forced to stand down, and the same day, JFK announced he would call for sweeping civil rights legislation. Three weeks later, on July 2, a coalition of civil rights leaders and organizations announced a March on Washington for Jobs and Freedom to take place that August. Mal was exhilarated. A sea change seemed underway.

Mal saw the power of the media, especially television, which magnified the campaign's impact, especially when protesters were ferociously attacked. He followed the planning for the march on Washington and wanted to be a part of ABC's coverage. But before Mal could leverage the acclaim that came with his reporting on Cuba, he was asked to go to Africa.

No continent was changing more than Africa in the 1960s, and no part of the world exercised a greater hold on Mal. Although distant from Homestead and the Hill, Africa had long gripped his psyche. He had followed its transition from colonialism to independence since he was a boy, watching films about Africa at Clark Memorial Baptist Church, attending lectures at the Centre Avenue YMCA, and readings dispatches from the *Courier*'s foreign correspondents. They made sure that neither the continent's cultures nor its struggles for autonomy were ignored. During the 1930s Mussolini's invasion of Ethiopia and Joe Louis's ascent to the heavyweight title were the most widely covered stories in the Black press. But Mal longed to know more about Mother Africa, and once at the United Nations, he paid special attention to its envoys and their concerns. He doubted that many other journalists would. And then he got the chance to go there.[12]

He could hardly have found a more exciting time to go. Two years earlier, UN Under-Secretary for Political Affairs Ralph Bunche told a symposium at Wellesley College that "1960 will be 'the year of Africa' because at least four, but maybe seven or eight new [UN] member states will come from the continent."[13] Bunche was right; the year 1960 did become known as the Year of Africa, and seventeen new African states joined the United Nations by year's end.

African independence was the fruit of decades of anticolonial struggle that brought together militants from labor unions, football clubs, peasant organizations, and European-educated sectors. Adapting the civil rights movement's tactics and strategy to their liberation struggles, they gained control over a score of colonies.

Mal followed their nation-building projects, their gains in per capita income, literacy, and life expectancy, and a cultural eruption that extended from dance halls to literary circles. He watched coverage of the Sharpeville Massacre in South Africa, as well the prolonged bloody Algerian war for independence and ethnic clashes. His hopes for Africa's future were tempered by the violence and the difficulties undercutting any efforts to move forward. An important symbolic victory came in December 1960, when African nations persuaded the United Nations to adopt the Declaration of the Granting of Independence to Colonial Countries and Peoples. The resolution condemning colonialism passed unanimously and was lauded for its defense of human rights. But nine nations abstained, including the United States.[14] These cross-cutting currents filled Mal with both hope and trepidation for Africa's future.

When asked by the African-American Institute (AAI) to help lead workshops in Addis Ababa, Dar Es Salaam, and Lagos in the summer of 1963, Mal was delighted. The foundation wanted to build educational and social capital on the continent by working with students and professionals. It believed that developing African mass media was "a matter of transparent urgency" and that radio, television, and the press were set to play critical roles in the aftermath of colonialism.[15]

In July 1963 Mal and two other veteran newsmen were sent overseas to initiate the collaboration. John McCormally, the editor of the

Hutchinson News in Kansas, was a tough, no-nonsense editor well-versed in print journalism. Professor Burton Marvin, dean of the William Allen White School of Journalism at the University of Kansas, brought exceptional academic and administrative experience. Dr. Sydney Head, who had taught journalism for twenty years before arriving in Africa in 1960 and becoming the AAI's field coordinator, coordinated their efforts.[16]

When the AAI asked Jim Hagerty to suggest a correspondent for the team, he nominated Mal. Hagerty never explained why he had decided to place Mal at the United Nations in the first place, but it was an excellent posting for all concerned. The United Nations' culture was remarkably tolerant, and Mal smoothly connected with its diverse assemblage of ambassadors and staff. Adding Africa to Mal's resume would only heighten his access to the African delegates.

Excited about the prospect of visiting Africa, Mal was nervous about the reception he would receive. "I felt some misapprehension because of the strong criticism of my country for its racial policies by the African delegates I knew." Their censure of US domestic policies was well founded, and Mal was no apologist for his country when it came to race. But, he asked: "What kind of criticism would I face as an American Negro, the grandson of slaves, and unarmed as far as answering the criticism of discrimination and bigotry, so comparable to apartheid and colonialism which every African knew so well?"[17]

Mal had confronted these contradictions at the United Nations. In less than a year, he had become a familiar face to the African delegates and their staffs. Introducing himself to everyone he met, Mal interrogated them about their countries and attitudes about the United States. His thirst for understanding African realities won their respect. The more he listened, the more regard he gained for their grasp of global politics and the continent's complexities. They, in turn, saw that Mal was trustworthy.

Mal discussed the trip with a friend, George Enninful, from the Ghana News Service office. Ghana, the first sub-Saharan colony to win independence from European colonialism, was led by Kwame Nkrumah, who had been exposed to Garveyism as a student at Lincoln University and later to W. E. B. Du Bois at a Pan African congress in England. Nkrumah, who embraced Pan Africanism as a strategy to guide the continent toward independence and development, was among the continent's most influential leaders. In order to figure out what he might face, Mal turned to Enninful, who assured him that Africans were not unreasonable about the United States, but they were distrustful. "It would be my task to refrain from justifying any American shortcomings in race relations," Mal concluded. Instead of defending the indefensible, Enninful encouraged Mal to emphasize efforts to resolve racial problems in the United States. That was something that he could honestly communicate to Africans.

Enninful dispelled notions that Africans were ignorant of the world. Radio and the press, he explained, were popular throughout the continent. "Little could be hidden," he told Mal, "for the wire services carry world news as rapidly to Ghana, Nigeria, Tanganyika, and Ethiopia as to Atlanta." Enninful schooled Mal about the mechanics of African newspaper publishing and the critical impact of radio. In the countryside, a radio was often a communal set, with villagers gathering in someone's home to listen to the news. That reminded Mal of rural Blacks gathering at a home or a general store—the only places with electricity and a radio—to listen to Joe Louis fights in the 1930s and 1940s. "In more developed areas, George explained, individual sets were an important part of the furnishings of homes and huts. This I found to be very true."

In June, Mal, John McCormally, and Burt Marvin were briefed at the State Department's African desk in Washington, DC. Mary, still living in Pittsburgh, joined him in New York City for a few days afterward. Despite Mal's excitement, he and Mary were apprehensive when they took a taxi to Idlewild Airport on a hot Monday morning in early July for the first leg of the journey, to London. "She was upset," Mal recalled, "partly about the long separation, the longest in our 26 years of marriage, and also about that long flight across the ocean, my first overseas."

Mal was too excited to be apprehensive. He was thrilled to travel overseas and, after landing in London, could hardly believe that he was walking down Picadilly Road, shillings and pence jangling in his pockets. "I was seeing historic sites I had read about but never really expected to see." The transatlantic flight to London was the first leg of the six-flight, five-day journey, and the thrill of travel soon wore thin. After two nights in London, they flew to Madrid and stayed for thirty-six hours, before touching down in Athens, Cairo, and Khartoum along the way.

But by the time he arrived in Addis Ababa, Mal had no adrenaline left. He was physically drained, and his six-foot frame was stiff from flights in cramped seats. Addis Ababa offered scant relief. Overpowering heat and humidity hit him with palpable force when he stepped onto the tarmac. After clearing customs, receiving health permits, and retrieving his luggage, Mal was wrung out. Stepping outside into mist and a light rain, he could not get over how "extremely dreary" it was.

By then, Mal, McCormally, and Marvin had shared meals and endured the hassles that travel entailed. They bonded during the next two months but adjusting to Africa was difficult. Their State Department briefings in Washington, DC, had misled them about what to expect. They had not mentioned the need to acclimate to Addis Ababa, which was almost eight thousand feet above sea level, nor how to deal with monsoon season, much less what they would encounter in the course of a day. While their journey was steeped in African history and politics, which Mal relished, he wasn't so sure about the food and lodgings.

In Addis Ababa, the team stayed at the Ras Hotel, the nicest hotel in Ethiopia's capital city. "It wasn't a bad stopping place," Mal conceded, "but it certainly had none of the embellishments of a newly-built American Hilton." He was sleep deprived and grumpy, overcome by bleakness. But Mal was gracious enough to appreciate the hotel staff's welcome and introductions to US Information Agency (USIA) and embassy personnel. He listened intently to a confidant of Emperor Haile Selasssie Selassie who met with them later that day. "He was able to offer us some sage advice and counsel on how to adjust to this new living, how to get along with the Ethiopians, and more important the attitude to have toward those who were certain to criticize us as Americans when discussions arose about our policies towards Negroes." Mal appreciated the man even more a few days later when invited to his home "for some American food, a real delicacy for one who had found it difficult to adjust to the Ethiopian bill of fare at the Ras Hotel."

That weekend, Mal questioned whether he should have to come to Africa. "Our first night I found it hard to sleep until I obtained a supply of insect repellant which I used profusely on my bed to massacre the fleas that found my body so palatable." The next morning, a Saturday, they toured the countryside with the chairman of the teaching team. Sydney Head, often described as the founder of modern broadcasting studies, was not simply an erudite scholar. The London-born, California-bred professor had taken advantage of a hiatus from teaching to live in Addis Ababa for a year. He knew his way around the city and was well connected to businessmen and government officials.[18] "We visited a section owned by the Queen, a beautiful spot in the countryside, but getting there was a problem as we moved slowly along the narrow Ethiopian macadam roadway, waiting for flocks of goats, sheep and donkeys to move to the side to allow our passage." At a roadside inn, his colleagues ordered a noodle and meatballs dish, which Mal declined. "I satisfied myself with a Coke, having observed the cats and dogs that were making themselves very much at home until the waiter shooed them from a tabletop and from underneath a chair or two." Mal was no prima donna, but food and its preparation were high priorities.

Mal wasn't sure he should stay in Africa. "After this experience on the road, coupled with a miserable night of little rest, I began to wrestle with the possibility of returning to the States post haste." But he rallied. By Saturday evening, most of the participants for the first workshop had arrived at the Ras. They won Mal over with their charm and sense of purpose. He jousted with a twenty-two-year-old Kenyan at dinner over the race question in the United States. When the young man, after listening to Mal, agreed that the US government at least recognized that there were problems and was making an effort to solve them, Mal felt his presence could matter.

The following day, a Sunday, convinced him that he belonged there. He attended services at a Methodist church where the sermon was delivered in a language he did not understand, but the hymns, "The Old Rugged Cross" and "Nearer My God to Thee," were familiar. So was the fellowship afterward. Two young men walked with him to a hotel where they ate peanuts and drank soda from a stand in the lobby as they talked. "Their friendliness was unbounded," he wrote. Later in the day, USIA staff took him into the countryside. The narrow rural roads reminded him of rural western Pennsylvania and Virginia. They visited a Peace Corps encampment where Mal met a young woman from Morehead State College, where he had spoken the previous spring, and a young man from Philadelphia who knew some of Mal's friends. Whatever misgivings he harbored about US policies toward Africa, the Peace Corps project was heartening. He felt even better after spending Sunday evening at Sydney Head's home, where he feasted on stuffed pork chops. "Later I knew the meaning of this fine meal," he joked. "It was to prepare us for the hard weeks of teaching ahead of us."

The seminar was held at the Ras Hotel, where generations of politicians, businessmen, and activists had negotiated deals and plotted revolution. Nelson Mandela had taken refuge there after he fled South Africa in 1962, not long before Mal checked in. Mandela, traveling with a fake Ethiopian passport, took part in a conference of Pan African freedom fighters that led to the formation of the Organization of African Unity. While in Addis Ababa, Mandela marshaled support for the African National Congress's recently created military wing and studied guerrilla tactics. But he never had a chance to use them. By the time Mal arrived, Mandela had returned to South Africa, where he was put on trial and imprisoned for the next twenty-seven years, eighteen of them on Robben Island. Mal knew little about Mandela when he arrived in Ethiopia but soon began to cover the fight to overturn apartheid and would live long enough to see Mandela released from prison and win election as South Africa's president in 1994.[19]

In Ethiopia, Mal encountered Pan Africanism, a movement that blossomed as the continent decolonized. He already knew of Marcus

Garvey and Pan African efforts to forge solidarity among descendants of the African diaspora in the Western Hemisphere. This Pan Africanism was rooted in Africa and sought to unify the continent's disparate people in order to forge a common future. Although realistic about how difficult that would be to achieve, Mal reveled in its energy.

Ethiopia's ruler Haile Selassie was among Pan Africanism's most prominent advocates. A quasi-legendary figure, he led the only African society that had not succumbed to colonialism in the early twentieth century. In 1936, after Benito Mussolini's Italian military invaded and occupied his country, Selassie rallied resistance. Five years later, he returned to power when Ethiopian and Allied forces ousted the Italian military early in World War II. Selassie's defiance of Italian fascism had made Ethiopia a leading story in the Black press during the 1930s. "Negroes became interested in world affairs after learning of the Italian invasion of Ethiopia," Mal explained. "The Negro press in the United States, including the *Pittsburgh Courier*, spread the word and pushed, as did many Black leaders, for lasting peace and a chance to live and prosper as free men and women."

Selassie's influence extended as far as Jamaica where the Rastafarians saw him as the Lion of Judah. They considered Selassie a prophet or an incarnation of Jah, a godlike figure, and called themselves after the name that he went by, Ras Tafari Makoonen, before he assumed the throne in 1930. Although Mal was in Ethiopia to teach, he was also there to learn. He soaked up as much as he could about Ethiopian history, its culture, and the fervor over Pan Africanism and regretted not getting the opportunity to meet Selassie.

There was little time in the agenda for the team to travel beyond the confines of Addis Ababa and explore rural Ethiopia, where 90 percent of its people lived, mostly by farming and herding. Mal, McCormally, and Marvin were disappointed that they had not being able to spend even a week "in the bush" before initiating the workshops. They realized how profoundly rural areas lagged behind the cities. A deep rural-urban divide cut through each African country, and low levels of literacy and inadequate infrastructure made it difficult to reach those living in rural areas.

Nor did they have sufficient time to assess the state of African media before beginning work. With little opportunity to adjust to a setting far from their comfort zone, Mal and his colleagues struggled to find their footing. They soon dismissed the State Department briefings they had received in Washington as a waste of time. "We found out the main characteristics necessary to adjust and get along with the Africans was plain common sense," Mal wrote. "The 'Briefers' actually misled or better still misinformed us at some points. I recall specifically one of the 'desk' men advising us not to tell jokes to the Africans. I think John McCormally established a fine rapport, particularly in Addis and Dar-es-Salaam, with our students because he knew so many good stories they heartily enjoyed. John was 'a hale fellow, well met' man who found favor in the eyes of each participant." It took longer for the AAI, which had never attempted this sort of tour, to appreciate how poorly they had prepared their team.

But Mal, McCormally, Marvin, and Head overcame those obstacles. Burt Marvin, though not as effusive as McCormally, was respected for his experiences in and knowledge of journalism. "Sydney Head, our leader, was just the catalyst that our four-man teaching team needed." He kept discussions focused. "In times of tension either between us and the students, or between Burt, John, and myself, Sydney had just the knack for easing that tension."

The seminar participants had been carefully scrutinized. They came from fifteen nations and worked for forty-one different publications, twelve broadcasters, nine information ministries, and three news agencies. Most were experienced newsmen or officials from government news agencies; all were eager to learn more. None was female; women were excluded from participation. Each day combined daily assignments based on journalism texts, press conferences, guest speakers, and workshops focused on newsgathering, reporting, and production.

After a few weeks, the team had absorbed enough about these participants, Africa, and its media culture to establish rapport with seminar attendees, who quickened their learning curve. "In all frankness," Mal confessed, "they were prepared to give us an academic workout." The Africans pushed back when Mal and his colleagues assessed the continent's newspapers by US standards and told them that their methods were inappropriate for the African press. With gentle humor they pointed out that, while weather reports mattered to Africans, they already knew that, if it was rainy season, it would rain today and again tomorrow. The media did not need to state the obvious. Nor, they chuckled, did people whose diets were based on a few staples prepared in customary ways find cooking columns of much interest. Recognizing that African journalists were more sophisticated and knowledgeable about many parts of the world than he was, Mal suggested that future workshops include local newsmen on the team. They could critique each session and bring their American visitors up to speed regarding the state of the media in each region. He began to see the wisdom of those urging the team to "Seek African solutions for African problems." The only African American on the team, Mal endeared himself to workshop participants. They hailed him as their "fellow African."[20]

Enthralled by his exposure to Pan Africanism in Addis Ababa, Mal was eager to find out more when he arrived in Tanganyika's capital, Dar Es Salaam, for the second workshop. The country—first a German and then a British colony—had become a democratic republic on the eve of Mal's arrival. Its leader, Julius Nyerere, was trying to unify the nation's more than one hundred language groups while also forging continental solidarity. A vocal proponent of Pan Africanism, Nyerere campaigned against South Africa and Rhodesia, two of colonialism's remaining bastions, and espoused a progressive African socialism known as *ujamaa*.

Mal wanted to understand what that meant on the ground. Consequently, he practiced what he had preached to Puddin' Grayson when he had taken Jackie Robinson to meet the young athlete in McKeesport in 1962—be a quick listener. He spent evenings interrogating Africans about their politics and problems and cultivated contacts he tapped for the next quarter of a century. Just as his parents had left the southern countryside for Pittsburgh, Africans were embarked on a rural to urban migration that was reconfiguring the continent. He saw that in Tanganyika, where immigrants were flooding into Dar es Salaam, a former fishing village whose population was topping two hundred thousand.[21]

During the third and final workshop, in Lagos, Nigeria, Mal confronted colonialism's aftermath. Riven by overlapping tensions rooted in religion, ethnicity, and region, Nigerians grappled with the same question that was plaguing Tanganyika. How could they create a cohesive democratic republic when there were so many different ethnic groups and languages? Colonialism had left these new countries with little experience in building viable democratic cultures, and Mal had few illusions about what they faced. But the Africans with whom he talked left him invigorated.

Nigeria, after a millennium of self-rule, had succumbed to British colonialism in the middle of the nineteenth century. Regaining self-rule in 1960, it struggled to overcome tensions between Muslim and Christian regions. Although independence leaders proclaimed a federal republic months after Mal left, a military junta seized power a few years later, and the country fell into civil war. Given colonialism's often violent aftermath in Africa, Mal was hardly sanguine about its future.

Team members worked from early dawn to well after dusk each day, intent on equipping participants with a tool kit of journalistic practices. They asked as many questions as they answered, trying to understand African media, constantly recalibrating their approach. In each venue, they met with a group of about thirty men for seven hours on weekdays and for half a day on Saturdays. After dinner, they spent evenings in private conferences with workshop participants and evaluated the daily assignments completed by each attendee. Although they had a few days off between venues, the workload was exhausting and the accommodations and logistics taxing. Conference rooms were often hot, noisy, and cramped. One of Mal's colleagues said the trip was the hardest work of his life. After three months, Mal described his experience as "grueling and exacting." But, he concluded, "we managed to survive the ordeal and it is my hope that our work was a credit to our country, to the African-American Institute, to Africa, and to our God."[22]

Exhausted by day's end, Mal fed off the enthusiasm of the African attendees, who rated him as the team's friendliest and most helpful member. They were struck by his narrative as the grandson of slaves who had struggled against the odds to reach the pinnacle of African American achievement in network television. They believed that he could relate to their own challenges on a gut level and sought him out after class, even on Sundays.

Mal understood that the trip bolstered the United States' stature on the continent and would "enhance the African's image of America with regard to the racial question." While okay with that, he was more concerned with how the workshops could inject higher standards of reporting and production by print, radio, and television journalists. He, John McCormally, and Burton Marvin were impressed by the attendees' sophistication when discussing politics and socioeconomics but underwhelmed by their journalistic craftsmanship. The three men were taskmasters, exacting in their demands for accuracy, objectivity, and tight well-prepared copy. The AAI wanted to provoke African journalists to examine their own unconscious assumptions and find ways to build a vibrant and effective media in countries with little experience in building democratic, independent cultures. That goal could only be achieved if standards were raised across the board, and Mal saw the workshops as a step in a long-term process. Embracing his part in it, he worked with the AAI for years to come. His specialty, broadcasting, was the weakest and least developed of African media, in part because the medium was only just taking shape. After independence, most of the BBC staff in place had been dismissed. Nor was English ubiquitous; indigenous languages prevailed in many regions.

Most nights, Mal was exhausted by the time he bid adieu to the Africans with whom he had spent the evening. But their enthusiasm kept him going. Mal saw himself in many of them and wrote of "an inherent bond between the young African and the Negro who has attained some measure of success in his profession." He gave what scant free time he had to them unstintingly but still found time to walk through the market in each stop, bartering for wooden figures, carved horns, and gifts, and soaking up the smells, colors, and energy engulfing him. He returned home with masks, a zebra skin, a leather-topped coffee table, a tiny animal skin purse for Rosalia, and a red footstool that his grandson Randy still has. At the end of each workshop, he and his colleagues were on the receiving end of speeches of praise and gifts from the participants. Mal gave away most of his shirts as well as other pieces of clothing and basked in their transatlantic camaraderie.

Africa resonated with Mal both personally and metaphysically. The men and women he met confirmed his belief in African intellectual and social equality and gave him a better sense of his own heritage. He was deeply impressed with their understanding of the world, and every day offered visceral proof of their humanity. Although he never returned to Africa, Mal stayed engaged with the Africans he encountered and tried to voice their perspective on the world in his reporting. They, in turn, reached out to him after the seminar for advice, help to defray the costs of traveling to London for a fellowship, or to further their education. Some asked him to invest in ventures that would market African wares and resources, others sought materials regarding the United Nations, and most of all, they wanted him to represent them to the United States.

Mal did just that, while at ABC and afterward when he worked at the United Nations for African American news agencies. He called on the people he met that summer when chasing down stories or seeking comments for broadcast. Mal would not let Africa's stories remain untold. Before he left Africa, one attendee declared to the workshop: "Mr. Goode, my fellow African, has shown real brotherhood." He lauded Mal's knowledge of Africa and intuitive understanding of its challenges. He admonished Mal not to "forget that AFRICA calls you with a voice, 'Do it again!'" Mal did not forget.[23]

But there was one incalculable downside to the time Mal spent out of the States. He missed the August 28, 1963, March on Washington, which came near the end of his stay in Lagos. "The morning after the march, one of my young students ran into my room and yelled at the top of his lungs: 'Mr. Goode! Mr. Goode! The March on Washington, did you hear?' 'No,' I said, 'but they said there would be upwards of 50,000 people there.' The youngster's eyes lit up and he said 'There were a lot more than that, Mr. Goode. Over 250,000 were there. Over a quarter of a million people!' That student wanted to be the first to tell me the good news about something was dear to me." He was spot on. Mal devoured what little news he could discover on the historic demonstration for civil rights and the speech that catapulted Martin Luther King Jr. to global prominence. "I was able to hear the King speech before I left Africa," he recalled. It confirmed his impressions of King as a man and as a leader. That filled him with inordinate hope for the future, but he hurt not to be part of it. On the long journey back home, Mal thought about how to use his ABC platform to cover the struggles ahead. It was a year since he first began working at ABC, and he sensed the energy building to confront America's racial dilemma. He knew he would be part of that effort.[24]

8

THE LONG HOT SUMMER

Returning from Africa in September 1963, Mal landed in a news cycle driven by civil rights. Days before he landed at LaGuardia Airport, a quarter of a million people gathered at the Lincoln Memorial during the March on Washington to hear Martin Luther King Jr. call for comprehensive civil rights legislation to make real the promises of democracy. "I have a dream," King declared, "that one day this nation will rise up and live out the true meaning of its creed: 'We hold these truths to be self-evident, that all men are created equal.'"[1] Mal, who had been fighting this fight most of his life, read King's speech while he was in Africa and returned to the States heartened that the struggle was finally capturing the nation's attention. He wanted to be on its front lines, where he could use ABC's news platform to reach the widest possible audience.

Maintaining his base at the United Nations, where the Cold War and decolonization dictated the agenda, Mal began splitting his time between the UN headquarters and ABC's studios at 7 West 66th Street. Traveling and teaching in Africa had expanded his web of sources and deepened his understanding of the continent, assets he tapped throughout his career. But civil rights campaigns were rattling the status quo, and the leadership at ABC called on Mal to cover them on the street where most of his colleagues were out of their element. Mal knew he belonged there. For the next five years, as assassinations, civil strife, and war in Indochina pushed the country into a frenzy, he did what he could to help people make sense of confounding times.

His race, for once, was an asset. Mal could enter any Black community, as he had since boyhood. No other network television correspondent had his intimate knowledge of African American politics. Nor did movement leaders and rank and file accord them comparable respect and access. Mal could catch the eye of Martin Luther King Jr. or Malcolm X when they were surrounded by throngs of reporters and speak with them privately when the chaos subsided. He connected with everyday people, making him a rare voice.

Although there was strong African American representation in print journalism by then, few Black professionals reported for the networks. Among those few, Mal was the only one with a national platform. Executives at CBS and NBC took note of his success and began to realize they needed to diversify their newsrooms. ABC hired other African Americans, notably John Johnson in 1968, Max Robinson in 1978, and Carole Simpson in 1982. But until they, too, were on-air, it rested on Mal to capture Black America's volatility and its disparate experiences, interpreting them for African Americans as well as for ABC's mostly white audience. For ABC, that made him the go-to guy, especially in moments of crisis.

The first year at ABC was a whirlwind for Mal. After living out of a suitcase he longed to be reunited with his family. Mary was anxious about leaving Pittsburgh but was ready to make the transition and bring the family under one roof. Commuting back and forth to Pittsburgh on weekends his first year at the United Nations, living in a new city, and learning how to cover a global beat in a new medium had pushed Mal to his limits. As grateful as he was to the Harlem YMCA where he first lodged, and Henry Kempton Craft, who hosted him in his comfortable Harlem apartment afterward, it was time to settle down in New York. But where? Several Negro Leaguers whom Mal had befriended before they crossed baseball's color line were determined to help him figure that out. Jackie Robinson urged Mal and Mary to consider Connecticut, where he and Rachel resided, while Roy Campanella recommended Queens or Glen Cove, Long Island, the neighborhood where he was living when a 1958 auto accident left him paralyzed from the shoulders down. New York Yankee catcher Elston Howard had something else in mind.

Mal became friends with Elston Howard when he and *Courier* sport editor Bill Nunn Jr. covered spring training in Florida during the late 1950s. Black and Latin ballplayers were still forced to live apart from their teammates in substandard accommodations, and the *Courier's* spotlight had embarrassed several major league franchises enough that they hastened to bring an end to these discriminatory practices. Many ballplayers, including Howard, saw Mary and Mal as their friends. They had confided in Mal and savored Mary's home cooking on road trips to Pittsburgh and relaxed in the Goodes' front yard afterward as neighborhood children came by to gawk at their heroes. When in New York City for the World Series, which the Yankees had been in most seasons since 1947, Mal had dinner with Arlene and Elston Howard at their home in Teaneck, New Jersey, across the river from New York City. When the Howards were in Pittsburgh for the 1960 Series, the Goodes reciprocated.

After word of Mal's hiring hit the New York papers, the Howards were among the first to call. When Mal arrived in Manhattan, they had him over for dinner and discussed where he and Mary would live. Hearing that the family would stay in Pittsburgh for the school year, Elston said: "That's good. I might have something you'd be interested in." Mal didn't realize he meant their house in Teaneck. Elston and Arlene had bought a nearby lot to build a new home and thought the Goodes would be comfortable in their current residence.[2]

Teaneck was a logical spot for the family. On the New Jersey side of the George Washington Bridge, it was a direct commute to Manhattan. Lauded as "America's Model Community" in 1949, it had a reputation for welcoming minorities. Teaneck grew during the 1950s, as millions of Americans, including African Americans, moved to the suburbs. Their transition to the perimeters of big cities was influenced in part by racial steering practices among realtors. In Teaneck, majority Black neighborhoods and schools formed in the northeast section of town. In 1961, the newly hired school superintendent Harvey Scribner worked with Black community groups to integrate the schools. A volunteer busing program failed in 1962, but in 1965 Teaneck became the first white majority town in the United States to voluntarily integrate its schools ahead of a court order demanding it do so. Its diversity and proximity made it attractive; the connection with the Howards made it desirable.[3]

It was fitting that Mary and Mal bought the Howards' home. Both Elston and Mal were barrier breakers. A former Negro Leaguer, Elston became the first African American to crack the Yankees roster when he debuted in 1955. A few weeks after the Goodes moved in, he was named the 1962 American League Most Valuable Player (MVP). Mal was jubilant. "Dear Elly," he wrote. "It may be sentimental of me to send this note but I just want it on the record. When Mary told me yesterday morning she heard on the radio of your selection it was as much a relief to me as to you for I've sweated out these past couple weeks myself, just hoping this honor would come to one of the finest guys it has been my privilege to meet in public life." Mal said he had as much regard for Elston as he did for Jackie Robinson, Roberto Clemente, and Martin Luther King Jr. "As I travel around the country speaking to young Negroes, I try to point out to them careers such as yours to encourage them to prepare for tomorrow."[4]

By the time the Goodes moved into their new home, the four oldest children were out of the house. Russell was in the US Air Force, Bob was starting his career in Pittsburgh, Richard was a student at West Virginia University, and Roberta was attending Bennett College. The two youngest—Ronnie, a high school junior, and Rosalia, a sixth grader—were still at home. For the Goodes, Teaneck was a step up the socioeconomic ladder. They marveled at a split-level home with two and a half bathrooms, a screened-in porch, a stone patio, and a big backyard where Mary edged the yard with flowers. Teaneck had a suburban ambience to it, with many of the male heads of households, Mal among them, heading into Manhattan for work each day. Black and white families were interspersed on their block. Mal, who slept in on Saturday mornings whenever he could, often went outside in his bathrobe to sweep the sidewalk in front of the house when he awakened. Teaneck, he felt, offered evidence that racial harmony was attainable. But Teaneck was not as idyllic when it came to race as it was sometimes pictured, and Mal would lay bare that contradiction.

Although he spent most of his time at the United Nations, Mal wanted to enhance ABC's dismal coverage of African Americans. Out of sight, they were an afterthought in the news, rarely appearing unless there was trouble. Knowing Jim Hagerty's affinity for politics, Mal prepared a memo, "A Look at the Negro Vote for November 6, 1962." Working the phones, he tapped his contacts to analyze what Black voters cared about in Chicago, Philadelphia, Pittsburgh, Ohio, and California. Most southern Blacks were unable to even register, but Black voters were pivotal in northern states. A White House veteran, Hagerty knew that African American voters had propelled Harry Truman's comeback in 1948 over Thomas Dewey (the candidate he was working for at the time) and had provided John Kennedy with his margin of victory over Richard Nixon in 1960. Mal spoke with aldermen, local bosses, Dr. King, NAACP president Roy Wilkins, and Black editors as he handicapped congressional and state races for ABC. His analysis was granular, focusing on which elected officials had delivered on their promises and who had stumbled, who controlled voting blocs and how their constituents were likely to vote in November's off-year elections. "The Kennedy image has faded somewhat because of his failure to push Civil Rights legislation and Fair Housing," Mal reported. Black papers criticized the president for failing to "make that stroke of the pen" he had promised would eliminate discrimination in federally assisted housing. On the other hand, Kennedy had appointed an unprecedented number of African Americans to federal positions. Thurgood Marshall's elevation to the US Circuit Court of Appeals, Carl Rowan's selection as deputy assistant secretary of state and Marjorie Lawson as an attorney for the District of Columbia, and Leon Higginbotham's appointment to the Federal Trade Commission had been warmly received.[5]

Nobody at ABC had as clear or detailed a perspective on Black voters, and Mal parleyed this knowledge into assignments to cover the Democratic and Republican Party conventions in 1964. Nor did ABC have another correspondent who could so easily enter distressed neighborhoods and get people talking. When Mal covered a wave of New York City rent strikes, his crew filmed people living without heat and electricity and tenants carrying pictures of dead rats into civil court. Residents who were worried about addicts squatting in vacant apartments, upset that nobody seemed to care, turned to him to tell their story.

Circulating proposals for assignments that would dig deeper into race, Mal tried to get ABC to focus on efforts that embodied change for the better. He wanted to cover solutions, not just problems. Kennedy had focused national attention on Appalachia, the region stretching from western New York into the Deep South where one of three people lived in poverty. Mal, no stranger to Appalachia, proposed a feature on a multiracial summer program in Tennessee helping youth fill the gaps in their education caused by underfunded segregated schools.[6] He also pushed for a program about Atlanta, which he considered a harbinger of racial progress, and segments on Staunton, his mother's hometown in Virginia. ABC did not bite on Staunton, but green-lighted Mal's proposal on Atlanta—six years later.

He suggested a documentary series, "The Winds of Change: The Other Side of the Coin," that would range from the workplace and education to the church, armed forces, and politics. "This is not to be a campaign," he cautioned, "nor a crusade but rather a dramatic presentation of a process of change that will eventually lead to America becoming the real Citadel of Democracy which the founding fathers intended it to be." The series would "serve as an answer to the Carmichaels, the Ku Klux Klan, the Rockwell Nazis and all those 'hate mongering' groups without even referring to them or giving them any kind of recognition for their ideas. The dramatizations would graphically show how much out of place they are in this country."[7] Although this proposal and most of those Mal made fell on deaf ears, he kept on pitching.

His difficulty getting traction greenlighting stories was due to several reasons. Mal was an outlier at ABC. He was the network's only African American national correspondent, already in his mid-50s, and without the benefit of traditional journalism training. While consumed with meeting the standards of his new job, Mal was navigating uncharted terrain. No longer in Pittsburgh where he knew everybody and nearly everybody knew him, he was starting a career in an unfamiliar, often uncomfortable, setting where his actions were scrutinized by millions. While ABC was trying to boost ratings and broaden its audience, reporting on racial realities was a double-edged sword, attracting some viewers, alienating others. Additionally, his UN beat meant that he was not especially visible at ABC headquarters. Most of his reporting was on the radio and he was frustrated that he had not joined the elite core of television correspondents who entered people's homes daily. According to one of Mal's closest colleagues at ABC, David Snell: "He wasn't on their radar. He was off at the United Nations most of the time and most of the UN stories he was involved with were radio stories. He wasn't on television a whole lot and so they just didn't think of him as one of their go-to guys."[8]

More often, Mal became ABC's go-to guy when racial troubles flared. Those once infrequent moments began occurring with troubling regularity.

On June 12, 1963, the civil rights movement suffered a searing loss when thirty-seven-year-old Medgar Evers, civil rights activist and the first NAACP field secretary in Mississippi, was assassinated at the hands of the Ku Klux Klan. Evers's stepped-up campaign to overturn segregation had put him in constant danger. He was struck down when walking to his front door after returning from an NAACP meeting, just hours after Kennedy announced on television that he would propose civil rights legislation. "It is better," the president said, "to settle these matters in the courts than on the streets."[9]

Mal, energized by his time in Africa and elated by the March on Washington, was hopeful. But that bubble popped when four young girls were killed when white supremacists set off a bomb at the 16th Street Baptist Church in Birmingham on September 15, 1963. Two Black youth died during the ensuing protests, and Governor Wallace sent more than one thousand Alabama National Guard and officers to the city. Concerned they might overreact, Dr. King said that the US Army ought to take the city over. The same day, President Kennedy spoke to the nation. "If these cruel and tragic events can only awaken that city and state," he implored, "if they can only awaken this entire nation to a realization of the folly of racial injustice and hatred and violence, then it is not too late for all concerned to unite in steps toward peaceful progress before more lives are lost."[10] Kennedy, many hoped, would finally meet the lofty expectations they had placed on him. At the funeral for the four girls, King delivered the eulogy. He called Denise McNair, Addie Mae Collins, Carole Robertson, and Cynthia Wesley, whose age ranged from eleven to fourteen, "martyred heroines of a holy crusade for freedom and human dignity."[11] And then two months later, Mal and the entire nation were stunned when an assassin's bullet felled John F. Kennedy on November 22, 1963.

Mal took the train to Philadelphia two days later to fulfill a speaking commitment at the anniversary breakfast of a Catholic fraternal group, the Philos. He was in the midst of what he called four awful days when he and other journalists hardly slept. "Prepare for a long, hard fight—your champion is gone," he told the Philos in the ballroom of the Benjamin Franklin Hotel. "We are in one of the darkest hours of our nation and when we boil it down, it comes to just one thing—hate. We have allowed some groups to grow under the cover of freedom of speech—the Ku Klux Klan, the American Nazi Party, the John Birchers. They hate the Jews, they hate colored people, they hate the Catholics, they hate everything that stands for the American way of life." Kennedy's assassination was traumatic, but only the first of many ordeals marking the decade. "My most striking recollection in this terrible period," Mal recalled, "was hearing the trembling words of tribute from an African ambassador, 'A great oak has fallen in the forest of men.'"[12]

He watched with trepidation as Lyndon Johnson picked up the baton that JFK had first raised for civil rights legislation. "Everything I had ever learned in the history books taught me that martyrs have to die for causes," Johnson told biographer Doris Kearns. "I had to take the dead man's program and turn it into a martyr's cause. That way Kennedy would live on forever, and so would I." For Johnson, that meant passing a civil rights bill ending racial discrimination and segregation in public accommodations, public education, and federally assisted programs. Johnson was hardly the orator that Kennedy was, but he was an adroit politician and seized his moment of maximum leverage to press for the bill's enactment. "No memorial oration or eulogy could more eloquently honor President Kennedy's memory," he declared, "than the earliest possible passage of the Civil Rights Bill for which he fought so long. We have talked long enough in this country about equal rights. We have talked for one hundred years or more. It is time now to write the next chapter, and to write it in the books of law."[13]

Mal wanted to believe in Johnson but wasn't sure he would follow through and worried that momentum for the bill would dissipate. One thing was certain; it would provoke fierce opposition in Congress. But for Mal, its passage was nonnegotiable and his estimation of Johnson changed when the president remained steadfast. Neither was blind to the political hit Democrats would incur for years to come if it passed.[14] Many white southerners were unwilling to leave segregation behind. As Senate majority leader, Johnson had pushed a mild civil rights bill through Congress in 1957. That bill had been watered down to win passage and dismayed activists seeking stronger measures; this one would be much tougher to enact into law because southern Senators vowed to filibuster the legislation to prevent a vote on it. During a filibuster, senators who opposed the legislation could hold the Senate floor indefinitely, talking without time constraints. When one senator tired, he could cede his time to another filibusterer, thus blocking a vote. To force a vote, the Senate needed to pass a cloture measure. But cloture required sixty-seven votes and Johnson had to forge a bipartisan supermajority to bring discussion of the bill to an end and allow a vote. No president had never done that with a civil rights bill.[15]

Just how far some people were willing to go to stop civil rights became apparent in Mississippi that June. Violence and retribution against civil rights activists had bloodied the state. Mal had seen as much when he went to the South for the *Pittsburgh Courier* in 1950. No injustice did more to rivet his attention on the state than the brutal murder of a fourteen-year-old boy from Chicago who was visiting relatives in a Mississippi Delta town in the summer of 1955. Emmitt Till's alleged transgression was speaking to, and possibly smiling at, a white woman clerking in her family's grocery store. A few nights later, the woman's husband and another man seized Emmitt from his uncle's home. They tortured and killed him and then tried to sink his body in the Tallahatchie River. Three days later the battered body rose to the surface. Mamie Till Bradley brought her son's corpse back to Chicago where it was placed in an open casket for his funeral. Photographs of his disfigured body seared Mississippi into the nation's psyche as a bastion of white terror. After an all-white jury acquitted Till's murderers, the two men admitted to the crime in an interview with *Look* magazine for which they were paid several thousand dollars. That infuriated Mal, who spoke about the murder on Pittsburgh radio and connected it to local incidents of police brutality. One of the most gripping episodes in civil rights history, it spurred passage of the fairly weak, but still controversial, 1957 federal civil rights law that Johnson had backed.

Mississippi became the focal point of white terror again in 1963. Mal did not cover Medgar Evers's murder that June before he left for Africa, but ABC and the national media did. Evers, the secretary of the Mississippi NAACP, was shot dead one evening after parking in his driveway. His murderer, Byron De La Beckwith, belonged to the White

Citizens' Council, a network of white supremacists that formed after the 1954 Supreme Court ruling declaring that segregation in public education was unconstitutional. An all-white jury failed to convict De La Beckwith. Nor did another all-white jury when he was retried. He was not found guilty until 1994 after new evidence led to a third trial.

In the summer of 1964, as civil rights became a litmus test for democracy, Mississippi again seized center stage. The catalyst was the Mississippi Summer Freedom Project, which brought over one thousand Black and white volunteers to the state to register voters. The Congress of Racial Equality (CORE) and the Student Nonviolent Coordinating Committee (SNCC) had mobilized these volunteers to work with local activists to combat voter suppression. Mississippi had denied African Americans the franchise since the collapse of Reconstruction. In 1962, only 7 percent of eligible African Americans voted in a state with a substantial Black population. Once in Mississippi, the volunteers were threatened with violence. On June 21, a few weeks after Mississippi Summer began, three activists who were investigating a church bombing in Neshoba County vanished. The disappearance of James Chaney, Andrew Goodman, and Michael Schwerner made the national news, in part because two of them were white northerners. But in Washington, filibustering senators refused to budge and blocked a vote on the civil rights bill that Johnson had championed. Breaking the filibuster would require Johnson to use every political maneuver at his disposal.

Johnson's relentless push to make that happen encouraged Mal, who longed to see the civil rights bill become law. But he worried about the backlash coursing through the South. He knew many of the young women and men who had joined the Mississippi Summer campaign and understood the risks they faced. Back in Pittsburgh, Mary's brother and sister-in-law, Robert and Adah Lavelle, were facing the hardest summer of their lives when their son insisted on joining the campaign. Robert Lavelle Jr. (Bob) had grown up in a home where fighting for change was as normal as daily prayer and was surprised his parents tried to stop him. Adah remembered him responding: "but I thought you'd be so pleased." The Lavelles reluctantly agreed to let him go with the understanding he would return to Penn State that fall.[16]

Bob wrote to his uncle Mal from Columbus, Mississippi, ten days after Chaney, Goodman, and Schwerner went missing. "From the reports we receive," Lavelle reported, "the Mississippi Summer project parents are raising quite an uproar about their sons' and daughters' safety.... I am glad because this action and the news coverage prompts the Mississippi Authorities to think almost twice before plotting a sinister action of harassment or detainment." Ten of Lavelle's coworkers had just been arrested in Columbus for handing out leaflets about the civil rights bill that Senate segregationists were filibustering. Bail was set at four hundred dollars, which the activists had difficulty raising. Even more problematic was finding lawyers to represent them. Only three attorneys in Mississippi were willing to take on civil rights cases. When lawyers from outside the state offered to defend them, the presiding judge ruled they had no standing in Mississippi courts. Expecting more arrests, Lavelle feared a difficult summer. "It is clear that this was an attempt to harass the summer project workers and impede our work." If arrested, Mississippi Summer workers might not find legal representation anywhere in the state.[17]

Bob Lavelle wanted to convey the gravity of the situation but was careful not to strike an alarmist tone. He knew that anything he told uncle Mal would get back to his parents. "Columbus so far is not noted for its violence but I don't know how long this period will last. People, hoods, police and others ride past headquarters here constantly." In town, he encountered derogatory remarks but not overt intimidation. Rather than violently suppress the activists, local authorities tried to isolate them. The proprietors of the "colored cafes" where they ate were "mysteriously contacted by the person who holds the mortgage and are told that if they continue to serve us something bad will happen to their business." They had also been forced out of their lodgings after landlords were told either evict them or lose their property. Problems with food and housing had dampened morale. "Add this to the phlegmatic attitude of most of the Negroes here and it amounts to quite a problem," Bob confessed.[18]

"As you are probably aware," he wrote, "most of the Negroes are steeped in Uncle Tomism and do not believe they have the right to vote. Some Negroes are not aware of what a vote is! They agree that we are right in our cause but don't ask them to do anything! Of course, we expect this and combat it. We have also had a difficult time getting the church to cooperate." Not wanting to portray too negative a judgment, Bob concluded: "Well, it is going to be a long hot summer; having a hard time eating and we're on the verge of being evicted from the headquarters." But, he added: "The future looks bright." His handwritten postscript said: "Not really so bad. There's a lot of work to be done and if we keep busy we might stay away from trouble and get the job done. Bob." He was both realistic and hopeful, but mother Adah Lavelle recalled it as "a miserable summer."[9]

By the time Bob's letter arrived in Teaneck, Lyndon Johnson had marshaled the support to win a cloture vote, ending the filibuster after sixty working days in the Senate by persuading twenty-seven Republican and forty-four Democratic senators to shut down debate. It was the first time that cloture ever forced a vote on a civil rights bill. On July 2, 1964, after both houses of Congress passed the civil rights bill, President Johnson signed it into law with Martin Luther King Jr. and other civil rights leaders at his side. Mal joined millions of citizens watching on television.

But elation over the Civil Rights Act was dampened by the counterattack coursing through the South. A month after this landmark victory, an informant tipped off federal investigators that the bodies of Chaney, Goodman, and Schwerner had been buried beneath an earthen dam. On August 4, forty-four days after they had been murdered, their corpses were dug up. The two white activists, Schwerner and Goodman, had been shot in the heart; Goodman was most likely alive when he was buried. Chaney, the local Black civil rights worker, had been beaten, shot three times, and castrated. Although the nation's laws were bending toward equality, the backlash was becoming deadlier.

With the 1964 election approaching, ABC assigned Mal to the Republican and Democratic Party conventions that summer. He went first to San Francisco, where Republicans anointed a candidate from the party's right flank as their presidential standard bearer. On July 16, as Mal roamed the convention floor at the Cow Palace, James Powell bled out on a sidewalk along Manhattan's upper East Side. The fifteen-year-old's death at the hands of an off-duty policeman triggered six days of turmoil that swept through New York City's Black neighborhoods. "So," the *New York Times* declared, "the 'long hot summer' of Negro discontent" has begun.[20] The unrest started in Harlem, jumped across the East River to Brooklyn, then returned to Manhattan. Within days, frustrated African Americans in Rochester upstate joined in. These disturbances were a harbinger of a "long hot summer" that lasted five years. The race issue, which many northerners viewed as a distinctly southern problem, was no longer confined to the South. It was a national dilemma. Nor would white supremacists continue to monopolize the use of force and violence, as they had during most of the century. Angry young African Americans were picking up rocks and making their voices heard as notions of Black power, armed self-defense, and revolution gained traction.[21]

James Powell died just two weeks after Lyndon Johnson signed the 1964 Civil Rights Act. The landmark legislation outlawed discrimination based on race, gender, nationality, and religion at work and in public places. It also revamped national politics, placing civil rights at the heart of the election. The night before Powell died in New York City, Mal interviewed GOP delegates and party luminaries as Arizona senator Barry Goldwater secured the presidential nod. After returning to the Cow Palace for Goldwater's acceptance speech the next day, he heard that a Black teenager had been shot and killed in Manhattan. But he was more focused on Goldwater's remarks in which the militant conservative called for law and order but offered little that appealed to African Americans.[22] The death of a young Black male at the hands of a policeman was hardly a rare event. Goldwater's nomination, however, was ominous.

After witnessing skirmishes at the Cow Palace where men carrying "Goldwater for President" signs disrupted civil rights demonstrators, Mal was skeptical of the nominee's commitment to racial equality. In a radio commentary twenty years later, he remarked that there were hardly any Black delegates and only one other Black correspondent, Bob Teague, at the convention. Teague and Mal hardly looked alike, but Goldwater didn't process the differences. "We were so rare that after interviewing Goldwater, he went out of his way to thank me and say: 'Thanks, too, for your interview yesterday.' But he had talked with Bob the day before, not me." Pausing to let those listening to his report process what he said, Mal deadpanned: "You understand; we all look alike." Mal added that Goldwater supporters had set afire the coat of Pennsylvania's secretary of labor, Bill Young, a Black delegate sitting with his state's delegation.[23]

Bob Teague, a local reporter for WNBC-TV in New York who sometimes worked for NBC News, was twenty years younger than Mal. After starring in football at the University of Wisconsin, he declined offers from four teams to play professionally, instead pursuing journalism. Teague worked for CBS radio and the *New York Times* before joining WNBC-TV, a local affiliate. His television career as a reporter, producer, and anchor spanned three decades before he retired in 1991. He might have been amused by Goldwater's confusion and later wrote that, when Mal had debuted in 1962, his "hair was so straight and his skin so white that his arrival had been virtually unnoticed."[24] That was an exaggeration, but there had been muted criticism that ABC chose Mal because he was lighter skinned. Teague's *New York Times* obituary noted that he followed in Mal's footsteps and cited a *TV Guide* report that "Mr. Goode was assigned to the ABC News United Nations bureau because network executives feared his presence in the main studio would be too disruptive." While Mal was sensitive to the relative privilege lighter-skinned African Americans sometimes had, nobody complained about that publicly or said that to his face.[25]

Mal caught a flight home the next day. Although he longed for a few days to recover from the convention, he was quickly back on the street covering the reaction to James Powell's death. Mal went first to Harlem, then followed the strife to Bedford Stuyvesant and lower Manhattan, chronicling the outbursts as they played out. His reports and commentaries did more than describe confrontations that left over a thousand injured or jailed and hundreds of storefronts gutted.

He questioned what had caused them and addressed what might prevent their reoccurrence, something he tried to do whenever urban revolt erupted.

The catalyst to New York City's unrest was the death of a fifteen-year-old African American student on Thursday, July 16. James Powell had been hanging out with friends on the stoop of an apartment building in a white working-class section on the Upper East Side awaiting summer school classes to begin that morning. The building superintendent, incensed that Black youth were ignoring his demands to stay off the steps, began spraying them with a hose, purportedly yelling "Dirty niggers, I'll wash the black off you!"[26] The students responded by chasing him inside the building. An off-duty police lieutenant saw the altercation and intervened, fired three shots, and killed Powell. He claimed that Powell, who was five foot six inches tall and weighed 122 pounds, was about to attack him with a knife. Witnesses disputed his allegations. More than two hundred students from Powell's school took to the streets, chanting "Stop Killer Cops!" and "End Police Brutality!"[27]

Not much happened that day or the next other than name-calling. Although activists pressed demands for a civilian review board that could investigate allegations of police violence, they were unable to speak with Mayor Robert Wagner, who was in Geneva, Switzerland, for a conference on the impact of automation. But on Saturday July 18, as temperatures climbed into the 90s, people sought relief from sweltering tenement apartments by taking to their stoops, the streets, and rooftops. After an emotional funeral service for Powell in Harlem, crowds surrounded the West 123rd Street precinct house, where lines of steel helmeted officers stood on guard. When a policeman urged protesters to go home, someone replied, "We are home, baby!" Veteran civil rights activist Bayard Rustin tried to calm the crowd but was taunted as an Uncle Tom. Some protesters chanted "We want Malcolm X!"[28]

But Malcolm was out of the country during a four-and-a-half-month trip to the Middle East, and he was not a factor as the riots played out. He was taking part in the Hajj and attending an Organization of African Unity conference in Egypt. When Mal tracked

Malcolm down in his hotel room in Cairo, Mal pressed him about militant protestors on the streets and whether their approach was the best way to respond to James Powell's death. Malcolm mentioned the call in his autobiography. "Mal Goode asked me questions that I answered for his beeping tape recorder, about the 'Blood Brothers' in Harlem, the rifle clubs for Negroes, and other subjects with which I was being identified in the American press."[29]

Demonstrators milled around the station house, demanding that the officer who shot Powell be arrested. They were incredulous that the six-foot-tall, two-hundred-pound lieutenant could not have defused the situation without deadly force. Bottles, bricks, and garbage can lids began flying, some tossed from surrounding rooftops. A few shots were fired by police and Molotov cocktails thrown by demonstrators. One man was found dead afterward, shot by a 38 caliber pistol, hundreds were arrested, and looting lasted until dawn.

Spiraling out of the control, disturbances continued for another six days. Because the riots began in Harlem, the capital of Black America, and spread throughout the metropolis, they captured national attention. Harlem encompassed several segments of Black America—families born in the South, in the Caribbean, and in the North—as well as whites of various classes and nationalities. Despite the aura of the Harlem Renaissance and an educated, well-off strata of African Americans, the neighborhood suffered the same indignities and difficulties plaguing other urban neighborhoods. Nor was it free of internal tensions. Frustration was palpable, and many residents had questioned the city's efforts to host the recently opened 1964 World's Fair in Queens instead of investing in Harlem.

Mal joined the press corps covering the tumult, prowling city streets and attending city hall briefings. After Harlem settled into a surly calm, he crossed the East River into Brooklyn, where the next storm was gathering. Bedford-Stuyvesant was larger and poorer than Harlem, its residents crammed into one hundred square blocks. "I moved into the Bedford-Stuyvesant area of Brooklyn," Mal reported on the air, "only to witness a restless crowd showing its resentment." The riots exposed fault lines that reflected widening ideological, generational, and organizational tensions. "I was there when they booed the NAACP sound truck speaker as he urged them to return home," Mal told listeners. The NAACP sought to avert violence, considering it counterproductive. "The speaker in the truck said: 'We've been telling them [city officials] all hell might break loose unless you saw real progress and they wouldn't listen. But now they're willing to listen, with both ears. The message has been delivered! Now, it's time to cool it and let the message sink in.' The crowd still booed," Mal reported. The NAACP speaker tried to speak over them, proclaiming that "Violent demonstration and looting hurt our cause!" At that, Mal reported, "the teenagers booed with more vigor."[30]

Their response troubled Mal, but he wasn't surprised by their vehemence. He knew the Black community was far from monolithic in its politics. Leaders had egos, and organizations had agendas. Deeper conflicts between the nonviolent protest strategy of the NAACP, SCLC, and King on the one hand and the more militant, separatist voices speaking for Black nationalist and radical groups on the other were coming out in the open. The NAACP leaflets handed to bystanders on Harlem streets said: "Cool it baby! . . . Violent demonstrations and looting hurt our cause. Think!" But that message was not winning the day. Instead, Mal reported, it was "like red flags before a bull."[31]

Although Black power politics had yet to explode on the scene, Mal worried about its strident rhetoric. He had listened to Malcolm X declare that "1964 will be America's hottest year, her hottest year yet, a year of much racial violence and much racial bloodshed."[32] When he heard calls for "Guerilla warfare!" against the New York Police Department as he stood in the street, Mal worried that somebody might act upon their rhetoric. Malcolm, when asked about the riots while still in Cairo, had said: "There are probably more armed Negroes in Harlem than in any other spot on earth. If the people who are armed get involved in this, you can bet they'll really have something on their hands."[33] Mal feared the worst.

Militant rhetoric and carnage in the streets were a perfect foil for those opposing change. Although the 1964 Civil Rights Act had come about because of peaceful protest and the democratic process, it amplified white anxieties and sparked violent reprisals against integration in the South. Johnson, as politically astute as anyone who ever sat in the Oval Office, was well aware of the damage he and the Democratic Party would incur because of the new law. Johnson's longtime ally, Georgia senator Richard Russell, told him that it could cost him the South as well as the election. "If that's the price I've got to pay," Johnson answered, "I'll pay it gladly." It didn't cost Johnson that November, but Democrats paid a stiff price in future elections as the South lurched from solidly Democratic to solidly Republican. Johnson was the last Democratic candidate to win a majority of white votes in the South, heralding a national shift by white voters. Almost two-thirds of white southerners had called themselves Democrats in 1964. Twenty-five years later, when asked the same question, more answered that they were Republicans than Democrats by a 37 to 34 percent margin.[34]

Riots and inflammatory rhetoric exacerbated white fears, scaring many otherwise sympathetic to civil rights. Apocalyptic statements about the future fueled their anxieties. Malcolm X was not the only one forecasting that trouble would spread from the South to the North. Barry Goldwater had also predicted that northern cities would confront civil disorder. The previous July, he had warned that "if there is rioting in the streets it'll occur in Chicago, Detroit, New York, or Washington, probably to a greater extent than it will occur in the southern cities." Condemning "fire-eating talk" by Black leaders and their white allies, he tied crime, violence, and disorder to civil rights activism and had the chutzpah to blame these troubles on King's philosophy of nonviolent civil disobedience.[35]

In the meantime, Mal watched mounted patrolmen ride on to sidewalks along Brooklyn's Nostrand Avenue to disperse crowds. Street smart and nimble at fifty-six, he avoided being run down. "I saw plainclothesmen arrest a youngster 30 seconds after he needlessly tossed a brick through a window of a delicatessen store," Mal reported. "I heard some shots at a distance, just about eight, and later learned they were fired to break up a crowd. At midnight the toll included at least one suspected looter shot, 30 others arrested for defying police."[36]

His interviews with a minister, a physician, and an insurance agent underscored Brooklyn's concerns. They voiced disappointment about the mayor's failure to promise an impartial civilian review board and condemned Police Commissioner Michael Murphy's hard-line stance. Mal assessed the moment: "The early morning brings calm, but it's the same uneasy calm we've had since Sunday and the long-time residents of these areas fear what follows the daytime calm." They were prescient. "In New York this morning," Mal said, "there's a continuing wave of bitterness, defiance, police brutality, and worst of all a deep-seated fear has gripped the city, fear that's dormant in the daytime and none dares predict what the night will bring." The next day, he described what night had brought. "There's a strange square mile in Brooklyn this morning, ravished, demolished, a picture that would ideally fit the title, 'After the Storm,' for during much of the last night there was a storm of demolition, violence, and destruction. A familiar pattern the past three days that seemed to merely shift locale. In this case from across the East River in New York's Harlem to the Brooklyn Harlem known more familiarly as the Bedford-Stuyvesant section of Brooklyn."[37]

Bob Teague, one of the other Black correspondents covering the riots, observed that his supervisors "felt black reporters would be invulnerable in a riot." He knew otherwise.[38] Even Black reporters, heckled as sellouts, were hiding their press credentials. Mal did not encounter problems with the police or protesters, but some journalists did. Joseph Lelyveld and two other white *New York Times* reporters covering the Sunday demonstrations on July 19 were attacked as they walked along 7th Avenue. Ironically, Lelyveld's father, Cleveland Rabbi Arthur Lelyveld, had been beaten by the police just days before in Mississippi where he was working with Freedom Summer activists. A few weeks later, Rabbi Lelyveld would speak at Andrew Goodman's and Michael Schwerner's funerals.[39]

Mal was deeply troubled by the violence but knew it was his responsibility to report the story accurately and to cover the destruction and bloodshed as well as dig deeply into what caused the troubles. He began developing a template for covering riots that he would deploy for years to come. Frustrated that the mainstream press amplified the destruction instead of uncovering the community distress that sparked it, he refused to sensationalize violence. Rather than focus on broken windows and looting or the day's tally of arrests and injuries, Mal wanted his audience to think about what caused the riots and why they were so difficult to resolve. He did not ignore the arrest totals or the hundreds of shops in Brooklyn ransacked by looters. Those costs were significant, but he believed there was a more profound loss. "It will take weeks to determine what the real damage is to the moral fiber of this, the largest metropolitan community in the world," Mal reasoned. "The end does not seem in sight. The daylight brings a respite, but the night brings a new wave of hell and damnation." Scolding Robert Wagner, he said that while the mayor would deliver a fireside chat appealing to New Yorkers' sense of citizenship, it's "wishful thinking at its best. Mayor Wagner must know this as do his many aides who have been warned—by the history of 1935, again in 1943." Riots had mangled Harlem in both years.[40]

Transcending the moment, Mal asked: "What's the answer?" He was more than ready to offer one. "Change the posture, the image of New York's finest; eradicate the slums; create a new outlook for the disheartened, the disillusioned, the disfranchised. Improve hospital facilities, upgrade some Negro policemen, even clean up the streets." He enumerated other remedial measures: end practices restricting Blacks to "the Negro ghetto," improve an educational system that sent the least qualified teachers to Harlem while providing better teachers, books, and supplies to white schools. Mal knew that little of what he suggested would be done immediately, if ever, but he wanted to chart a course that could break the patterns of poverty, disenfranchisement, and violence.[41]

His ABC colleague Bill Beutel accompanied him to Brooklyn during the riots. "Bill turned to me and said, 'Mal, do you think this is the right way to go about it?' And I said, 'Hell no, but what is the best way to go about it after 300 years?'" When Bill responded: "I see what you mean," Mal snapped: "You don't see what I mean. You've never been a Negro like me, and so there's no way for you to see." Beutel paused and said: "I guess you're right."[42]

A week after the disturbances began, Mal stood on a Harlem street, describing a return to quiet. A thousand people had been injured or arrested and hundreds of stores and businesses devastated, but now normality was reasserting itself. "Fingers are crossed, and hopes are high for continued peace in Harlem this Saturday night, which marks the end of a week of the worst rioting and plundering this city ever experienced." Mal described children playing, people shopping, and families enjoying ice balls. "There is hope too, that out of this crucible of rioting, plunder, and hatred will come the end of frustrations, that political, religious, and civic leadership will continue meeting and working to eliminate any smoldering embers that might lead to this type of hate and destruction in the future." He closed by saying: "Tomorrow morning, Harlem churches will be packed with thousands wanting to give thanks for a peace which finally came, and to ask for guidance in a plan to prevent any recurrence of the past week's nightmare. Mal Goode, ABC, New York."[43]

The riots crystalized the nation's fears and divides. Many whites watching the disturbances play out on television worried that violence would soon be at their own doorstep. African Americans, whose experiences with the police were fraught, felt caught between indifference to their concerns and suppression of their protests. Moreover, friction was evident among supporters of the NAACP, SCLC, CORE, SNCC, Black nationalist, and revolutionary groups. They openly scorned each other. Nor was there consensus about how the country should respond. Some of those seeking racial transformation urged a domestic Marshall Plan; others sought revolution. And many who resisted change cheered Barry Goldwater's call to crack down on civil rights and black power agitators.

Four days after rioting subsided, Mayor Wagner invited Martin Luther King Jr. to the city. "I do not think that violence can solve the problem in New York City, nor can it solve the problem in Mississippi," King told reporters. While he called for people of goodwill to press nonviolently against racial and economic oppression, the riots had placed him on his back foot. King called for "honest, soul-searching analysis and evaluation of the environmental causes" spawning unrest. Although a majority of African Americans adhered to nonviolent protest as the most effective course of action, King knew that without better housing, better schools, and better jobs, that could change. He headed next to Harlem and Brooklyn to talk with community leaders, but militants dismissed his visit and belittled his emphasis on nonviolence.[44]

The *New York Times* editorial on July 26 after the city quieted down condemned the violence but addressed why it occurred. Those writing the editorial reasoned that "The cycle of discrimination that confronts the Negro in these and other Northern ghettoes is hard to break. . . . There is job discrimination, resulting in low Negro income. The low income plus housing discrimination condemn the Negro to living in the slums. There is apathy toward education, disqualifying many Negroes for many jobs that might otherwise be available. The bleakness of the Negro's future often puts him in conflict with the authority wielded by the dominant white man and breeds hostility toward the enforcer of that authority, the policeman." Despite years of struggle, African Americans in the North had made scant headway. "As a result the talk this year of a 'long, hot summer' has grown. The potential for explosion was clearly there. Ten days ago came the spark."[45]

A week later, Mal was back on the street, covering outbursts in nearby Jersey City as the long hot summer continued to boil over. Jersey City reprised New York City, but on a smaller scale. Mal traced the genesis of the disturbances, describing looting, bottle throwing, and confrontations with police, and then tried to explain what caused them. "Last night's action," he explained, "was triggered by the cold answer of Mayor Thomas Whalen to representatives of CORE, the NAACP, the ministers, and a delegation of Jersey City youth." Presented with demands seeking more Black police, better-equipped playgrounds, cleaner streets, and an end to police brutality, Mayor Whalen responded: "We will meet force with force" and called the trouble "the work of hooligans." That failed to placate Jersey City's African American leaders, and twenty minutes later, Mal reported, disturbances flared. Episcopalian ministers who had just returned from Mississippi told him unrest would persist for months. In closing, Mal observed: "Jersey City has experienced some of the worst in destruction and hate. Like the second act, there's more to come."[46]

Later that month, Mal was part of the ABC team at the Democratic Party Convention in Atlantic City. There were no confrontations in the streets, but Democrats clashed over the makeup of the Mississippi delegation. After Lyndon Johnson had signed the Civil Rights Act of 1964 that July, white resistance escalated in the Deep South. When the Mississippi primary excluded African Americans, Mississippi Freedom Democratic Party (MFDP) activist Fannie Lou Hamer and Aaron Henry sought to be seated as the state's rightful delegates to the convention. But the state party's white leadership refused to step aside and dismissed efforts to incorporate African Americans into the delegation.

In a convention spot that Mal produced, the camera tracked shots of a burned-out car before cutting to a bell, all that remained of a church torched by an arsonist in Philadelphia, Mississippi. It showed members of the Ku Klux Klan and finally MFDP delegates demanding credentials to the convention. The footage Mal chose as the story's backdrop illustrated how far segregationists would go. In Mississippi, violence lurking in the background often came into the open. Although the convention was inclined to back the MFDP's integrated delegation, President Johnson feared losing even more white voters in the South and pushed through a compromise. The MFDP rejected it as woefully inadequate and left Atlantic City questioning the integrity of the Democratic Party. So did Mal. He had known Aaron Henry since 1950 and considered Fannie Lou Hamer an exemplar leader. The MFDP, meanwhile, invited Malcolm X to address its ranks and broke with Johnson on Vietnam. Despite efforts to allay white concerns, LBJ failed to carry Mississippi and four other southern states in the November 1964 election in what was otherwise a stunning electoral romp over Barry Goldwater.

After the Democratic Party convention, there were more riots to cover, this time across the river in Philadelphia. Most coverage gravitated toward scenes of destruction, but Mal interviewed Dr. King, Mayor James Tate, and religious and civic leaders, questioning them about what had triggered the trouble. With outbursts occurring with numbing regularity, Mal was ABC's correspondent for what many were calling the Black rebellion.

Civil disturbances waned after Labor Day, and Mal spent more time at the United Nations. On October 14, 1964, the Nobel Committee announced that Martin Luther King Jr. would receive its Peace Prize. In Norway that December at the Rådhuset, Oslo's city hall where the peace prize is awarded, King accepted the prize on the behalf of "a mighty army of love," the thousands who had sacrificed to secure civil rights. Mal was proud to have marched with them. Like King, he knew that a movement needed more than leaders, no matter how charismatic and visionary they were. King declared the prize validated the nonviolent approach that the civil rights movement had embraced.[47] But as much as Mal admired King, he saw signs of a more militant strategy emerging in Black America. And then, the leading voice for that approach—Malcolm X—was shot dead.

9 *"OUR OWN BLACK SHINING PRINCE"*

MARY AND MAL WERE SETTLING DOWN IN THEIR TEANECK dining room on a cold, sunny Sunday afternoon, February 21, 1965. This day was particularly special because of the company of their eldest son, Russell. Lieutenant Goode had been stationed at Stewart Air Force Base in Newburgh, New York, since returning from Germany three years before. He drove an hour south to spend his day's leave with his parents and sister Rosalia. The youngest of the six Goode children and the only one still at home, Rosalia had no memory of sharing a home with her oldest brother. She was only two when Russell, then seventeen, left for Penn State University, and she associated him with the dolls he sent her from around the world. Now thirteen, Rosalia eagerly anticipated visiting with her brother in uniform. Mary prepared her trademark Sunday meal with entrees, side dishes, and brimming platters that seemed to magically appear out of nowhere.

But then the phone rang. Mal rose to answer and shuddered when the ABC producer on the line informed him that Malcolm X had been shot multiple times as he addressed a gathering of his newly established Organization of Afro-American Unity (OAAU). He was declared dead at 3:30 p.m. at Columbia Presbyterian Hospital. Mal was visibly agitated when he ordered Russell to drive him to the scene of the murder, the Audubon Ballroom in the Washington Heights neighborhood of upper Manhattan. Mal dashed upstairs to change into a suit and tie before he met Russell in the car outside. The eight-mile trip across the Hudson River to 165th Street took half an hour, but Mal hardly spoke as he contemplated what he would do when they arrived. He needed to find the ABC crew dispatched to the scene and determine how to cover Malcolm's murder. He was also concerned about Malcolm's family. His wife, Betty Shabazz, was just thirty years old, pregnant, suddenly on her own with four young daughters, and facing ongoing death threats.

The scene was chaotic as they approached Broadway and 165th Street where police, camera crews, and onlookers swarmed the streets. Mal was devastated, but he knew that Malcolm's death had been sadly predictable. After his expulsion from the Nation of Islam (NOI) for so-called acts of heresy, Malcolm had anticipated retaliation. His home had been firebombed in the early hours of the previous Sunday, February 14. Two days later, Malcolm told Gordon Parks, the first African American photographer at *Life* magazine, that he believed the NOI intended to kill him.

Russell pulled the car as close as he could to the Audubon Ballroom. Without a goodbye, Mal leapt from the vehicle to search for his crew. Within seconds he disappeared into the pandemonium. Russell had faced threatening situations in the military, but the scrum of angry people made him uneasy. He tried to process the meaning and consequence of Malcolm's death as he sat for a moment in the idling car, observing the confusion of police and people on the street. His daze was disrupted when two men sprinted out of the crowd and jumped into a car that screeched to a sudden stop beside him. Russell glanced over and spotted a pile of guns on the backseat. He lingered no longer. Quickly putting the car into gear, Russell sped away and returned to his mother and sister in Teaneck, leaving his father somewhere in the crowd.[1]

Mal and Malcolm were unlikely friends. Each was committed to civil rights, but they disagreed about how to gain them. Mal mistrusted Malcolm's radically defiant separatist agenda and had not hesitated to tell him that. A civil rights activist and integrationist since he was a boy, Mal took his lead from Martin Luther King Jr. and saw nonviolent resistance as the path forward. Accustomed to forging relationships that crossed racial lines, he believed that those alliances were essential to achieve equality. Moreover, he feared that Malcolm's radical rhetoric would trigger a crippling backlash.

But Mal was in a unique position. By and large, Americans misunderstood Malcolm's politics and reporters portrayed him as a hatemonger. Mal, however, believed that Malcolm was principled and thoughtful. His ABC platform meant Mal could counteract what he saw as an otherwise distorted and caricatured portrayal. By seeking to find common ground, not only because it was his job but because he believed that racial progress demanded it, Mal gained Malcolm's trust. "These were two smart men who contended with one another intellectually," Bob Goode reflected. "Dad was not afraid to criticize Malcolm to his face, just as he did to an Alpha brother who wasn't paying child support."[2]

Despite dramatically different backgrounds, they liked each other. Mal was seventeen years older and raised in a family that viewed Christianity, hard work, and education as its guiding principles. Malcolm's parents, Louise and Earl Little, were adherents of the Universal Negro Improvement Association (UNIA), the Black separatist organization that Marcus Garvey founded in Jamaica in 1914. Its espousal of Black nationalism and Earl Little's unflinching embrace of Black pride made the family a target of the Ku Klux Klan and the Black Legion, a white supremacist militia. Malcolm was born in 1925 in Omaha, Nebraska, but the family fled to Wisconsin and then Michigan to seek safety. Earl Little found that elusive. The Baptist lay speaker and UNIA leader died in 1931, allegedly run over by a streetcar. It was widely speculated that the Black Legion had murdered him.[3] Malcolm was only six years old at the time, but his father's messages of self-reliance and the threats that tortured his family seared his memory.

Malcolm's Grenada-born mother, Louise, tried to provide for the family by working as a domestic. Overwhelmed by raising seven children on her own, she collapsed and was institutionalized for the next thirty years until Malcolm initiated her release. The children were separated and moved among foster homes. Malcolm, soon on his own, moved from Detroit to Boston to Harlem. Gravitating to the streets, he became a petty criminal, hustling and depending on street smarts to survive. Malcolm was convicted of burglary and sent to prison in 1946 after a clumsy colleague precipitated his arrest.

Malcolm transformed himself during his six-year incarceration. Devoting himself to reading and learning, he joined the Nation of Islam, also known as the Black Muslims, under the leadership of Elijah Muhammad. After his release in 1952, Malcolm became the NOI's most identifiable leader other than Elijah Muhammad, who saw Malcolm as his acolyte and chose the mesmerizing speaker to lead Temple Number 7 in Harlem. Malcolm's eloquent declaration of devotion to Allah and fiery separatist rhetoric, along with his magnetic presence and unapologetic embrace of Blackness, boosted his stature. Malcolm became a familiar presence on Harlem streets as Temple Number 7 flourished.

Despite their differences, Mal and Malcolm shared critical core beliefs, especially their commitment to family and their anger over what African Americans endured. Each was tireless in confronting racial injustice and had developed sharp analyses of the forces oppressing Black people. They put themselves on the line every day, boldly and unabashedly, to secure justice. Nor was Mal blind to Malcolm's appeal. Although he was a steadfast integrationist, Mal realized that Malcolm's surging popularity was a sign that nonviolent resistance was falling out of favor, especially with Black youth. But Mal, ever the bridge builder, tried to prevent the civil rights movement from splintering by straddling its diverging positions. Realistic about these rifts, he knew that might be impossible, but he was determined to try.

Mal pushed Malcolm X to clarify his position when he invited him and his youthful protégé Cassius Clay for a tour of the United Nations in March 1964. After winning gold in the light-heavyweight division at the 1960 Rome Olympics, Clay had danced through the ranks of professional boxing, mixing poetry with devastating jabs. On February 25, 1964, the twenty-two-year-old Clay beat heavily favored Sonny Liston for the heavyweight title in Miami. He handled Liston for the better part of six rounds before the champ conceded and failed to come out in the seventh round.[4]

The sporting world was in disbelief, and the newly crowned champ's celebrity exploded. Boxing was enormously popular in the 1960s, and the February fight drew exceptional coverage, especially because it came during sport's dead season between the end of football and the beginning of baseball. Clay's style amplified his presence. Young and brash, he taunted his opponents with lyrical barbs, predicting the round he would take them down. Unapologetic, absurdly confident, and able to take a punch, he was Black pride incarnate. But many whites loathed him. The sports world had not encountered such an outspoken and flamboyant African American in decades. He reminded some of Jack Johnson, the first African American heavyweight champ, who was known for his prowess in the ring as well as his defiance of racial norms, especially when it came to his relationships with white women. After Johnson defended his title in a 1910 bout with Jim Jeffries, whites incensed over this challenge to white supremacy attacked African Americans in more than a score of cities.

But another dimension to the Clay story began bubbling to the surface. The young fighter was preparing to join the Nation of Islam. After meeting Malcolm at a NOI rally in Detroit in 1962, Clay began showing up when Malcolm spoke. The fighter invited Malcolm and his family to his February 1964 bout with Sonny Liston in Miami as a sixth anniversary present for the couple. "I liked him," Malcolm wrote. "Some contagious quality about him made him one of the very few people I ever invited to my home. Betty liked him. Our children were crazy about him. Cassius was simply a likable, friendly, clean-cut, down-to-earth youngster."[5]

The NOI initially denied Clay membership because his boxing career violated the group's rules, but his success in the ring softened Elijah Muhammad's position. Before the Liston fight, Ali joined

Malcolm in prayer. During the bout, Malcolm X sat near the ring as Clay's guest. Later that night, he and Clay, joined by NFL star Jim Brown and singer Sam Cooke, talked about the Black athlete's duty to align with the freedom movement. The evening foreshadowed the direction each was going to take. Brown, among the best football players ever, retired a season later. Brown, who Mal had befriended during his career when he was in the vanguard of African Americans integrating professional football, visited the Goodes when the Cleveland Browns played in Pittsburgh. He said he was leaving football because "I want to have a hand in the struggle that is taking place in our country, and I have the opportunity to do that now." Cooke had recorded what became one of the era's most iconic songs, "A Change Is Gonna Come," just weeks before the fight. By then, Malcolm X had quietly become Cooke's mentor. But at the same time, Malcolm was falling out of favor with Elijah Muhammad. His time in the NOI was coming to an end.[6]

A week after defeating Liston, Cassius Clay renounced his surname, dismissing Clay as his slave name. When he joined Malcolm at the United Nations for meetings and a luncheon with foreign dignitaries that Mal arranged, he declared he was now Cassius X. Warmly received by representatives from Mali, Congo, Liberia, and Gambia, Malcolm and Cassius explained their Black nationalist politics.[7] Mal could hardly conceal his pleasure while interviewing the brash young champion. Moving seamlessly from one question to the next, Mal interrogated Cassius, then Malcolm, and finally Nigerian ambassador Simeon Adebo. The ambassador told Cassius: "You are not now what you were before the fight."[8] As the first Muslim heavyweight champion, he mattered on the global stage and was no longer just an athlete. Mal, mindful of that, asked Cassius and Malcolm to connect their Muslim faith and the Nation of Islam with the African American condition and the UN mission. "Do you feel being a follower of the Muslim religion had anything to do with your winning the championship," Mal asked. "My religion is the only thing I can give credit for pulling me through," Cassius answered, "because 99 out of 100 people could see no possibility of me winning and condemned it as a mismatch."[9]

When Mal asked Malcolm his opinion of the United Nations as a body dedicated to brotherhood and world peace, Malcolm responded with approval. "As I heard you explaining to Cassius this afternoon about, first, the ability to sit down and discuss the problem, well, this is what makes the United Nations what it is. They discuss the problem. Whether they disagree or not, at least they discuss the problem." Pivoting to the United States, Malcolm argued: "But America needs to do the same thing on the domestic level where the race problem is concerned. They need to discuss the problem, but they don't need to discuss it with Uncle Tom whom they themselves have placed up as a spokesman for Negroes because that Tom is not going to say anything but what his master wants him to say and you can't get to the root of the problem by listening to some parrot say what you already told it to say." Lapsing into the rapid-fire delivery he used when delivering a speech, Malcolm continued. "So, the first thing they've got to do is to discuss the problem, analyze it, get to the root of it and then they can come to a solution. And the only one, the only black man in America, who will spell out the real causes and the facts of the problem is the Honorable Elijah Muhammad."[10]

Differentiating his views from those of civil rights leaders advocating integration, Malcolm maintained that only the Honorable Elijah Muhammad understood the race problem and spoke the truth that would help the Black man. Mal asked Malcolm to "clear up" why so many people think members of the Nation are "purveyors of hate." Malcolm grinned and declared that Cassius is the "most likable, friendly person in the world and has been following the Muslim religion for the past four to five years. I think you'll find all people who follow the Honorable Elijah P. Muhammad have the ability to make friends with everyone." Where then, Mal asked, did this misconception come from? Malcolm grinned as he looked at Mal, leaned into the microphone, and said: "the press."[11]

Mal pushed Malcolm to clarify whether he was a member of the Nation of Islam in good standing, given speculation to the contrary. Malcolm did not equivocate. He answered that he still belonged to the NOI. But not for long. The interview was unlike the grilling Malcolm typically encountered. He was more relaxed talking with Mal, who gave him the chance to express his views without making him defensive.[12] Despite the inner turmoil that Malcolm was experiencing, he came across as composed and upbeat.

That moment of calm ended abruptly. Three days later, on March 8, 1964, Malcolm X broke with Elijah Muhammad and the NOI. Malcolm had grown increasingly disillusioned with Elijah Muhammad both personally and ideologically. "I remain a Muslim," Malcolm told the *New York Times*. "But the main emphasis of the new movement will be black nationalism as a political concept and form of social action against the oppressors."[13]

The catalyst to Malcolm's suspension was his controversial comment about the assassination of John F. Kennedy. After the president's death on November 22, 1963, Malcolm stated that his assassination was a case of "the chickens coming home to roost." Elijah Muhammad, Malcolm said, had misinterpreted those remarks. Malcolm said he was referring to a prevailing atmosphere of social hatred that had encouraged violence, including Kennedy's assassination. He connected JFK's death to the savagery the United States was inflicting elsewhere in the world, particularly the nation's support of a coup in Vietnam in which President Ngo Dinh Diem and his brother were murdered, just weeks before Kennedy's death. But Elijah Muhammad used it as a pretext to silence Malcolm, whose rift with the NOI had been widening for months. Elijah Muhammad had been unsettled by Malcolm X's growing celebrity among militant Black youth. "Envy," Malcolm said, "blinds men and makes it impossible for them to think clearly. This is what happened."[14]

Malcolm X remained a devout Muslim, but his departure from the NOI meant he was no longer obligated to comply with its demand to stay at arm's length from the civil rights movement. although he was critical of the nonviolent movement that King led, Malcolm said: "I am prepared to cooperate in local civil rights actions in the South and elsewhere and shall do so because every campaign for specific objectives can only heighten the political consciousness of the Negroes and intensify their identification against white society." Calling the "Negro revolution" a deception that had accomplished little, he added: "I shall tell them what a real revolution means—the French Revolution, the American Revolution, Algeria, to name a few. There can be no revolution without bloodshed, and it is nonsense to describe the civil rights movement in America as a revolution."[5]

The day after his expulsion, Malcolm X sat down for an interview with Mal. Malcolm seemed to relish his freedom from NOI orthodoxy and, with characteristic self-possession, critiqued the nonviolent movement. "Well," he said with a roguish grin, "they're doing the best they know how, and I think they're probably doing it as they see it. I don't agree with their method of operation, nor with their objectives. Some of their objectives I agree with, but most of them I don't agree with." Mal shot back. "*What do you agree with*, Malcolm?" Malcolm responded: "If they are against the injustices that are running rampant in the Negro community. . . . If they have a program to eliminate alcoholism or drug addiction or . . . to eliminate the deteriorating housing conditions . . . I mean if they have a program that will show us how to uplift our own community and keep our own community at a high level—then I go along with that." Malcolm's new sense of pragmatism was evident. When civil rights groups came up with plans that would uplift Black communities, he would be on board.[16]

Free to speak without adhering to Elijah Muhammad's dictates, Malcolm delivered what many consider his most important and prophetic address a few weeks later in Cleveland. At the Cory Methodist Church on April 3, 1964, he offered a warning. Noting that the title of his talk was "The Ballot or the Bullet," Malcolm said that the choice of one or the other was self-explanatory. Thanking Elijah Muhammad for opening his eyes to Islam, Malcolm declared: "I'm a Muslim minister, and I don't believe in fighting today on any one front, but on all fronts. In fact, I'm a Black Nationalist freedom fighter." Most of his remarks underscored the importance of electoral politics and building Black economic power. "We must know what part politics play in our lives," he said. "And until we become politically mature, we will always be misled, led astray, or deceived or maneuvered into supporting someone politically who doesn't have the good of our community at heart." Black people must open their eyes and become "more politically conscious, politically mature." And then, "whenever we are ready to cast our ballot, that ballot will be cast for a man of the community, who has the good of the community at heart."[17]

But, Malcolm stated, "The government has failed us. You can't deny that. Anytime you're living in the 20th century, 1964, and you walking around singing 'We Shall Overcome,' the government has failed you. This is part of what's wrong with you, you do too much singing. Today it's time to stop singing and start swinging." When the laughter and applause subsided, Malcolm described the upsurge of nationalism that liberated most of the African continent from colonialism. If the twenty-two million "Afro-Americans here in this country" wanted to get colonialism off their backs, they needed to adopt Black nationalism, as had African freedom fighters. "And 1964," he warned, "looks like it might be the year of the ballot or the bullet. . . . Negroes have listened to the trickery and the lies and the false promises of the white man now for too long, and they're fed up." That has led to a degree of pent-up frustration "that makes the black community throughout America today more explosive than all of the atomic bombs the Russians can invent." That racial powder keg, Malcolm warned, could easily explode. A few months later, it did.[18]

"This is why I say it's the ballot or the bullet. It's liberty or it's death. It's freedom for everybody or freedom for nobody. . . . I hope that the white man can see this. 'Cause if you don't see it you're finished." After predicting that US forces could not triumph in Vietnam, Malcolm concluded by encouraging his audience to join whatever churches or organizations, including the NAACP, that were advancing their common struggle. "Join any organization, —civic, religious, fraternal, political or otherwise that's based on lifting the Black man up and making him master of his own community.[19]

Malcolm then delivered the same message in Detroit to a crowd of two thousand people before departing for a five-week sojourn to the Middle East and West Africa. His travels brought him an epiphany. In Saudi Arabia, he fulfilled the hajj, the pilgrimage to Mecca that devout Muslims seek to make during their lives. There, he realized that Islam embraced diverse people regardless of race and that the faith was based upon unity and universal respect. "In my thirty-nine years on this earth, the Holy City of Mecca had been the first time I had ever stood before the Creator of All and felt like a complete human being," he wrote.[20] In many ways Malcolm returned to the United States much the same, a devout Muslim intense in his resolve. What had changed was his perception of the race problem. At the airport in Frankfort, preparing to board for Cairo, he observed: "Throngs of people, obviously Muslims from everywhere, bound for the pilgrimage [who] were hugging and embracing. They were of all complexions; the atmosphere was warm and friendly. The feeling hit me that there really wasn't any color problem here. The effect was as though I had just stepped out of a prison." Malcolm wrote that he would "return to the United States . . . with new, positive insights on race relations," and that while in Mecca, "for the first time in his life he had felt no racial antagonism toward whites nor had he sensed any antagonism on their part against him."[21]

Malcolm kept Mal apprised of his itinerary while abroad and let him know when his Pan American flight would arrive in New York City. Before Malcolm returned, he called Mal. "I remember seeing a replay of Dad's overseas call with Malcolm X," Bob Goode recalled. "Malcolm was about to return from his pilgrimage to Mecca and the technology was very primitive by today's standards. The visual was a map of eastern US to North Africa with a photo of Dad on the phone in a circle by New York City and a marker showing the location of Malcolm X. The audio was the conversation between them. I believe this was one of the first times the network broadcast a live intercontinental call."[22]

Upon his return, Malcolm X announced the creation of a new Black nationalist organization, the Organization of Afro-American Unity (OAAU). Like Mal, Malcolm had been impressed with the Pan African approach of the Organization of African Unity and made it the model for the OAAU. It emphasized Black control over Black communities and focused on social and political concerns, including housing, education, drug addiction, and voter registration. Malcolm

257

also wanted to make Africa—its history and culture as well as its post-colonial problems and prospects—real to African Americans. These were dramatically different issues than those topping the NOI agenda. Malcolm said that whites were not welcome to join but quipped that "If John Brown were still alive, we might accept him."[23] He also declared that he "would lead his newly formed black nationalist organization into the forefront of the civil rights struggle."[24] These sentiments brought Malcolm closer to how Mal perceived the world. According to Bob Goode, Malcolm called his father upon his return from Mecca and told him, "Mal, you were right."[25]

But if Mal was willing to challenge Malcolm, Malcolm in turn questioned Mal's core beliefs. Mal had grown up in a family and social milieu that subscribed to W. E. B. Du Bois's notion of the Talented Tenth. The African American community's best-educated, most upwardly mobile members were destined to lead the struggle. That ideology underlay the NAACP, of which Mal was a fervent, lifelong advocate. Malcolm's radical adherence to achieving change "by any means necessary" and his emphasis on racial separatism tested Mal's assumptions about integration and nonviolent struggle. But Mal hoped these positions would now converge.[26]

As much as Mal was willing to follow King, he could not dismiss Malcolm as a reckless provocateur. Malcolm's separatist rhetoric had attracted a sizeable following, and his radicalism made King's approach more palatable to mainstream Americans. Encouraged by Malcolm's break with the NOI, Mal felt that Malcom X was evolving in ways that could forge greater unity in the movement. And then, less than a year later, on Sunday February 21, 1965, Mal found himself on the streets of Harlem reporting Malcolm's murder.

The assassination shocked the nation and devastated Harlem, but it was sadly in sync with the times. Another long hot summer was already on the horizon. The firebombing of Malcolm's home the previous Sunday had foreshadowed his assassination. It underscored divisions among militant Black groups that could turn deadly. J. Edgar Hoover's FBI Counter-Intelligence Program (COINTEL) had exacerbated these tensions as it broke laws to harass radical groups. COINTEL covertly financed white nationalist extremists who attacked antiwar groups and incited Black militants to attack each other by forging threatening documents and spreading disinformation that had them at each other's throats.[27]

After the murder, Mal tirelessly canvassed Harlem, gauging the despair he saw on people's faces and heard in their voices. He had been on these streets a few months before, after James Powell's death triggered a week of devastating outbursts. Deeply troubled, Mal feared more violence, but he did not surrender to the disquietude pervading the streets. His friendship with Malcolm persuaded Betty Shabazz to talk with him. Unlike most of the reporters covering the assassination, Mal was concerned about the family that Malcolm had left behind and wanted to allow her to tell her story. They spoke the next day as she left the city's Office of the Chief Medical Examiner. Betty Shabazz had a kerchief tied around her hair; her eyes were sad and partially shut. "Did he ever discuss with you the likelihood that he would be assassinated?" Mal asked. "Yes, we discussed it many times," she answered. "Several attempts had been made on his life. The police and the press tried to make it look like he bombed his own home, which was ridiculous. I mean, he had no insurance on the furniture or himself or anything like that, and now I guess they'll say he shot himself." As they spoke, with Mal holding the microphone close to her face, she seemed to come alive.[28]

"Mrs. Betty Shabazz is naturally bitter about the murder of her husband," Mal reported afterward, "but she is also bitter because of charges made last week that Malcolm actually staged the bombing of their home. She complained, too, because the press charged her husband with receiving financial support from Red China. 'We have no money,' she said. There are four children and she expects a fifth one in the fall."[29] To her surprise, she had twin girls.

They spoke again in a lengthy interview that focused on how Malcolm's worldview changed after his trip to Mecca. "Malcolm wanted to internationalize the race problem" through his new organization, she explained, and she insisted that he respected Dr. King. Her husband, Shabazz declared, believed in self-protection, not violence, and "came to realize the world was made up of many different colors of people and all must work together for peace and normal living."[30]

Mal got little sleep that week. He took the measure of Harlem's mood, subtly inserting his own perspective into his coverage. "A tense quiet in Harlem," he reported:

> Mrs. Malcolm X made another visit to the bier of her husband last night while the curious and those who admired him also passed through the Unity Funeral Chapel . . . just a few steps from the spot where Malcolm swayed hundreds in outdoor meetings with his fiery oratory. The man on the street is worried . . . some fear the memorial service planned for 125th Street Thursday may trigger repercussions. Malcolm's murder, the firebomb that destroyed Muslim headquarters on 116th St, and bomb threats have stunned the Harlem community. The hope is that quiet can continue, with no retaliation, and authorities bring to justice those responsible for the crime.[31]

The question on the street was who had killed Malcolm. Mal, like others, suspected that the NOI had been behind the assassination, but he was careful not to spread speculation regarding what had happened. "The tenor in Harlem last night, even from those who disagreed with Malcolm, is that the guilty must be punished." Mal applauded Malcolm's political evolution, reasoning that "his toned-down attitude on hatred for whites, his more recent agreement with other civil rights leaders and pleas for joint action, improved his image."[32]

Mal feared that in their distress, Harlemites would turn against each other. He canvassed the streets the night before Malcolm's funeral and witnessed an altercation at Bunny's Wig Shop on 124th Street. Bunny Jones was frustrated that a small band of picketers had blocked the entrance to her shop because she had refused to close operations after Malcolm's death. The picketers chanted "lock her up," and claimed that Jones came to the door with a shotgun threatening

to shoot them. After the police calmed everyone down, Mal continued to walk the streets, like a chaperone making sure all were safe.
He concluded the day by noting: "Harlem quiet with some degree of
tenseness. If there is trouble it will most likely occur after the funeral
Saturday." With that, he told his crew to pack it in at 10:45 pm.[33]

Mal covered Malcolm's funeral at the Faith Temple Church of God
on Saturday, February 27, where Ossie Davis delivered a stirring eulogy. The activist and actor told attendees that "Harlem has come to
bid farewell to one of its brightest hopes—extinguished now and gone
from us forever. . . . Many will ask what Harlem finds to honor in this
stormy, controversial and bold young captain—and we will smile."
Davis answered his own question. "Malcolm was our manhood, our
living, black manhood! This was his meaning to his people." By honoring him, he said, we are honoring "the best in ourselves." He read
from a letter that Malcolm had written a friend while in Africa the
year before. "'My journey is almost ended, and I have a much broader
scope than when I started out, which I believe will add new life and
dimension to our struggle for freedom and honor and dignity in the
States. . . . The main thing is that we keep a United Front wherein our
most valuable time and energy will not be wasted fighting each other.'
However we may have differed with him," Davis said, "or with each
other about him and his value as a man—let his going from us serve
only to bring us together now."[34]

Mal could hardly have agreed more, but he knew that Malcolm's
death would make that harder to accomplish. Davis ended his eulogy
with uncommon eloquence. "Consigning these mortal remains to
earth, the common mother of all, secure in the knowledge that what we
place in the ground is no more now a man—but a seed—which, after
the winter of our discontent, will come forth again to meet us. And
we will know him then for what he was and is, a Prince, our own black
shining Prince, who didn't hesitate to die, because he loved us so."[35]

Malcolm X's assassination was a prelude to prolonged turmoil,
not a catalyst for peace and sober reflection. And Mal was in the

thick of it. As riots broke out, Mal covered them, but he wanted to move beyond scenes of tumult and destruction so that viewers would see the underlying poverty and discrimination that caused them.

That brought him back to Mississippi in the summer of 1966. When Henry Hampton produced his acclaimed documentary series *Eyes on the Prize*, he titled one episode: "Mississippi, Is This America?" After the murders of Emmitt Till and Medgar Evers, the rise of White Citizens Councils, and countless mind-numbing atrocities, many had their doubts that it was. Despite the Mississippi River Delta's rich alluvial soil and prosperous cotton crop, African Americans living there were mired in poverty. For them the 1964 Civil Rights Act and the 1965 Voter Rights Act were hollow victories, doing little to raise their standard of living or deliver any semblance of political power. If anything, conditions were deteriorating as mechanization wiped out their jobs in the cotton fields and threw sharecroppers and tenant farmers off the land.

In 1962, James Meredith, an Air Force veteran trying to make the state live up to the US Constitution, defied segregation by enrolling at the University of Mississippi. Four years later, after receiving his degree, Meredith set off alone on what became known as the March Against Fear. He planned to walk 220 miles through the Mississippi Delta to protest the abysmal poverty plaguing African Americans and persuade them to register to vote. But on June 6, 1966, the second day of the march, Meredith was shot by a sniper and hospitalized. The assassination attempt spurred civil rights organizations to carry on Meredith's campaign. Dr. King, his close SCLC collaborator Andrew Young, SNCC chairman Stokely Carmichael, and other organizers joined the march. They walked side by side along Route 51 during the day and hotly debated movement strategy in the evenings. While united by their stand against racism, they differed in age, temperament, and ideology; those fissures soon split the movement.

As the March Against Fear captivated much of the nation, Mal organized ABC's coverage. There was nobody else at the network so plugged in to the civil rights community, especially in the South.

Mal spent hours on the telephone, then shared his contacts, telling correspondents how to reach spokespeople in towns along the route. Mal let them know what he considered newsworthy and helped them understand the backstory they might otherwise miss.

Aaron Henry alerted Mal to a memorial service for Medgar Evers, who had been slain three summers before. Evers, the NAACP's first field secretary in the state, had played a critical role in Meredith's fight to gain admission to the University of Mississippi. He told Mal that after the service, attendees would join the march. Charles Evers, who replaced his brother at the helm of Mississippi's NAACP, declared: "We may catch Hell but we're going to see this thing through." Mal impressed upon ABC news directors that carrying Meredith's campaign to a conclusion could trigger a political earthquake in the state. He made sure they understood the psychological dimensions of the struggle. "A successful march," he stressed, "will have great impetus on the movement to eliminate the awful fear which has gripped most parts of Mississippi since Reconstruction days." Ever attentive to political power, he underscored the importance of registration efforts in Jefferson County. Voter registration could make the landmark 1965 Voting Rights Act more than words on paper that were routinely ignored in southern states. He pressed ABC to highlight the gains achieved, not just the setbacks endured. "Jefferson County has 9,000 residents and 7,000 are Negroes," he pointed out. "Today there are 3,485 Negroes registered to vote and last Tuesday almost every registered voter went to the Polls."[36] Flipping the county would generate enormous momentum.

As the march entered its second week, Mal stayed in touch with activists in Yazoo City, Belzoni, Canton, Tougaloo, Greenwood, Swifton, Louise, Lake City, Berryville, and Itta Bena. His memos included the walk's day-by-day route and phone numbers for organizers in each town along the way. One contact was Tougaloo College president George Owens, who Mal explained was the first African American to head the school and "more forthright on Civil Rights than most Negroes in similar school positions." Some phone numbers were for funeral homes and furniture stores, which relayed messages to organizers in the field. ABC personnel in the field would have been lost without Mal's guidance. Mal alerted crews to where trouble was expected. Charles Darden, the NAACP's former state chairman, warned him that violence could break out in Belzoni, where "they have driven all the NAACP and Civil Rights workers out." Mal made sure his ABC colleagues knew something about Belzoni, where in 1955 the local NAACP president, the Reverend George Lee, had been murdered in his car as retaliation for trying to register Black voters. "No one was ever tried, or even arrested for this murder," Mal related. "It is still considered a difficult area and we should be prepared for a possible confrontation between 'locals' and the marchers when they reach Belzoni about the 19th."[37]

After organizing coverage from afar, Mal joined the march before it reached Jackson, its final destination. His crew filmed protesters making their way through Winona, Vaiden, and Durant, their feet crunching in the gravel alongside the highway. White bystanders waved at the camera while African Americans looked on impassively, most unwilling to be interviewed. Many of the marchers would never return to Mississippi, but those living there feared retribution after the camera crews left.

Some marchers looked exhausted; others determined and jubilant. One sixty-eight-year-old man said he had lived his entire life in Mississippi. When asked what he thought about Meredith's march, he responded: "I feel it's going to be a great help to us, and so far, we have come quite a few miles ahead." The man observed that while many Blacks were reluctant to register and vote, "It seems like a lot of them have, you know, overcome that, and come on in and registered." When asked if he had registered, the man said: "That's right." Would he vote on August 8th? "Believe it!" What lay ahead? Mal asked. The man smiled and answered unequivocally: "We're going to overcome. There *ain't* no other way but to overcome."[38]

A second man, forty-four, declared: "It's going to show that there's going to be no more fear amongst the Negro race. If we can march in Vietnam, we can march in the state in which we were born. . . . We have a right to march here and I don't think we have a right to march over in Vietnam." Despite the specter of violence, he exclaimed: "This is a wonderful thing! I think we need a little more marching. There will be no more fear with the Negroes. We have some few that have fear but the majority of the Negroes? No fear whatsoever!" Mal let them have their say, before asking what town he was in and telling his cameraman to film a nearby Coca-Cola sign that read: "COLORED POOL ROOM." Then, without notes or pausing to think about what he would say, Mal delivered his closing:

I have just talked with two men who have lived in the state of Mississippi all their lives, one forty-four and one sixty-eight. Both are in agreement with Jim Meredith. They believe that his march is going to help to dissipate the climate of fear that has been in existence. Both of these men are registered and plan to vote in the state elections on August the 8th. I've traveled this tour for three days now with Jim Meredith and there's no question that there has been a climate of fear in the past. There's also no question that Jim Meredith's march is going to have a great deal to do with eliminating that fear. Here in Durant, Mississippi, less than forty miles from the capital of this state, there are the remnants of discrimination and segregation. Just to my left is a pool room which has a sign that says colored, C-O-L-O-R-E-D. There's still some places in this area where Negroes cannot be served meals, but they're permitted to spend their money in the other business places.

This is what Jim Meredith's march against fear is all about. The general feeling of more than sixteen people I've talked with so far in the past three days—five white, and eleven Negro, is that Jim Meredith is right in this particular march. I talked with a twenty-year-old white boy yesterday who said not only that he has a right to march, but that Negroes have the same rights and privileges as others. You heard the statement of this man a few moments ago . . . who says that if Negroes have a right to march in Vietnam, they have a right to march in Mississippi. They have a right to freedom in the state of Mississippi. This is Mal Goode, ABC news, forty miles from Jackson, Mississippi in a town called Durant.[39]

Mal exposed ABC's audience to those striding along the macadam road, not just their leaders. He showed them singing and clapping in unison to a gospel song whose lyrics had been adapted. Rather than march into "glory land" or "heaven land," they were seeking freedom land. "*Ain't* gonna let nobody, turn me round, Lord, turn me round, turn me round. *Ain't* gonna let nobody, turn me round. I just keep on a-walkin,' keep on a-talkin,' marching up on freedom land." Mal joined the marchers, mostly women, teenagers, and children, with a few whites, as they filed into a church where a man preached. "I'm getting madder and madder and madder. Every time I look into a white cracker's face and he seems to look so pleased. He looks like life is good for him and he gonna be that way forever. He doesn't have to worry about us no more, things so good." The speaker concluded: "Well, this country belongs as much to my people as it belongs to anybody! And there's no reason that we shouldn't have everything in it that we deserve."[40]

But the movement was divided over how to make that happen and by the time Mal joined the march, tensions over strategy were exploding. After SNCC chairman Stokely Carmichael was arrested and briefly detained in Greenwood, Mississippi, he spoke to fifteen hundred marchers at a local park. There, he called for the movement to embrace Black power. "We been saying freedom for six years and we *ain't* got nothing," he declared. "What we got to start saying now is Black Power! We want Black Power."[41] Those sentiments had been building within the movement, especially among younger activists. Malcolm X had anticipated the emergence of a more violent, separatist arm of the movement that was no longer willing to embrace nonviolent civil disobedience and cross-race alliances. Now, with national media covering the march, the notion of Black Power reverberated across the country. Although King was still the movement's most visible and acclaimed leader, Carmichael, H. Rap Brown, and other younger leaders were pushing for a militantly separatist direction, and they were gaining traction.

After marchers left Greenwood, a sharecropper from Marks, Mississippi, named Armistead Phipps collapsed and died along the road from a heart attack. That brought Martin Luther King Jr. to Marks, a town he would never forget. After King delivered Phipps's eulogy at the Valley Queen Baptist Church, Marian Wright Edelman escorted him and the Reverend Ralph Abernathy through the town. Edelman, who became King's counsel during the 1968 Poor People's Campaign and later founded the Children's Defense Fund, was working with the NAACP Legal Defense Fund in Mississippi. She took King and Abernathy to a Head Start program in Marks that had lost federal funding. "After watching the teacher divide a single apple into quarters for four hungry children at lunchtime," Edelman recalled, "Dr. King uncharacteristically broke down in tears and had to leave the room. Later, he said to Dr. Abernathy, 'I can't get those children out of my mind. . . . We can't let that kind of poverty exist in this country. I don't think people really know that little school children are slowly starving in the United States of America. I didn't know it.'"[42]

Hungry children with bloated bellies were inescapable in Marks, where Black children attended school sporadically. Students left the classroom in March and April and again in July and August to work in the cotton fields, planting, weeding, and picking cotton. A year later, Edelman brought Senator Robert Kennedy to Marks, where they talked about how to stress poverty in their civil rights efforts. She conveyed their conversation to King. "I told him that I'd just seen Robert Kennedy and he had seen the hunger of children in Marks." When she told King that Kennedy said bring the poor to Washington, he "lit up like a light bulb." Those visits to Marks by King and Kennedy, as well as Marian Wright Edelman's intervention, caused King to adjust his priorities. They were the genesis of the Poor People's Campaign, which brought King back to Marks and caused Mal to make his own pilgrimage there two years later.[43]

The following summer, in 1967, Mal found a message at work that James Meredith had called. He was returning to Mississippi the next day to repeat part of the previous summer's march and wanted Mal to join him. Mal quickly headed south. "I walked and rode eighty miles with James Meredith and witnessed a brand of hatred almost unbelievable," he reported.[44] He went from small town to small town, interviewing marchers and spectators, mindful of the threat from police and men brandishing Confederate flags who glared at him. But he was willing to engage with them, too. By then, Mal had been at ABC for five years. He had covered riots, assassinations, demonstrations, and funerals, while quickly acquiring the skills to succeed in the industry. Mal recognized that he had given voice to those who had long been ignored. But he was frustrated; he knew he could do more.

10

ON THE FRONT LINES

IN JULY 1967 PRESIDENT LYNDON JOHNSON EMPANELED the National Advisory Commission on Civil Disorders, what became known as the Kerner Commission, to study the riots that had erupted each summer since 1964. A month later, ABC president Elmer Lower turned to Mal Goode for advice about the media's role in those upheavals. Mal answered quickly, forecasting much of what the Kerner Commission would conclude the following February. The United States, the commission warned, was "moving toward two societies, one black, one white—separate and unequal" and American cities were careening toward "apartheid."[1] It was a scathing indictment of the deeply embedded racism causing urban centers to explode. The report was prescient; a month after its release Martin Luther King Jr. was assassinated, triggering a cascade of riots in 125 cities leaving at least 46 dead, 2,600 injured, and incalculable financial, structural, and emotional devastation.

The Kerner Commission, like ABC's Lower, probed how well the media were covering these urban rebellions. But unlike Lower, the commission's conclusions were biting and offered concrete recommendations to improve coverage of civil disturbances. The report described a "significant imbalance" between media coverage and urban reality. "We found that disorders, as serious as they were, were less destructive, less widespread, and less a black-white confrontation than most people believed."[2] Interviews of "ghetto residents and middle class Negroes" revealed they believed reporters focused more on police and officials "than on what Negro citizens or leaders are doing or saying."[3] Media coverage, it added, was often at odds with how the residents of affected communities perceived the disorders. The report claimed that the press had relied on unreliable sources, including local officials who were inexperienced with civil disorders. They were not, the commission observed, "always able to sort out fact from rumor in the confusion."[4]

Many Black inner city residents told commission investigators that they viewed the media as little more than an extension of the white power structure which consistently portrayed Black people unfairly and failed to cover the widespread efforts of Black residents to help the police and those wounded during disturbances. According to the commission report, African Americans trusted mainstream print media the least and television the most, not because it was more "sensitive or responsive to Negro needs and aspirations but because ghetto residents believe that television allowed them to see the actual events for themselves. Even so, many told researchers . . . they noted a pronounced discrepancy between what they saw on the street during the riots and what they saw on television."[5]

The Kerner Commission focused on the lack of Black representation and called mainstream media "shockingly backward in seeking out, hiring, training, and promoting Negroes." It blasted tokenism and declared that "Negro reporters are essential, but so are Negro editors, writers and commentators." African Americans, it concluded, must hold positions allowing them to influence media policy and its coverage of Black communities.[6] This had always been Mal's mantra.

Since walking through the doors of 47 West 66th Street six years before the Kerner Commission issued its report, Mal Goode had challenged conventional media's assumptions about race and their coverage of Black America. He was always willing to call out anyone he thought was slighting him or anyone else because of their race. When he read Elmer Lower's memo in August 1967, he realized that, after five years of jousting at windmills, he might be seeing his primary goal at the network coming within reach.[7] Lower sought Mal's counsel regarding how he should respond to charges that the media had sensationalized the urban rebellion rippling across the land. Turning to his only African American correspondent, he posed the question that Mal had been trying to place on ABC's agenda: How should the network cover Black America? Mal had nudged and prodded producers to realize there was more to Black America than riots and rhetoric, but he had not been able to persuade them to comprehensively cover the Black experience. As he read Lower's memo, Mal finally sensed he was being taken seriously, and maybe so would the African American community.

When Mal joined ABC in September 1962, there were no African American mentors to smooth his transition from self-taught radio newsman to network correspondent. Nor was there any seasoned Black journalist to help chart his course toward professional success or to define what a breakthrough in media might mean for the race. But Mal's drive and the expectations of Black Americans that his success should matter for them, too, compelled him to do both. A self-made man with a blue-collar background whose grandparents were born in slavery, Mal was a blend of his father's toughness and his mother's pursuit of education and racial uplift. He mastered television reporting and network protocols in short order and, at 60 years of age, was no stranger to negotiating pitfalls on the job. Striding into hostile crowds, confronting foreign despots, or interviewing white supremacists gave him little pause. But he had struggled to define the role he could play as a broadcast pioneer. Although success at ABC filled him with enormous satisfaction, he held barrier breakers to higher standards. What, Mal asked, could he do for the race from his position as a national media figure?

Mal saw himself as maintaining Black journalism's tradition of informing Black audiences while advocating for the race. James Mc-

Grath Morris, who wrote about the Black press and the pioneering journalist Ethel Payne, observed that through national crises and triumphs, the Black press had "unremittingly chronicled racism, eloquently protested injustices, impassionedly educated its people, and remained—like most African American institutions—completely out of sight of white America."[8] Mal experienced this mission at the *Courier*, but he ran into walls each time he attempted to crack local Pittsburgh television stations. His career embodied the changes of the postwar period. The dismantling of legalized segregation forced white mainstream society to recognize the realities of racial injustices and pressured white institutions to include Black voices. When the riots in the 1960s brought racial problems to the front page, Mal was positioned to report on them for ABC.

In the late 1960s, Black journalists—in print, on the radio, and those breaking into television—still faced an uphill battle. Mal was blazing that trail, as were other Black journalists and non-air staffers at outlets across the country. They often risked personal and professional peril, but putting themselves on the line did not necessarily win them respect and fair treatment on the job. Those like Mal, who were determined to make the leap to television, had little company if they were successful. They were consistently excluded from the big stories and were sent to cover racial conflict zones that were considered too dangerous for white reporters. Robert Richardson was working as an advertising messenger for the *Los Angeles Times* when violence erupted in Watts in August 1965. He walked into the newsroom late on the second night of the disturbance to share what he saw happening in his neighborhood. The all-white staff welcomed his firsthand observations since, according to one reporter, "we had no blacks on staff at the time, and he gave us a much needed measure of credibility. He was bright, observant, and hard working." He delivered dispatches from a phone booth in Watts and within a week was listed as part of the "news staff." After the Watts riots cooled, he was kept on staff but was assigned the night shift to cover fires, or "the disaster desk," as Richardson dubbed it.[9] According to the *New York Times* reporter Earl Caldwell, putting Black people—prepared or not—into the center of racial uprisings was referred to as "battlefield commissions. They'd send you right on out."[10] Black reporters were useful to white editors at mainstream outlets when their race served a specific purpose, typically to fill a token role, to cover a riot, or to deliver "Black" stories. But they could not access positions of authority that allowed them to shape the coverage of Black America.

News directors routinely assigned Black reporters stories with the expectation that their reporting would confirm racial stereotypes. Norma Quarles was the morning anchor at WNBC in New York when she was assigned a story on "welfare mothers." She profiled a white woman and was asked "back at the office. . . . How come the welfare mother is white? We thought she was going to be black." Quarles explained: "there are more white women and children on welfare than there are blacks" to her disgruntled producer. "I fought that all the time," Quarles concluded in an interview for *Cosmopolitan* in 1986.[11] Max Robinson, who became the first Black national co-anchor when he held that position at ABC from 1978 to 1983, was deeply committed to exposing injustices and improving conditions for Black people. As a journalist he had always confronted discrimination and was not about to stop fighting when in the anchor's chair. When a story on home buyers didn't include a single person of color, Robinson raised his concern. A colleague replied: "but Max, it has nothing to do with black people."[12]

Penetrating that ignorance was a constant struggle. Mal and his cohort of barrier breakers struggled to expand respectable coverage and confront racial stereotypes while advocating for a strong Black presence on air. Mal Goode demanded that ABC pay attention to African Americans beyond moments of conflict. He relentlessly pitched proposals to cover grassroots politics, Black enterprise, and community initiatives, pushing ABC to examine the systemic problems plaguing African Americans and to focus on solutions.

Getting his bosses' attention was another matter. No matter how perceptive his memos were when suggesting stories, he got little feedback. Producers might have sensed that Mal was ahead of the curve—on the mark when he said that Massachusetts attorney general Edward Brooke would become the first African American elected to the Senate since Reconstruction, or that efforts underway in Cleveland might avert a riot like the one that had struck Watts in 1965. But his approach strayed from network orthodoxy about what to feature.

Mal searched for nuance and the dynamics of change in stories. Alabama, he told producers, was not defined solely by Governor Wallace's 1963 inaugural address proclaiming: "segregation now, segregation tomorrow, segregation forever." There was a counterpoint, he argued—Attorney General Richard Flowers. Paradoxically, Alabama voters had chosen Flowers, the governor's antithesis, in the same election that propelled Wallace into the statehouse. Flowers had prosecuted the KKK, pushed schools to desegregate, and won voting rights cases in the US Supreme Court that strengthened African Americans' grip on the franchise. Mal wanted to juxtapose the two men in a piece about the contradictions shaping Alabama. But this was not the sort of story that fitted easily into a nightly newscast. Covering a world in turmoil left ABC with little time to do what Mal wanted—proactively produce stories that plumbed poverty, depicted the Black experience, and showed how people could change the world.[13]

Mal followed up his poised performance during the Cuban missile crisis with polished interviews at the United Nations, fearless reporting from riot-torn cities, and appearances on ABC specials. He covered disarmament talks, Nikita Khrushchev's ouster in the Soviet Union, and the rebellion in the Dominican Republic that brought US troops there the same month in 1965 that US Marines landed in South Vietnam. Throughout it all, he remained focused on an honest portrayal of Black America, and the struggle for Black influence in newsrooms and representation on the air.

Mal was affable but relentless when digging into a story. Although he held Adlai Stevenson in high esteem, he cornered the US ambassador at the United Nations, peppering him with questions about the war in Vietnam. Nor did he pull punches when interviewing Papa Doc Duvalier, the Haitian despot whose Tonton Macoute paramilitaries coerced dissidents. After Duvalier was elected president in 1957, his rule devolved into a reign of terror. Reelected unanimously in 1961 in an election without opponents, Duvalier declared himself president-for-life. Mal knew that Duvalier would deflect his questions, but this didn't stop him from exposing the brutality keeping Duvalier in power. Mal asked why he had empowered his secret police force to kill enemies on sight, why Haiti's poverty was so deep, and whether Duvalier had banked huge sums of money outside the country, money given as US aid to Haiti. Did he consider Haitian refugees in the United States a threat to his regime? Would their relatives face retribution? Asking those questions, even if Duvalier evaded answering them, meant that Papa Doc's cruelty would not go unnoticed.[14]

Mal was not easily intimidated, knowing that the Tonton Macoutes couldn't touch him at the United Nations. But neither did Mal, tall, fit, and self-assured, evince worry about the danger he faced reporting in the South. To the contrary, he relished grilling infuriated segregationists or challenging militant Black radicals on camera. After growing up in Homestead, working in the mill, and serving as a probation officer, neither the United Nations, Congress, nor haughty police chiefs frightened him. He felt that the ABC logo protected him even more than his affiliation with the *Courier* had done in Pittsburgh. And he knew that the balance of power was shifting, weakening hard-core segregationists.

Encountering George Wallace in Manhattan in November 1963, Mal asked to interview him in Montgomery. Although a Black journalist was an anomaly in the governor's office, he persisted and finally sat down with Wallace two years later. Mal spoke about the interview on local radio, prompting parents of students at Booker T. Washington High School to visit Mal at the home of his Montgomery host, Dr. Moses Jones. Mal often tapped his fraternal connections and stayed at somebody's home when on the road. The parents had heard his exhortation on the radio to keep children in school to "prepare them for the new opportunities opening to Negro children." What they told Mal reinforced his concerns that, without better facilities, seizing opportunity would be difficult. He wrote Wallace, itemizing the disparities in resources for Black children and reminding the governor that he had lamented dropout rates for Black youth. "Don't count me as interfering," Mal wrote, subtly chiding Wallace's failure to adequately fund Black students' education. "I just thought you would like to have this information." Mal let few chances pass to raise matters concerning African Americans. He was emboldened by the surge in Black voting in Alabama that had persuaded Wallace to speak to him. Ever gracious, Mal thanked "My dear Governor," for the interview and invited Wallace and his family to visit the United Nations, where he would escort them on a tour, and then come to dinner at his home in Teaneck.[15] Wallace wrote back, thanking Mal for the invitation and telling him his staff would investigate his concerns. "Of course, we are very much interested in improving educational facilities, and I will see what can be done. I appreciate your calling this matter to my attention, and we will look into it immediately. . . . Come by the office again anytime you are in this area."[16]

The Wallace interview caused ripples in Alabama. "Since returning from Montgomery December 7, I've had letters from several friends who tell me Wallace is having a real 'change of heart,'" Mal explained in an ABC memo. "This is probably due to the tremendous increase in Negro voter registrations across the state since last August. At any rate, this guy is so vocal, and so personable, that I'm certain a forthright, no-holds-barred interview with him would be the talk of the nation." His bosses at ABC were astounded when Wallace offered Mal an exclusive when he left office on December 31, 1965. "With the proviso already agreed upon, that this would be a no-holds-barred session," Jack O'Grady wrote, "I think Mal could give him a good run for his money, and ours. I think it would be a hell of a way to start the new year on the race beat. Mal has personally assured me that he does not plan to pull any punches. . . . I think it will make a hell of a half hour."[17] But on the eve of the interview, Wallace's press secretary called to postpone after the governor had fractured his hand working out on a punching bag in Miami. He suggested rescheduling in late January. The second interview never happened.[18]

Mal connected with Wallace because they understood each other. Both maintained an aura of genial propriety even when dealing with steadfast opponents, and each understood political power. "I need not tell you George Wallace has changed his tune since 1963," Mal told a Black audience, "not because he got religion, but because 450,000 Black people vote in the state of Alabama."[19] That got Wallace's attention.

Mal recognized that a Black reporter questioning militant segregationists was good television and that it empowered African Americans. He showed up unannounced at the American Nazi Party's headquarters after an irate party member murdered its founder, George Lincoln Rockwell, in August 1967. Disconcerted by Mal looking them in the eye and smiling as he asked questions, the Nazis were thrown off-balance. His composed, straight-forward coverage won kudos from his bosses for "a job well-done."[20]

By then, the winds of change buffeting the nation had spurred sit-ins, freedom rides, and legislative battles. A greater focus on race was unavoidable, and ABC began paying attention to the issues Mal believed mattered—but never as much as he felt they warranted. Producers did not hesitate to send him into the fray. While not unduly confrontational, Mal never backed down, whether interviewing powerful politicians or furious people on Harlem streets after Malcolm X's assassination. His supervisors were especially impressed with his reporting from Newark during the Black Power Conference in July 1967.

The three-day event began days after the beating of a Black cabbie by the police triggered fierce rioting. Twenty-six people had died as Newark police, National Guardsmen, demonstrators, and looters clashed over four days. Network brass were jumpy about the reception their crews would receive at the conference, and the few white reporters there were barred from the proceedings. But Mal was welcomed inside the hall, and other reporters interviewed him so they could file their stories. When he questioned Rap Brown, Dick Gregory, and Floyd McKissick, the schisms troubling the movement quickly surfaced. Black nationalists called for a separatist agenda while McKissick, the CORE director, was quick to criticize other leaders. "The Civil Rights movement itself," he proclaimed, "is a thing of the past.... The struggle is not one of legal status [but] black power—political power, the use of the vote, use of buying power." When pressed, McKissick responded: "I'm not at variance with King or Roy Wilkins. I just think they are out of step with reality."[21]

Despite his ties to King, Mal knew that McKissick had a point. Soon after the Newark riots, trouble flared in the nearby city of Plainfield. Mal did a stand-upper for the nightly news. As the camera panned broken windows, angry crowds, and demolished vehicles, Mal spoke with the Reverend A. Ross Brent of the Shiloh Baptist Church, who said he had seen trouble coming after incidents with the police. "I can't see how it could have been avoided. Too much talk about a long hot summer planting seeds in minds that hadn't given it a thought." Trying to explain why Plainfield had erupted, Mal spoke to the camera: "Here in Plainfield, New Jersey, seventeen miles south of Newark, there's a population of fifty thousand. Forty percent is Negro. Last night's devastation is a sample of what happened in Newark. The format was the same. The causes, too, the same." Not enough had been done to improve schools and housing or create jobs. "One looks at Newark and Plainfield and concludes the obvious, there was no concern for the ghettoes. *Now* there is, after wanton destruction of property and more than twenty deaths in Newark. Why must we pay this high price to learn the obvious?" A week later, it was déjà vu in nearby Englewood, where First Baptist Church pastor Isaiah Goodman lamented: "We've been talking to the power structure for nineteen years. People here are forced to live like rats.... Two wrongs do not make a right, but conditions must be corrected!"[22]

Mal was on the air frequently that month. California congressman Lionel Van Deerlin requested a copy of a Black Power Conference story in which Mal reported that the fairly liberal Democratic representative had been targeted for defeat in the 1968 elections. "I would like to thank you in advance for your cooperation, and also, as a former newsman, to commend you for your initiative in recording the Black Power sessions under conditions which must have been—to say the least—highly adverse."[23]

Van Deerlin wasn't the only one who saw Mal as the go-to-guy when racial conundrums surfaced. So did ABC News president Elmer Lower.[24] When Sigma Delta Chi, the forerunner of the Society of Professional Journalists, asked Lower to address charges that television news was mishandling coverage of the riots and race relations at a forum in Buffalo in September 1967, he asked Mal how he should handle them. Lower, who assumed ABC's presidency a year after Mal was hired, had adroitly remade the network, tripling the number of correspondents, expanding nightly newscasts to thirty minutes, and bringing Peter Jennings, Ted Koppel, Frank Reynolds, and Sam Donaldson aboard. He later became dean of the University of Missouri School of Journalism, where he had been a student. His 2011 *New York Times* obituary praised him for turning ABC, long dismissed as the "Almost Broadcasting Company," into a respected news operation. But ABC and the other networks were under attack for provoking trouble and exacerbating rebellion.[25]

Criticism ramped up after television crews were charged with encouraging people to play to cameras to boost ratings during the 1965 Watts riots. A reporter was accused of telling a boy: "Hey Kid! Throw a rock! Throw a rock! Throw one!. . . . I haven't seen you do anything yet!" Other reporters coached youth to pose in threatening ways. Footage of looting was blamed for bringing more people into the streets, prolonging disturbances, and spreading trouble. Polling confirmed that a large percentage of white respondents believed that news about a riot prompted "copycat" rioting. With the frequency and intensity of outbursts increasing, Lower knew that the issue would not disappear. Besides, the accusations had some merit.[26]

Perplexed, Lower turned to Mal, noting the unique role he played for ABC. "I would greatly appreciate your detailed thoughts on what should go into such a speech," he wrote. "This is important to all of us. I urge you to give it your most serious thought."[27] Mal obliged. This was the opening he wanted. Describing encounters from Syracuse, New York, to Jackson, Mississippi, Mal responded that people often blame "us for the demonstrations and for the riots . . . some even accuse us of 'making' Stokely Carmichael and Rap Brown." Race had not shielded Mal from criticism coming from Black militants. "It's not easy to interview a Carmichael as I did last May in Cincinnati, ask him why he is 'leaving a trail of blood and violence wherever he goes' and then hear one of his colleagues say: 'Now you've got your news, take it back to whitey!'" His interview with Mattias Koehl, the ex-Marine neo-Nazi who succeeded Rockwell as president of the American Nazi Party, was also unsettling, forcing him to maintain his cool when faced with racial hatred. "It's not easy to ask a Matt Koehl on the porch of the Nazi Party headquarters in Arlington, Virginia: 'Have you found your members increasing since the riots?' and have him answer 'Yes, we have and we are determined to stop the Black Revolution as our Commander would have wanted us to do.'"[28]

But those blaming journalists for provoking trouble, Mal countered, "must remember the News Media did not 'make' a Carmichael nor a Rap Brown any more than we 'made' a Martin Luther King, a Whitney Young, a Lester Maddox, or a Ralph McGill. These men are newsmakers, whether we like them personally, their philosophies, or the causes they represent." Mal's three-page singled-spaced memo stressed that journalism's mission was to "present them and their philosophies and permit the viewing, listening, and reading public to make up their own minds and reach their own conclusions."

Lower, whose journalistic credentials were impeccable, knew that. But Mal urged him to be as forceful as possible, contending that, without coverage of civil rights, "many of the changes for the better would hardly have come about." Mal reminded Lower that racial inequities on the job, church bombings, voter suppression, inner-city squalor, lynchings, and police brutality had long existed. "But our media," he said, "dramatized them so forcefully that inept and apathetic Americans finally realized the printed words of Booker T. Washington, Walter White, and W. E. B. Du Bois earlier in this century . . . were not words of fantasy, but facts."

The media, Mal stressed, made America's racial dilemma real to people who would have ignored it. "We showed the pictures and taped the voices and the sounds of the thuds to prove the same. There's no distortion when the picture records someone smashing one of our cameras, or a thug tossing a brick at a group of innocent marchers, or a criminal tossing a Molotov cocktail into the store window of a reputable businessman or a policeman flaying a woman with a night-stick . . . it is all there, recorded for the viewing public to see." Mal could stay within the tight confines of a radio or television spot, but his fingers galloped over the keys of his typewriter as he answered Lower. "Neither is there any distortion when our cameras and tape recorders follow National Guardsmen searching a home in Plainfield, or record a Senator moving through a plantation walking with hungry children with distended stomachs, or a Mayor walking through alley-ways cluttered with garbage and rats skipping along the curbstone. These are the 'facts' of life, raw as they may be, and show clearly the need for solutions."

Although Mal believed that the media could not shy from upheav-al, what he wanted the most was greater balance in their approach. He called it journalism's greatest shortcoming. "I just cannot believe the public wants only 'blood and thunder' and 'X marks the spot where the body lies.' I believe our viewers, our listeners, would also like to have more of the constructive side of the news." Mal wanted ABC to spotlight efforts like Operation Breadbasket or President Johnson's Plans for Progress for which his son Bob was working while on leave from Mellon Bank.

"Our task is not to inflame," Mal concluded, "yet there are times when adequate and proper coverage can do no less. . . . It is my honest conviction that Americans are strong enough to 'take' the news as it happens, without sugar coating and without any cover-up. This is the only way we can ever right those conditions which are wrong, correct the evils which exist."[29]

Lower toned down Mal's language but affirmed his arguments. His remarks in Buffalo, later placed in the *Congressional Record*, con-tended that the media had covered the "long hot summer" of 1967 both credibly and responsibly. "Racial problems are the biggest news of this generation," he said, making it incumbent on ABC to thor-oughly cover them.[30] Addressing charges that reporters had incited people to jack up ratings, Lower painstakingly laid out the ways in which the networks had avoided fanning the flames. He detailed ABC's conduct in half a dozen hotspots the previous summer. The network had endeavored to ensure comprehensive coverage that informed audiences, particularly during trouble, so that citizens could navigate their lives safely. And he maintained that it had minimized demonstrators playing to the camera.

He agreed with Mal that demonstrations had become "part of the American scene" and must be covered. "Who created Stokely Carmichael?" he asked? "Who created Rap Brown? I really believe that these two agitators have gotten under the skin of white man more than any colored person in memory. And by their irresponsible behavior, they have caused irreparable damage to the legitimate civil rights movement. But who created them?" Blaming the media, Lower argued, was naïve nonsense. To the contrary, media coverage had caused the public to repudiate them and their ideas. Not covering them would betray the public trust. The networks, he maintained, had a responsibility to cover this social revolution in all its manifestations, from looting and shooting to neighborhood cleanups and efforts to help dropouts. He stopped short of Mal's advice to credit their coverage for making African Americans and their problems palpably visible. Without that coverage, Mal had said, "many of the changes for the better would hardly have come about." Mal would have liked to see Lower go further than his boss did, but he was influencing ABC's coverage. This was deeply satisfying, even though he knew he was waging an endless fight to keep the focus on Black America.[31]

During his eleven years at ABC, Mal tried to shift the network's approach to Black America. But he also spoke directly to that community, crisscrossing the country on the lecture circuit. By the mid-1960s, he knew people just about everywhere he went. Some he had met on the road for the *Pittsburgh Courier* during the 1950s. Many were Alpha Phi Alpha brothers, Pitt grads, or NAACP members. Others showed up to embrace one of the only African Americans they had encountered on national television or radio. Mal never led an organization or authored a civil rights manifesto, but he was the glue that connected people in the archipelago of towns, cities, coal patches, and rural hinterlands comprising Black America. Mal brought them into dialogue with each other.

Mal relished each chance to speak, capturing audiences with his resonant voice, rhetorical flourishes, and biblical allegories. But his gift was communicating in ways that hit home. He was accessible, able to explain issues and why they mattered without talking down to people. Many found him mesmerizing and inspirational, especially when his emotions surfaced. They knew he spoke from the heart, and they came away looking at the world differently, remembering some of the evidence that built his case.

Mal especially treasured speaking to young people, where he combined lessons in African American history with political analysis and heartfelt podium-thumping homilies about faith and family. When students wrote, he replied, often at greater length than their missives to him. In addition to school assemblies, university forums, conferences, conventions, churches, and fraternal groups, Mal spoke to virtually every NAACP and Alpha Phi Alpha chapter in the country. By the time he left a city, he had a clear sense of its power structure and knew who to call when their locale was in the news. ABC counted on those connections.

Each event invariably triggered new invitations. After addressing more than five hundred Alpha Phi Alpha members in Columbus, Ohio, following the missile crisis, Mal basked in the ovation from proud fraternity brothers, who told him what watching him on ABC meant to them. Before leaving Columbus, he was invited to sixteen other cities.[32]

Raised in a culture that valued public speaking, Mal developed his own style of debating at Homestead High and around the table of his parents' home when he and his siblings held forth at Sunday meals. Mal used those oratorical skills on the behalf of the *Courier* and then on Pittsburgh radio. He could speak extemporaneously, arriving at the studio minutes before he went on-air, or work with a carefully edited text. By the time he decamped for Manhattan, his reputation as a fiery orator able to bring people to their feet extended far beyond Pittsburgh.

Shunning sectarianism, Mal prioritized unity and crossing racial boundaries, and this led to invitations to speak to white organizations willing to confront the race question. His bosses at ABC were more than willing to accommodate these requests, realizing that every time Mal spoke, he built their audience. And if Mal sometimes went offscript, they could live with that. Besides, trying to silence or constrain him would have backfired. He was able to maintain a professional demeanor on the air, but he bridled at any interference with what he said on the lecture circuit.

The talks boosted his income and helped send six children to college. Although making far more at ABC than he had in Pittsburgh, Mal believed that he was the network's lowest paid correspondent, a grievance that rankled. After living through the Great Depression, he and Mary never escaped its shadows. They kept close tabs on finances and counted on his honorariums. Still, Mal often waived his appearance fee of $250 plus travel expenses if talking to students or church groups and often turned NAACP honorariums into lifetime memberships in its chapters for family members.[33]

Appearances invariably generated follow-up—a request for advice, a copy of his remarks, or participation in a project. After Mal spoke at Tougaloo College in Mississippi, Thelma Sanders asked if he would connect her with Harry Belafonte, the talented and influential Jamaican American performer and activist who was a confidant of Martin Luther King Jr. "We are trying to raise money on this swimming pool I told you about," she wrote, explaining that authorities had closed the pools to block their integration after the passage of the 1964 Civil Rights Act. "The kids would love to have somewhere to swim and we need a pool on the campus anyway."[34] Could Mal convince Belafonte to perform at a fundraiser?

Public appearances boosted his ego and his reputation. Having worked in a steel mill until he was almost thirty, Mal felt compelled to advance his own career. He didn't expect anyone to do it for him and sent copies of speeches to people he wanted to meet. Vice President Hubert H. Humphrey received his commencement address at Alabama A&M, and Under Secretary of Commerce LeRoy Collins got a speech titled "We Ought to Remember" and an offer to assist his Senate campaign in Florida. Unable to help overtly because of his ABC position, Mal offered to write campaign literature and connect Collins with his contacts in the state.

He wrote LBJ after his 1965 State of the Union and again after the president's gall bladder surgery, letting him know that "Our family is praying that you will soon be up and about and as good as new real soon."[35] Mal added that he was honored to have spoken in twenty-eight cities for the President's Plans For Progress initiative and that his son, Air Force Captain Russell Goode, was stationed in Thailand. President Johnson replied that Mal's letter had deeply moved him. "I don't know your children but I feel—after reading your message—that I do. I am proud of them and you and will be praying with you for God's guarding hand to be on your son and all his comrades in Vietnam."[36]

Mal saw himself as a bridge builder. Sometimes, however, his anger and candor blew those bridges up. No stranger to Evansville, Indiana, he was on a first-name basis with its NAACP leaders when keynoting the chapter's fiftieth-anniversary celebration in September 1965. Most attendees knew Mal, but few anticipated they would be squirming before he finished speaking. Genial and quick to smile and joke, Mal was dead serious when lecturing and not adverse to confrontation. Emphasizing the tremendous progress African Americans had made, he warned against complacency and questioned their resolve. Mal pointed to the 1964 Civil Rights Act and the 1965 Voting Rights Act as historic victories and underscored the bravery of young people who were risking their lives registering voters in the Deep South. "They're going to win this battle in the South," he assured them, "but what frightens me is they'll win in the South before we win up here in the North!"[37]

"We no longer need to say to our children, 'Son, it's not for you, but someday it will be." Then he went for their jugular. "That's not to say that all is well." Shifting into reportorial mode, Mal cited Urban

League reports decrying racial disparities in income and horrifically high Black infant mortality rates. If these remarks would have made Evansville's chamber of commerce sweat, he saved his heaviest salvos for African Americans who failed to embrace the struggle. Extolling the courage of those who had lost their jobs, freedom, or lives registering to vote in the South, Mal excoriated northern Blacks who did not appreciate the power of the franchise. He scorned those who "sit at home and wait for some two-bit politician to drive up in a big black car and drive him two blocks to register or vote. The greatest gift you have is your right to vote!" he roared. They needed to use it.[38]

Mal condemned those who "made it" but turned their backs on others. "The successful Negro," he warned, is the greatest obstacle to moving forward. "He's real sickening." When asked to join the NAACP, they respond: "You don't need that. Work and you can make it. I made it. Nobody," Mal thundered, "made it on his own in this life! Everybody who had somebody to raise him, and others outside to help him, has an obligation to help someone else coming up. . . . If you have cousins down South who are not first-class citizens and you don't help them, then neither are you a first-class citizen!" Nor did athletes escape his vitriol. They're not in the major leagues "just because they're good enough" to play ball he said. "The NAACP put these boys there and they ought not forget it." This brought people to their feet.[39]

Although Mal was ecumenical about Black politics and abhorred infighting, he was an NAACP loyalist. Little, he argued, would have changed without its presence on the front lines, where some died and others were beaten and jailed. Mal, however, was not blind to rival groups coming to the fore. Nonetheless, he felt that the NAACP, America's longest-standing civil rights organization, had brought significant legal and political advances.[40]

Mal spoke in Pittsburgh later that year, appearing for the ninth time since he had left for ABC two years before. He began his lecture at the Wesley Center AME Zion Church by quoting the third-century B.C. Greek mathematician Archimedes: "Give me a lever and a place to stand and I will move the earth. Pittsburgh," Mal declared, is "the place where you can stand." No matter how much they had done, he said, it was not enough. He exhorted them to "keep driving to make this city the kind of place it ought to be for all of its citizens." That was standard fare for Mal.[41]

"You ought to know some of the shortcomings of YOUR city and Mine," he said, citing one dismal statistic after another: that only Detroit had a higher percentage of unemployed African Americans; that twice as many Black as white children died in infancy; and that 54 percent of African American renters lived in substandard dwellings. Few in Pittsburgh held professional, technical, or managerial positions, while more than one-third of families fell below the poverty line. In 1960, Mal said, 75 percent of Black Pittsburghers had not completed high school, leaving them in a "vicious cycle." Quoting Lorraine Hansberry's *A Raisin in the Sun*, he said, "It's like I can see the future stretched out in front of me just plain as day ... the future, Mama ... hanging over there at the edge of my days. .... Just waiting for me, a big looming black space ... full of nothing."[42]

Few institutions escaped his wrath. He targeted Pitt's medical school for quotas, city realtors for segregating neighborhoods, and local hotels for not according respect. "Our own self-respect and status as a nation and as a people demand that we eradicate these social carbuncles." Reprising Whitney Young's remarks, he warned that if the nation wanted to avoid "angry men in the streets, let us convert those streets from avenues of despair to highways of hope." As he spoke, listeners punctuated his remarks with exclamations of approval. For many, Mal was akin to a favorite preacher.[43]

Pittsburghers must struggle to achieve the "Four Freedoms," he said: freedom of speech and worship and freedom from want and fear. He quoted John Kennedy's 1963 civil rights message to Congress: "The Negro baby born in America today, regardless of the section or state in which he is born, has about one half as much chance of completing high school as a white baby born in the same place on the same day, one third as much chance of completing college, one third as much chance of becoming a professional man, twice as much chance of becoming unemployed, a life expectancy which is seven years less and prospects of earning only half as much in that lifetime."[44]

Pausing to let that sink in, he bellowed "AND SOME NEGROES SAY 'You're pushing too fast!'" He berated "the lucky ones whose bellies are filled, and subsequently turn their backs on the needy." New laws alone would not bring fundamental change. "The true enemies are the appalling interlocking vicious cycles of abject poverty, ill health, leading to school drop-outs, school drop-outs due to lack of skills, lack of skills to poor jobs or no jobs, no jobs leading back to the lower income and then back to the sickness which the people cannot afford to cure. . . . This is the unfinished business which the Civil Rights bill does not remedy." Reminding them that the fight against injustice must be waged relentlessly, Mal repeated: "THIS IS YOUR PLACE TO STAND, PITTSBURGH!" This was where they should use Archimedes' lever.[45]

For Mal, the Great Society was the next great leap forward. After winning election in 1964 and gaining large congressional majorities, Lyndon Johnson revamped the nation's domestic agenda. Seeking to build on FDR's New Deal, Johnson called for a Great Society, one that "rests on abundance and liberty for all [and] demands an end to poverty and racial injustice, to which we are totally committed in our time."[46] Johnson used his mandate to push through a staggering array of programs, including Medicare, Head Start, urban mass transit, federal aid to education, environmental legislation, and the War on Poverty.

Mal could see the impact these reforms would have domestically, but he also wanted Pittsburghers to be global citizens. He argued that the United States had the potential not only to resolve its domestic shortcomings but also to harness its technological and medical capabilities to eliminate poverty, disease, and illiteracy elsewhere. "Equality is the guiding principle of this century," he declared. "What we decide to do, we can do! . . . We can accomplish what we aim at and our aim should be equality under the law for all our citizens. GIVE ME A PLACE TO STAND AND I CAN MOVE THE WORLD. MY FRIENDS, THIS IS *YOUR* PLACE TO STAND."[47]

Mal leveraged his roots in Black sport to encourage athletes to commit to civil rights. He implored them to raise their voices and open their wallets when interviewing them in Pittsburgh. Others had kicked back with the Goodes in Belmar Gardens, the city's Black housing cooperative where the family lived before leaving for Teaneck. They savored Mary's cooking after ballgames and relaxed in polo shirts and chinos in the front yard afterward. Perched on the hillside, they looked out at the city and at felt at home.

When Donn Clendenon was a freshman at Morehouse, his "big brother" was alumnus Martin Luther King Jr. A terrific athlete who received offers to play professionally in three sports, Clendenon gravitated to baseball and finished second in the 1962 National League Rookie of the Year voting. That December, he wrote Mal from Puerto Rico, where he was playing winter ball, to congratulate him for his debut on ABC. "Mal, you know, I am quite proud of you. Your accomplishments have given all of us a thrill. You are and have been an asset to our race. Keep up the good work, my blessings and prayers are for you."[48]

When Mal asked Clendenon to get involved, it wasn't a hard sell. Henry Aaron felt the same way. After a brief stint with the Indianapolis Clowns in the Negro Leagues, the Mobile, Alabama, native forged a Hall of Fame career. He, too, had sat at the Goodes' table and regarded Mal as a mentor, especially when it came to politics. They spent time together whenever the Braves visited Pittsburgh, where Mal took him to an NAACP meeting that prompted Aaron's lifelong commitment to the organization. "I've always felt closest to the NAACP," Aaron observed, "because it was there at the beginning."[49] Mal also showed Aaron the city. "I was walking Downtown with my two boys, Kerry and Dennis," *Pittsburgh Post-Gazette* columnist Joe Browne recalled, "and I ran into Mal, who was with Hank Aaron, then at the height of his career. My boys were pop-eyed. Hank Aaron! Mal, always kind to kids, introduced them to the great home run hitter—who, too, was super nice to Kerry and Dennis—and invited the boys to a ballgame to see Hank play." Before the game, Mal took them to the dugout. "You have to be a father—or mother—to know how grateful I was to Mal."[50] So was Henry Aaron, who years later at an Urban Scouting Dinner in Pittsburgh years said: "I don't know where I would be today without people like Mary and Mal Goode."[51]

When Mal asked Aaron to join the National Sports Committee and back the NAACP Legal Defense Fund, he quickly agreed. The all-star ensemble, which included Mal, Buddy Young, Monte Irvin, Joe Black, Sam Lacy, and Bill Nunn Jr., met in May 1966 to tap athletes' celebrity with a wider audience. Buddy Young, a National Collegiate Athletic Association (NCAA) track champion at the University of Illinois, had played in the NFL. Monte Irvin, a Negro League and National League All Star, was inducted into baseball's Hall of Fame in 1973. Joe Black, another Negro Leaguer, was the 1962 National League Rookie of the Year with the Dodgers. Veteran sportswriter Sam Lacy, the first Black member of the Baseball Writers' Association of America, was voted into the writers' and broadcasters' wing of the Hall of Fame. Mal and Nunn had worked together at the *Courier*, where Nunn's father, who had played with the Homestead Grays before becoming the paper's editor, was Mal's mentor. Bill followed in his father's athletic and journalistic footsteps before joining the Pittsburgh Steelers' front office. There, he tapped Black college football, boosting their Super Bowl ascent. Nunn was inducted into the Pro Football Hall of Fame in 2021.

Mal told Aaron that the NAACP Legal Defense Fund needed ball-players to step up and cover legal fees, especially in the South. "Many seem to feel the battle is over when actually it is just really beginning.... there is a hard core of people in this country who just do not want Negroes to have total equality. There's still much to be done."[52] Mal also reached out to Jackie Robinson and Willie Mays. He wrote Mays that while there were more than five hundred Black professional athletes, many had little sense of the battle waged to make it possible for them to play professionally and be well compensated. "Few of them know about players like your Dad, Ernie Banks' Dad, Josh Gibson, Martin Dihigo, and hundreds of other great players who were not permitted in the major leagues in their day." Mal's efforts paid off. In January 1967, Bill Russell, Bill White, and Gale Sayers, the Sports Committee's cochairs, announced its agenda. More than ever before, the athletes he knew—Aaron, Muhammad Ali, Roberto Clemente, and Jim Brown—were making themselves heard on and off the field.[53]

In hundreds of speeches to a total audience he counted as being upward of 150,000 people, Mal never followed any particular organization's line. He was free with his criticism, but he avoided polemics and sought common ground with those working for civil rights. That struggle came first. Apprehensive about white backlash and enduring poverty, Mal relished both small breakthroughs and game-changing victories, especially the Civil Rights Act in 1964 and the Voter Rights Act of 1965. Moreover, in Martin Luther King Jr., Mal had found his North Star, the leader who could take his people across the River Jordan to the promised land. But King could be a vexed figure for Mal, forcing him to wrestle with long-held views about foreign policy and the Cold War. King spoke out against the US presence in Vietnam in March 1965, long before antiwar sentiment had reached critical mass. That made him an outlier, even among civil rights leaders.

Few in the United States could have found Vietnam on a map in the late 1940s, much less thought the French colony mattered to American interests. That the United States wound up waging counter-insurgency warfare somewhere in the world after World War II was hardly surprising. But fighting an insurgency in Vietnam was tragically difficult. Those at the helm of the US government and military knew almost nothing about Vietnam—its history of conflict with China, France, and Japan, its Buddhist culture, its Mekong Delta topography, or its languages. Their sense of warfare was based on combat in Europe and the South Pacific during World War II. No one heeded T. E. Lawrence's warning that "to make war upon rebellion is messy and slow, like eating soup with a knife." Few even knew of Lawrence till Peter O'Toole played him in *Lawrence of Arabia*, and even then, they ignored the challenge of suppressing insurgency in a distant land.[54]

The United States could have had Ho Chi Minh on a platter, Archimedes Patti, an OSS agent who met often with the Vietnamese leader reflected.[55] Instead, President Harry Truman considered France a bulwark against Soviet aggression in Western Europe and backed its military efforts in Vietnam as a quid pro quo. But the French, unable to quash Vietnamese independence forces, abandoned the colony after the catastrophic defeat at Dien Bien Phu in 1954. The peace conference in Geneva that followed divided Vietnam pending an election and reunification in 1956. Until then, Ho Chi Minh, a founder of the Indochinese Communist Party, would lead in the North, and Ngo Dinh Diem, an anti-communist Catholic, would rule in the South. Rather than exit Vietnam gracefully, subsequent US presidents sank deeper into the quagmire. When Diem refused to hold the election in 1956 that Ho Chi Minh would easily have won, President Dwight Eisenhower backed him.

In 1961 John Kennedy challenged citizens in his inaugural address to "ask not what your country can do for you," but rather, "what you can do for your country." By then, US forces were fighting guerrilla fighters and North Vietnamese regulars entering South Vietnam along infiltration routes known as the Ho Chi Minh Trail. Kennedy increased aid despite Diem's authoritarian bent and lack of popular support. Diem's heavy-handed repression of opponents and widespread corruption did little to win Vietnamese hearts and minds. Realizing Diem was losing his grip on power, the United States blessed a coup d'état in early November 1963 in which he was killed. After Kennedy was assassinated later that month, Lyndon Johnson maintained US commitments lest the nation be perceived as weak.

The United States, however, was not winning the war, and Mal began to see that. Stymied by resistance from National Liberation Front guerrillas and North Vietnamese regulars, Johnson ramped up the US military presence in March 1965. The same week that King was declaring his opposition to the war, the US Air Force launched Operation Rolling Thunder. Bombers attacked North Vietnam, attempting to disrupt the flow of fighters and supplies heading south. Planned as an eight-week operation, Rolling Thunder lasted three years.

Days after Rolling Thunder began, the first US Marines landed in South Vietnam. Deploring the escalation, King urged Johnson to negotiate a settlement.[56] Wary that his antiwar stance could derail support for the Voting Rights bill, King tried to avoid rupturing ties to the president. Endorsing administration efforts to begin talks with the North Vietnamese government, he couched his antiwar stance as a moral question.

Mal was not sure what to make of this. His oldest son, Captain Malvin Russell Goode Jr., had deployed to Southeast Asia that August as part of Rolling Thunder. Only his superior officers called him Malvin, and that was only on formal occasions. Everyone else called him Russ. Stationed in Thailand, Russ oversaw communications with aircraft sent to bomb North Vietnam. For the next year, he directed crews communicating with pilots as their fuel tanks were topped off while in the air heading to drop zones. After a period of radio silence, his team resumed contact as the pilots returned to base. Many never made it back. Nor did Rolling Thunder deter the infiltration of fighters and supplies into the South or force North Vietnam to submit. Mal and Russ hardly spoke about the war during the rare times they were together. Russ knew his father was proud of his service and eventual promotion to major, but like his brother Bob, a Marine reservist, he could see his father's growing unease over the war.[57]

King was ever more certain that the United States was making a tragic mistake. Unlike civil rights leaders who separated the war from domestic problems, King tied them together. He focused on the war when he spoke at the University of Pittsburgh in November 1966. An overflow crowd of one thousand, the largest ever to hear a speaker at the student union, rose to greet him when he strode into the room. Hundreds unable to find seats stood against the walls or listened to loudspeakers in nearby hallways. King connected Vietnam to racial and economic justice. Mustering his oratorical skills, King reasoned that "if the United States could spend 24 billion dollars a year to fight the war in Vietnam and almost as much to put a man on the moon, then billions could be spent to upgrade the Negro. Some people," he declared, "are more concerned about winning the war in Vietnam than they are about winning the war on poverty right here at home. I must say to you, no matter how much I'm criticized for it, I never intend to adjust to the madness of militarism."[58]

Nonviolent protest, King argued, remained the "most potent weapon" in the fight for equality. A riot, he said, was "the language of the unheard." But it was an understandable reaction to indifference. Because the nation had failed to "listen to the plight of the poor Negro," King reasoned, winters of delay had become summers of riots.[59]

King spoke frankly, acknowledging tensions within the civil rights movement and a growing white backlash. Mal, whose perspective on foreign affairs had changed during his UN posting, was moved by King's passion and appreciated how he connected domestic realities to global matters.[60] Though not at Pitt for King's speech, Mal heard about it from friends. Many were unsettled by King's strong language about Vietnam. Uncertain about the war but not ready to oppose it, they wanted to know what Mal thought. He had always considered himself a patriot and opposing American foreign policy was difficult, but King was the most compelling figure in his life. "My suspicion," Russ Goode said, "is that he followed Martin Luther King on Vietnam."[61]

For King, ending the war became a priority. In Chicago that March, he declared that as "bombs in Vietnam explode at home—they destroy the dream and possibility for a decent America."[62] A few days later, he ducked out of an SCLC board meeting to confer with Muhammad Ali, who had announced he would refuse his army induction orders. Ali told King that he might defy Elijah Muhammad's proscription against participating in politics and speak at the Mobilization Against the War in April 1967.[63]

On April 4, 1967, King addressed three thousand people at the Riverside Church in Manhattan. Decrying the "deadly Western arrogance" destroying Vietnam, King claimed that "we are on the side of the wealthy, and the secure, while we create a hell for the poor." Mal agreed with his analysis. King saw Vietnam as a reflection of America's colonial approach. The United States, he said, had made "peaceful revolution impossible by refusing to give up the privileges and the pleasures that come from the immense profits of overseas investments." He blamed the war for taking young Black men "crippled by our society and sending them eight thousand miles away to guarantee liberties in Southeast Asia which they had not found in southwest Georgia and East Harlem."[64] These were concerns Mal shared.

King, never more impassioned, called for the United States to declare a unilateral ceasefire and to extricate itself from the conflict. Antiwar activists applauded his remarks, but editorial writers at the *New York Times* and the *Washington Post* excoriated him, arguing that King was undercutting his advocacy of civil rights.[65] They called his arguments faulty and simplistic. Even the NAACP and Ralph Bunche decried King's stance.[66]

Mal instinctively leapt to defend King who, undeterred by public censure, stood with 150 young men burning their draft cards in Central Park on April 15, 1967, and then joined Harry Belafonte and pediatrician Benjamin Spock at the head of ten thousand demonstrators who marched from there to the United Nations. Addressing the crowd, King said, "I speak out against it not in anger but with anxiety and sorrow in my heart, and above all with a passionate desire to see our beloved country stand as the moral example of the world." Mal, who preached an ethic of peace, endorsed those sentiments even as he covered the protest. "In his speeches," Bob Goode recalled, "my father often said: 'There will be no peace in the world until there is peace in the hearts of men.'"[67]

Mal was no longer simply a correspondent. He had become a public intellectual whose opinions about the state of the nation were solicited. A confidant of Martin Luther King Jr., Jackie Robinson, and scores of activists and civic leaders, he was a link to older generations and struggles. In March 1968, the House Subcommittee on Labor requested his testimony during hearings on a bill to create a National Commission on Negro History and Culture. Blurring the line between journalism and activism, Mal joined James Baldwin, Betty Shabazz, Jackie Robinson, and scholars to call for a museum of African American history. By unearthing the largely neglected saga of African Americans, the museum could begin the arduous task of restoring them to the mainstream of US history.

Mal spoke about his own education in Homestead, which had written African Americans out of American history. Their role in the making of the country had been ignored or caricatured. Historians Carter Woodson and E. Franklin Frazier, Mal explained, made it possible to recapture and reimagine the past, demolishing the racist mythology about slavery and Reconstruction that had been created by *Birth of a Nation, Gone with the Wind,* and a legion of apologists for the Confederacy. Mal recalled *Birth of a Nation*—a grotesque caricature of African Americans and glorification of white supremacists—playing in Homestead in 1916. Even then, its twisted portrayal of history and its corrosive effect on popular culture appalled him.

Mal disputed these versions of the past by offering the congressional subcommittee a counternarrative. He described critical junctures when African Americans had made a difference, detailing the number of Black soldiers who died in Korea or who served in Vietnam. He loaded his remarks with evidence, something he had favored since debating in high school. But his data was designed to buttress more polemical arguments. The commission, he argued, could address "a deliberate void in our nation's history [and] help narrow-minded and bigoted Americans" understand how central African Americans were to the national saga. This was familiar ground for Mal, who often lectured on Black history. "The history of Africans and Americans of African descent has been belittled, ignored, and submerged in the education of black and white children in this country," he testified. "Because of it, this very day we are tortured with a threatened revolution that emanates from the struggle of black Americans for human rights and dignity. That revolution has already cost the deaths of almost 100 persons and property damage that approaches a billion dollars, and the end is not in sight unless we move rapidly toward the establishment of equality with a capital E." Pausing for emphasis, he concluded: "The Negro is not challenging basic American values. He wants to join the system, not upset it; he wants to come into the house, not bomb it, and he feels an inherent right to come into that house because he helped to build it."[68]

Jackie Robinson, addressing the committee after Mal, called his friend the embodiment of progress: "I remember when they were looking for a guy to go on ABC. It was a tremendous thing for them to choose a man like Mal Goode. I knew him to be the fighter that he is. He won't say and do things simply because it is going to push Mal Goode." That's why he asked Mal to join the committee supporting the legislation he chaired. Though neither Jackie nor Mal lived long enough to see their campaign bear fruit, President Barack Obama opened the National Museum of African American History and Culture on the Mall in Washington, DC, in 2015. But Mal made it to the Mall in the spring of 1968 when the Poor People's Campaign set up camp there.[69]

Jackie Robinson, ever more outspoken about politics, confided in Mal. By then, Jackie was engaged with Africa, and he tapped Mal's understanding of the continent and his contacts. Robinson had chaired the Emergency Conference on South Africa in 1960 when it condemned apartheid and colonialism. In February 1968, he and Boston Celtics star K. C. Jones issued a statement protesting South Africa's readmission to the 1968 Olympic Games, and a raft of prominent athletes affixed their names. Jackie and Mal conferred about the politics of sport, especially the boycott that African American athletes were organizing to protest the upcoming 1968 Mexico City Olympics.[70]

Drawing ever closer to King, Mal met him in Newark in late March. After the previous summer's riots there, South Side High School's class president, seventeen-year-old Winthrop McGriff, wanted to bring a speaker to campus to help students make sense of the outbursts. He spoke with his grandfather the Reverend William McGriff, who wrote a telephone number on a piece of paper, handed it to him, and said call it. When Winthrop did, Martin Luther King Jr. answered. King, who respected William McGriff, the pastor at Canaan Baptist Church, readily agreed to speak.

King told Mal he had another reason for the Newark trip. "I'm here seeking support from my brother ministers and their churches for the Poor People's March. We're going to dramatize the hunger and poverty that exists in a rich country that grows enough food to feed the world." Neither the Civil Rights or Voting Rights Acts had reduced poverty.[71] Moreover, Lyndon Johnson's anti-poverty efforts were sputtering. King hoped that a campaign of nonviolent civil disobedience would make it impossible to ignore poor people and would press Congress to act.[72]

The Poor People's Campaign reflected King's shifting priorities. "I'm fighting not just for blacks," he told Mal, "but for whites and for Indians, for Mexicans, Puerto Ricans, Chicanos—whoever. Nobody should ever be hungry in this country. Nobody!" Mal, who had grown up straddling social divides within the Black community, knew that poverty transcended race. An anti-poverty campaign could cross racial lines and a poor people's coalition, if successful, might become a powerful force for change.[73]

As King preached and fourteen hundred mostly Black and Hispanic students listened, Mal marveled at his ability to reach them. King spoke of Memphis, where he had gone earlier that month to support Black sanitation workers who struck after two coworkers were crushed to death on the job. He described the Poor People's Campaign and linked inequality to the war in Vietnam. Appropriating some of the rhetorical flourishes of Black power militants, King's voice, rich and resonant, rose in volume as he implored them to "Burn, baby, burn! Burn that midnight oil!" King peppered his lecture with references to Jackie Robinson, Joe Louis, and prolific inventors Elijah McCoy and Garrett Morgan. "King talked to those kids about who they were, and the contributions blacks had made to building this country," Mal recalled. "He wanted them to get ready and prepare for their coming years. They mobbed him as he left the school, coming close to shake his hand or just to touch him."[74] Mal valued every encounter with King, but Newark left an indelible impression. It was the last time they talked.

Vietnam remained a paramount concern for King, who argued that racism, poverty, and the war were the nation's most pressing problems and could not be disentangled. On March 31, days after he spoke in Newark, King preached to three thousand people at Washington's National Cathedral. In the last sermon he ever delivered, King called US intervention in Vietnam "one of the most unjust wars that has ever been fought in the history of the world."[75]

By then, Mal echoed King on the war. When addressing the Foreign Affairs Council in Philadelphia in 1968, he couched his disapproval of the war in scripture. "Just how far are we," Mal asked, from "the love that would cause us to beat our swords into plowshares and our spears into pruning hooks?" He condemned "the awful holocaust of Viet Nam" and criticized all sides for failing to resolve it. "We have no right to be there in the first place and we ought to come on home for we cannot police the entire world. Moreover, the facts prove conclusively that we are really not wanted there." A big nation, he argued, would admit its mistakes. "In Viet Nam," Mal said, "we made a tragic mistake that has already cost us 28,000 boys, 200,000 wounded, billions of dollars and a nation divided against itself."[76]

Although Mal rarely covered the war and missed more of King's speeches than he heard, he tracked the conflict and King's peripatetic agenda. On March 31, days after speaking with King in Newark and hours after King's sermon at the National Cathedral, Mal joined those watching President Johnson address the nation from the Oval Office. Seated at his desk, Johnson announced the United States would unilaterally cease attacks on North Vietnam and seek peace through negotiations.

Johnson's address came after the Tet Offensive in January had shaken the president's resolve. Coordinated attacks by NLF guerrillas and North Vietnamese forces, while not sparking the uprising they anticipated, shattered the US administration's claims that the war was being won. Almost sixteen thousand US soldiers had died and one hundred thousand were wounded in 1967 alone and there was little to suggest that 1968 would be any better.[77] Support for the war was crumbling even among Johnson's closest advisors. In a special report after Tet, CBS anchor Walter Cronkite delivered a dire warning as he ended the broadcast. "To say that we are mired in stalemate seems the only realistic, if unsatisfactory, conclusion."[78]

Johnson was under duress from all sides. The Kerner Commission, which had examined the riots shaking the country, had released its report a month earlier, citing racial inequality as their cause. "What white Americans have never fully understood," it stated, "but what the Negro can never forget—is that white society is deeply implicated in the ghetto. White institutions created it, white institutions maintain

it, and white society condones it."[79] Nor was Johnson immune to criticism within his own party. Minnesota senator Eugene McCarthy,
challenging Johnson for the Democratic Party's presidential nomination on an antiwar platform, had rocked the president by winning
42 percent of the votes in New Hampshire's primary election in mid-
March. Bobby Kennedy by then had resigned as attorney general
and won election as a senator from New York. McCarty's showing
prompted Kennedy to enter the race.

Johnson followed his declaration of a unilateral halt to the bombing with an even more unexpected announcement. "With America's
sons in the fields far away, with America's future under challenge
right here at home, with our hopes and the world's hopes for peace in
the balance every day, I do not believe that I should devote an hour
or a day of my time to any personal partisan causes or to any duties
other than the awesome duties of this office—the presidency of this
country." After giving his audience a chance to absorb what he said,
Johnson continued. "Accordingly, I shall not seek, and I will not accept the nomination of my party for another term as your President."[80]

King, encouraged by Johnson's new stance, addressed an audience
at the Mason Temple in Memphis in support of striking sanitation
workers on April 3, 1968. After speaking at length and discussing some
of the threats he had faced in recent days, he said: "I don't know what
will happen now. We've got some difficult days ahead. But it really
doesn't matter with me now. Because I've been to the mountaintop."
The audience, rising to their feet, interrupted him with cheers and
applause. "And I don't mind," King continued when the crowd stilled.
"Like anybody, I would like to live a long life; longevity has its place." As
he spoke, rain pounded the Mason Temple roof. "But I'm not concerned
about that now," King declared. "I just want to do God's will. And he's
allowed me to go up the mountain. And I've looked over. And I have
seen the promised land. And I may not get there with you, but I want
you to know, tonight, that we as a people will get to the promised land.
So I'm happy tonight. I'm not worried about anything. I'm not fearing
any man. My eyes have seen the glory of the coming of the Lord!"[81]

Mal never forgot those words.

FIGURE 13. Mal Goode was hired by ABC news director James Hagerty in 1962, making him the first Black correspondent on network news. Photo courtesy of E. Azalia Hackley Collection of African Americans in the Performing Arts, Detroit Public Library National Automotive History Collection, Detroit Public Library.

FIGURE 14. Mal Goode with Nigerian foreign minister Jaja Wachuku in Lagos, Nigeria, during his tour of Africa in 1963. Photographer unknown. Courtesy of the Goode Family.

FIGURE 15. In the summer of 1963, Mal led seminars for media in Ethiopia, Tanganyika, and Nigeria. He returned with a better understanding of the difficulties facing newly independent countries as they emerged from colonial rule. Photographer unknown. Courtesy of the Goode Family.

FIGURE 16. Mal Goode providing his son Robert with a personal tour of the UN Security Council Chamber. Mal offered countless personal tours of the United Nations for family, friends, colleagues, and acquaintances. He was popular with the staff who grew accustomed to his tip of the hat and greeting by name. Photographer unknown. Courtesy of the Goode Family.

FIGURE 17. Mal Goode interviewing Andrew Young, year unknown. Young worked close-ly with Martin Luther King Jr.; he and Mal interacted frequently throughout Mal's long career in journalism. "There was nothing eccentric about Mal," Young recalled. "He was around, he was reliable, he was accurate, and he was lovable." Photographer unknown. Courtesy of the Goode Family.

FIGURE 18. Mal Goode interviewing Bayard Rustin, one of the key organizers of the March on Washington in 1963. Photo by George Rowen. Courtesy of the Goode Family.

FIGURE 19. Mal Goode at the United Nations, likely in the late 1960s. "The U.N. is," Mal avowed, "the last, best hope for man. That includes man's hope for his civil rights, because the two, the U.N. and civil rights, go hand-in-hand." Photo by Max Machol. Courtesy of the Goode Family.

FIGURE 20. The Goode family at son Richard's wedding to Lois in 1967. Mal was delighted to have the "6 Rs" together. He caught the photographer and asked him to take a picture, leaving the bride out of the frame. The photographer captured the family's laughter as they looked toward their new sister-in-law. Photographer unknown. Courtesy of the Goode Family.

11

AND THEN MARTIN

MAL WAS AT THE AIRPORT IN SYRACUSE, NEW YORK, ON THE
evening of April 4, 1968. His flight from Washington, DC, had landed
early, giving him time to relax before heading to a speaking engagement. Afterward, he would catch a flight back home and spend some
time with Mary before calling it a day. Savoring the down time, Mal
ducked into an airport restaurant. He had been on the go for months,
covering the wave of rebellion and upheaval that had begun with the
Tet Offensive in January. Shattering any claim that the United States
was winning the war in Vietnam, Tet dissuaded Lyndon Johnson
from seeking reelection and instead to begin negotiations with North
Vietnam to find a peaceful end to hostilities. As antiwar forces gathered momentum, the Democratic Party fell into disarray. Alabama's
former governor George Wallace, the country's most prominent hard-
line segregationist, was attracting surprising support in the North as a
third-party candidate and Republican Richard Nixon was rising like
a phoenix from the ashes of electoral defeats. Mal was in the thick
of it. A student rebellion in Paris in May, Prague Spring, campus
uprisings on three continents, Robert Kennedy's assassination in
June, Soviet tanks crushing Czech dissidents, chaos in the streets of

Chicago during the Democratic Party Convention that August, and the massacre of students protesting the Mexico City Olympic games in October followed in mind-blowing succession. Mal moved from one storm to another, apprising ABC audiences of what was making 1968 such a consequential year in global history.

Long in demand as a speaker, requests for Mal's input ratcheted up as people wanted to listen to someone who might make sense of what was happening. He had begun the day in Washington, DC, at a press conference held by a congressional subcommittee advancing a bill to create a national museum of Black history and culture. Mal had testified before the committee in March, and its chairman requested his participation in the April 4 press conference. Turning sixty that February, Mal had spent the last six years in a whirlwind. His ABC duties demanded that he perform with objectivity and profession-alism, but Mal was at heart an activist and advocate. And he was worried.

He fretted over the vicious counterattack to civil rights surging through the South as politicians, vigilantes, and police undermined newly enacted laws. Terror was not an abstract notion for Mal, who had grown up when the KKK was on the march and lynchings went unpunished. The savagery he now saw in Alabama, Mississippi, and pockets of the North made him question whether those times were returning. Still, he marveled at what had transpired since he returned from Africa in September 1963—especially Dr. King's Nobel Peace Prize and passage of the 1964 Civil Rights and 1965 Voter Rights Acts. It seemed as if the nation had embraced a second Reconstruction, one that would address problems unresolved after the Civil War. These victories had emboldened campaigns for equality, and Mal sensed the movement's gathering momentum wherever he spoke, even if his hopes for the future were tempered by sporadic violence and recog-nition of the degree of difficulty achieving those changes.

And then, a week after he traveled with King in Newark, Mal was shattered as he sat in a restaurant at the Syracuse airport. "As the girl brought my order, a fellow walked up to the counter and said, 'Did you hear Martin Luther King just got shot?'" Mal froze.

> I didn't ask that man anything. I didn't question him about where he had heard the news. I just left the sandwich and ran to the nearest telephone to call ABC assignment editor Charlie Schuman in Manhattan. When he picked up, I couldn't believe what he said. "We've been trying to reach you, Mal. King is dead!"
>
> "Martin Luther King is dead?" I repeated, hoping I hadn't heard him correctly.
>
> Charlie responded: "He was shot about an hour ago in Memphis at the Lorraine Hotel, and he died. Come in right away. We've already chartered a plane for you."
>
> I was numb but heard Charlie tell me to head back to the city. They had a small airplane waiting for me, but I never did like riding [in] one or two motor jobs.

Mal rushed to the American Airlines counter and asked to get on board the next flight to New York City. ABC would go on air to cover the assassination at 10:00 p.m. That was cutting it close, but he dreaded getting aboard a tiny plane even if it would arrive earlier. "I told the reservations agent to give me a seat and if they were filled, I'd pay anybody whatever they wanted for their seat. She said that wouldn't be necessary."

Once aboard, Mal felt disoriented. Over and over he thought, "How could King be dead? All of his energy, his goodness, his willingness to fight, and now he was gone?" After they first met in Pittsburgh in 1960, their paths had crossed in Birmingham, Atlanta, at the Republican and Democratic Party conventions in the summer of 1964, and in Chicago where Mal was covering Operation PUSH (People United to Save Humanity), a program designed to feed the poor and hungry. Their relationship was based on friendship, mutual respect, and self-interest. Men of faith, they were simpatico, committed to family, and focused on gaining freedom and equality for those denied their full measure. Access to King helped Mal do his job while access to Mal allowed King to reach a large, multiracial, audience.

King went out of his way to accommodate Mal, alerting him to impending actions to make sure he would be there. After a press briefing in Chicago, King, Ralph Abernathy, John Lewis, and Jesse Jackson were leaving for Northwestern University when Mal's cameraman, John Fletcher, rushed over to say: "Mal, we had a serious problem with the camera. We're in real trouble." Mal flagged King down to say his film was out of focus. "Could I get you to answer a couple of the questions again?' King turned to Abernathy and said: 'Ralph, Mal's in trouble. You all just wait a minute. I'll be right back.' And with that, we went back inside, just him and me and my crew. He answered my questions and I had my story. We shook hands and they were off to the next stop. And he didn't think it was a big deal. I had interviewed him all over the South by then and he knew I had to have film to tell my story on television."

Nor was it difficult for him to reach King.

If there was something hinted about King that ABC wanted to know, I would call Dora McDonald, his secretary, or call SCLC on Auburn Avenue in Atlanta and tell them I was trying to reach Dr. King and they'd tell me where he was. The instructions came from Dr. King himself. Two years before he died, J. Edgar Hoover called Martin a liar. My office called at five o'clock in the morning and asked if I knew where I could reach him.

I called Dora and said, "I hate to bother you at this hour of the morning, but I need to get in touch with Dr. King."

She said: "'He's down on the island working on his book. It'll take about five minutes for him to get to the telephone, but you promise me you won't call him before seven o'clock." I promised and she gave me his number.

I called about five minutes to seven and they brought him to the telephone. When I told him ABC wanted to interview him about Hoover's statement, he said: "Sure, I'll be glad to do it," and it was settled. At 7:55 that morning, 1,100 radio stations across America aired one of ABC's most popular programs. Martin was featured and spoke about what had happened with Hoover after he criticized the FBI. Although no one knew it at the time, Hoover had bugged King and doctored tapes, piecing them together to make King look like an untrustworthy man. Even after Dr. King's death, Hoover desecrated this man's name and tried to tarnish his memory. Hoover was a vicious, angry man and I don't think a single black ever worked for the FBI during his reign.

But an assassin's bullet had done what Hoover could not do, silence King.[2]

The plane landed at LaGuardia Airport at 9:40 that evening. "I hopped a cab and told the driver to go as fast as he could." By the time Mal arrived at ABC, coverage of the assassination was already airing. Still in shock, he sat down, adjusted his microphone, and joined the discussion. He talked about his encounters with King and described the inspirational speech he witnessed him deliver in Newark the week before. But it wasn't easy tamping down emotions that made him want to scream and cry. Mal described King's determination to "gain freedom and the rights guaranteed not by any man, but by God Almighty Himself." He chronicled King's last years as the movement confronted Jim Crow in the South. "It is imperative," Mal implored, "that one understand the events that led him to do what he did in Birmingham, Selma, and Montgomery."

Connecting King to those who fought alongside him, Mal recalled his declaration that those who came before him deserved "their just due if the future is to grow prosperous and bright for blacks through-out the free and oppressed world." When King received the Nobel Peace Prize in 1964, Mal said, "An entire nation of concerned Negroes felt they had won the prize, too. Martin accepted the award with them in mind." Mal stressed that those who marched and risked their lives but were never acclaimed for their courage had enabled King to persuade President Johnson and Congress to pass the most important civil rights bills since the constitutional revolution after the Civil War.

By the time Mal made it back to Teaneck after midnight, he was numb. ABC called soon after he got home, asking him to find out the details of the funeral. Mal thought about who in King's family and SCLC he needed to reach in the morning. Exhausted, he and Mary prayed before falling into a fitful sleep. Morning brought little relief.

"I made the telephone call to Atlanta early Friday morning; my second call was to ABC. I told them the funeral was going to be Tuesday, the 9th." He then headed to ABC's Manhattan headquarters, where that afternoon ABC posted a list of ninety-four people assigned to cover the funeral. As Mal scanned the names, he was dumbfounded. His name was not there. "I was furious." Masking his hurt and anger, he called ABC News vice president Bill Sheehan, and said: "Bill, I've got some information about the King funeral that all of you fellows, the producer and associate producers, should know. You get them together. I'm on my way up."

Sheehan's office was a floor above Mal's. Striding into the room where the vice president and three producers were waiting, Mal declined to sit. Instead, he barked: "My name is not on that list, but I want to tell you, Bill, I'm going to the funeral. I'll be there on Sunday in Atlanta and I'm staying at a hotel that I know real well on Hunter Street."[3] Mal, in his own words, went on a rant as the frustration he felt from years of slights surfaced. Dumbfounded to be left out of the funeral's coverage, he demanded: "How could you have fourteen network correspondents there and not include me?"

There was an uncomfortable silence. "Then Bill Sheehan hit the ceiling. He claimed he didn't know my name wasn't on the list. Maybe he was putting on a show for me, but he said: 'Sure you ought to go to Atlanta, Mal.'" That hardly appeased Mal, who retorted: "You're not going to treat me like this!" and walked out. That Sunday, he left for Atlanta.

But his anger smoldered. "I had been at ABC for six years," he reflected. "Everyday, something came up to remind me I was black and still considered second class. Many times I got the dog assignments—riots or trivial, irrelevant stories. After King got killed, I got to the point where I said I wouldn't cover any more riots. And I didn't."

He wasn't the only one lacking respect. "Women had some of the same problems," he recalled. "Marlene Sanders for one." After joining ABC in 1964, Sanders broke barriers for women in the industry, covering the Vietnam War and anchoring newscasts before becoming an Emmy-winning documentary filmmaker.[4] For several years, Mal and Marlene shared a tiny cubbyhole at ABC's West 66th Street complex with David Snell. They called it "the Correspondents' Ghetto." Mal was as close to her as anybody at ABC. "They treated her terribly. She was Jewish and one of the first women in the business. She had two strikes against her." Sanders later wrote: "Mal and I were both minorities and had many shared experiences, not all of them pleasant." After King's death, the frustration he had held in burst out.[5]

Arriving in Atlanta on Sunday, Mal began calling people he wanted to interview. The following morning, he covered the viewing of Martin Luther King Jr.'s body at the Sisters Chapel on Spelman College's campus. "Since Saturday night," he reported, "the body of Dr. King has been viewed by more than one hundred thousand people from every walk of life . . . some old, some young, some on canes. I watched the faces of hundreds today slowly walking in the line, single file with somber faces, waiting their turn to get the last view of the man that many termed 'our leader.' A few had tears in their eyes, but most seemed stunned, yet resolved that the voice which was raised so many times with the words 'I have a dream' was really stilled." Silent for a moment, Mal asked: "Who will take his place?"[6]

The camera panned long lines of mourners in the rain, some weeping, others grim, as Mal stood outside the church, sunglasses concealing his grief. "The body of Dr. Martin Luther King," he intoned, "has come for the last time, here in Atlanta, to the church which he co-pastored with his father and the church which he attended as a boy, and the church from where he preached the doctrine of nonviolence, hoping that someday he would attain full equality for his Negro brothers. Tonight, the people who felt the closest to him, the poor, the average citizens, will have a final opportunity to view his body."

Mal's television spot closed by focusing on a banner hanging from an overpass that read: "Gone . . . But NOT forgotten. WE SHALL OVERCOME."[7]

That night, Mal appeared on an ABC special, *Journey to the Mountain Top*, to discuss the assassination, racial strife, and the sanitation workers' strike with Ted Koppel and other reporters. He was the only African American on the show. The next day, when Mal looked around at the news crews covering the funeral, he found that with one exception, "All of them were white except me." The only other African American was Bob Teague.[8] The *Atlanta Journal* and other print reporters noted the dearth of Black correspondents. "There he was," Mal later said, "probably the most prominent American of the 20th century, and they had only two black network correspondents covering his funeral. Neither I nor Bob Teague got too much exposure on air, not anything like we should have received, but that was the temper of the times."[9]

African Americans, however, sought Mal out on the street. Reversing the usual journalistic protocols, a young man outside the chapel asked him what would happen to the movement without King.

> I could only answer him on the basis of what that man lying in state across the street meant by "the dream . . . " His dream was that black men in America would one day be totally free and have full citizenship as guaranteed under the 13th, 14th, and 15th Amendments. He dreamed that his children and my children and their children unborn, would have every door of opportunity opened to them that was open to white American children, have the equality due them, and hold the respect for each other as required by the Laws of God and Men.

Channeling King, Mal concluded that: "as long as one man was enslaved to hate and the passions of prejudice, poverty and deprivation, all were enslaved."[10]

Mal covered the funeral differently than his white counterparts. For him it was not only a tragic moment but a teachable one. The month before, when addressing the congressional subcommittee on creating a museum of African American history, he lamented that African Americans had been left out of the American story. Broadcasting from Atlanta, Mal wrote them back into it. He introduced his audience to Dr. Benjamin Mays, Gordon Parks, Ralph Bunche, and Dick Gregory, offering a window into Black culture and politics.

Mal sketched the history of Morehouse College, the historically Black college in Atlanta that King entered when he was fifteen years old. Its president, Dr. Hugh Gloster, explained how Morehouse shaped King when he was a junior in college by exposing him to Mahatma Gandhi, whose struggle for Indian independence culminated with the British withdrawal in 1947. King then developed his own take on nonviolence at the Crozer Theological Seminary in Pennsylvania, an unorthodox clerical school with a liberal theological agenda. At Crozer, King connected Gandhi, pacifism, and nonviolence to civil and social reform.

Mal acknowledged that King had been partially eclipsed by a vocal minority of students who had "drifted from nonviolence to the philosophy of black power." He agreed with Gloster, who hoped that "Dr. King's death will serve to awaken the conscience of white America." But, Gloster added, "That will not be done in a short time and while adjustments are being made there will be disorders."[11] Those disorders were already breaking out.

Mal interviewed photojournalist Gordon Parks, who like Mal, had broken a color line when he began shooting photos for *Life* magazine. Each had been close to Malcolm X and to King. Parks underscored the respect he saw on Atlanta's streets that day. "White and Negro will miss him," he stressed. "He was the symbol that brought understanding between both races. I don't expect we will run into another Martin Luther King soon." He was not the only one wondering if a leader of King's stature would emerge again.[12]

Dr. Benjamin Mays, the president emeritus of Morehouse whom King called his spiritual mentor, confided that they had an understanding. "I was to do his eulogy if he died first and he would do mine if I died first." Mal asked Mays what lay ahead. "It is difficult to say where we go in the Civil Rights movement, but I know where we should go. . . . We should now dedicate ourselves to the cause for which Dr. King gave his life. . . . If we are not successful in bringing about brotherhood, then he will have died in vain."[13]

Dick Gregory, who had been fasting for social justice, was less restrained. "I don't see America awakening," he said bluntly. "We are following the path Rome followed." An African American comedian who achieved rare crossover popularity, Gregory was a social justice warrior, and King's assassination left him seething. "I see only chaos—not black against white—just right against wrong. We are the most morally unethical country on the face of the earth! I could not believe it took so long to kill King," he added bitterly, enumerating a wave of assassinations that included JFK, Medgar Evers, and Malcolm X. In each case, Gregory said, investigators found the gun but not necessarily the actual assassin. "In this country," Gregory declared, "if anyone speaks the truth, they'll bust them."[14]

Ralph Bunche, the distinguished scholar whose efforts mediating the conflict in Palestine for the United Nations led to the 1950 Nobel Peace Prize, was in disbelief. Like Gregory, he was uncompromising. "Less than a week ago, so many were maligning him," Bunche protested "Now, in unprecedented ways, the nation is mourning him so deeply that the country has almost closed down." The assassin's shot, he said, had been heard around the world, not just "in this racist-infected country." Referring to the Nobel Prizes he and King had received, he confessed, "I sometimes think we should have sent them back." Mal concluded his reporting for the day by noting that the closing hymn at the service where King's body lay in state was "We Shall Overcome." But he wasn't sure they would.[15]

There's no way of knowing how many people heard Mal that day, nor whether African Americans turned to ABC radio so they could hear a Black correspondent reporting. But it's likely that more people listened to Mal cover those two days in Atlanta than at any other time in his career with the exception of the Sunday when the Cuban missile crisis came to a head. For some, his words were consoling. But that did little to stop people taking to the streets in anger.

The next morning, Mal covered the caisson as it left Ebenezer Baptist Church, where a private service had been held for family and close friends. King's body was then carried to Morehouse College for a public service. Mal climbed atop a platform that ABC built on the route, ready to participate in the live broadcast set to begin at 10:00 a.m., two hours before the service. Mal chafed as time went by and he wasn't put on the air. "I was just sitting there watching the program on the television monitor perched in front of me and seeing other correspondents telling their stories, all emanating from New York, but they still hadn't come to me." Finally, he picked up a telephone on the platform and called ABC president Leonard Goldenson. When Goldenson, who grew up in Scottdale, a small town near Pittsburgh, came on the line, he said: "Mal, how are you?" Mal responded: "I'm mad as hell! I've been up here waiting for them to switch to me and after forty-five minutes, almost an hour, I still haven't gotten on the air!" Goldenson let him vent, then intervened.

Mal's emotions were raw and he wasn't sleeping well. Sensitive to any slight, he seethed. "Here I was, probably the closest network correspondent to Dr. King in the world and I stood the chance of never getting on the air to report on his death." Mal felt that King had accorded him special treatment because he trusted him. "I never violated his confidence, not one time." Sometimes, King came to him first with stories. "I was special to Dr. King. Being black, for once, gave me the upper hand and I used it to tell my stories."

Moreover, Mal believed the networks had consistently slighted King. "Oft times I had to insist that King get media coverage before ABC editors even brought up the subject." He fought to make ABC understand that the civil rights struggle was paramount. "King left a legacy and it's a real pride of my life to have known him over eight years and to watch him up close. So for ABC to keep me standing up there on that platform for close to an hour without putting me on the air—it just got me upset." Ten minutes after he hung up with Goldenson, a producer told Mal to get a forty-second piece ready. "And I was off and running on national television, across the U.S.A."

He described the mule train preparing to carry the caisson bearing King's body through the Morehouse College campus, where he had graduated in 1948. "The casket," he intoned, "will be borne along the streets of Atlanta that were so familiar to Dr. King, carried on a mule-drawn caisson to symbolize his identity with the poor." Afterward, he interviewed an eleven-year-old whose grandmother had brought him from California. "'My grandmother thinks I ought to be here,' was the heart of what he said, and it was enough." Mal's television and radio spots continued throughout the day. "I came to this city thirty years ago," he reflected. "A Negro could not buy a sandwich downtown. Now he can, but most Negroes do not have the money."[6]

He spoke with Harry Belafonte and Senator Robert Kennedy, whose presence in Atlanta was a turning point for Kennedy's relations with Black activists. Kennedy, seeking the Democratic Party nomination, had endorsed the Poor People's Campaign. His main competitor for the nomination, Vice President Hubert Humphrey, had entered the race after Lyndon Johnson declined to seek reelection. Although Humphrey was a well-respected liberal, Kennedy's campaign was gathering momentum. If he captured the California primary in two months, he would likely become the party's nominee.

Kennedy won over many activists before leaving Atlanta. "We couldn't grieve over Martin because we had to keep his movement going," Andrew Young remembered. "But Bobby Kennedy had come to Martin's funeral. He came to Daddy King's room in the hotel where a bunch of us were gathered around and stayed for close to an hour, talking about his reaction to the assassination of his brother. That was the first time most of us had ever identified with him."[7]

In the days after King's assassination, America burned. So did Mal. Something changed after he was left off the list of correspondents assigned to King's funeral. Like Jackie Robinson, he had held in his anger and frustration long enough. In 1945, when Branch Rickey spoke with Robinson about how he would respond to racial attacks if he was brought to the majors, the Dodgers president was clear. "I'm looking for a ballplayer with guts enough not to fight back."[18] Rickey feared that a vocal, combative Black player would trigger a backlash to what historian Jules Tygiel famously called baseball's great experiment. He urged Robinson to respond with his play, at least for the first few seasons. Robinson did, winning the National League Rookie of the Year award and spurring the Dodgers into the World Series.

Mal relished comparisons to Robinson, although he never thought he came close to matching his friend's courage or accomplishments. He realized, however, that his breakthrough at ABC could inspire others to confront segregation and challenge discrimination. He behaved accordingly, maintaining his composure even when technicians sabotaged his television shoots with shoddy work or editors gave him the runaround. The second time a cameraman deliberately twisted film of an interview so that it couldn't be used, Mal confronted him. "I know what you're doing," he said. "We're both just trying to make a living and take care of our families." Pausing he said, *"Don't do it again."* The cameraman never sabotaged his work again and, when Mal retired, gave him a set of luggage as a gift.[19]

But like Jackie, Mal kept silent for only so long. Robinson abided with Rickey's marching order for two seasons before becoming more vocal both on and off the field. And after being left off King's funeral coverage, Mal became more assertive at ABC. He told his boss he was going to Atlanta anyway, even if it was on his own dime. He challenged what he called "efforts to break my will . . . innuendos like 'Who does that nigger think he is?'" He no longer checked himself when desk men failed to assign him stories or coworkers challenged his right to work at ABC. Mal made it clear that he "would not allow any small-minded bigot" to stand in his way. And none did during the remainder of his ABC tenure.[20]

Devastated by King's death and drained by his funeral, Mal was dismayed by the riots breaking out afterward. The uprising, which spread to more than one hundred cities, eclipsed the scale of any civil disturbance since the Civil War. The Hill in Pittsburgh was in flames, as were other parts of the city. Although understanding the impulse to burn America down, Mal saw little to be gained by rioting, which repudiated King's belief in nonviolence. Most of all, he refused to give in to despair, which he considered a cause for the eruptions.

When Mal had spoken with King just days before in Newark, he sensed King's determination to address poverty and broaden the movement's emphasis beyond civil rights. Riots would not do that, but the Poor People's Campaign could. Although SCLC leaders were reeling from the loss of King, they were compelled to carry on the campaign. "What we really needed was a long break before attempting to rekindle our energies," Andrew Young later acknowledged, but "this was not the time to rest. . . . I didn't really grieve. I just let my work consume me." So did Mal, but neither held illusions about the campaign. "Without Martin," Young reflected, "it would be very difficult to convey our message." That message was about poverty and power. "Poor people in America were out of sight and out of mind," Young said.[21] Because they lacked power, politicians ignored them and the policies that perpetuated poverty. The Poor People's Campaign aimed to empower the powerless so as to confront the persistence of poverty in a land of plenty.

Nowhere was poverty more dire than in the Mississippi Delta, where the seeds for the campaign were planted. "The Poor People's Campaign was Marian Wright Edelman's idea," Young explained.[22] Working in the Delta for the NAACP Legal Defense Fund, Edelman had escorted King around Marks, Mississippi, during the 1966 March Against Fear initiated by James Meredith. King saw children with bloated bellies and hollow expressions and could not put them out of his mind. Nor could Senator Robert Kennedy, who Edelman later walked through Marks. Although Great Society programs and a roaring economy had cut the poverty rate almost in half during the 1960s, those gains bypassed Marks, Mississippi.[23] Kennedy listened as Edelman analyzed how agricultural subsidies—an artifact of Great Depression policies that paid landowners to take land out of production—had devastated sharecroppers and tenant farmers. Limiting the supply of agricultural commodities boosted prices but pushed small farmers off the land. With few nonfarming jobs available, families sank deeper into poverty. Before leaving Marks, Kennedy urged Edelman to convince King to make poverty visible to the nation. She soon did.

In September 1967, Edelman brought four Delta farmers who had worked the land since childhood to SCLC's Atlanta office. "These were sharecroppers," Andrew Young remembered, "who no longer had jobs. They couldn't even grow corn or raise chickens or hogs on the land anymore because it wasn't theirs. . . . They were desperate to do something, and after we listened to them, Marian proposed that Martin and other religious and labor leaders join them in a fast and [a] sit-in at the Department of Labor."[24] King went further than that, much further, and proposed a campaign of civil disobedience more massive and longer lasting than any previous civil rights drive. It would bring poor Americans to the nation's capital and render them visible. "We intended to arouse the conscience of the nation around issues of poverty as we had challenged the nation to reject segregation," Young explained.[25]

SCLC organizers were determined to see it through, despite King's death. The Poor People's Campaign, which embodied his message of economic inclusion, would kick off in Marks. The small beleaguered town in the Delta that haunted King was central to their effort to place poverty on the nation's agenda. "I was in Marks, Mississippi the other day," King said as he announced the campaign at the National Cathedral in Washington, DC, just days before his death. "And I tell you I saw hundreds of black boys and black girls walking the streets with no shoes to wear."[26]

The campaign focused on extending economic justice and human rights for poor Americans, not just civil rights for African Americans. Civil rights laws had accomplished only so much, and a diverse multiracial group of activists, dismayed that Johnson's War on Poverty had lost momentum, joined the campaign. "With Martin's death," Andrew Young explained, "the Poor People's Campaign became the venue through which his coalition of conscience came together."[27]

"We ought to come in mule carts, in old trucks, any kind of transportation people can get their hands on," King had said. "People ought to come to Washington, sit down if necessary in the middle of the street and say, 'We are here; we are poor; we don't have any money; you have made us this way . . . and we've come to stay until you do something about it.'"[28] They would press Congress to consider an economic bill of rights that stressed meaningful jobs at living wages and a secure income for those who could not find or were unable to work. By then, King was talking about fundamental economic change and was willing to disrupt business as usual in Washington, DC, in order to make that happen.

Mal's coverage of King's death showcased his exceptional capacity as a reporter and commentator. No other network correspondent had comparable access to African American leaders or people in the community, much less such an intimate understanding of Black America. With greater latitude to focus on what he covered afterward, Mal decided there was no better way to confront his grief over King's death and his doubts about the future than to focus on the Poor People's Campaign. His first stop was Washington, DC, where he filmed the Reverend Ralph Abernathy holding an impromptu news conference in the lobby at the Department of Agriculture. Abernathy warned that "the most militant nonviolent action in the country's history will take place unless all poor people are taken care of with food, clothing, and jobs." This, Abernathy declared, was King's dream. As protesters belted out "Ain't Gonna Let Nobody Turn Me Around" and "We Shall Overcome," Mal kept the camera rolling. Strong language and impassioned singing made for good television.[29]

Privy to movement infighting, Mal was realistic about the difficulties confronting organizers, but he avoided reporting on those conflicts or the logistical difficulties they faced. King's death had made the campaign a rallying cry and caused far more people to join Resurrection City on the Mall in Washington, DC, than the organizers could accommodate. Nor could SCLC convey its message nearly as well without King. "Even if Martin had been alive it would have been difficult to pull that off," Andrew Young acknowledged. "Without him we had no voice of reason that everybody had to listen to." Mal realized this, making him even more determined to do what he could to get the campaign's message out.[30]

In May, Coretta Scott King led marchers seeking an economic bill of rights through the streets of Washington, DC, while caravans assembled in Selma, Atlanta, and seven other cities. Mal anticipated that the caravan that would catch the nation's attention was the one made up of mule-drawn covered wagons leaving from Marks. He decided to join it, but first he toured the South, stopping in venues where activists had shed blood to change the country. In Atlanta, which had long intrigued him as a city with great potential for African Americans, he covered Muhammad Ali presenting Martin Luther King Sr. with a portrait of his son. Mal then returned to Selma, where he had covered protests three years before.

As 1965 began, despite repeated efforts, only 2 percent of eligible African Americans were registered to vote in Selma. Resolved to claim their right to vote, SCLC, SNCC, and local groups took to the streets that January. They anticipated that the Selma sheriff Jim Clark would respond with violence, but they saw no alternative if they were to claim their right to vote. On February 18, after a month of police attacks and mass arrests, state troopers shot Jimmie Lee Jackson, a church deacon trying to protect his mother from being clubbed. When Jackson died, SCLC's Hosea Williams and SNCC's John Lewis called for a march from Selma to Montgomery. On Sunday March 7, as marchers crossed the Edmund Pettus Bridge in Selma, Sheriff Clark commanded them to disperse. When they stood their ground, Clark ordered his men to attack. As television cameras rolled, troopers battered demonstrators, fired tear gas, and rode their horses into the crowd. The day became known as "Bloody Sunday."

A national audience, including Lyndon Johnson, heard future Congressman John Lewis, his head matted in blood, declare: "I don't see how President Johnson can send troops to Vietnam—I don't see how he can send troops to the Congo—I don't see how he can send troops to Africa and can't send troops to Selma."[31] King, meanwhile, called for religious leaders of all faiths to join him in Selma to resume the march. Faced with a federal restraining order calling for a delay until protection could be afforded marchers, King led two thousand people on to the Edmund Pettus Bridge, where they knelt and prayed before returning to Selma. Militants decried this as a retreat, but King's strategy bore fruit.

The protestors' courage and Bloody Sunday's violence swayed national opinion and prompted President Johnson to send the voting rights bill to Congress. A week later, he spoke to Congress, declaring he stood with the marchers. "Their cause must be our cause, too. Because it is not just Negroes, but really it is all of us, who must overcome the crippling legacy of bigotry and injustice. And we shall overcome."[32] A few days later, King, Lena Horne, and Harry Belafonte led marchers out of Selma with FBI agents and National Guardsmen protecting them along the way. Although the federal permit to march limited the number of participants to three hundred people, they were twenty-five thousand strong when they arrived at the steps of the state capitol in Montgomery five days later. "There never was a moment in American history," King proclaimed, "more honorable and more inspiring than the pilgrimage of clergymen and laymen of every race and faith pouring into Selma to face danger at the side of its embattled Negroes."[33] That evening, Viola Liuzzo, who had driven from Michigan to take part in the campaign, was heading back to Selma when Klansmen opened fire on her car and killed her. An African American teenager accompanying her was also shot but survived. The death of the young mother of five children, the only white woman to be killed during the civil rights struggle, was widely publicized. It caught the attention of those who otherwise paid little attention to the backlash in the South. Outrage over her murder boosted support for the Voting Rights Act, which Johnson signed into law on August 6.[34]

Now, three years later, Mal returned to Selma, accompanying Ralph Abernathy to the Tabernacle Baptist Church from which a caravan departed. Mal's piece featured Abernathy leading congregants in prayer and lambasting politicians for ignoring poverty. The Poor People's Campaign would be nonviolent, Abernathy stated, and apply maximum pressure on Congress to enact legislation to help the poor. Those worried about violence, he countered, should concentrate on ending the war in Vietnam. Mal was standing with the mostly white press corps as the audience burst out in applause.

Mal spent the next few days in Montgomery. After talking with a maid at the Governor's House Motel, he wrote Pittsburgh Pirates general manager Joe L. Brown about her son, who played ball at the Alabama State College for Negroes:

> I know mothers are usually proud but this boy sounds like a wonderful prospect, six feet tall, 175 pounds, all-round athlete. . . . What impressed me most was that he wants to make good and stop his mother from working. I wish you would have your scout in that area talk with him, Joe, and try to see him in action. . . . I am in the South almost every month and if you want me to talk to him, just say the word. My only handicap is that I'm not a judge of baseball talent, *per se*, but I know character.[35]

The Pirates never signed Tommy James Riley, but Mal was always willing to try to help somebody get a chance.

After Montgomery, Mal went to Birmingham, then back to Atlanta, where he interviewed the Reverend Hosea Williams. Mal's footage featured a floral cross in front of a church, people departing for Washington, DC, and a service at King's grave. Mal, his hair carefully parted on the right side of his head, wore a dark suit and white shirt. "Here at the grave of Dr. Martin Luther King, Jr.," he said, "participants in the Poor People's March stopped long enough to pay their respects to the man. The idea is now functioning and in operation. Poor people from the Southwest, from the East, from the North, and from the South—Mexicans, Indians, Puerto Ricans, Negroes, and the Appalachian poor are on their way to Washington to present their case to the executives of this great nation, the richest in the world, but where 20 percent of its population is oft times hungry." After Atlanta, Mal headed to Marks, Mississippi.[36]

Mal began his coverage seated atop the running board of a mule-drawn wagon heading toward Grenada, Mississippi. "About eighty people," he said, "most of them from Mississippi, are on the mule train to Washington this morning. They are the rural poor. I'd like to introduce some of them to you."[37] The camera panned fifteen covered wagons rolling by. Slogans painted on their white canvas sides said: "Jesus Was a Poor Man," and "Feed the Poor."

Mal interspersed shots of the wagon train with children seated on a porch, their legs hanging over the edge as they stared at the caravan. No one could have confused these men and women with well-off citizens. They looked prematurely aged, with hollowed cheeks and missing teeth. Leadora Collins, a kerchief around her head, spoke about her ten children and husband, a mechanic. "He makes a very low income; sometimes he makes twelve dollars a week and sometimes that runs in a month's time." Asked why she was going to Washington, she said, "Well, I hope this will accomplish something in bringing our income up. . . . We going to try to make it there if we live, and if we don't, I'd rather die going than die back there starving to death."[38]

William Miller, aged seventy-one, said he had made two dollars a day chopping cotton when he was younger, a bit more now doing yardwork. When Mal asked what he did in the wintertime, he shrugged "Nothing." Miller said he hoped the campaign would bring more work. When asked why he had joined it, he declared, "I'm going to Washington for my rights." Another man, aged sixty-seven, said he still worked in the fields when he could. "I chop cotton for three dollars a day, twelve hours, sun to sun, sunup to sundown." But he hadn't worked for a year. An unlit cigarette hanging from his lips, he lapsed into profanity while describing his life. That didn't make it into the final cut. When asked if he had money in the bank, he retorted: "WHAT! What the hell you talking about? No money. Go away!" Mal refrained from embellishing their remarks. He let people have their say, with the clip clop of the mules' hooves on the pavement a staccato soundtrack. He shot his closing several times, changing words and modulating his tone as he stood in front of a wagon. The final cut was to the point: "So that's but a glimpse of the face of poverty which exists here in rural Mississippi, and in urban ghettos, and all around us, poverty that so few of us ever get to see. This is Mal Goode, ABC

News, in Mississippi."[39] He stayed with the caravan for a few more days, then headed north.

On Tuesday, May 21, 1968, when a few thousand people set up a tent encampment called Resurrection City on the National Mall, Mal was in New York City covering demonstrations at Columbia University. The student unrest that paralyzed Paris earlier that spring quickly crossed the Atlantic. Columbia students were protesting both the university's plans for a gymnasium opposed by its Harlem neighbors and the school's complicity in the Vietnam War. Their agitation, which began before King's assassination, culminated on April 23 in a dramatic takeover of Hamilton Hall, which housed administrative offices. The Columbia University occupation—the first student takeover in the United States that spring—captured the news cycle when police forcefully evicted the students a week later. Mal's crew filmed chanting students climbing over police barricades and retaking Hamilton Hall before the police countered, beating and arresting hundreds.

Mal went back and forth between New York and Washington, DC, for a few weeks before focusing exclusively on Resurrection City. Campaign organizers wanted to convince Congress to adopt an economic bill of rights but eventually shelved the massive civil disobedience that King had planned. Instead, smaller groups sought meetings with congressmen and used the encampment to call attention to poverty.

They garnered the attention they sought, but providing shelter, food, medical care, and sanitation for Resurrection City became a logistical nightmare. Organizers had planned on bringing fifteen hundred people to Washington and recruiting a few more locally. "When Dr. King was killed," Andrew Young recalled, "we ended up with five thousand people and were not prepared to feed that many." Heavy rains turned Resurrection City into a swamp with people sinking into mud up to their knees as they walked the grounds. Bickering among SCLC leaders seeking to claim King's mantle of leadership made matters worse. So did government agents and informants, some posing as journalists, who tried to discredit the campaign by disrupting it.[40]

And then another assassination rocked the nation. Robert F. Kennedy had quickly become a contender after entering the race for the 1968 Democratic Party presidential nomination. Charismatic, thoughtful, and carrying a name that evoked Camelot, Kennedy's antiwar stance and domestic advocacy resonated with activists as well as with working and poor Americans. On June 4, he won both the California and the South Dakota primaries. That made him the front-runner to secure the nomination and take on former vice president Richard Nixon in November. After speaking to jubilant supporters in the Embassy Room of the Ambassador Hotel in Los Angeles shortly after midnight on the East Coast, he left for another gathering. Escorted by retired FBI agent William Barry, former NFL star Rosey Grier who lived near the Goodes in Teaneck, and 1960 Olympic gold medal-winning decathlete Rafer Johnson, Kennedy was cutting through the hotel kitchen when Sirhan Sirhan, a twenty-four-year-old Palestinian enraged by the candidate's support for Israel, shot him three times. Kennedy was declared dead twenty-six hours later.

Mal and those who had begun investing their hopes in Robert Kennedy were shaken. First JFK, then Malcolm, Martin, and finally RFK had been felled by assassins. "We were in Resurrection City when Robert Kennedy was killed," Andrew Young recalled. "I was in a daze." Kennedy had won over Young and other SCLC leaders at King's funeral in Atlanta when he had spoken with them about grieving for his brother. They bonded both personally and politically. "As soon as Martin died," Young remembered, "we started placing hope and faith in Bobby Kennedy."[41] Kennedy had prompted Marian Wright Edelman to urge King to make poverty a national issue, and he backed the Poor People's Campaign from its inception. Kennedy, Young wrote, "embodied all that was good and promising about his brother John and the best ideas of the Johnson era." If he could win the presidency, the nation's commitment to equality might gain purchase. Remembering that moment decades later, Young paused and said,

"And six weeks later," without finishing the sentence. After pausing, he continued. "Deep in the recesses of our subconscious, we always expected that Martin would eventually be killed, but the death of Robert Kennedy shocked us into a state of disbelief and incomprehension bordering on total despair. . . . We had thought we might be able to rebuild a forceful national consensus around Kennedy, salvaging at least something in the wake of Martin's death. Now even that hope was gone."[42]

At home the night Kennedy was shot, Mal filed stories from the United Nations and Manhattan the next day and joined ABC's studio coverage. He interviewed Secretary General U Thant, Ralph Bunche, Manhattan Borough president Percy Sutton, state assemblyman Charles Rangel, and Jackie Robinson. After Kennedy's funeral at St. Patrick's Cathedral in New York City on June 8, a train carried his body to Arlington National Cemetery, passing by an estimated one million mourners.[43] Mal reported on the cortege as it passed through New Brunswick, New Jersey.

Helen Wright listened as she did her ironing in Pittsburgh. "Your words were so moving and your voice so full of feeling," she wrote Mal. "When you described the people around you, I felt as if I could have reached out and held your arm." She sensed Mal's vulnerability. "Your voice trembled a little, I thought. It was a little deeper; I could almost feel your pain." Wright, who had listened to Mal for years, said his comments consoled and strengthened her for the challenges ahead. "I thought of the old days when you used to tell stories on radio. At the end you would say 'The walls keep tumbling down, ladies and gentlemen, the walls keep tumbling down.' It was you all over again here in Pittsburgh trying so hard to encourage progress." Wright bared her feelings. "Our country is in such a bad situation today I cannot grasp the real meaning of it all. . . . I was so sad, I cried as I listened to you. Tears were dropping all over my ironing board. . . . I guess I cried more that day than I did when King died." She described confrontations on the streets of her Homewood neighborhood after King's death. "Your brothers must have told you about the 'Storm Troopers' we had on every corner," she wrote. "I got so sick of the helicopter flying over my house every day for four days. . . . it was so frightening and it made me angry."[44]

A preacher in Indiana wrote, "I was never so proud of you in all my life as I was last night when I saw you on television, discussing the awful dilemma that America's racism, bigotry, hate mongers, and hate mongering have brought us. . . . God bless you and keep you." ABC Executive Producer Walter Pfister replied to a letter from Miss Ruth White, 118 West 12th Street, Homestead, telling her, "He did a remarkable job of reporting during the tragic days surrounding the assassination of Dr. King. The acid test for television correspondents, unfortunately, often occurs during times of tragedy or calamity. It is in such times that these men are put to their severest tests, and Mal Goode rose to the occasion. ABC News is proud of him. We're glad you are, too." Pfister had no idea just how proud she was. Mal was her big brother.[45] When the train carrying RFK arrived in D.C. and the cortege passed Resurrection City, its residents stood in a silent tribute. They joined throngs at the Lincoln Memorial, who sang "The Battle Hymn of the Republic" in homage.

While SCLC kept the campaign going, Mal covered it with respect and empathy.[46] By then, the Poor People's Campaign's relations with the media were shot. King could have cogently explained its goals, but nobody else commanded comparable respect. In his absence, the campaign could not keep the focus on poverty. SCLC leaders thought highly of a few journalists but were hardly sanguine about most reporters. "The press had apparently made up its mind to condemn the Poor People's Campaign and Resurrection City long before we even arrived in the capital," Young rued. "The Washington press in particular didn't know anything about the civil rights movement, and even the black reporters were surprisingly unfamiliar with our philosophy and history. With few exceptions, reporters were interested only in dirt-digging—unearthing the internal conflicts, disputes, and backbiting from our sea of mud. There was no real interest shown in issues we were attempting to elucidate."[47]

Mal was an exception, a network correspondent whom they trusted. It had been that way since Mal began showing up in the South with a television crew in tow. "The black papers couldn't afford to send a reporter to the scene and cover protests in the South," Young explained in an interview. "Mal really stood out and we put him in a special class, because he was." Their sense of mission aligned. "What we were trying to do was to educate the public. That's what he was trying to do; we never saw him as an adversary." Some reporters distorted and twisted their comments in ways that made them seem more controversial than they were. Mal didn't play that way. "Mal was normal, a good guy who loved his work, and did it extremely well," Young maintained. He bridged racial and class divisions, could speak to anybody, and understood how programs like food stamps and agricultural subsidies worked and affected people. Most reporters, Young said, did not. "There was nothing eccentric about Mal. He was around, he was reliable, he was accurate, and he was lovable."[48]

As the campaign settled in, Mal filed stories from Resurrection City. When James Earle Ray was arrested at London's Heathrow airport on June 8, 1968, Reverend Abernathy told Mal, "All of us here in Resurrection City are delighted to have the news that Mr. Ray, the man accused of assassinating our leader, Dr. Martin Luther King, has been apprehended."[49] But he and Mal suspected that others were involved. They knew that Ray, a petty criminal who had escaped from the Missouri State Penitentiary the year before, was a stone cold racist. But neither of them believed he could have avoided the manhunt and fled the country on his own. "I don't think there's any question about there being a conspiracy in King's assassination," Mal concluded. "I think it was designed that this guy would do it, get away, and never be caught. Ray was a ne'er-do-well, but those behind the assassination paid him well to do the job. He was able to get out of Memphis undetected, go to Nashville, on to Canada, and end up in London without a hitch. How could a dishwasher do all of that on his salary?"[50]

The SCLC sought to bring the campaign to a dignified conclusion with a Solidarity Day Rally for Jobs, Peace and Freedom on June 19, 1968. That date held special significance for African Americans. Although the Emancipation Proclamation was issued in 1863, African

Americans in Texas did not learn that slavery had been abolished until June 19, 1865, when Union troops arrived in Galveston. Their jubilation led African Americans to make June 19—Juneteenth—a day to commemorate freedom, and upward of one hundred thousand people rallied on the National Mall that day. When the National Park Service permit for Resurrection City expired three days later, police cleared the camp. The campaign had not fulfilled King's vision but did make poor people and their plight more visible and did increase federal funding for anti-poverty initiatives. "The bottom line, Marian Wright Edelman stressed, "was hunger, hunger, hunger." She and others vowed to keep pressing that agenda.[51]

Mal covered Resurrection City's denouement, reporting on Reverend Abernathy's hunger strike in the District of Columbia jail. Abernathy said that he respected the law but could not always obey it. It was imperative to make "America conscious of the hunger Americans face." Dismissing concerns about his health, Abernathy said folks should worry instead about "the health of the nation." Mal filed one final story. As the camera panned tents in a field of mud and workmen picked up debris, he ended by saying that the encampment had been abandoned, but not the struggle that brought people there.[52]

The SCLC sent a caravan, including a mule train, to raise the Poor People's Campaign flag at the GOP convention in Miami Beach in early August. But Richard Nixon, who won the party's presidential nomination, was more inclined to use protesters as a foil than embrace their cause. From there, the campaign traveled to Chicago where Hubert Humphrey secured the Democratic Party nod as antiwar demonstrators and police battled in the streets. During the primaries, Mal had traveled with Humphrey, who denounced extremist groups and railed against the politics of fear. Mal caught up with him in Chicago on the day the vice president accepted his party's nomination. His interview juxtaposed Humphrey with shots of the late Robert Kennedy and protesters in Chicago's streets that captured the presidential candidate's dilemma.

Mal shuttled between the campaign and protests the rest of the year. In early August, he interviewed Jackie Robinson, who was endorsing a boycott of the upcoming Olympic Games in Mexico City. Black athletes, led by a doctoral student and former athlete Harry Edwards, had initiated the Olympic Project for Human Rights (OPHR). It dismissed efforts to showcase Black athletes as window dressing to conceal racial realities. Contending that the "oppression of Afro-Americans is greater than it ever was," the OPHR proposed boycotting the Olympics unless reforms were made. "We must no longer allow the Sports World to pat itself on the back as a citadel of racial justice when the racial injustices of the sports industry are infamously legendary." OPHR's demands ranged from reinstating Muhammad Ali as the heavyweight champ to excluding South Africa and Rhodesia from the Olympics and hiring more Black coaches.[53]

Former Olympian Jesse Owens opposed the boycott, as did several Black newspapers, but Jackie Robinson emphatically backed it. Mal, for whom sport had always mattered, listened as Robinson lauded athletes who were sacrificing their chance at the Olympics. "I respect their courage. We need to understand the reason and frustration behind these protests." Robinson added that the campaign to desegregate major league baseball had struck a moderate tone, but that much had changed since then. "It was different in my day," Robinson said. "Perhaps we lacked courage." Mal didn't think that, nor did Martin Luther King Jr., who had told Dodgers pitcher Don Newcombe a month before his death that "You and Jackie and Roy [Campanella] will never know how easy you made it to do my job." Robinson bristled when asked if he was an Uncle Tom, too moderate to speak for African Americans. He replied that Stokely Carmichael was a creation of the news media without the knowledge to be a leader. "We don't need him," he said. We need people like Dr. Martin Luther King."[54]

But ten days before the Olympic torch was lit that October, Mexico City was traumatized. Ten thousand students were assembled on the Plaza de las Tres Culturas to hear speeches protesting government corruption, the cost of the Olympic Games, and police intrusions on campuses when shots began striking troops surrounding them. Believing that student radicals were attacking them, the troops fired into the crowds, killing an estimated three thousand students. Trying to play down the massacre, the government claimed that only four people had died and that "communists" infiltrating the student movement had instigated the violence. It took forty years for the truth to emerge. An investigation that gained access to secret government documents revealed that members of the Presidential Guard had fired at the troops to incite them to attack the students and closed off exits to prevent the students from escaping. They wanted to provoke a confrontation that would stifle student activism and place blame on them for the clash. A few days later, with blood still staining the plaza, the Games began.

Kareem Abdul Jabbar, who was in the midst of leading UCLA to three consecutive NCAA basketball championships, and other prominent athletes stood on principle and declined to participate. Others took their protests to Mexico City and used their medal-winning performances to take a stand. After Tommie Smith, Peter Norman, and John Carlos finished first, second, and third in the two hundred meters, they climbed atop the podium. As the US anthem played, Smith and Carlos bowed their heads, raised fists covered by black gloves, and stood shoeless in black socks. The gloves emphasized Black power; the socks but no shoes represented Black poverty. Norman, the son of a butcher from Melbourne, Australia, who was deeply committed to racial equality, wore the OPHR badge on his chest in solidarity with Smith and Carlos. It became one of sport's iconic moments.[55]

Their protests triggered vicious condemnation, and Smith and Carlos were summarily expelled from the Olympic Village by the US Olympic Committee (USOC). Norman, at odds with his country's "White Australia Policy," was ostracized and denied the chance to represent his country in future competitions. Several Black sportswriters joined white sportswriters in excoriating Smith and Carlos, but the *Pittsburgh Courier* captioned its front-page photograph of the athletes: "Black and Proud."

ABC, unlike the other networks that initially downplayed the protest, ran a long piece about Smith and Carlos the next day. Anchor Frank Reynolds described what happened and explained their motivation without condemning them. ABC showed them on the winners' podium as the national anthem was played in its entirety. The network's loquacious sports commentator Howard Cosell, who had long supported controversial Black athletes, followed the clip by asking Smith to explain his actions.

The next day, Cosell angrily defended Smith and Carlos in a commentary from the Olympic Stadium. Speaking rapidly and with unusual emotion, Cosell dismissed USOC as "a group of pompous, arrogant, medieval-minded men who regard the games as a private social preserve for their tiny clique." USOC, he said, called the Olympics sport, "separate and apart from the realities of life." The Black athlete, Cosell countered, "says he is leading a revolution in America, a revolution designed to produce dignity for the black man and that he is a human being before he is an athlete. He says his life in America is filled with injustice, that he wants equality everywhere, not just within the arena." Echoing OPHR's stance that Black athletes were unwilling to be used once every four years on behalf of those who otherwise ignored them, Cosell said that they had earned their right to compete, won fairly, and were justified in using their prominence to seek change. "And so," Cosell concluded, "the Olympic Games for the United States have become a kind of America in microcosm, a country torn apart. Where will it all end?" Dripping in sarcasm, he concluded: "Don't ask the U.S. Olympic Committee, they've been too busy preparing for a VIP cocktail party next Monday night in the lush new Camino Real. Howard Cosell reporting from Mexico City."[56]

Mal wasn't in Mexico City, but he appreciated Cosell's impassioned defense of Black athletes as well as his network's respectful coverage of their protests. After all, he had been fighting to get ABC to take the Black experience seriously ever since he was hired. But as much as he would have liked to cover the Olympics, he was ABC News, not ABC Sports. With the 1968 election weeks away, ABC sent him on the road.

Mal covered a contentious strike by the United Federation of Teachers in the Ocean Hill–Brownsville neighborhoods of Brooklyn that pitted teachers against a Black and Latin community. The strike raised issues of community control and exposed tensions between a heavily Jewish faculty and Black families. Mal let the stakeholders speak. A teacher at Public School 88 told him that his teaching came first, while students said that they just wanted to go to school, and residents affirmed their goal of community control. From there, Mal headed to Cleveland to cover the aftermath of the Glendale riots, which broke out after a police shoot-out with militant Black nationalists. Returning to Mississippi, he interviewed NAACP state field director Charles Evers and filmed him addressing a congregation and pinning buttons on Black children's shirts after services. Mal took heart in seeing Evers exhorting the children to tell their parents to vote. At a meeting of the Loyal Democrats in Jackson, he interviewed Aaron Henry and Spencer Oliver, the state president of the Young Democrats of America, who called for the party to "reject the racist appeal of George Wallace and reactionary appeal of Richard Nixon."[37]

Mal walked the line between advocacy and reporting that fall, troubled by the assassinations and worried about the crescendo of protest, incendiary rhetoric, and backlash. The Democratic Party was reeling from divisions over the war in Vietnam, undercutting Hubert Humphrey's appeal, and third-party candidate George Wallace was gaining traction with white workers in the North unsettled by the protests. Reliably Democratic mill towns in the Monongahela River Valley where Mal grew up were no longer so dependable when voting. Most of all, Mal was worried that Richard Nixon would become president. He didn't know what that would mean for the fight for equality and rights he had given much of his life to achieving. But he knew it wouldn't be good.

12

TELLING IT LIKE IT IS

Mal Goode wasn't sure what to expect after Richard Nixon was elected president in November 1968, but he doubted it would be good. Although disenchanted by Lyndon Johnson's failure to extricate the United States from Vietnam, Mal praised the outgoing president for delivering "the most forceful and effective thrust against discrimination of all the administrations which preceded him." Mal knew that, without Johnson, the 1964 Civil Rights Act, the 1965 Voting Rights Act, and a host of Great Society reforms might never have been enacted. Nixon, on the other hand, had campaigned against Johnson's vision of a Great Society and appealed to white voters' racial grievances. In a national radio commentary before Nixon's inauguration, Mal argued that getting out of Vietnam and reconciling domestic factions at each other's throats were the most pressing issues on America's agenda. But with Nixon taking office, he was uneasy about the prospects for either. "The success or failure of our efforts in the next four years in attaining domestic peace will depend largely on the type of leadership provided by the president-elect, Richard Nixon," Mal reasoned. But Nixon would take office with two "strikes against him." The country was badly polarized, and race relations were dismal. Mal castigated Nixon for ignoring Black communities during his campaign, omitting African Americans from his cabinet, and empowering his running mate, Spiro Agnew, who had sneered during the campaign that "If you've seen one slum you have seen them all." Mal knew when politicians were playing the race card and did not doubt that Nixon and Agnew would sacrifice racial progress for the slightest political gain.[1]

Nor could he ignore the degree to which fear, distrust, and hatred agitated the country. "Four years of carnage have polarized America into two camps, black and white," he told a crowd of twenty-two hundred at the World Affairs Council in Pittsburgh. "And when 13 percent of the New Jersey vote goes to George Wallace, you get an idea of just how far polarization has gone." But Mal resisted the urge to make matters worse. Instead, he wanted to show people that change could come. His mantra became "It can be done."[2]

Mal believed that someone's action was more telling than their race or rhetoric. Progress, he told an NAACP chapter outside Pittsburgh, would not come by speeches like the one he was delivering. "Neither can it be accomplished with Molotov cocktails, rioting, looting and debauchery, inflamed oft-times by irresponsible, loose-tongued hate-mongers suddenly thrust into notoriety by my profession, the news media." He vowed to challenge hatred "no matter what color it comes in," and no matter whether it was promoted by white supremacists or Black separatists.[3]

In the aftermath of King's death, yet another summer of discontent, and Nixon's alarming election victory, Mal was worried. The debates over race and poverty frustrated him. "It is not enough for us to talk about the wrongs of rioting or the money cost of rebellions and eruptions in our cities. We must talk about the causes and work together, black and white, to find the cures."[4] That, he knew, would be harder than ever given the backlash against the movements of the 1960s that carried Nixon into office. But Mal felt compelled to channel King's vision—even his talking points and metaphors—when speaking or building alliances. Like King, he deplored the domestic opportunities lost because of the cost of the war, which he calculated as surpassing one hundred billion dollars. He lamented spending millions to land a man on the moon while people starved on earth.[5] But rage would not bring about change. With the end of his time at ABC on the horizon, Mal was more determined than ever to recommit to his life's work. He would not give in to despair.

Sixty years old at a time when most workers were forced to retire at sixty-five, Mal was at the height of his oratorical powers. He had won the confidence of Black leaders and become a household name in Black America. Professional recognition also came his way as peers elected him the first non-white president of the Association of Radio-Television News Analysts, an august body that included Walter Cronkite, John Chancellor, Pauline Frederick, Peter Jennings, Marlene Sanders, Daniel Schorr, and Eric Sevareid.

But Mal was hardly satisfied. ABC wanted him on the street when trouble broke out and, on the air, delivering news and commentary, but he sought a different platform. He finally got it after flirting with termination. "They called me here at the house one day and told me to get a cab and come in right away. They were rioting in some city, and I said to Charlie Schuman, who was the desk man, 'Charlie, I'm not coming. You tell this to Bill Sheehan,' who was the Vice President of News, 'so he knows that I'm not coming, and don't you take responsibility.' Charlie was a nervous Nellie. He said, 'Mal, this could be your job.'" Correspondents didn't refuse assignments.[6]

Arriving at work the next day, Mal went upstairs to see Sheehan, who sighed, "'Mal, you know, I don't understand you. You're supposed to do what you're told.' I said, 'Bill, please don't give me a lecture. Fire me, do whatever you want. But I'm not going to do any more riots until I'm able to do a documentary—like the white reporters are doing.' He said, 'Like what?' I said I just came out of Atlanta covering a story last week and the mayor of Atlanta said: 'We're a city too busy to hate.' Let me go down there.' And he said, 'Give me a memo on it.'"[7]

Mal was referring to Mayor Ivan Allen Jr., originally an ardent segregationist who had then changed his stance on race at a time when most southern politicians were doubling down on segregation. After becoming head of the local chamber of commerce, Allen shrewdly labored behind the scenes to integrate the city. In 1961, with Black Atlantans giving him their votes, he thrashed a notoriously racist restaurateur named Lester Maddox to become the mayor. His predecessor, William Hartsfield, had coined the tagline—a city that was too busy to hate—in 1955. "We do not want the hatred of Montgomery or Little Rock," Hartsfield declared. He saw the handwriting on the wall—that refusing to accept racial equality was impeding economic change. Taking office in 1962, Allen continued Hartsfield's efforts. He desegregated the city hall's cafeteria and testified before the Senate in support of Kennedy's Civil Rights Bill, something that no other elected official in the South dared to do. Mal respected that; he had a soft spot for politicians who saw the light on race and partnered with Black people.[8]

After convincing Sheehan to greenlight his project, Mal and the producer Arthur Holch headed to Atlanta. They stayed for ten weeks, returning home on weekends. Their crew went to the top of Stone Mountain where the Klan had gathered, the Capital Club where the wealthiest white men in Atlanta met for lunch, and Vine City, a Black neighborhood that showed how much remained to be done. Interviews featured a multiracial, mostly male, cast of leaders and citizens. The documentary showcased Atlanta's futuristic skyline and building boom but did not soft peddle the poverty in its midst.

Mal saw the spirit and strength personified by Black Atlantans and applauded their gains at the ballot box and at work. Because a progressive white element had emerged, the city was changing for the better. Mal believed Atlanta would become the vanguard of the new South, if it was able to tap its potential, finding ways to address inequality and racism while flexing economic muscle. He saw Black Atlanta building Black power, not rhetorically, but materially.

Mal began the documentary with the Reverend William Holmes Borders standing by a stained-glass window at the Wheat Street Baptist Church. Few people had more authority to address Atlanta's past than Borders, whose radio show was the city's second-highest-rated program. "The Atlanta of thirty-two years ago, which I first came to know on arrival in '37," the veteran activist recounted, "was segregated from top to bottom, buses, trolleys, railroad stations, businesses, everything. Schools, even churches—I mean the church of the living God—were segregated." Dr. Benjamin Mays, Morehouse College's emeritus president, then jumped in, recalling past indignities. "But now there is an atmosphere of freedom, you feel more like an individual, like a man." That set up Mayor Allen, who declared that integration was essential to "trying to build something worthy of people who live here." Julian Bond, a SNCC cofounder and state representative, was more measured. If you think that a city "ought to provide citizens with a decent standard of living, decent housing, adequate police protection, sanitation services, then it's really not a great city to live in," he countered. "It's like any other big city. It's callous, it's very cruel, has large numbers of very poor people. It's just not a very happy place to live."

The tension between past and present and between and among white and Black Atlantans shaped the documentary. Mal didn't dodge these conflicts; despite his hopes for Atlanta's future, he knew integration was a work in progress. "Ever since Sherman left Atlanta in flames, the city has had two faces," he professed. "One is a shrine to the Old South embalmed in *Gone with the Wind*, the other is the image of a hustling, industrial, sometimes liberal, New South." That contradiction propelled the hour-long show.

As a jaunty version of "Yankee Doodle Dandy" segued into "Dixie," Klan members marched down a city street and Mal, off camera, said, "For a long time, Atlanta was the hub of the Ku Klux Klan. Now it's all a Grand Dragon can do to muster a hundred for a parade. This one is in 1968 and if the strength of the Klan is a barometer of racial bigotry, then the pressure is going down."

"Talk about change in Atlanta?" he asked. "United Klan Grand Dragon Calvin Craig resigned a year ago to join the Model Cities Program." Craig, who had followed his mother and wife into the Klan, was a heavy equipment operator. Tall and charismatic, he became a Grand Dragon before stunning Atlantans on May 1, 1968, when, with cameras rolling, he removed his hood and robe and handed them to a woman by his side. "I resigned as Grand Dragon of the United Klans of America," he declared, "for the simple reason that I am connected to the Model City Program of Atlanta and deeply involved in voter registration." From now on, Craig declared, he would work for a nation where "black men and white men can stand shoulder to shoulder in a united America."[10] Craig, who once burned crosses, said the best way to solve problems was at the conference table. "Violence in the streets of America, and by night riders, should be something of the past." And no matter how people felt about civil rights laws and Supreme Court decisions, they needed to accept them.[11] His on-camera transformation from Klansman to anti-poverty worker signified Atlanta's reinvention from a Confederate bastion to the poster city for the New South.

While the Klansman's about-face was compelling, Mal missed a chance to explore who prompted his conversion. He ignored the role that Xernona Clayton had played. Clayton, a relatively unsung civil rights leader, was close to the Kings, and she drove him to the airport for his fatal flight to Memphis in April 1968. The host of *The Xernona Clayton Show* on a CBS affiliate and the director of Atlanta's Model Cities program, she encountered Craig at a meeting in his mostly white neighborhood. When she mentioned that white friends had come to her home for dinner, Craig muttered that he could never do that. "You'll not only be eating at my house," Clayton retorted, "you'll be eating out of my hand." Knowing Craig was a Baptist deacon, she tapped their religious roots to find common ground. "I asked him what part of the Bible are you reading?" Clayton told Craig he was too intelligent to be so ignorant, and they argued, almost daily, until she won him over.[12] They began traveling together, holding joint interviews, and were called the civil rights' Odd Couple. Featuring Clayton, whose show was on CBS, might have been off-limits for Mal. But it's likely that he didn't fully appreciate the role women played in Atlanta. Whether at the steel mill, YMCA, or Alpha Phi Alpha, he had operated in a male world. Nor did he and Mary leave their traditional gender lanes. The documentary included few female voices and reflected that bias. Still, even without Xernona Clayton, former Grand Dragon Craig made for compelling television.

"Talk about change," Mal repeated. "Ten years ago, there really wasn't a tall building or a new hotel in Atlanta. Now there's skyscrapers at Peach Tree Center and a hotel with a lobby right out of Disneyland." Although a commanding presence at a podium, Mal let the footage and Atlantans tell the story. He paused to let viewers absorb the modern space-age architecture remaking the skyline. "Ten years ago, a black would be stuck as maid or busboy." Those times were raw and recent. "Now they work at the front desk and register blacks as well as whites. It's part of a resurgence marked by major league sports, a new arts center, new industry, as well as a kind of lifting of the racial lid."[3]

Atlanta's makeover conveyed progress in a city where almost half of all inner-city residents were Black. But as the camera zoomed in on a neighborhood, Mal cautioned: "They live in a paradox of racial change and memories of the Confederacy. Less insult and greater opportunity on the one hand, and monuments to the Confederacy on the other." The camera jumped to workmen sculpting the images of Confederate icons Jefferson Davis, Robert E. Lee, and Stonewall Jackson into a cliff face. "Here at Stone Mountain Park, long time meeting place of the Ku Klux Klan, just thirty minutes from downtown Atlanta, workmen continue to carve a monument to the Confederacy on a space on this mountain longer than a football field."

As a choir sweetly sang "Oh, I wish I was in the land of cotton," the camera cut to the eternal flame of the Confederacy. "It burns from a lamppost that was scarred in the battle of Atlanta when Sherman marched through here in the Civil War 106 years ago," Mal drily observed. The choir singing "Look away, Dixie Land" faded as "We Shall Overcome" welled up. "But perhaps Atlanta is better known for another eternal flame," Mal said, "the flame that burns at the grave of Dr. Martin Luther King Jr. We have come to Atlanta to investigate the theory that Atlantans, both black and white, are moving away from the Confederacy to a realization of the dream of Dr. Martin Luther King Jr., the dream that all men are equal."

Mal wanted to show that change could be achieved and how it had come about. He singled out the activists and religious leaders who put themselves at risk and refused to back down. By sitting in at lunch counters and forcing businesses to let them try on clothes, they had made King's dream tangible. Rev. Borders described the "battle of the buses" when preachers campaigned to desegregate the buses. "I told the mayor and the police chief that we were going to ride the buses desegregated or ride a chariot in heaven or push a wheelbarrow in hell." Protestors were jailed but remained defiant and ultimately achieved many of their goals. "Atlanta," Borders concluded, "has the greatest potential of any city in the world." Touting its cooperative approach to desegregation, he said, "We don't have all that we should have, but we are on our way."

The documentary segued to one of the city's enduring strengths, its complex of Black colleges—Morehouse, Morris Brown, Spelman, Clark, and Atlanta University. Against that backdrop, Dr. Benjamin Mays noted that "the great change that has come about in Atlanta is the fact that there is an atmosphere of freedom, freedom of movement and freedom of activity, thanks to the federal courts, thanks to the students' demonstrations, and thanks to a white leadership in Atlanta who saw the justice of the cause and were able to make concessions and move along."

Mal spoke to some of those white leaders at the Capital Club, Atlanta's most prestigious enclave. "We were all born in a segregated society," Mayor Allen acknowledged, "which most of the nation was, and certainly the South." But these men had adjusted to integration and seen its upside. Department store magnate Richard Rich, a leader in the city's cultural renaissance, added: "It's hard to realize that this ever existed and that it was ever tolerated." But those racial divides, he argued, were fading, with the "Negro . . . feeling he can go any-where and do anything a white man can do." They professed that enlightened self-interest had led them to embrace integration. As Opie Shelton, the head of the Atlanta Chamber of Commerce, put it, "We weren't going to build a great town unless we brought everybody along for a piece of the action."

But their Black counterparts at a club in a different part of town disagreed. Thomas Allen, a union organizer, snorted: "the only difference that I see is that I don't have to ride in the back of a bus, and I don't have to eat at a colored restaurant or hotel." The vision of Atlanta as Utopia, he contended, was branding, not deeply rooted substantive change. Charles Black, sitting nearby, added that, if there was any credit to be given, it should go to the people who boycotted downtown businesses and forced "the white power structure" to develop a social consciousness.

The back and forth between the two groups reflected the racial prism through which they viewed history. Powerful whites perceived integration as positive, bringing them new customers and competent employees. It cost them little more than a few ugly letters. But Lonnie King, who had led the sit-ins in 1960, described Atlanta as "a city of incongruities. On the surface, you have what appears to be a liberal, progressive community and I would say that you do have a small minority of people in Atlanta who are liberal and progressive. . . . But the power people, black and white, respond only to power. You have to have the most votes, or you have to have enough money or if you don't have the money you have to take away some from them in order to change their overt behavior." Lonnie King understood power. On March 15, 1960—the Ides of March—he and Julian Bond had initiated sit-ins at eleven downtown stores. Their protests continued through the fall when Martin Luther King Jr. joined them and was arrested at Richard Rich's department store. After months of protest, they finally won the day.[14]

"Not so long ago," Mal emphasized, "it seemed that never could happen." He turned to Julian Bond, a magnetic activist who had gained national prominence after his name was floated as a vice-presidential candidate at the 1968 Democratic Party Convention. Bond escorted Mal through Vine City, offering a more subdued take on civic progress. Mayor Allen, he believed, was trying to get things done, but a recalcitrant board of aldermen and a diminishing tax base due to whites decamping for the suburbs limited his options. Nor did a group of African Americans, seated around a kitchen table, buy into the notion of Atlanta as a city too busy to hate. They spoke frankly about poverty, welfare, crime, and fatherless households. Conditions, one man said, were deplorable, "bad enough to make you want to get drunk and walk on your head."[15]

Mal gave the final word to Morehouse alumni who had led civic organizations and thrived professionally. The cameras rolled while they voiced their frustration and argued with each other. A pediatrician expressed grave reservations: "If you show me one place in America where black folk move in, and the white folks don't move out, I can have some confidence in the future of America. . . . But white folks don't want to bother with Negroes." When challenged, he retorted, "America is sick like Atlanta is sick, and it is my candid opinion that white America is so infected with racism that white America would rather see America destroyed than to share with its black brother." Until the government insured that the constitution applied equally to all, "I don't think we should let America have one day of rest! We should paralyze this country; we should stop industry and everything else."

Older heads were more restrained. "It's going to come," Rev. Borders asserted. "It's ordained by God and nobody can stop it because it's better for everybody." Benjamin Mays seconded his appraisal. "I'm a realist. Atlantans need to see where we are now, see the improvements we made but also chart the future and see what areas we have not touched. . . . Atlanta has come a long way, but Atlanta also has a long way to go." Their pragmatism was the documentary's throughline.

Near its end, Mal showcased a clip of Dr. King at a local banquet after his Nobel Peace Prize. "We have come a long way," King intoned. "We still have a long, long way to go. I think we can all take consolation as a fact that as a region and as a people we have made some meaningful strides, and so I say goodnight quoting the words of an old Negro slave preacher who didn't have his grammar right but who uttered words of great symbolic profundity in the words of a prayer, "Lord, we isn't what we ought to be. We *ain't* what we want to be. We *ain't* what we gonna be. But thank God we *ain't* what we was."

Neither, Mal said, was Atlanta what it was. "This reporter, the grandson of slaves, has been visiting the city of Atlanta for thirty years, and at one time with great fear, for lynchings, jailings, and beatings were commonplace." Change began after World War II when African Americans began voting and the *Atlanta Constitution* editor Ralph McGill waged a journalistic crusade. During Mayor Hartsfield's tenure, Black voting surged, and students mobilized. They sat in, demonstrated, boycotted, and marched until restaurants and lunch counters opened up to them and theatres stopped sending them to the balcony. Then, Mal said, "Ivan Allen, the converted segregationist . . . convinced the white power structure that the late educator, Booker T. Washington, was right when he told Atlantans in 1897 that you can't keep a man in a ditch unless you stay there with him. And if you do that, neither is going anywhere."

"There are many opinions about Atlanta. This one is mine. Evaluate it as you will. Despite those who still resist, and those who would like to cling to the memory of the Confederate era, Atlanta's leaders, black and white, understand and know the evils of segregation." They also know, Mal stressed, that "keeping the Negro in his place will never work. And moreover, it will not be acceptable and must be overcome. And the pride of Atlantans has provided that will to overcome, a will that keeps saying over and over again, *it can be done.*"[16]

That's what he called the show, *It Can Be Done.* It aired on July 3, 1969, as part of ABC's *Time for Americans* series.[17] Mal was gratified by the response. "Oh, the mail they got! Why won't the networks do more stories like this?" he reflected. "The mail they got was fascinating." Equal Employment Opportunities Commission director Henry Ford gushed that the show was "superb; the topic was and is of utmost importance . . . clear and beautifully expressed. I wish more programs would emulate yours."[18] Mal also heard from Ernest Pharr, the editor of the *Atlanta Inquirer*, about what he had left out. Mal's typed, single-spaced, two-page response acknowledged those omissions. Pointing out that an hour of commercial television was actually only fifty minutes, Mal wrote that they had shot enough footage to fill three or four hours of airtime and wanted to do a follow-up. He knew that progress in Atlanta was incomplete.[19] ABC brass was thrilled with the show and relieved to hear from so many people affirming its positive message. They entered it as the network's Peabody Awards nominee in the public service category but did not give Mal the freedom to write his own agenda. Nor were they inclined to adopt the proactive stance toward covering Black America that Mal advocated. The documentary unleashed artistic energies that Mal felt had been stifled at ABC, but the show was a one-off and he never did another.[20]

Instead, Mal bounced between the United Nations and ABC, heading out of town weekly to report and deliver speeches. ABC, recognizing his capacity to reach across the racial divide while serving as its ambassador to Black America, encouraged Mal's roving schedule. He was a rarity, sought out by forward-thinking civic groups, politicians, and businessmen wanting to hear his take on a bewildering landscape. Mal thrived on these exchanges. A relentless self-promoter, he also initiated correspondence with influential people, believing they would benefit from his counsel and anticipating that those connections would redound to him professionally.

But while adept at addressing white crowds, Mal was renewed when speaking to Black audiences. He brought them to their feet, engaging in a call-and-response exchange. After he spoke to the Urban League's Equal Opportunity Day banquet in Louisville, a slew of letters arrived in Teaneck. "You had the delivery of a 'fiery Baptist minister,'" one woman wrote, "and I honestly feel if there were any souls in the audience who needed converting, they were converted by you! . . . You have a story to tell, and you certainly know how to tell it. You made me proud to be a Negro last Tuesday night." Mal wrote back, adding a dire postscript. "My travels indicate clearly to me that not only our country, but the world as well, are in deep trouble in this entire matter of 'Man's Humanity to Man' and unless we hurry up to bring about some kind of change the inevitable eruption has to take place."[21]

Mal wanted to educate, boost interracial cooperation, and encourage unity within the Black community. And though politic in his remarks, he relished telling it like it was, especially to whites. More enlightened or politically savvy corporate and civic leaders figured that his advice might help them navigate new racial terrain or at least reap goodwill. That put Mal in compromising situations. In April 1970, RJ Reynolds president A. H. Galloway requested he visit the conglomerate, which had diversified from its origins as a tobacco company into food and transportation. He implored Mal to offer a candid assessment of the company's efforts to provide equal opportunity and promote a better society.[22]

When Mal visited Reynolds' North Carolina headquarters, he was visibly impressed and said it was "heartwarming" to witness what had been done "to bring about total Equality for All the employees." After all, he preached, there is "no other answer to the turmoil, torture and frustration afflicting this nation but a total resolve by the Power Structure to guarantee every child from birth an equal opportunity in life." He lauded the company as "democracy in action," and said its work complemented his documentary, *It Can Be Done*. Social change, Mal now felt, was as much a top-down as a bottom-up effort. He wasn't turning his back on grassroots protest but was embracing what he considered progressive corporate action.[23]

Mal was not a naïf when it came to corporate interventions in the Black community, especially by tobacco companies cultivating Black consumers. RJ Reynolds had begun studying "ethnic markets" in 1969, advertising Kools to evoke coolness and promoting its association with jazz festivals to target African Americans. The company funded a segregated Black hospital near its Winston Salem headquarters and sought goodwill and political support through charitable and political donations. Reaching out to Mal was part of that strategy. He accepted these trade-offs, rarely questioning capitalism or corporate behavior as long as companies were doing right by their Black employees. Nor were tobacco's deadly consequences and the industry's deceit yet as apparent as they would become.[24]

While Mal gained greater leeway in what he covered, ABC still wrote the checks. And the network needed him to report on civil rights, Black power, and confrontations. In May 1969, Mal interviewed

James Forman, the Student Nonviolent Coordinating Committee's former executive director, in Manhattan. Two days before, Forman had disrupted services at the Riverside Church, a white, liberal congregation where King had delivered his searing critique of the Vietnam war in 1967. Seizing the pulpit, Forman read part of the *Black Manifesto*. Calling for reparations to address slavery and segregation, the *Manifesto* sought to achieve Black power by funding a southern land bank, the National Welfare Rights Organization, Black publishers, and a legal defense fund for striking Black workers. It demanded half a billion dollars, paid in part by white denominations. Although Forman had permission to read the *Manifesto* from the pulpit, Riverside's senior pastor ordered the organist to drown out discussion of it afterward. That backfired and drew media attention instead. Mal's piece featured shots of the manifesto being nailed to the door of church, reprising Martin Luther nailing his ninety-five theses to a church door in Germany to jumpstart the Protestant Reformation in 1517.[25]

When he wasn't responding to ABC producers, Mal was hearing from people seeking help. A Harlem teacher wrote Mal in May 1969. She wasn't looking for airtime but wanted Mal to intervene at her school. "We are having some acute racial problems at Wadleigh Junior High School. The situation may explode any day now. I need some help and advice from you. Would you let me know when you might be able to come to the school?"[26] She wasn't the only one asking Mal to intercede. A reverend in Erie, Pennsylvania told him that "it is likely that all Hell is going to break out soon in Erie because of a tense racial situation that has been brewing for months." Mass suspensions of Black students, canine units patrolling school hallways, and a lawsuit against the police chief for allegedly brutalizing a fourteen-year-old honor student had agitated the Black community. Meanwhile, Pennsylvania's Human Relations Commission warned that a group called "SPONGE"—an acronym for "Society for the Prevention of Niggers Getting Everything"—was threatening violence. So were some police in cahoots with the provocateurs.[27]

About the same time, friends alerted Mal to protests in Pittsburgh where African Americans had been shut out of most construction trades. The Black Construction Coalition was seeking a fair share of jobs on several mega-projects, including Three Rivers Stadium and the US Steel Building. The building trades, which offered well-paid jobs, had been run as guilds with membership largely based on race, nationality, and most of all, family connections. In September 1969, police confronted protestors, construction sites were shut down, and demonstrations held on "Black Mondays." Attorney Byrd Brown, the son of Mal's friend Judge Homer Brown, and the Reverend Jimmy Joe Robinson, the first Black football player at Pitt, were in constant contact with Mal as he coordinated ABC coverage. Mal also had a direct line to Pittsburgh Steelers president Art Rooney, a longtime friend whose team would play in Three Rivers Stadium upon its completion. Mal was too close to the principals to report on the struggle himself, but he made sure that ABC did. This was the sort of fight he relished, where victory meant tangible gains in the workplace.[28]

Along with UN assignments focusing on Africa, Mal held down the race beat, where the Black Panther Party had become a national obsession. While leery of the Panthers, he was more suspicious of the FBI. He drew attention to a Justice Department's investigation of police departments flagrantly conspiring against the group. His television piece showed children at the Panthers' free breakfast program, studying at Panther schools, and receiving treatment at their medical clinic. But Panther rhetoric left him cold and he recoiled at their inflammatory chants. "What is a pig?" one chant asked. The answer, sung with staccato verve: "A low-natured beast that has no regard for law, justice, or the rights of people, that bites the hand that feeds it, a foul, depraved traducer usually found masquerading as the victim of an unprovoked attack."[29]

Mal did his best to avoid incendiary rhetoric. After covering assassinations, the murder of Panther leaders by the police, and Nixon's hard line on dissent and protest, he thought the movement needed to recalculate its strategy. "I think there was a need for civil disobedience, but it has served its purpose," he said in March 1971. "The time for marching is over."[30] Nor did he favor separatist politics or identity politics. Despite his lifelong appreciation for African and

African American culture, he railed against Black studies. Instead, he championed the acquisition of skills. "I can't run an IBM machine with black studies. . . . I can't learn to be a brain surgeon with black studies. And you can't learn to drive that big trailer truck with 20 tons of merchandise on the back with black studies." He even questioned whether those pushing for Black studies courses harbored "deep-seated inferiority complexes."[31]

But his criticism of radicals, separatists, and Afrocentric studies paled in comparison with his denunciation of discrimination and inequality. He was especially upset at the lack of progress in the North and more hopeful about the South. After a moderate Republican, Linwood Holton, was inaugurated as Virginia's governor in 1970, Mal congratulated him for the progress Virginia had made and requested an interview. Holton had enrolled his children in majority-Black Richmond public schools, increased the number of African Americans and women in state positions, and upped state funding for mental health centers and the environment. Mal felt that Virginia was heading in the right direction. "Back in the thirties and forties, I could drive for miles and hardly be able to buy more than gasoline for my car, and the thought of a hot meal in some decent restaurant or a comfortable room in a decent hotel was out of the question." He no longer faced such indignities. "This is not to say that all is well, but the changes are taking place," and Mal wanted to explore Holton's agenda for ABC.[32]

RETURNING ABROAD

A familiar figure to African diplomats and media, Mal was less well known in European circles until his election as president of both the Association of Radio-TV News Analysts and the UN Correspondents Association. That prompted invitations to Europe, where his race gave him additional cachet. His visit to Germany went off without a hitch, but Sweden was an Alice in Wonderland—through the looking glass—experience.

In January 1972, the US ambassador Jerome Holland invited Mal to kick off his Black Editors Exchange Educational Project in Sweden. Holland had assumed ambassadorial duties two years before, but only after Richard Nixon left the position vacant for fifteen months to show his displeasure over Swedish opposition to the US presence in Vietnam. Nixon's behavior hardly helped Holland win over the Swedes, and when Holland's flight touched down in Stockholm, activists berated him, mocking the embassy as "Uncle Tom's Cabin." Mal, however, respected "Brud" Holland, who had washed dishes and tended a furnace while putting himself through Cornell University. The first African American to play football at the school, Holland was a two-time All American. Earning a PhD, Holland became the first African American on the board of the New York Stock Exchange and served as president of two Black colleges, Delaware State and Hampton. A conservative, he was convinced that progress came by working within the system, with education and job training offering a path forward.[33]

Holland's tenure at Hampton had been marked by confrontation with militant students, but he was unprepared for what he encountered in Sweden. Unable to escape Nixon's shadow, Holland sought Mal's help. While deeply impressed with Sweden's approach to social welfare, Holland was dismayed by the media's take on the Vietnam war and US race relations. Realizing that arguing with Swedes about the war was futile, he believed Mal had the bona fides to offer a counternarrative about race, something he had been unable to do because of Nixon. "Tell your counterparts here your personal experiences and opinions; you and your organization's work in finding solutions; the practical steps that have already been taken, the progress as well as the unfinished tasks." And do so, Holland stressed, not as a government spokesman but as somebody speaking from his experiences on the front lines. "This is a personal project of mine," Holland added, with funding primarily from foundations, not the US government.[34]

Flattered, Mal responded that he recognized the problems Holland faced. "This nation, like other nations, is tortured with internal dissension because we DO have problems." But that, he argued, was true all over the world. Mal painstakingly laid out his own story, from laboring for twelve years in a steel mill to joining ABC. His habit of self-promotion was deeply ingrained, but he also wanted to let Holland know he shared his pragmatism. Change was imperative, but it would not come about by yelling "tyrant" or "Uncle Tom" at someone and scorning mainstream activists. Mal, however, underestimated the depth of Swedish hostility to the war and Nixon's swerve to the right.[35]

Mal was no Pollyanna about race relations. "To indicate that every colleague I work with at ABC counts me as his equal would be a delusion; to say all our problems in America have been solved, would be hiding our heads in the sand; on the other hand, to say no progress has been made, or to intimate nothing is being done, or that we are going backward would be nothing short of total ignorance of the facts." Denying he was a gradualist, Mal testified that he wanted "EQUALITY" and that he wanted it "yesterday." But it would only come about "if we determine not to give up the fight. This does not mean that we as American Negroes should 'let America off the hook' by advocating some 'separatisms' policy, nor engage in total violence and destruction, but that we make full use of our political and economic strength to guarantee the needed changes." He looked forward to "rapping" with students, particularly the skeptics who "look upon me as someone 'special' and 'token.'"[36]

Arriving in Stockholm in March 1972, Mal met with editors and journalists, conducted interviews, and lectured to appreciative audiences. A US Information Service (USIS) field officer, delighted by the reception Mal received, called him "dynamic, articulate, and extremely well-informed about the racial scene in America." His talk to graduate students at the University of Gothenburg was "outstanding," even though the classroom was packed with "the Red Mafia," a reference to leftist students and radical expatriate American professors. Faculty and students described it as the best speech they had ever heard. "Mr. Goode spoke with force and to the point, with concrete, vivid, and often personal examples to illustrate his ideas."[37] Mal could hardly have been happier, lecturing, dining with politicians and foreign service officials, and relishing his celebrity. He even found time for a ballet premiere at the Malmö Stadsteater.

But at Gothenburg's School of Journalism, Mal entered a politically charged Twilight Zone where he was attacked as a race traitor and as Nixon's lackey. After his introduction, a student stood to raise a point of order. Margareta Larsson-Zorawska read a statement from the student union that had been approved by a contentious fifteen-to-fourteen vote by journalism students. It resolved: "WE DO NOT WANT REPRESENTATIVES OF THE AMERICAN IMPERIALISM AT OUR SCHOOL!" Furthermore, the student union voted that the record show that they rejected "American imperialism and all its effort to introduce its reactionary propaganda machinery at the school. Mr. Mel [sic] Goode is a part of this machinery. He's not just any American journalist. He's a hireling from the American embassy and the USIS."[38]

The students, whose politics skewed left, knew little about Mal or what he thought about race and Vietnam. What mattered was that USIS, the US Information Service, had brought him to campus at the behest of the ambassador. They considered his visit "American propaganda to reach those who in a few years will function as creators of opinion in press, radio and television." The United States, no longer perceived "as a home for democracy and freedom," was viewed as "the number one enemy of democracy and freedom." Given those headwinds, Mal stood slight chance of being heard, much less of neutralizing students' visceral distrust of US policy.[39]

They pegged him as a "U.S. imperialist propaganda lackey" sent "to convince Swedes that black people in the United States have left their slavery behind and attained freedom and equality." To the contrary, they contended, US capitalism, past and present, depended on slavery. "This is not changed by the fact that a handful of blacks let themselves be bought to represent that system which oppresses their race. This is what Mr. Goode lends himself to, and this is what ambassador Holland does."[40]

Mal sat quietly while Larsson-Zorawska spoke, bristling at some charges, bemused by others. She likened his invitation to the introduction of Nazi propaganda in Swedish universities in the 1930s on the grounds that "one must listen to both sides." She called for a vote that resolved: "We reject the mockery which in the interests of American racism and capitalism lets black renegades represent the black people in the U.S. Mr. Goode is to be regarded as such a renegade and he's not welcome to our school." The resolution passed forty-four to two.[41]

Rather than leave, Mal addressed a scrum of students who remained after the vote. He didn't need a podium or the decorum of a lecture to do that. Speaking with passion but keeping his anger in check, Mal countered their arguments. White students in their early twenties five thousand miles from the United States, he said, could not possibly tell him, a Black American, what it was like to live in his own country. "I've lived every facet of discrimination and ignominy and denial. In addition, I've been fighting this battle for Equal Rights for more than fifty years—as a Black man." Mal granted that the United States had shortcomings but pointed to the progress it had made. "We will not stop," he declared, "until every facet of discrimination and bigotry is erased." He later wrote that "the students who gathered at the door with their leader to listen to me got the message, and the leader, too."[42] While being belittled as a lackey for imperialism, an Uncle Tom, and apologist for the Vietnam war had his head spinning, Mal had heard worse before and faced much greater personal threat in the United States than the students' rhetorical assault. Shaking off the insults, he resumed his tour.

"The rest of the program went off without a hitch," USIS reported. "Mr. Goode literally stunned a group of approximately 80 business leaders at a Rotary Club Luncheon with his eloquence and forcefulness." Meanwhile, the attack made Mal a cause célèbre for Swedish media, who denounced the students for refusing to let him speak. Calling it a "scandal," they labeled the activists "Public Opinion Terrorists." And, as the USIS public affairs officer who wrote the report declared, Minister of Education Ingvar Carlsson criticized their stunning lack of respect for free speech. Their "course of action was grotesque . . . a serious insult to a man who has been pursuing a long fight for the democratic rights of the black." Prime Minister Olaf Palme, a vocal critic of Nixon and the war in Vietnam, tracked Mal down in Copenhagen to apologize on Sweden's behalf.[43]

Mal returned to Europe a few months later, this time as the guest of the West German government. He visited East and West Berlin,

Frankfurt, Hamburg, and Lubeck as president of the UN Correspondents Association. That trip went smoothly, and the Germans did not
attack him as Nixon's stooge.

Mal returned to a nation roiled over Vietnam, only to find his
friend, Jackie Robinson, in failing health. He succumbed on October
24, 1972. Jackie was only fifty-three years old, but heart disease and
diabetes had weakened the indomitable warrior. During ten seasons
in the majors, Jackie was the NL's 1947 Rookie of the Year, its 1949
MVP, and a perennial All Star who led the Brooklyn Dodgers into
six World Series. In 1955 Robinson and the team dubbed the Boys of
Summer finally beat the New York Yankees to win the World Series.
But after striking out to end the 1956 World Series, he retired. Taking
an executive position with Chock Full o' Nuts, Robinson backed
economic initiatives in the Black community and became ever more
vocal on politics, civil rights, and apartheid in South Africa. But now,
he, like Malcolm and Martin, had passed on. Mal was still standing,
but his time at ABC was hurtling toward an end.

That fall, an activist in Sweden still infuriated by Mal's visit
launched a second attack. Sherman Adams, a twenty-something
leftist African American expatriate, wrote vitriolic letters to ABC and
left-leaning US congressmen. He told ABC vice president Thomas
O'Brien that "ABC's progressive image" had been "tarnished here
in Sweden" and that Mal inferred that ABC supported the Vietnam
war. "Goode came to Sweden paid by the USIS," Adams claimed. "He
made propaganda for the Vietnam war and the Nixon administration." Adams, after leaving Atlanta in the 1960s, became a prominent
militant and journalist in Sweden. His 1980 memoir, *Mitt Amerika
(My America)* was a Swedish best-seller and was translated into
Russian and Danish.[44] His disdain for Mal could hardly have been
deeper. He wrote O'Brien that "Your boy Mr. Goode is all a part of
Nixon's *'Niggerpolitik'* against the Swedish people . . . part of a sinister
plot planned by the forces of genocide and racism." Just to make sure
O'Brien got the message, he referred to Mal as "Your house boy Mr.
Goode."[45] O'Brien, who had received several laudatory letters about
the trip, assured Mal he didn't take Adams seriously.[46]

In Sweden, Mal had responded to students with remarkable equanimity, but he unleashed his wrath on Sherman Adams. In October, he wrote Adams:

> I have just returned from the funeral of Jackie Robinson ... who did as much, or more than any single black man in his fight for the rights of all. Therefore, I'm in no mood to send you an answer but I did not want the weekend to pass without some recognition of the infamous, ill-conceived, second-hand, vicious appraisal of my remarks at several schools in Sweden last winter. Not only that, they represent a syndrome of outright LIES, nothing more, nothing less.

He warned Adams that he would answer his charges more fully:

> But in the meantime, I want you to send me just ONE NAME, just ONE SINGLE PERSON who heard me who can document either by transcription or reflection that I ever said I approved of the war in Viet Nam and in the next mail I'll send you a certified check for $1,000 with no questions asked. All I want is the documentation. I've been in more than 350 cities in the past ten years since joining ABC and NEVER, NEVER have I at any time even suggested that we were right in even being in Viet Nam and anybody who says I did is a Damn Liar.

Indeed, Mal had told students:

> Young people represent our last hope to get rid of the vicious, immoral, ungodly, unconscionable war not only in Viet Nam but the Middle East and at every other point of trouble around the world.... You talk about UNCLE TOM. Boy, you certainly have your men mixed. While in Pittsburgh, PA in the forties and fifties I went to Jail nine times in my personal fight against intolerance, bigotry, police brutality and hatred and all you need to do is check the record.

He left unsaid what he was probably thinking—what had Adams done other than leave the country? "My advice to you is to Blow your Mind with some facts and then make some determination about me." He signed off: "Yours for Total Equality which I was fighting for before you were born, Mal Goode."[47]

Jackie Robinson played a decade in the majors, Mal worked at ABC a year longer. At his retirement affair in 1973, ABC executives compared them. ABC Chairman Leonard Goldenson saluted Mal, noting: "You, like Jackie Robinson, were the individual who led the way to opening up opportunities for many others to become professional newsmen and women in the field of electronic journalism." Jim Hagerty seconded what Mal's success meant for African Americans entering the industry. "As Jackie Robinson did for baseball, Mal was the fella who led the way. And the men and women we have in TV, radio, not only on networks but all over the country, is a personal tribute to Mal, his professional dignity, honor, and the way he covered stories."[48]

Hagerty's revisionist history of Mal's hiring, however, downplayed Robinson's role as the catalyst to that decision. "When I came in from the government to help reorganize a news department that wasn't," Hagerty asserted, "one of the things that surprised me the most was that there wasn't a black reporter on TV or radio either on networks or stations around this country, and I immediately started a search for an individual who could pave the way." Hagerty called Jesse Vann at the *Courier* to ask about Mal. "She said she'd hate to lose him but go ahead. I called Mal and asked him to come in." When the search was completed, "I called his home in Pittsburgh and I talked to his wife, and told her who I was and said I'd like to talk to Mal. And she said 'Well, would you mind telling me your decision." And I said 'Yeah, if he comes to work on Monday next week, then he works for ABC News.' And then I talked to Mal and I think it was a Friday, and he said: 'Are you sure you want me to wait till Monday?'"

When it was his turn at the podium, Mal began by saying, "I don't know whether you want the $10 speech, $250 speech, and I have a $500 speech. Sometimes I give that one." Uncharacteristically brief, he refrained from challenging Jim Hagerty's spin on his hiring. Mal had always credited Jackie Robinson with confronting Hagerty over ABC's failure to hire African Americans for anything but menial positions. Instead, he graciously thanked the speakers for noting his ability to bond with doormen and typists as well as cameramen and editors. His years at ABC, he said, "have been much more than I ever dreamed they would be, and along the line of life I think I've made some trends at ABC that I wouldn't take any amount of money for. And I'm so glad [ABC president] Elmer Rule said what he did about making friends in every category." Mal mentioned that Manny Soriano, who cleaned his ABC offices, was at the ball game that evening with tickets that he had left for him from Henry Aaron. Mal thanked his cameramen for teaching him on the job. "So many times, they said to me: 'Mal you didn't mean to say it that way, did you?' because they didn't want me to stumble." No women spoke at the affair and Mal seemed oblivious to how patronizing his comments about women sounded. He thanked "all those little girls," who had assisted him over the years, including "little Lynn," "little Patsy," and "that little black girl who was Elmer's secretary who I met one Sunday afternoon in 1965 at a Junior Chapter meeting of the NAACP."

He wasn't about to leave ABC without taking a few shots. Referring to ABC's recent earnings report, its highest ever, Mal said: "I think I had something to do with that. I've been in 369 cities and 42 foreign countries. I've been on 54 affiliate stations from Bangor, Maine, to San Francisco." At many of them, he confronted managers for the monochromatic makeup of their staff and pushed them to do better. Mal said he recently told two thousand students at Arkansas A&M College "to get ready" because he wasn't done yet. "Get ready and if God give me strength there will be a group of us fighting to get the door open." Progress would come, but not without a fight.

"ABC got the cheapest investment in the world in me because when I go out of here, I'll be retired from the American Broadcasting Company, but I'm booked through the commencement season of 1974.... I'm gonna carry the name of ABC, and I'm gonna carry it with pride. I'm grateful, in some ways, for what has happened to me. I'm grateful for most of you who are here tonight." But Mal wasn't grateful to those who had slighted and doubted him or tried to impede his progress. Speaking faster, his agitation apparent, he said, "The ones who are not here, I know why they are not here and that's alright with me. . . . If you don't believe I'm your equal, get out of my way. You can only stop me from making money and I don't need it at this late date. I haven't had it my whole life and I don't need it now. All I need is my dignity and my self-respect."

Mal stopped short of blasting his audience for not doing enough but indicated he expected more of them. The evening allowed a momentary catharsis, releasing some of the anger he had held in check. Mal spoke just enough about the racism that had been part of his experience at ABC to make it clear he wasn't leaving the fight. He would keep challenging the country to do better.

Finally, he spoke of his children and how they had shaped him. "For those of you who didn't totally understand how I felt, this is the reason. It was because of those kids. And now I have four little grandsons, and you want to know something, for the rest of my life until they put me in the ground and say 'ashes to ashes, dust to dust,' I'm going to fight and fight and fight, until my children and grandchildren are treated like everybody else is treated everywhere else in the world." He defied ABC to match its record earnings by reaching new heights in "humanity, so that anyone who comes here . . . will know that every door is open, and there won't be some bigot standing there saying, like someone told me four years ago, 'You use your color as a crutch.' Imagine a man telling me I use my color as a crutch! Another one saying to me, 'if you're uncomfortable, why don't you leave?' He got his answer and I don't think that will ever happen again. God bless every one of you. My home is open in Teaneck, New Jersey, and thank you very much."

With that, his fulltime career at ABC came to an end. But Mal was not about to retire. He wasn't the retiring type.

13
THE LION IN WINTER

MAL GOODE'S JOURNEY FROM A MONONGAHELA RIVER MILL town to Manhattan meant climbing out of a Black working class whose roots were still entangled with slavery. But Mal never left behind the people he grew up with. They had been his neighbors on Hilltop in Homestead, the men whose shoes he shined at the Blue Goose Barbershop, the laborers he worked alongside at the steelworks, and the women who sustained Clark Memorial Baptist Church's social and spiritual missions. As a juvenile probation officer and boys' director at the Centre Avenue YMCA, Mal became their advocate. After joining the *Pittsburgh Courier* and taking to Pittsburgh's airwaves, that calling deepened. Mal Goode's commitment to advocacy and activism were throughlines he never abandoned, neither at ABC nor afterward.

Those commitments and a preternatural drive sustained Mal when he exited the "correspondents' ghetto" at ABC in 1973 and began working with the National Black Network (NBN).[1] It's unlikely he would have voluntarily left ABC if not for its policy that employees must retire at sixty-five, but his timing and connections were fortuitous. In July 1973, NBN powered up its operations intent on serving a national Black audience.[2] Eager to connect African Americans to the world, NBN hired Mal as a senior consultant and UN correspondent. Nobody was better suited to fulfill those duties. Not only was his voice familiar with NBN's target audience, Mal brought gravitas to the fledgling effort.

The new gig put Mal on a glide path for the next two decades. Rather than fade away, he sustained his professional affiliations and maintained an office at the United Nations, where he was a familiar face and knew everyone, especially the men and women whose labor maintained it. Mal might never have said to them what his father, William, declared: "You're no better than anyone else and no one is any better than you." But a tip of his hat and greeting by name had shown them respect since his first day on the job. In turn they went out of their way to reciprocate. They even held on to a coveted parking spot for him until he tired of driving and began taking the bus. His family, and by all accounts commuters on I-95, were grateful; Mal was a notoriously adventurous driver.

Mal thought highly of the United Nations and the people he met there. After his election as the head of the UN Correspondents Association in 1972, a reporter interviewed him in the ABC bureau's third-floor office overlooking the East River: "The U.N. is—and I don't like to use the cliché—but it IS the last, best hope for man," Mal avowed. "That includes man's hope for his civil rights, because the two, the U.N. and civil rights, go hand-in-hand. If the U.N. fails, where do we turn?" Anticipating the wave of globalization about to hit shore, Mal added: "The world is getting smaller by the hour. We are going to be living in each other's laps by the year two thousand."[3]

In addition to sustaining his UN presence, Mal was also welcome at NBN's office on the Avenue of the Americas. NBN was the perfect bridge for Mal after ABC. The young staff valued his expertise, and Mal enjoyed passing on what he had learned charting terra incognita for Black correspondents. He commuted most weekdays from Teaneck, conducting interviews, delivering radio spots, and making connections for NBN staff. The new venture revived what the National Negro Network (NNN) had attempted in 1954 when it brought together forty affiliated stations. But the NNN lasted only four years, leaving a vacuum for two decades until the creation of NBN in 1973. By 1978 the five-year-old network had eighty affiliates.

Mal first took to the airwaves for the *Pittsburgh Courier* in the late 1940s and witnessed Black radio's troubles when television took hold in the 1950s. Now, on the ground floor of its comeback, he smoothly transitioned to a new professional setting and happily shared his knowledge. His work at NBN sustained him for the next eighteen years, until he was eighty-three years old. Quick to distribute the bright red business cards that his son-in-law Lonnie Parker had printed for him, "Mal Goode: Senior Consultant" was ready to help a younger generation fighting for justice on journalism's front lines.[4]

After bidding farewell to the United Nations and Black radio in 1991, Mal intensified the dogged, often uphill, campaigns he had long waged. Writing lengthy and impassioned letters and keeping a speaking schedule that would have wearied someone half his age, he remained, as he liked to say, "in the thick of things." Mal rarely turned down requests from NAACP and Alpha Phi Alpha chapters, universities, policy forums, or community groups seeking support. He responded with the same attention to invitations from national bodies as he did to groups unable to cover his travel expenses. And he corresponded with some of the most powerful figures in the country as well as anyone else seeking his counsel.

A pacemaker implanted in 1981 hardly slowed him down, and when a reporter shadowed him for a day in 1988, he described Mal as a swirl of motion. "It's one of those clotted Tuesdays for Mal Goode, 79, re-tired but busier than much of the rest of the world," Leonard Reed, wrote for *The Record*:

> Up at 9 in the morning for a conference with faculty at Bergen Community College, afternoon at the United Nations "talking about that Mideast problem," home to Teaneck again at 6 to join his wife in shopping then straight to Town Hall at 8 to rail against the Teaneck Town Council for governing a city that is nothing less than "a cesspool of bigotry." It is vintage Goode—Mal on a roll, Mal "Call the cops if you can't stand to listen" Goode—and there

is no stopping him, the retired TV correspondent, even in a formal interview of finite length.[5]

As animated as ever, Mal was invariably a good interviewee and Reed captured his dynamism.

> And all the while he talks, he smiles. His arms flail, his hands paint circles, his glasses go on and off, his eyebrows rise and fall over worry lines—but always in the center of it is the smile, sometimes flickering and ironic, sometimes wide and celebratory and girded by a deep laugh. Goode is simply the unblocked conscience of a chunk of black America and he is having fun getting everybody upset in the unloading.[6]

Mal often smiled, but when gauging the degree of progress since the civil rights movement's landmark victories, he saw a bad moon rising. The nation's direction in the 1980s and 1990s angered him. He feared that much of what he had long fought for was coming undone. The 1964 Civil Rights Act and the 1965 Voting Rights were signal achievements, but progress toward equality had slowed, the civil rights movement had fractured, and the future was murky. Although his time on earth was running out, Mal Goode could not pull back from the fray. And just as nobody was too small or too big to be the recipient of his kindness, attention, or mentorship, nobody was too small or too big to escape his wrath. Mal's nature defaulted to optimism, but he roared at the slightest provocation. Ever the lion in winter, he was ready to defend what mattered the most to him. As he had for decades, Mal rose early, dressed with care, breakfasted with Mary, and got to work. Faith, family, and freedom had long framed Mal's life. The first two never wavered. Freedom, however, was becoming elusive.

Mal was as committed to freedom abroad, especially in Africa, as he was at home. He had kept his eye on Africa both professionally and personally since his transformative trip to the continent in 1963. The Africans he met had called him their brother, and he would not abandon them or turn his back on their struggles. Most of the continent had won independence from Europeans during the 1960s, but South Africa, although independent, continued to subjugate Blacks. The descendants of white colonists ruled the resource-rich state, and a racial system of apartheid was more entrenched and vicious than Jim Crow in the United States. After the Afrikaners—settlers descended from Dutch migrants—gained power after World War II, their National Party designated more than 80 percent of South African land for the exclusive use of the minority white population. Supplementary "pass" laws required non-whites to carry documentation when in restricted areas. The government then transferred citizenship for all Black South Africans to African Homelands known as Bantustans. Organized along linguistic and ethnic groupings defined by white ethnographers, they lacked any viable economic foundation. South Africa did little to improve conditions in the Bantustans, but its economy relied on their lowly paid, non-white workers.[7]

When opposition to apartheid escalated during the 1960s, the South African government responded forcibly. Although journalists were supposed to remain neutral, Mal was a partisan and made no bones about it. He watched in horror as the police massacred Black protestors during the 1960s and railed against the South African regime whenever he saw the chance. Mal had not met Nelson Mandela on his 1963 trip to Africa, but he followed the charismatic resistance leader's prosecution and imprisonment that took place months after he returned to the United States. Mal questioned US ambassadors to the United Nations about apartheid whenever given the chance. He applauded the General Assembly's 1973 denunciation of apartheid and the Security Council's unanimous vote to embargo arms exports to the country. By 1985, after the United States and the United Kingdom levied selective economic sanctions against South Africa, Mal anticipated apartheid's imminent collapse.[8]

Mal backed ever tougher sanctions because he believed South Africa's apartheid would not withstand an existential threat to its economy. The Reagan administration, however, opposed sanctions, and Mal despised its toothless policy of "constructive engagement" with South African leaders. Knowing that would do little for Black South Africans, he placed his hopes on a bill in Congress to enforce tougher sanctions. But when that bill proposed a two-year period before sanctions would be imposed, Mal blasted Senator Charles Mathias, a liberal Republican on the Foreign Relations Committee, arguing the bill would allow South Africa to continue receiving corporate investments, bank loans, and computers, and to export its Krugerrands. That would postpone justice for Black South Africans. "I had a picture on the wall of Nelson Mandela who is now in the Robbins Island prison where he has been for more than twenty-two years," he wrote Mathias. "The South African government will hear NO ONE but us and that means hearing that we are going to withhold financial support, sustenance, if you will, unless you end apartheid." He implored Mathias, a staunch civil rights ally, to reconsider, concluding with a flourish. "I only want my country to stand up for [what is] RIGHT." Two weeks later, the committee approved revised legislation banning new bank loans, computer exports, and nuclear technology flowing to South Africa. It bolstered economic sanctions that would commence in eighteen months unless South Africa made significant strides to eliminate apartheid.[9] While the bill could have been tougher, it was progress. After fighting for civil rights for more than a half century, Mal continued to appreciate change for the better but bristled at half-hearted solutions.

While Mal had reason to believe he could appeal to Mathias on principle, he didn't expect much from his next target, Alabama Republican Senator Jeremiah Denton. But Denton, narrowly elected, was vulnerable to increasing Black turnout at the polls. So Mal appealed both to his Christian sensibilities and to the specter of Black political power. Registering his "surprise" that Denton had appeared on a panel with Jerry Falwell, "whose total agenda seems to be Racial Hate," Mal questioned how Denton could endorse "the hate mongering of . . . a man supposedly of the 'clergy' who endorses the beating and killing of Black people in the streets of Soweto." Mal let Denton know that he was heading to Montgomery and Tuskegee where he would speak about the senator's "brutal, bigoted and biased discussion" with Falwell. "I am certain you have witnessed the pictures of the South African police whipping little children seven and eight years old, with bull whips and shooting them with rubber bullets . . . did it not remind you of the meanness and evil of the late Bull Connor . . . as he and his Cossacks flushed Black men, women, and children down the streets with strong fire hoses?" Mal had covered these protests. He had walked across the Edmund Pettis bridge in Selma and spoken from the pulpit of the 16th Street Baptist Church in Birmingham where four girls died in a bombing in 1963. "Mr. Senator . . . God is going to punish us if we do not stake a stand for that which is right, not only in South Africa but in our own country as well."[10]

Mal lived long enough to witness the end of apartheid and Nelson Mandela walk free after twenty-seven years of imprisonment. Like the passage of the 1964 Civil Rights Act, Mandela's election as South Africa's president in 1994 underscored that people could change the world. Mal would do that close to home, in Teaneck.

A New Jersey suburb across the Hudson River from Manhattan, Teaneck had enjoyed exceptionally positive press for its racial vibe since 1949 when it was described as "America's Model Community." It was touted as the first town in the nation to vote to integrate its schools. But Mal saw its shortcomings and was quick to point them out. For Theodora and Archie Lacey, he was the older comrade-in-arms they wanted alongside them as they fought to make Teaneck's rhetoric of progress real. For others, he was a gadfly, the town's prickly conscience they could not ignore.[11]

Mary and Mal bought Arlene and Elston Howard's house in Teaneck, New Jersey, in 1963 and made it their home for thirty years. The split-level redbrick house was their haven, where they celebrated both the landmark civil rights victories of the 1960s and the joys of watching their children and grandchildren emerge into their own. But there were stumbles and sadness. They lost friends and comrades to illness and assassination and witnessed a backlash to civil rights gain momentum. Mal spent more time there after leaving ABC, but this did not mean he was withdrawing from the issues that defined his tenure at the network. The struggle for freedom—securing civil rights, ending apartheid in South Africa, and confronting Teaneck's shortcomings—still shaped his life. For most of the next eighteen years, Mal commuted weekdays to the United Nations and NBN's Manhattan headquarters. Once there, he prepared radio spots for the network, fired off letters, and kept to a relentless schedule of out-of-town speeches. But Mal also had more time for friends, comrades, and family, and 80 Howland Avenue was the crossroads for the Goode clan.

Not long after they moved to Teaneck, Mal's younger sister, Mary Dee, paid a visit. Mal had been flying high in 1963, making the leap from local radio to national television and about to head to Africa for his first foray abroad. Mary Dee, a vivacious barrier-breaking pioneer for women on the airwaves, had boosted Mal's career in radio. They had partnered on the air on WHOD and its successor station, WAMO. Now aged fifty-one, Mary Dee was living in Philadelphia where she hosted her own program, "Songs of Faith," on WHAT-AM. But she had been diagnosed with colon cancer and the prognosis was grim. Mal and Mary knew that, but the cancer's impact was demonstrably worse than they anticipated. Mary Dee sat on the couch, weak and thin but smiling, when Mal walked in the front door after a day in Manhattan. He greeted his sister warmly and excused himself to go to his room to complete his nightly ritual of changing clothes and kneeling in prayer before heading back downstairs. While upstairs, he wept at the sight of his beautiful and beloved sister decimated by disease, muffling his sobs so she wouldn't hear his grief. Mary Dee was resolute. That courage, *Pittsburgh Courier* journalist Hazel Garland wrote, had allowed her to "surmount the barriers she faced as the nation's first Negro woman disc jockey" and then endure "unimaginable pain without uttering a complaint."[12] Mary Dee succumbed in March 1964.

More than three thousand mourners paid her tribute at Jones Memorial Baptist Church in Philadelphia before she was brought to

Pittsburgh. Hundreds more filed in and out of the Frederick Funeral Home and attended services at Clark Memorial Baptist Church in Homestead, a few blocks from where she grew up and debuted on WHOD. Mary Dee's two sons, Franklin and Sherwood Dudley, and two daughters, Sherlynn Reid and Yvonne "Bonnie" Pendleton, joined their mother as she was taken to her final resting place at Restland–Lincoln Memorial Cemetery. It was fifteen miles away from the church, but a cold rain did not deter hundreds from accompanying her to her grave.[13] Mal was skilled at keeping his emotions in check, but Mary Dee's death was hard to take.

The only other time his family recalled Mal collapsing in emotion was on January 1, 1973, when he learned that Roberto Clemente, just thirty-eight years old, had died in a plane crash while traveling to deliver aid to victims of the 1972 Nicaraguan earthquake. His plane plunged into the ocean after taking off in San Juan, Puerto Rico, on New Year's Eve. Mal sobbed with grief when the news broke the next day. Roberto had often sat at Mary and Mal's table after arriving in Pittsburgh in 1955. One of sport's *nonpareils*, Clemente, like Jackie Robinson and Henry Aaron, was in the vanguard of those seeking social justice in sport. He had escorted Martin Luther King Jr. during his visit to Puerto Rico and led major leaguers in their refusal to begin the 1968 season until after King's funeral that April.

By the time Mary and Mal settled into Teaneck only their two youngest children, Ronald and Rosalia, were still at home. Mal had lodged in Manhattan the previous year without his family, commuting to Pittsburgh on weekends when he could. But he was unaccustomed to living alone and wanted family surrounding him. He and Mary waited to relocate the family until Roberta finished high school, unwilling to interrupt her senior year. Mal also wanted to get the lay of the land and find the best place for the family to settle. Once he did, the Goodes accepted an offer from the Howards to buy their home as they prepared to move into a larger home on the other side of Teaneck. Mal first met Elston when the Kansas City Monarchs played in Pittsburgh. Now at the peak of a two-decade career that began in the Negro American League in 1948, Howard was a versatile All-Star for the Yankees and had just won the American League MVP award.

The Goodes planned on moving into the ten-year-old, fourteen-hundred-square-foot house before the 1963 school year, allowing Roberta to start at Bennett College in Greensboro, North Carolina, and Ronald and Rosalia to enter the Teaneck system for the new school year. But the Howards' move was delayed, postponing the Goodes' arrival until October. The school year did not start well for Rosalia. "I was lost at school," she reflected. "I was used to easily making straight As but the Teaneck school system was far more advanced, and I floundered in the sixth grade." Nor was it easy to feel accepted. "People on the street were outwardly friendly, but there was a secretive, closed atmosphere." Mary had been pulled away from her church, family, and friends. With Mal at work or on the road, "We had to confront Teaneck, the town with its NYC bedroom town sensibilities." But Rosalia regained her academic footing, with Mal patiently tutoring her in math and her parents' confidence steadying her. From then on, she excelled. Teaneck's teachers and coursework prepared her for college and sharpened her writing skills. "My folks just said study, study, study and go to college. As Roberta always says, 'It wasn't *if* you were going, just *where . . .* but you *were* going!'"[4]

When it was time for Rosalia to make that decision, Mary told her she could attend any college she chose but had one request—visit Spelman College in Atlanta. Mary enlisted Roberta and her husband to take Rosalia there on a spring weekend. On that visit, Rosalia's world expanded. Marvin Gaye's music reverberated from dorm windows as Black students circulated on campus, laughing, chatting, and heading to class. Returning to Teaneck, Rosalia announced she would attend Spelman. Mary just smiled. She later revealed she thought it best for her to attend a Historically Black College or University (HBCU), because life in Teaneck was so white dominated. She wanted Rosalia to experience a proud Black environment. After Spelman, Rosalia entered Duke Law School. Among its first Black female students, she was one of seven African Americans in the 1977 graduating class.[15]

Mary was happy about her husband's breakthrough and ABC's paychecks, but she struggled to anchor the family to 80 Howland Avenue. She monitored household finances and managed their affairs, and she was, as she had been in Pittsburgh, the beating heart of the household. But Teaneck was not the Steel City. Household rhythms revolved around Mal's ABC job and speaking engagements—packing and unpacking, good-byes and hellos, reminders and catch-up sessions. These rituals, born of necessity, as well as habits acquired coping with layoffs at the mill, the Great Depression, and World War II, grounded them. Mal still gathered left over napkins from restaurants on the road and stashed them in his suitcase, delivering them to Mary who stored them with kitchen supplies upon his return.

Mal and Mary had lived in Homestead, the Hill, and East Liberty their entire lives before leaving the city. Pittsburgh was home to a sparkling array of Black leaders, performers, and entertainers, but Teaneck had a different sort of cachet. Its proximity to New York City attracted people from sports, the arts, and industry. The *New York Herald Tribune* wrote about crooner Pat Boone living on Mildred Street and coaching his Little League team. Teaneck residents, the *Tribune* noted, "are pretty proud" of novelist Robert Molloy, songwriter Moe Jaffe, singers Al Hibbler and Eddie Ames of the Ames Brothers, jazz trombonist J. J. Johnson, New York Giants tackle "Rosey" Brown, and Manhattan ad executive Jean Wade Rindlaub.[16] The Goodes were now a few doors down from Hibbler, a civil rights activist and baritone vocalist who sang with Duke Ellington, living in a more upscale neighborhood than any they had ever known.

The neighborhood was home to Black and white families with the latter in the majority. By the mid-1960s, more than one-fifth of Teaneck's population was Jewish, and 7 percent African American.[17] The Goodes became friendly with their next-door neighbors, including African Americans Jessie and George Bennett. Mal talked shop with George, a PhD who worked at the United Nations. On the other side was another Black family, the Davises, whose daughter Holly was

Rosalia's age. The neighborhood "know-it-all" lived across the street. Mal, however, grew tired of his white neighbor's visits to offer unsolicited advice and confronted him when he harangued Ronald for using a push mower, extolling the virtues of a gas lawn mower. "George," Mal started, "I've been around grass my whole life. I know how grass works. My son will be using the push mower to mow my grass. And George, I don't care about the grass." The nebby neighbor quieted down after that, but the family delighted in retelling the story. It was even better than Mal confronting Papa Doc Duvalier or the Klan.[18]

No longer part of the bedrock of the Black community as they had been in Pittsburgh, the Goodes assumed different roles. Mal was more absent than before; his travel for work and lectures grew more frequent and their durations longer. He spent nine weeks on assignment in Africa in 1963 and three weeks in Atlanta producing the documentary *It Can Be Done* in 1969. There were few weeks when he wasn't flying somewhere to speak or report. When in town, Mal routinely showed up with hungry guests in tow, including his younger ABC colleagues Peter Jennings and David Snell.

Mary could not re-create the community they had relished in Pittsburgh, but she did her best. She coped with being at home without Mal. When a bedroom space heater sparked a fire on New Year's Eve of 1969 only Rosalia and Roberta's infant son Randy were with her. Mal was on assignment. As smoke filled the house, Mary scooped up Randy and pushed Rosalia out the door. She frantically banged on neighbors' doors yelling for someone to call for help but nobody was home. They were out celebrating. The newly decorated second floor bedroom was destroyed (it had been a surprise from Mal for Mary), but they were otherwise unscathed. Mary was terrified, while Mal focused on the goodwill and concern the neighbors later conveyed.[19]

With fewer children at home and Mal out of town, Mary had more time to explore and discover. She had abandoned her own educational and professional aspirations as a young woman in Pittsburgh to help her widowed mother care for younger siblings. After graduating Peabody High School in East Liberty in 1931, Mary had foregone a career to care for family. Despite raising six children and Mal's frenzied commitment to work and civil rights, she had sacrificed without complaint. Now she relished new flexibility, even though it came in unfamiliar surroundings and without a driver's license. The family maintained its split church affiliations. Mal became a parishioner at the First Baptist Church of Teaneck and served as a Sunday School teacher and trustee for the next thirty years. Mary joined the Prophetic Church of God in Paterson, New Jersey, where she met "Sister" Betty Lawson, who became her closest New Jersey friend. Betty and her husband, Robert, shuttled Rosalia and Mary to church every Sunday. Although Mary tried twice to obtain a driver's license, which would have expanded her own vistas, both times nerves prevented her from passing. That added a wrinkle to the story she often told—that she never wanted to learn to drive because "I'd be driving Mal around all day."[20]

Mary briefly secured part-time work proofreading for a check printing company and delighted in the small paycheck. She discovered the magic of frozen meals and prepared dishes from the grocery store and took to "doctoring" them, adding her own twist before placing them on the table. Children and grandchildren were puzzled when a pie seemed a little different than Mary's baking. When asked by skeptics if she had made the dish, Mary looked them in the eye and playfully countered, "It came out of my kitchen, didn't it?"[21] Despite all the praise heaped on Mary's cooking and its place in family lore, the truth slowly emerged: she did not like to cook. That reality was obscured by a remarkable talent to produce sumptuous meals out of a sparse refrigerator. David Snell, Mal's ABC News colleague, was a frequent guest. "I always had the feeling that she had a feast every night. Mal brought whoever he brought, and she was always ready for it."[22] Despite her legendary culinary skills, one of Mary's favorite possessions was a sign she was gifted that boldly declared, "MARY'S KITCHEN IS CLOSED."

David Snell had unique insight into Mal and Mary. Snell joined ABC in 1967 and was instantly drawn to Mal's professionalism and avuncularity. The Michigan native had worked in radio before entering the military and heading overseas for a tour of duty in Vietnam before injury brought him back to the States. While recuperating and making plans to reenter radio journalism, Snell turned on ABC News and saw Peter Jennings anchoring the national news. ABC had hired Jennings for the anchor desk in 1965 when he was only twenty-six years old, making the Canadian the youngest national news anchor. Snell immediately applied to ABC. "I figured if they hired someone as young as him, they might hire me."[23]

Snell arrived at "7 West" and met his "cubicle mate" who became his colleague, mentor, and friend. "Mal was a gentleman," Snell recalls as he recounts the story of Lem Tucker, who started at NBC in 1965 and joined ABC in 1972. A highly recognized journalist who notched two Emmys, Tucker often clashed with colleagues and supervisors. Snell once suggested to Mal that had the peripatetic Tucker been the first Black correspondent in network news, there wouldn't have been a second one for ten years. Since the first was Mal, Snell concluded, the door stayed open for other Black professionals.[24]

Snell was younger, white, and more radical than his sage adviser, but the two became fast friends who debated reporting ethics in a turbulent landscape affected by office politics and the radicalization of the civil rights, antiwar, and women's movements. As with most of Mal's relationships, the barrier between professional and personal disappeared. Snell and his wife, Mary Lou, were frequent guests at the Goodes' house and quickly felt at home. "You never worried about where you should sit and what you should do. Mary was so welcoming." When Snell began socializing with other young professionals at ABC, Mal invited them to dinner, too. After they became parents, their first trip with the baby was to visit the Goodes. When they moved to Atlanta, Mal stayed at their home during his frequent trips to Georgia. He was always welcome, Snell laughed, recalling that Mal once left his pajamas behind in the guest room. They joked that Mal was leaving a message that the guest room was actually *his room*.[25]

The 370 miles between Teaneck and Pittsburgh didn't prevent 80 Howland Avenue from becoming the hub for the extended Goode family. Friends from Pittsburgh visited, especially Mary's brother Bob Lavelle and her sister-in-law Adah. Bob, who worked as a realtor,

had opened Dwelling House Savings and Loan on the Hill, the first
Black-owned, FDIC-backed financial institution in the country. His
obituary called him "as much a preacher as a banker in his evangelistic
crusade" to increase homeownership among low-income Pittsburghers unable to secure mortgages.[26] Adah relished Broadway shows
and VIP tours at the United Nations. She had always expected Mal
to become prominent but figured that would happen in Pittsburgh.
Instead, she saw her brother-in-law interacting with diplomats and
global leaders.[27] Roberta, the oldest of the Goodes' two daughters,
and her son young Randy, moved in with her parents after a divorce
and began her teaching career in Teaneck. By then, Russell was stationed in Hawaii, Bob and his wife, Phyllis, had made their home in
Pittsburgh where he became a senior vice president at Mellon Bank,
and Reverend Richard and his wife, Lois, were in Anderson, Indiana,
where he was at the Church of God before settling in Atlanta in 1984
to serve as the pastor of the Sherman Street Church of God.

Mary and Mal's children were soon building families of their own.
While their sons and daughters mostly left after brief visits, the seven
grandchildren often stayed for weeks or months at a time, especially
during the summer. Russell and Antje's children, Tamiko and Christopher, were in Hawaii and rarely made the long trip. Bob and Phyllis's
son, Michael, and Richard and Lois's children, Troy and Christee,
frequently visited. Randy lived at 80 Howland before moving nearby
with his mother. The youngest grandchild, Lonnie IV, lived in Pittsburgh with Rosalia and Lonnie III. Mal and Mary's values and the
sense of rectitude they modeled influenced their grandchildren. They
set high expectations for gaining education and joining the fight for
freedom. But it wasn't all politics and pressure to excel academically. Cards, long letters, and birthday checks arrived without fail, and
Mary and Mal's love and affection were never doubted. Granddaughter Christee remembers that Mary had her own checking account
in addition to sharing one with Mal. Mary told Christee, whom she
called "Grandma's Doll," that "it's good to have a little something of
your own" and popped an additional check from her account into
birthday cards each year.[28]

Grandchildren remembered the Teaneck home as being suffused with warmth and often abuzz. Mary made sure that they felt welcome and secure while Mal kept things humming. Mary dished out fried apples and peanut butter cookies served with bursts of playfulness, gentle correction, and spiritual depth. Her children and grandchildren delighted in her distinctive wit, warmth, and wisdom. She might have been disappointed in people's conduct—grandson Randy remembers her shaking her head and mumbling when somebody foolishly blundered—but moved on and never focused on the negative for long.[29] Mary often offered insight while washing dishes. If she thought someone needed "a word," she called the grandchild into the kitchen while she stood firmly planted in front of a full sink and gestured with whatever was in her sudsy gloved hands to make her point. They knew that she meant business if her voice was hushed and she was washing knives.[30] Mary was smart, tough, and tender, and her love for Mal undeniable. Their grandchildren saw that love when with a slight toss of her head and eye roll, she murmured: "Oh Mal" in reaction to her husband's antics. They heard "Oh Mal" a lot.

Mal, meanwhile, was always on the go and that worked for everybody. As Christee laughed, "Grandpa was *busy*." Constantly in motion, engaging, writing, planning, meeting, and speaking, Mal's seemingly boundless energy hardly flagged as he grew older. He often returned to cities where he had been decades before, including a trip to deliver the 1983 Honors Day Address at Saint Paul's College in Lawrenceville, Virginia, near where he had been born on his grandparents' farm. The $350 honorarium he received was almost as much as they paid for the land. Mary knew how to manage Mal's comings and goings, and the grandchildren adjusted to his rhythms. When in Teaneck, Mal spent time with them, trying to guide them along what he saw as their best paths. Richard and Lois Goode thought their son, Troy, would find Teaneck a refreshing change of pace from their home in Indiana and left him there for a summer during high school. Mal secured a job for Troy at the Parks Department, and he bonded with Roberta's son, Randy, "more like a brother than a cousin." Mal delighted in having his teenaged grandsons at his side, and they enjoyed the time with him, at least until Mal had cataract surgery. The surgery went well but his recovery nearly killed them all. Mal was ordered not to leave the house, cutting him off from the throes of activity and conversations that sustained him. Mal grumpily insisted that everyone else stay home with him. He needed their company and attention. The family dutifully sat together watching the news while Mal provided a running commentary. As Troy recalled, "if he couldn't go out, *nobody* was going out."[31]

Randy and Troy both matriculated to Howard University, a decision that Mal had quietly guided. HBCUs were an important institution in the Goode family. Roberta studied at Bennett in Greensboro before finishing college at another HBCU, Virginia Union in Richmond, and Rosalia attended Spelman in Atlanta. By the time the next generation went to college, HBCUs were facing pressure as predominantly white institutions actively recruited top Black students. Howard appointed thirty-seven-year-old James Cheek to the presidency in 1969. According to the *New York Times*, Cheek boldly challenged "the belief that black men and the institutions which serve them are inherently, intrinsically and generically inferior."[32] Mal heartily approved.

Cheek led the university for two decades, overseeing growth, confronting controversy, and welcoming Randy and Troy into its ranks. At Howard they discovered their grandfather's stature. Randy arrived at Howard in 1987 with a partial swim scholarship and was immediately greeted with a message to stop by the president's office, where Cheek told him to come by if there was anything he needed. Randy slowly realized that his grandfather personally knew most of the nation's HBCU presidents. Troy started at Howard in 1988 as a journalism major and was stunned when he opened his first textbook and saw pages about the significance of his grandfather. When attending a lecture by Ted Koppel, Troy was shocked when the ABC correspondent stopped his remarks to recognize him as the grandson of a journalistic great and estimable colleague. The young men had known that their grandfather was important, but his constant activity had blurred the people with whom he was interacting. Mal did not pressure either grandson to join Alpha Phi Alpha and neither of them did. What mattered to him and Mary was that they graduated from Howard University and were launched for the future. A 1992 photo captured Mary beaming, flanked by the two radiant, capped, and blue-gowned Howard men at commencement.

A PLACE TO STAND

Mal embraced Teaneck as his home but wasn't about to cut it any slack when it came to racial justice. On the speaking circuit, he had often exhorted audiences to follow the words of Greek mathematician Archimedes, who proclaimed: "Give me a lever and a place to stand and I will move the earth." Teaneck was now where Mal stood, and he would do whatever he could to move it toward equality for all. Confronting its failings, he repeatedly slammed the town as "a cesspool of bigotry." Bonding with younger activists, Mal grabbed his lever and went to work.[33]

Fifty-five when he moved to Teaneck, Mal became the local movement's elder statesman, able to tap decades of experience, media savvy, and a Rolodex that facilitated connections throughout the country. His first step was to join the Bergen County Chapter of the NAACP. He eventually joined its board of directors but did not seek to lead the movement in Teaneck as much as stand beside those crusading for change.

Theodora and Archie Lacey were part of that vanguard. Born in Alabama in 1932, Theodora Smiley Lacey plunged into the Montgomery Bus Boycott after her mother's childhood friend and life-long activist Rosa Parks was arrested for refusing to give up her seat on a bus to a white person in December 1955. Theodora's parents were educators, and her father chaired the board at the Dexter Avenue Baptist Church that had hired Martin Luther King Jr. as its pastor the previous year. The church became its command center when the boycott began. Theodora, an Alabama State College graduate who was teaching science at George Washington Carver High, joined the campaign. She raised money, typed press releases, and mobilized supporters outside Montgomery. That's how she met Archie Lacey, an Alabama State science professor also volunteering. They married a few months later. Dr. King was scheduled to officiate their ceremony but was called away to an out-of-town meeting. He would baptize two of their children.

After the boycott achieved its goals, the Laceys led voter registration efforts and mounted legal challenges to Alabama efforts disenfranchising Black voters. They then took teaching positions in Louisiana but chafed at segregation and decided to see whether the North would be better. They didn't want their son to ask why he could not play in "whites only" public parks or drink from some water fountains. "I knew it would be better," Theodora recalled, than "them being subjected to that kind of daily abuse." Moreover, she knew the educational deficiencies of southern classrooms. Archie began teaching at Hunter College in Manhattan, and the family settled in Teaneck in 1961, not long before the Goodes arrived.[34]

In Teaneck, they continued to fight, focusing on fair housing and school integration. Theodora taught science locally while Archie commuted to Hunter. For all the praise Teaneck received for racial progress, the Laceys' welcome to the neighborhood was mixed. Some neighbors moved out, and a homeowner across the street set up a lawn chair and glared at their children playing in their front yard, all the while clutching a rifle. But the Laceys, after years of coping with irate whites in the South, were undaunted.

Along with younger citizens who did the day-to-day grassroots organizing, the Laceys sought Mal's advice and depended on his celebrity and commanding presence as a speaker to advance their struggles. "There were lots of issues in Teaneck with integration of schools," Theodora Lacey explained, "and on every issue you could count on him to speak out. People would almost freeze when he spoke. He was intense, deliberate, unabashed, and unashamed in what he believed in. He was really a spark!"[35]

Lacey emphasized Mal's fearlessness in the face of authority, particularly when confronting white board members and community leaders. "Some of them were petrified. He knew everybody and they cringed when he stood up because they knew he was going to call them out and question their actions. And he wanted a response." Yet,

Lacey noted, Mal was liked and admired. His critiques were harsh but "unvicious." Mary Goode displayed similar strength, Lacey remembered, as well as an aura of kindness and security.[36]

But the longer the Goodes lived in Teaneck, the more it vexed Mal. As he saw the promise of federal civil rights legislation fading, Mal fought not only those opposed to Black progress but Black apathy. At times, his frustration with the latter reached a fevered pitch. He reprised arguments he had been making for years, lauding the South for achieving substantive change while calling out the North for lagging behind, largely due to Black inaction. "Although equality is slow in coming it's closer at hand in the South than elsewhere," he said in 1973. He spoke of seeing more Black mayors, executives, and professionals in the South than in the North and blasted both Teaneck and Pittsburgh for their lack of progress.[37] When asked who was to blame, he often pointed to the Black community. "The sheer apathy of Blacks is largely responsible for our inability to overcome." The only indication of "fair play" in Pittsburgh, he noted, came in sport, where the Steelers and Pirates fielded Black and Latin players and even had a few African Americans in the front office.[38]

Mal didn't hold back when excoriating northern Black communities. "Blacks need to go down South to see real progress being made," he railed. "I'm tired of [people] who are satisfied because they have a bottle of whiskey or believe that we have arrived because they might have two pair of shoes or own a house in Squirrel Hill. What we need to correct all of this is young aggressive men and women who won't take no for an answer."[39] Addressing an audience in Rockford, Illinois, he said that outside the South some were "too lazy, too shiftless, and too pathetic to even register and cast their vote."[40]

When interviewed for an oral history of Teaneck in 1984, Mal paired his critique of white power structures and discriminatory hiring practices in Teaneck with a scathing rebuke of Black faintheartedness.[41] Capable of pounding his points home with fevered rhetoric, Mal laced his arguments with evidence, statistics, and data that he delivered with practiced ease. "Break it down," he said, "five black policemen out of ninety, four black firemen out of sixty-eight?"

He blamed nepotism, arguing that family connections were the key to a position on Teaneck's municipal payroll. "You got a Police Department with three white families with nine members on the force. A father a son and a daughter, a father and two sons, and father and two sons." Mal cited similar patterns in other municipal branches. And (as Theodora Lacey had pointed out) he named names. But Mal believed that the Black community needed to confront its culpability. "Only about two or three of us ever complain," he rued. Nor did he feel that he was able to reach many people. "It got to the place where it was meaningless because the attitude was, well here he is again."[42]

Mal believed that decently paid jobs were critical to the Black community's overall health and its potential to attain economic power. He pushed whites with the power to hire to deliver those jobs and Blacks to raise their voices and apply pressure so they would. "We need black people to stop the attitude of I am glad to live here. I can't get involved." He called out those who said, "Well, they are going to do what they are going to do." Mal argued that Black mayors in the South, numbering two hundred in eleven southern states, by his count, were using "their political clout to get something done for the Black people. Why not in Teaneck, Pittsburgh, and other northern towns and cities?"[43]

"I don't want everything, but I'd like to share. . . . I just happen to be a black man who believes he is as good as anybody else is. My father taught me that." But Mal felt that intimidation and fear among African Americans held back progress in Teaneck. "I know they have families and I respect them for that. If I knew their names, I wouldn't tell you. But they are frightened to death. . . . I am sick of reading about this great municipality, this township of liberality, and I call it, and I've said it to the council, this town is a cesspool of bigotry, and I can't find five other black people in this town that will agree with me. They are just so happy to be living in Teaneck."[44]

The longer Mal spoke during the 1984 oral history session, the more outraged he became. For change to come to town, he implored citizens to show up en masse at council meetings. He was not hopeful about Black residents' commitment, nor could he reconcile their lack of outrage. He recoiled at the argument that there were few good

Black candidates for jobs. Detailing the dearth of Black teachers in its school system, he discussed a strike that had imperiled instruction. To help keep the schools open, the district hired 150 Black substitute teachers. Yet when the strike ended and the school hired eight new full-time teachers, none was Black. "If there was a semblance of decency in the community, in the power structure, in the administrative body, if there was a semblance of decency, they would have said, well let's hire one."[45]

By Mal's count, only 44 of the 392 teachers in Teaneck, only 1 of 9 school board trustees, and 1 of 7 high school coaches were Black at a time when they comprised 30 percent of the population and half of the student body. He denounced those in power who never even considered hiring Black teachers. "There are so many 'liberal' white people who keep pointing out to me that things are so much better than they once were, but those are the people who turn around and hire people on the basis of their being white." Mal, aged seventy-six, was not about to stop agitating for change. "I am going to keep on doing it as long as God gives me health and strength, until something is done to rectify this vicious, patronage system in Teaneck. I am not going to sit idly by."[46]

Drawing upon his experience at ABC, Mal stressed how entrenched bigotry functioned. "The pity is that they don't even understand what they are afflicted with." He said he once told a supervisor at ABC: "Nick, you are a bigot and that's not what bothers me. You don't even know it. It is a part of you, it is a part of your makeup. And I am not going to spend the time I have allotted to me by God almighty trying to convert you because it is hopeless." Instead, he adhered to what *Chicago Evening Post* journalist Finley Peter Dunne's fictional newspaper character Mr. Dooley said in 1893: "The job of the newspaper is to comfort the afflicted and afflict the comfortable." Mal was putting the comfortable on notice.[47]

While dismayed at Richard Nixon's reelection in 1972, Mal grew disenchanted with the Democratic Party after it regained the presidency in 1976. Even though President Jimmy Carter had honored Mal and civil rights stalwarts A. Philip Randolph, Roy Wilkins, and Dr. Benjamin Mays at the White House in April 1979, that did not stop the lifelong Democrat from casting his vote for Republicans Ronald Reagan and George Bush in 1980.[48] Mal's decision had more to do with his disenchantment with Carter than any confidence in Reagan. He was willing to give the Reagan administration a chance because of what he had witnessed in Bush's tenure as the US ambassador to the United Nations and his respect for his father, Prescott Bush, who as a Connecticut senator had supported anti-lynching legislation.

Mal wrote Bush after the GOP's landslide 1980 victory, extending his best wishes but confessing he hardly knew Reagan. He laid out his expectations that the administration would "lead this nation out of its present morass of unemployment, inflation, racial hatred, and divisiveness and just plain 'bumbling along' in domestic affairs as well as in foreign policy." The GOP had a chance to rewrite history, he reasoned, and if it gave "proper consideration to blacks in this nation, it will be a long time before another Democratic President wins an election."[49]

Mal's flirtation with the GOP was short-lived, and he voted for Democratic candidate Walter Mondale in 1984. By then, Mal had concluded that Republicans had no interest in addressing Black Americans' concerns, working with African nations, or appointing Blacks to positions in the administration or the courts. He dismissed the party's platform in a radio commentary as nothing more than vacuous clichés about equality amounting to "Lincoln freed the slaves." Mal was more encouraged by the 1984 Democratic convention where he saw five hundred Black delegates and alternates, as well as Black reporters everywhere he looked. "I cannot count the news people, floor reporters, field producers for TV, news anchorpersons like Carol Simpson of NBC, Max Robinson of Chicago, NRN's Ron King."[50]

Mal's detour to the Republicans reflected his sense of desperation. But as Reagan was about to leave office, Mal said the country was in a mess. Checking off problems—apartheid in South Africa, counterinsurgency in Central America, just four minorities among three hundred judicial appointments—he concluded: "You can't change things with Reagan in office."[31] On the speaking circuit, he vented. "He just does not understand. His VP George Bush once said when campaigning himself for the presidency that Reagan proposed 'Voodoo Economics' and that's what it has turned out to be. Robin Hood in reverse, robbing the poor to give to the rich." Exasperated, he thundered: "That man Reagan! Let us stop lionizing him. First, he is not GOD and there is a way to get him out of office."[32]

By 1984 Mal was vexed and wanted people to know just how upset he was. He had always been willing to debate anyone, whether they were close friends and allies or people with radically opposing views and values. If he thought someone was backsliding on a commitment or taking positions he opposed, Mal made clear what he thought in detailed, typed, and single-spaced letters. He had even chastised his comrade-in-arms Thurgood Marshall in 1966 for remarks that the future Supreme Court justice replied had been taken out of context. Nor did he let Black activists off the hook. Mal bristled when a younger generation of race rebels chided him and his generation for their moderation. A student at Fisk University challenged him at a talk, asking, "Why didn't your generation stand up and fight like we did? We marched and we went to jail." Mal asked the student his father's age, which was about fifty. Pausing, Mal replied, "How many of you were killed, son? If your father had done what you did, he would have been dragged off and arrested."[33]

No longer at ABC or the NBN, Mal had more time to challenge those he found wanting. Professional and calm on television, he rarely revealed his emotions when reporting. Those sentiments had been harder to hide in radio commentaries, such as the ones he did for KABC in Los Angeles in the early 1960s. When confronting troublesome issues, emotion crept into his voice. And when he spoke at a church, to an NAACP or Alpha Phi Alpha chapter, or a civic group, Mal was a smoldering volcano that usually erupted. In letters to US senators on both sides of the aisle, government officials, and commentators, he rarely held back. Mal would be in somebody's face no matter who they were.

Nearing eighty, Mal focused his ire on those he saw as betraying the institutions and causes he cherished. On the air less frequently now, he corresponded with those he sought to influence. He typed rapidly, using just two fingers, at his UN and NBN offices, or on the dining room table at home, using carbon paper to keep copies. Mal never stopped corresponding, convinced that a personal letter might have an impact or at least cajole, criticize, and challenge. Quick to praise and celebrate an accomplishment, especially when it meant that another segregated workplace or institution had been breached, Mal was even quicker to confront politicians and commentators with whom he disagreed. He critiqued an athlete's diction, reprimanded behavior that might cast the race in a bad light, and blasted those who slighted people he held in high regard.

A person's politics or race did not offer immunity if he or she offended Mal's sense of propriety or policy. In 1984 he chastised New York Democratic senator Daniel Moynihan for his "useless and insensitive tirade" at the United Nations. The following year, he blasted Pennsylvania Republican senator Arlen Spector for supporting Edwin Meese's nomination as attorney general. Meese, he said, had callously dismissed the notion that there was hunger in America and would "destroy all that was done in Civil Rights. . . . Does it matter to you, Senator? In great sorrow. MG."[54] Mal also berated George Will, calling the commentator's criticism of President Carter for the Iranian hostage crisis disgraceful, ridiculing his defense of the invasion of Grenada and human rights abuses in Central America, and decrying his conduct in recent presidential debates as shameful. "Tell me, Mr. Will, just how do you sleep at night?"[55]

Mal gave special attention to African Americans in the public eye. He wrote to Clarence Thomas, the future US Supreme Court justice then chairing the Equal Employment Opportunity Commission. Why was Thomas fighting with the Urban League and the NAACP, he asked, given that they had made it possible for him to enter Yale Law School? "Surely you do not believe you would be in your present position had it not been for the pressure of Rosa Parks, MLK Jr., Adam Powell, Roy Wilkins, Whitney Young, and Malcom X?" If the federal government and the courts did not address discrimination, he asked, who would? "Tell me Clarence, without some quotas, some affirmative action, when will the inequities be adjusted? In 2,050 or 2,100 A.D?"[36]

Thomas had said when speaking in Pittsburgh that "I hate discrimination. I despise those who discriminate and will fight both with every breath in my body." Mal threw those words back at him, not so subtly implying that Thomas was a hypocrite betraying the people and principles that had made it possible for him to succeed. Mal invited Thomas to come see him in Teaneck where he could confront discrimination firsthand. "I hope you will," Mal implored, "before I get arrested because, call it a threat, call it what you will, I'm not going to live in Teaneck, pay the kind of taxes I pay, and permit my family to be subjected to what we are subjected [to] from a crew of second generation Americans who hardly want us to share the jobs on even a token basis."[37]

Mal was relentless. Two months later, he beseeched Thomas to push back against President Reagan's judicial appointments and challenge him about an upsurge of Ku Klux Klan activity. If Thomas thought that the country had solved the race question, Mal said, "Then come travel with me one week and I'll show you pockets of denial, bigotry, racism, so deep, so wide, so strong that generations of Affirmative Action and Quotas will hardly erase UNLESS there is pressure from the TOP."[38]

Dubious of Thomas's civil rights bona fides, Mal expected more from Black journalist Carl Rowan. They had shared common ground politically, but Mal unleashed his fury after reading Rowan's memoir, *Breaking Barriers*. The book's buzz focused on what a US congressman had told Rowan about a tape that FBI director J. Edgar Hoover had played to a House committee. Seeking to undermine King, Hoover implied it suggested that King had engaged in a sexual encounter with Ralph Abernathy.[39] Rowan defended his use of the controversial and unverified material, stating "It's about J. Edgar Hoover's monstrous usage of these rumors and allegations to try to destroy Dr. King." But Mal was furious, believing that Rowan had disparaged King. David

Garrow, the civil rights leader's biographer, dismissed it as second-hand conjecture that could not be confirmed, until the tapes were released by the National Archives in 2027.[60] Mal was less politic and went for the jugular. "This is not easy but I felt compelled to write because of your attack on Dr. King to help publish your shameful book." Noting that he had often congratulated Rowan for sticking up for African Americans, he admonished him for trying to sell

a few lousy books by defaming Dr. MLK Jr. The real shame is that you have dropped so LOW. . . . Could it be possible that Hoover "used" you. . . . I suspect some bigots will buy your book, but thank God, most will ignore some little fellow with a warped inferiority complex who needed to peddle a book written by one with a jealous mind in the evening of a career. . . . Look up, Carl, and ask forgiveness for your shame. . . . I feel sorry for one I considered intelligent and once even a friend. I too, will ask HIS forgiveness for you, one who knows not what he doeth or sayeth. In great sorrow, MG.[61]

In addition to rebuking those with whom he disagreed, Mal leveraged connections, brokered contacts, and provided guidance and comfort, even for total strangers. When a woman in La Habra, California, read about Mal in the *Orange County Register,* she sought his advice on the identity challenges and harassment facing her mixed-race son, Jamal. Mal responded, "I wish I had the kind of wisdom that would provide for you, but I don't. I can only tell you that my father, the son of slaves, used to pound into our heads and hearts day in and day out, 'you're no better than anyone else and NO ONE is better than you, now go out and prove it.'" His lengthy letter offered historical context, examples of Blacks other than athletes she could discuss with Jamal, and the titles of books he could read.[62]

Mal freely offered unsolicited advice, especially to prominent Black athletes and powerful figures in sport. He urged outfielder Mickey Rivers, who had won two World Series with the Yankees but often needed an advance on his salary, "to turn his life around," stop playing the horses and poker, and live within his means.[63] Mal gently chastised O.J. Simpson long before his 1994 arrest on murder charges. He wanted O.J. to use better diction in his role as a television commentator and sent him a page-long list of phrases O.J. had misused on television, correcting his diction and choice of words. His English teachers in Homestead would have loved that. When O.J. continued to offend Mal's linguistic sensibilities, he scolded him again:

> It is not only embarrassing to your friends and those like myself, who are proud but it is a negative reflection on four years of supposed college and/or university training. I also think you ought to let Howard Cosell know he did not MAKE you. . . . One thing about Muhammad Ali, not blessed with the education you were exposed to, he never failed to let Cosell know "I made you fellow" and that is the truth. No one ever heard of Cosell beyond New York until he supported Ali in his refusal to enter the draft or serve in Viet Nam. Cosell likes to take credit for any black athlete doing well that he ever talked with.[64]

Mal wrote NFL commissioner Pete Rozelle asking him to place African Americans in positions of authority. "Black players now make up 44% of the NFL, [they've] made their contributions to the point where surely in 1980, there should be some in the top positions. . . . [T]ake the real first step to make Professional Football the kind of American sport it out to be . . . truly Democratic AND American, adhering to the true traditions of Justice, Equality, and Fair play." Mal recounted how Pittsburgh Steelers owner Art Rooney hired Ray Kemp in 1933. Kemp, who had played on Rooney's semipro teams, was on the roster for his squad's first NFL season. Criticized for signing a Black player, Rooney said on radio: "Ray is practicing and if he makes the team, he will play and those who don't want to see him play can stay home." Mal implored Rozelle to hire more Black officials and coaches. Sport, he said, has shown the country that color, creed, and religion should not prevent people from developing to their full potential. "But it will not happen," he stressed, "unless men in high positions TAKE A STAND FOR THAT WHICH IS RIGHT." Mal closed by inviting Rozelle to lunch at the United Nations.[65]

While chastising Rozelle for not hiring more Blacks, he praised Roone Arledge, the president of ABC's News Division for diversifying the staff and "dealing with the problems this nation faces—bigotry and bias." He told Arledge that his heroes had long been Branch Rickey, Joe L. Brown, and Art Rooney. "I now feel I can add a fourth, Roone Arledge, and if it sounds like apple polishing so be it."[66]

But he rebuked ABC chairman Leonard Goldenson after leaving a stockholders' meeting in 1980 "with a heavy heart." He was upset that ABC had not protected the daughter of a close friend, a USC grad the network employed in Hollywood, when coworkers belittled her Jewish background, causing her to quit. The incident was a way to address a bigger story:

> I know ABC Sports makes great use of Black athletes and Black entertainers and in turn, has made substantial money from Sports events, most of them involving Black athletes. However, I also feel . . . Blacks can do something else other than dance and sing, or stuff a ball in a basket, or skip in the end zone for a touchdown. As one Black man and former ABC employee who was grossly underpaid for almost eleven years, I have carried the name of ABC across this country and halfway around the world and carried it well with dignity. I was hurt, Leonard . . . to listen to you read a credo of "We are committed to Equality" or whatever those empty words may mean. I repeat, take a look at the Management team the next time you sit down for a session on policy then call me and tell me how many Black faces are represented.

He ended with a comparison intended to strike deeply. "The Jewish people suffered, thousands more years than have mine and I would think there would be more empathy."[67]

Mal's letters had a common thread. During a 1986 interview, he observed that, all too frequently, gains made were soon reversed. And despite the success Mal had experienced, he was not taking a victory lap. Nor was he reluctant to recount the daily provocations he encountered.

There has never been a day in my career I was not reminded, whether it was mentally or actually that I am still a Negro. That was what we called ourselves back then. It could have been something small like beginning to say the word nigger and stopping, or I would call for an interview and they think they are talking to a white man and begin to tell me about the Niggers wanting their equal rights. When I walk in with my note pad and camera crew, they begin to squirm. I asked, what is it you're apologizing for? Was it something you said? What was that something? It was all very entertaining.[68]

Mal might have been bemused but the anger he felt smoldered.

FIGURE 21. Mal Goode with Ossie Davis, actor, director, writer, activist, and close friend of Malcolm X. Photographer unknown. Courtesy of the Goode Family.

FIGURE 22. Mal Goode interviewing his friend Jackie Robinson, who broke major league baseball's color line in 1947. The two shared a friendship and connection as pioneers. Photographer unknown. Courtesy of the Goode Family.

FIGURE 23. Mal meeting with a Black student group at the University of Florida in 1971. Mal captioned the photo, writing that he was urging students to "apply themselves and get ready to share in this nation's good." Photographer unknown. Courtesy of the Goode Family.

FIGURE 24. Mal Goode interviewing George H. W. Bush, UN ambassador from 1971 to 1973. Photographer unknown. Courtesy of the Goode Family.

FIGURE 25. Mal Goode with US representative Yvonne Braithwaite Burke at the National Democratic Party Convention in New York City in 1976. Burke was the first Black woman to represent a congressional district on the West Coast, serving from 1973 to 1979. Photographer unknown. Courtesy of the Goode Family.

FIGURE 26 (ABOVE). Mal Goode representing the National Black Network on a panel interview for "World Chronicle," at the United Nations in 1982 (interviewing Philippe de Seynes, the UN under-secretary-general for economic and social affairs). Photo Credit: UN Photo 160 821. Courtesy of the Goode Family.

FIGURE 27 (RIGHT). Mal Goode pictured with Max Robinson in 1981. The first Black network correspondent to co-anchor the nightly news, Robinson held the position for ABC World News Tonight from 1978 to 1983. The two shared experiences as Black professionals at ABC and would articulate similar critiques. Photographer unknown. Courtesy of the Goode Family.

FIGURE 28. Mal Goode at the NAACP Diamond Jubilee Freedom Fund Banquet held February 18, 1984. Although Mal abhorred infighting, he was an NAACP loyalist. Little, he argued, would have changed without its presence on the front lines, where some died and others were beaten and jailed. Photographer unknown. Courtesy of the Goode Family.

FIGURE 29. Mal, a guest speaker at a Mellon Bank event, delights the crowd. Son Robert on the far left watches his dad at work. Photographer unknown. Courtesy of the Goode Family.

FIGURE 30. Mal and Mary shared a sixty-nine-year marriage. Letters, cards, and notes between the two reveal a loving partnership that prevailed throughout the demands of lives committed to public service, family, and faith. Photographer unknown. Courtesy of the Goode Family.

FIGURE 31. Mal Goode, in his Teaneck home in 1990. After leaving the United Nations and the National Black Network in 1991, Mal kept himself, as he often said, in "the thick of it," working from home in Teaneck. Although his pace slowed, his activism continued through his writing and speaking engagements. Photographer unknown. Courtesy of the Goode Family.

FIGURE 32. By the end of his television career at ABC, Mal Goode was often called the dean of Black journalism.

FIGURE 33. Mal Goode's career took him from Homestead and the Hill to Europe and Africa.

AFTERMATH

Mal's forays into Manhattan became less frequent and his days at the United Nations and the National Black Network dwindled. But it wasn't easy winding down when a younger generation of activists, journalists, and commentators continually turned to him as a voice of experience and wisdom. Mal, once a barrier breaker, was now a fiery connection to the movement that had called out the nation's shortcomings. He basked in the adulation but was not about to forego the activism that sustained him. While making as few concessions to aging as possible, he gradually relinquished his role reporting from the front lines and became the story instead.

Learning how to balance advocacy with accolades, Mal remained on the go. After unloading on Teaneck council members on a September evening meeting in 1987, he flew to Orlando to speak at the Radio-Television Directors News Association (RTDNA) conference.[1] Since Mal debuted at ABC, a more substantial cohort of non-white media had coalesced. He was asked to offer a retrospective assessing those changes. But unlike the out-of-town jaunts he took in his fifties and sixties, Mal no longer attempted to squeeze half a dozen appearances into a two-day trip. After addressing the conference, he would return to Teaneck.

Houston's CBS news anchor Felicia Jenkins moderated the session, which was billed as "Talking Back: Minorities Tell Us What We're Doing Wrong." The Kerner Report, she observed, had criticized the media in 1968 for looking at the Black community from a mostly white perspective and with mostly monochromatic newsrooms. But balanced multidimensional coverage remained an aspiration yet to be realized. "Here to talk back is Mal Goode," Jenkins said, "one of our national treasures." As Mal began speaking, the multiracial and multi-generational crowd hushed. Peppering a compelling evidence-driven chronicle with stories of his encounters with Jackie Robinson, Rosa Parks, and Martin Luther King Jr., Mal demanded respect for the courage these rebels had displayed and the doors they had opened. For Mal, the past, present, and future were entangled, both personally and professionally. Framing a sweeping narrative that began with his enslaved grandparents in Virginia, he smiled and said, "I am an arrogant Negro." Pausing for a beat, he added: "Now some of my best friends are white. But I don't let them live in my neighborhood or walk through my front door." With that, whites in the room laughed along with Black and Latino attendees.[2]

A quarter of a century had passed since Mal began confronting the challenge of making mainstream media reflect America's diversity. Acknowledging the gains made, he left no doubt that neither the country nor the media had fully embraced equality. For Mal, that meant the media must stay locked in on the big picture, hold leaders accountable, and apply pressure. After Mal stirred the waters, the audience shared stories about their experiences as people of color navigating a white-dominated industry. Mal's career showed them that it was possible to make it without abandoning principle. Concluding his remarks, he thundered, "Do not let them break your will!"[3]

Mal was proud that he had neither given in nor compromised his beliefs. Just days before, he had railed against elected politicians and public servants at the council meeting in Teaneck. He mocked them as "public thieves" who made deals for personal gain. He held the media to higher standards. Mal often recounted the story of his confrontation with Pittsburgh mayor David Lawrence over the death of Al Spalding, a Black man accused of killing a policeman in 1954. After Spalding died in a police station cell and the authorities claimed he had committed suicide, Mal took to the airwaves demanding an investigation. Lawrence, he said, had tried to buy his silence with a well-paid city job "doing nothing." Mal barked at Lawrence, "Let me tell you one god-damned thing. I don't want anything you've got."[4]

What Mal didn't have was time; he was wrestling with an eighty-year-old body. He and Mary spent more time with their children, grandchildren, and friends while his frenetic schedule gradually slowed down. Mal started a journal in 1990 and logged their train ride in January to Fort Lauderdale, where they boarded a cruise to the Bahamas. When he stopped contributing entries, Mary then made it her diary. The journal captured the prayer and board meetings they attended, the Sunday school classes they taught, and the doctors' appointments to keep. Mary logged their children's and grandchildren's adventures and travels as well as their own trips, especially those to Pittsburgh. She was candid about her own and Mal's growing fatigue.[5]

Mary described Mal's trips to the United Nations in early February 1990 and his birthday on February 11. "He got lots of cards and calls," she wrote, adding mischievously, "82—gosh he is old." She and Roberta, who was teaching in Teaneck, attended most of Mal's local talks. When he spoke in other cities, Mal invariably saw friends, family, and longtime acquaintances, many who had heard him speak so often they already knew many of his stories. Mary tracked visitors to their Teaneck home, what she cooked for guests, and daily phone calls with family and friends. She relished hearing about what was happening in Pittsburgh from her sisters-in-law Sara Jane Goode and Adah Lavelle. One night in March, she wrote, their grandson Randy, then a junior at Howard, arrived at midnight with four friends—three male and one female—to spend the night. "Fixed dinner. And breakfast." A few weeks later, she lamented, "So sad. Sara Vaughan passed away."

The diary captured how much civil rights still shaped their lives. They took the train to Washington, DC, for a dinner celebrating the

National Association of Black Journalists' inaugural Hall of Fame induction. Unsurprisingly, she logged, her husband knew the two men sitting behind them and "They talked all the way to Philly." She and Mal stayed at the Mayflower Hotel and many family members attended the event. Mary found herself uncharacteristically impressed by the celebrities drawn to her husband at the affair. He was the one who opened the door for many in the room. Sam Donaldson hosted the evening, and Ed Bradley, Carole Simpson, and other media notables honored Mal from the dais or via video. "Mal was the big pull," she wrote. "Everyone was talking about how he had helped them. We were really in the limelight." Although Mary had always kept Mal grounded, she smiled at the respect he was accorded. "I'm really married to a big shot," she told her diary.

The glow snapped the following week when a white police officer killed a fifteen-year-old Black teenager, Phillip C. Pannell, as he ran from a Teaneck elementary school playground, allegedly carrying a loaded gun. Details were contested and tension flared.[6] "Phone won't stop ringing," Mary wrote on April 10. "Mal is home and very upset." They attended the peaceful vigil held for Pannell but worried about the scattered violence his death provoked. Three days later, on Good Friday, Mary reflected, "Thank God for seeing another day. A gift of life. So much turmoil in Teaneck, so close to home. Thank God for peace." But unrest lingered. The following day, she wrote, "Teaneck is still brimming with celebrities. Jesse Jackson was here today." Two days later, she mentioned that the Harlem activist preacher Al Sharpton was en route. "I hope and pray there is no violence." Mary knew that Mal was too connected to local and national activists to stay on the sidelines and that concerned her.

As the remainder of 1990 ticked away, Mary recorded "bad nights" and weariness. "Our life should be spent in a love for learning—books, good records," she affirmed. "Learning to absorb everything good and worthwhile before it disappears." Entries chronicled her grandchildren's relationship breakups and triumphs as well as her sleepless nights and Mal's bad days. He was stoical, she wrote, but "I can always tell." She ended the journal by anticipating the future. "This is the year I will turn 80 if I live to July. I have lived longer than any of the Lavelle women. I thank God for his loving mercies that he gives me each day. I thank him for my family and for Mal who has taken care of me all these years. For my children and all my grandchildren who are about to bring me to death. Glad to see them come and especially glad to see them leave." Beyond keeping her faith and serving her Lord, she told herself that from now on, she should be responsible to her eighty-year-old self. "I know that I don't have to do one thing that I don't feel like doing—so there." But there was one thing she wanted to do, to go home, to Pittsburgh.

In 1993 Mal and Mary Goode returned to Pittsburgh. Their son-in-law Lonnie Parker learned of a house going on the market on Lavern Street, a few homes away from where he, Rosalia, and their son, Lonnie IV, lived. Mal bought their home in Teaneck without Mary seeing it first. This time, Mary took the train to Pittsburgh to look at the house on Lavern Street without Mal. She gave it a resounding yes. Living a stone's throw from the Parkers and her youngest grandchild outweighed any other considerations.

Mary and Mal were ready, eager to head home. Mal's days of riding the bus into the city and protesting at Teaneck council meetings were over. Although three decades in New Jersey had embedded the Goodes in Teaneck and the greater New York City community, returning to the city at the headwaters of the Ohio River was inevitable. Three of their children—Bob, Ronald, and Rosalia—were well-established in the city. Russell's family remained in Honolulu, Richard and Lois in Atlanta, and Roberta's career kept her in Teaneck, but she, too, soon returned to Pittsburgh. Mal's older brother, Bill, and younger sister, Ruth, were also there. Bill, who had retired, had trained generations of pharmacists in the city. Ruth, like her siblings, had made a mark on the city. After earning her master's degree at Pitt, she transformed a storefront on the Hill into the country's first comprehensive sickle cell facility, a place where patients could be screened, counseled, and tested genetically for sickle cell anemia.

Moving back was bittersweet in that it signaled their twilight years had arrived. Mal could no longer stave them off through force of will. Gone was the indomitable warrior ready to take to the barricades, but he wasn't ready yet to give in quietly. At a welcome back reception at the Crawford Grill, Mal was asked how he would like to be remembered. "Well," he grinned, "I'd really like to not go anywhere."[7] He and Mary settled easily into their new routines. Eight-year-old Lonnie IV ran in and out of their house, and his mother, Rosalia, stopped by weekday mornings on her way to work. Mary was ready with a steaming bowl of cream of wheat and a hug for her youngest daughter, who afterward headed downtown where she was a workmen's compensation judge for the state. Roberta moved back to Pittsburgh and taught kindergarten at St. Edmund's Academy, and Ronald was working as an electrician. Mary and Mal settled back into the city where they had lived until ABC called in 1962.

But their bodies were weakening, and Mal's health inexorably deteriorated. So did that of his brother Bill, who died in July 1995 at the age of eighty-eight. His death left Mal and Ruth, the youngest sibling, the last of the six who had grown up on West 12th Avenue in Homestead. Mary and Mal's son Richard, the pastor of the Fellowship of Prayer Church of God in Atlanta, officiated the service, and Ruth Goode delivered the eulogy. Mal was devastated and did not speak at the service. Bill was his closest brother; they had slept in the same bed as kids, sold blocks of ice together, and double-dated in their blue 1929 Ford Coupe with a rumble seat.

Later that summer, a series of strokes landed Mal in St. Margaret's Hospital in Aspinwall, across the Allegheny River. Mary and their son Bob were at his bedside when he died on September 12, 1995. He was eighty-seven years old. Although his death was not unexpected, it left a void. Mal's niece Sharon Goode described him as "the gatherer," who not only brought family together but brought Jackie Robinson, Roberto Clemente, and Henry Aaron into their lives. He encouraged each of them to understand they were part of a larger struggle. "He was the person to show the best of what an African American could be, the uncle you would sit and have a conversation with. He knew people, and if you were in trouble, you could go to him." She prized how he understood "what you were going through." And "nobody could intimidate him," she added.[8]

In their obituaries, the *New York Times* and other papers focused on Mal's public persona as the man who "breathed fire." Frank Bolden, his colleague at the *Pittsburgh Courier* and a brother Alpha, said, "He could make you believe. He fought discrimination all his life. He was God's angry man on that. He wasn't afraid of anybody."[9] ABC anchor Peter Jennings, who considered Mal a mentor, emphasized his uncompromising professionalism: "Mal could have very sharp elbows. If he was on a civil rights story and anyone even appeared to give him any grief because he was black, he made it more than clear that this was now a free country."[10] ABC medical correspondent George Strait stressed that part of Mal's legacy was his rejection of the limitations placed on Black journalists: "He refused to be pigeon-holed. He wouldn't let them assign him only to so-called black stories. He opened the way for the next generation. And that's why I'm on the medical beat."[11]

The *Pittsburgh Post Gazette* flagged Mal's death on the front page. CNN anchorman Bernard Shaw described Mal as having "the calmness of a church deacon and the probing mind of a Marine drill instructor. The man was a journalistic patriot. His challenge was always live up to your principles and to your claims."[12] ABC colleague Lou Cioffi added, "He was a damn good reporter. He knew just about everybody, and there was no story that was too small to him." Those who worked alongside Mal spoke of his love and pride for his family. Cioffi added, "he was a great man for family values before that became fashionable. He always said he told them—his children—that without a sense of family values you're not going to get anywhere in this world." Henry Aaron conjured up memories of Black ball players at the Goode home feasting on Mary's "greens and cabbage and ox tails" while absorbing Mal's take on society. Most of all, they felt they could "relax" there, secure and happy to be in a home where "they knew the problems we were having being young black players."[13]

On September 16, 1995, at the Lincoln Avenue Church of God, Richard Goode delivered the eulogy for his father's "Homecoming

Celebration." Although Mal had been a lifelong Baptist, he joined the Church of God in 1994. The service concluded with his nieces, nephews, and friends sharing stories and feelings. "The Bridge Builder" was printed on the program. Mal had committed the poem to memory years earlier and often recited it at the conclusion of his speeches. It told of an aging man who forded a deep river despite its stiff current. Once on the other side, rather than rest, he began building a bridge over the chasm. A fellow pilgrim asked why he was spending his last days on earth laboring to build something he would never use to return to the other side. The bridge builder told the pilgrim he was building it for those who would come after him. Mal always reminded people that the bridges they built remained after they crossed them.

For the family, it was hard to accept that Mal was gone. For Mary, it was unfathomable. But her faith and friendships fortified her. David Snell, who traveled from Atlanta for the funeral, took a seat in the back of the sanctuary. When Mary spotted him, she insisted he move to the front to be close to her. "You are family," she told him, recognizing that Mal's young protégé was devastated.[14] Mary stayed in the house on Lavern Street. Roberta moved in to keep her company and help with her care. But faith, family, and "sweet treats" did not prevent life becoming harder. Her doctor prescribed medication to bolster her mood, but at the next visit she told him she had not taken them and instead stashed the pills under her pillow. The doctor wryly asked if the pillow felt better. Mary laughed.[15]

Mary's congestive heart failure depleted her energy and will. As spring turned to summer in 1998, she told her children that she was ready to join their father. Mary died in her sleep at home on August 10, 1998. Family and friends gathered at the Lincoln Avenue Church of God a few days later, and the Reverend Richard Goode eulogized his mother. The program included a message from Mary's children: "A precious wind beneath all our wings, we thank you Heavenly Father for giving us a more than extraordinary mother."[16]

The family gathered afterward at the house, their loss inescapable. There was something missing that everyone felt, the sights and smells of the comforting spread Mary always provided for them. Nor was she there to greet them. Mary Goode was gone, and with her, so was an era. They drifted outside, onto the street. They had lost their "rock" when Mal died in 1995. Now the family's "glue" was gone. Their musings and memories kept returning to Mary's counsel, care, wisdom, and never-ending support, not to mention her cooking and housekeeping. From the day that Mary Lavelle Goode was thrust into the role of taking care of her siblings, she had rarely had a day's rest. Despite their grief, her children and grandchildren began to see this day differently. One of them said that Mary must be in heaven by now, together again with Mal, looking down upon them and pleading, "please, just give me one day of peace." They laughed until they cried.

Mal Goode and Mary Lavelle were born in the dawn of the twentieth century and departed on the eve of the twenty-first. Although born decades after slavery was eliminated, their epoch was driven by America's enduring "race question." For most of their lives, they challenged segregation and fought to dismantle the legal, political, and social apparatuses sustaining it. Mal's work, especially at the *Courier*, on the radio, and with ABC, was in the public eye. Mary took a back seat, but she was his comrade, and they depended on each other for more than half a century. Without her, it's hard to imagine Mal becoming the sort of figure that he did. She made it possible for him to attack entrenched systems and their implacable protectors, offer expertise and guidance to those he encountered, and to walk the earth with the steadfast commitment to his family, faith, community, and justice.

A sea change in media followed Mal when he walked through the doors of ABC headquarters at 7 West in the late summer of 1962. He did not precipitate those changes, but his success facilitated the remaking of broadcast news. Although lacking formal journalistic training, Mal had been well schooled by the breadth of his experience—from his grandparents' farms in Virginia to Hilltop streets and those of the Hill; from Manhattan and Teaneck to Addis Ababa and Stockholm; from shining shoes at the Blue Goose Barbershop to night turns at the Homestead Steel Works; from classrooms at the University of Pittsburgh to the YMCA, city housing projects, Forbes

Field, and WHOD; from working for the *Courier* and the NAACP to the United Nations. Those experiences gave him the insight about the world and an understanding of people that allowed him to succeed as the first Black correspondent on network news. At ABC, Mal continued his lifelong campaign to tear down the walls blocking Black Americans and fought to make media reflect America's diversity. He made progress on both, but those battles were uphill. Black media professionals continue to cross bridges into newsrooms across the nation, communicating a textured portrayal of America's complicated truths while shaping the industry. Mal's unshakeable dedication, advocacy, and mentorship was at the foundation of those bridges. His father William admonished his children to go out and prove what they could do; Mal Goode proved it, and on a national stage.

ACKNOWLEDGMENTS

OUR CONNECTION TO MAL GOODE BEGAN IN THE 1980S WHEN Ronald Goode handed Rob a bright red business card bearing his father's name during a Western Pennsylvania Historical Society discussion about the Great Migration. Rob was talking about the Homestead Grays and the Crawfords, the sandlot clubs that became Negro League champions and made Pittsburgh the crossroads of Black baseball during the 1930s and 1940s. Ronald said that if Rob wanted to know more about their emergence in Homestead and the Hill, he should talk to his father.

A decade later, he did, and Mal Goode was featured in a documentary about sandlot and Negro League baseball in Pittsburgh along with August Wilson, John Edgar Wideman, and Monte Irvin. During an interview for the piece, Mal Goode spoke not only about his Homestead neighbor Cumberland Posey Jr., the numbers baron Gus Greenlee, and his close friend Jackie Robinson but also about working night turns at the Homestead Steel Works while he was a student at Pitt, joining the *Pittsburgh Courier*, and how integration reshaped the country during the 1950s and 1960s. He hardly mentioned his pathbreaking role in the media, but his intimate knowledge and passionate recall of Black Pittsburgh's history were astounding. Mal Goode died in 1995. Decades later, when Robert and Roberta Goode, asked if we would write their father's biography (at the suggestion of our colleague Richard Smethurst), we were all in.

To our delight, Marie Brown was already involved in this effort. If Mal Goode was regarded as the Dean of Black Journalism, Marie Brown played that part for African American literary agents. Marie's life has been surrounded by books and the drive to deliver marginalized voices and writers to the reading public. She graduated from Penn State University, started a teaching career, pivoted to publishing, and worked in bookstores before becoming the first Black woman to be named a senior editor at Doubleday. She launched Marie Brown and Associates in Harlem in 1984 and guided the careers of an array of outstanding authors and influential figures, including Dr. Johnetta Cole, Beverly Guy-Sheftall, Faith Ringgold, Randall Robinson, Susan Taylor, and Van Whitfield. Marie was changing the literary world as her close friend Ed Bradley and their generation of African Americans were doing the same for the mainstream media. Marie knew Mal and was deeply committed to getting his story told. Marie was our agent and, more important, our editor and most insightful critic. Her skill and friendship made this book possible.

Mal and Mary Goode's six children—Russell Goode, Robert Goode, Richard Goode, Roberta Wilburn, Ronald Goode, and Rosalia Parker—shared their memories, stories, photographs, DVDs, family treasures, and insight into their parents. So did their relatives and grandchildren, colleagues, and friends. Without them, we could not have told this story. We mourned the loss of Russell and Robert while in the midst of the project. Mal and Mary Goode put faith and family above all else. The seven grandchildren—Christopher, Tameko, Michael, Christee, Troy, Randy, and Lonnie V—were central to Mal and Mary's purpose. Conversations with Christee, Troy, Randy, Lonnie, nephew W. Allan Goode Jr., and niece Sharon Goode Ryan revealed vivid characterizations of the Goode family ethic, which surrounded them with love, imbued them with a commitment to God, family, and community, fed their bodies and souls, and encouraged their ambitions. Through them, we were reminded that family activity and joy softened the challenges of lives lived with conviction. The grandchildren celebrate the privilege of having had first row seats at the crossroads of history while innocently adoring these very special folks. Mal and Mary continue to guide them as they live and honor the legacy built by the Goodes and Lavelles.

Mal's sister-in-law Sarah Jane Moore, married to his brother Bill, and Mary's sister-in-law Adah Lavelle, married to her brother Robert Lavelle, as well as some of their children, helped us understand the private side of a very public figure and made us appreciate that

Mary Goode was indispensable, if largely overlooked, in accounts of her husband's career. Their friends and colleagues, including Leon Haley, Hop Kendrick, Theodora Lacey, John Reiser, and David Snell answered our questions and deepened our sense of ABC, Pittsburgh, and Teaneck. Andrew Young, a civil rights leader, US ambassador to the United Nations, and Martin Luther King Jr.'s confidant, illuminated Mal's special relationship with King and walked us through the backstory to the Poor People's Campaign and the devastating months following King's assassination in April 1968.

Any author knows how critical librarians and other writers are to their efforts. When we visited Stanton, Virginia, Nancy Sorrells showed us around Folly Farm and introduced us to the people living there, guided our research in city archives, and shared her writing about the region. Her colleague Sue Simmons explained the history of the Shenandoah Valley, giving us a sense of context for Mal Goode's roots in Staunton. Both of them went out of their way to find records about Mal Goode's mother and grandparents. Doug Cochran, who grew up on Folly Farm, and historian James Caknipe answered innumerable questions and dug through voluminous historical records for us. Wanda Brooks at the Mecklenburg County Public Library and Melissa Davidson at the Staunton Public Library retrieved records and documents we would otherwise have never found. Brunswick County Clerk Ann Kanell helped us navigate the records and resources regarding White Plains, Virginia, where Mal's father was born and raised.

At the State Historical Society of Missouri Columbia Research Center/University of Missouri, Heather Richmond oriented us to the vast Mal Goode collection and John Konzal provided good humor and professional service as we churned through files and audio collections in a compressed period. Finally, Senior Archivist Elizabeth Engel provided invaluable photo retrieval and critical guidance at the University. In Pittsburgh, Daniel Ramseier at the Homestead Carnegie Library, the staff at the Pennsylvania Room of the Carnegie Library in Oakland, and the ever competent and hardworking staff at Hillman Library at the University of Pittsburgh helped us navigate their holdings and explore the ever-expanding digital research universe. David Rotenstein, an indefatigable researcher, was always willing to share his knowledge of the Hill during the years when it was called the crossroads of the world.

Patricia Beeson, the provost at the University of Pittsburgh, provided research funds and just, as important, the institution's affirmation of this endeavor. Those funds allowed us to travel to the University of Missouri to look at Mal Goode's papers, to Virginia to research his roots in both White Plains and Staunton, to Atlanta to interview Andrew Young and David Snell, and to Teaneck, New Jersey, where he and Mary lived for three decades after he began working for ABC.

In Pittsburgh and Homestead, Robert Hill and Mark Fallon shared their contacts and sense of how Mal Goode fitted into the story. Mary Ellen Butler and Peggy Preacely did so from afar, remembering "Uncle Mal" and his part in the civil rights struggle as well as their own time on the front lines. Suzanne Gobstein researched the NAACP in Pittsburgh as an undergraduate research assistant, Sade Tukuru did substantial African research as a first experience in research undergraduate, and Alex Cohen dug through hours of news footage. Cory Brazile provided quick fact-finding, analysis, and technical skills, only a scintilla of her immeasurable contribution.

Our colleagues, especially Richard Blackett, Sy Drescher, Van Beck Hall, Ted Muller, Marcus Rediker, Joe Trotter, and most of all Laurence Glasco, shared their enormous knowledge of slavery, the South, civil rights, and Pittsburgh. Larry Glasco is the foremost historian of Black Pittsburgh. His work is the foundation on which anyone studying the saga of African Americans in the city and region builds her or his own studies. This biography relied heavily on his insights about the making of Black Pittsburgh during the twentieth century and the influential migration of African Americans from the Shenandoah Valley to the city.

For Liann, the first-time book author among us, Reid Andrews, Alex Finley, Niklas Frykman, Debbie Gershenowitz, Leslie Hammond, James Hill, Alex Mountain, Tony Novosel, Richard Pierce,

Lara Putnam, Pernille Røge, John Stoner, and Molly Warsh, offered professional and personal support that steadied the nerves and helped to integrate the diverse demands of work and life. Additionally, researching and writing was a journey shared with many students, particularly as the project was in its final stages. Nick, George, and Jia offered humor, camaraderie, and an occasional word or two while deadlines were clamping down on us all.

The History Department has depended on the skills and commitment of a talented cohort of people, especially Meg Caruso, Kathy Gibson, Cynthia Graf, Patty Landon, Katie Palmieri, Kimberly Thomas, and Grace Tomcho. They helped us evade the clutches of bureaucracy with their characteristic panache.

The editorial and production teams at the University of Pittsburgh Press were indispensable partners in this book. We are especially appreciative of Josh Shanholtzer's deft editorial touch and ability to guide us through the production maze and Pippa Letsky's scrutiny in the copy-editing process. She saved us from many unforced errors.

Finally, our families, who didn't sign up for this project but could not escape its effects, our thanks for being along for the ride. Many thanks go to Alison Perrotti and Alex Ruck, a native daughter and native son of Pittsburgh, who care about its past as well as its future, and Sia, Lee, and Diana Beasley, who have sustained so much because they have a mother who absolutely *must* talk through her thoughts, and also to the patient Shadow Ridge family, Diane and Ron Beasley, Pennee Tsoukas, and especially Elias Tsoukas, because he's the best.

Most of all to Scott Beasley and Maggie Patterson.

NOTES

INTRODUCTION

1. President John F. Kennedy, "Address during the Cuban Missile Crisis," John F. Kennedy Presidential Library and Museum, https://www.jfklibrary.org/learn/about-jfk/historic-speeches/address-during-the-cuban-missile-crisis.

2. Tanya Swails, "Exclusive Interview with Mal Goode," *Columbus Onyx News*, February 26, 1977.

3. Bernard Shaw quoted from Matthew P. Smith, "Malvin Goode, Rights Activist, Pioneer Journalist," *Pittsburgh Post-Gazette*, September 14, 1995.

4. Sandy Hamm, *Pittsburgh Courier*, September 16, 1995, A-1.

5. Peter Jennings to Mary Goode, February 28, 1996. Family collection.

6. Herbert Mitgang, "Howard K. Smith: TV History," *Washington Post*, April 16, 1996. (This quote from Burke might, in fact, be falsely attributed.)

7. Howard K. Smith Interview, The Interviews, Television Academy Foundation, October 24, 1997, https://interviews.televisionacademy.com/interviews/howard-k-smith.

8. Alissa Krinsky, "Norma Quarles: 'I Fought to Dispel Stereotypes. I Fought It In My Work,'" TV Newser, October 14, 2009, https://www.adweek.com/tvnewser/norma-quarles-i-fought-to-dispel-stereotypes-i-fought-it-in-my-work/27914.

9. Dennis Hevesi, "Malvin R. Goode, 87, Reporter Who Broke a TV Color Barrier," *New York Times*, September 15, 1995, Section D, 17.

10. Wayne Dawkins, *Black Journalists: The NABJ Story* (Sicklerville, NJ: August Press, 1993), 2.

11. Bob Teague, *Live and Off-Color: News Biz* (New York: A&W Publishers, 1982), 33.

12. DVD recording, Goode family collection.

13. Kristin Stewart, "NABJ Calls on Disney to Appoint First Black ABC News President," NABJ, February 3, 2021. https://nabjonline.org/blog/nabj-calls-on-disney-to-appoint-first-black-abc-news-president/#:~:text=%E2%80%9CIn%201962%2C%20ABC%20hired%20Mal,Roland%20S.

CHAPTER 1: VIRGINIA'S LEGACY

1. A rich body of literature describes and analyzes the Great Migration, including Isabel Wilkerson, *The Warmth of Other Suns* (New York: Random House, 2010); Nicholas Lemann, *The Promised Land: The Great Black Migration and How It Changed America* (London: Vintage, 1992): Joe Trotter, ed, *The Great Migration in Historical Perspective: New Dimensions of Race, Class, and Gender* (Bloomington: Indiana University Press, 1991); Peter Gottleib, *Making Their Own Way: Southern Blacks' Migration to Pittsburgh* (Champaign: University of Illinois Press, 1997).

2. Mal Goode's notes for an unpublished and untitled autobiography, with J. J. R.

Ramey, 1988 (hereafter cited as MG and Ramey, "Notes for an autobiography"), folder 306, Mal Goode Papers, University of Missouri Archives (hereafter cited as MG Papers). Copies of these notes are also in authors' possession. They include multiple drafts of different stories.

3. MG and Ramey, "Notes for an autobiography."

4. Sue Simmons, "Slavery in Antebellum Augusta County and Staunton," *Augusta Historical Bulletin* 32, no. 1 (Spring 1996): 2, 7–9 (Brethren Church elder quoted from p. 7); also Writers' Program of the Works Projects Administration in the State of Virginia (hereafter cited as Writers' Program of the WPA), *The Negro in Virginia* (New York: Hastings House, 1940), 168–69.

5. W. E. B. Du Bois, *Black Reconstruction in America* (1935; repr., New York: Simon and Schuster, 1999), 30.

6. In 1973, Folly Farms was listed in the Virginia Historic Landmarks Register and the National Register of Historic Places. See Joe Nutt, *Historic Houses of Augusta County, Virginia* (Waynesboro, VA: Humphries Press, 2007), 28–29.

7. William G. Thomas III and Edward L. Ayers, "The Differences Slavery Made: A Close Analysis of Two American Communities," *American Historical Review* 108, no. 5 (2003): 1299–307; Richard K. MacMaster, *Augusta County History, 1865–1950* (Staunton, VA: Augusta County Historical Society, 1987), 26; *Staunton Spectator* 65, no. 29 (March 28, 1888), http://virginiachronicle.com/cgi-bin/virginia.

8. Edward L. Ayers, *Momentous Events in Small Places: The Coming of the Civil War in Two American Communities* (Milwaukee, WI: Marquette University Press, 1997), 14.

9. Writers' Program of the WPA, *Negro in Virginia*, 162–163; Gay Neale, *Brunswick County, Virginia, 1720–1975* (Richmond, VA: Whatlet and Shipperson, 1975), 193.

10. The *Staunton Spectator*, n.d., quoted in Simmons, "Slavery in Antebellum Augusta County," 8. See also Writers' Program of the WPA, *Negro in Virginia*, 168–69.

11. Writers' Program of the WPA, *Negro in Virginia*, 27, 120.

12. This system offered an option to masters who cringed at the thought of destroying families while allowing farmers who did not own slaves to rent their labor. Without the hiring-out system, historian Nancy Sorrells noted, Augusta was "a marginal slave society." Nancy Sorrells, email, June 16, 2016.

13. The best sources for Smith and the hiring-out system are Simmons, "Slavery in Antebellum Augusta County," 1–11; Nancy Sorrells, "I Mourn in Bitterness over the State of Things: Francis McFarland's Community at War, 1860–1865" (master's thesis, Department of History, James Madison University, Harrisonburg, Virginia, 1995). Shorter-term contracts were also executed throughout the year. Many who were hired out lived alone with a white family, working alongside their master or mistress. Toiling together was a departure from most of the South, where whites who worked alongside Black men were stigmatized. In Augusta, physical proximity may not have fractured racial boundaries, but it did chip away at them. More important, it held families together and allowed them to sink roots. That might have been the biggest advantage enslaved people had at Folly Farm.

14. Joseph Smith Will, recorded March 10, 1864, *Augusta County Will Book*, 35–40. This can be found at Augusta County Courthouse, 1 East Johnson Street, Staunton, VA 24401-4302.

15. Sorrells, "I Mourn in Bitterness," 81.

16. MacMaster, *Augusta County History*, 23–27.

17. "Memorial of the Ladies of Augusta to the General Assembly of Virginia, January 19, 1832," manuscript in the Virginia State Library and Archives, Richmond, cited in J. Susanne Simmons, "They Too Were There: African-Americans in Augusta County and Staunton, Virginia, 1745–1865" (master's thesis, Department of History, James Madison University, Harrisonburg, Virginia, 1994), 62.

18. The pro-slavery, pro-secession candidate John Breckenridge, who became the Confederacy's Secretary of War, won just 5 percent of the vote; Abraham Lincoln was not even on the ballot.

19. Thomas and Ayers, "Differences Slavery Made," http://www2.vcdh.virginia.edu/AHR.

20. Ayers, *Momentous Events in Small Places*, 11; Sorrells, "I Mourn in Bitterness," 15–20, 93.

21. Douglas Cochran (Elizabeth and James Cochran's great-grandson), email, June 24, 2016; Excerpts from Robert J. Driver Jr., "14th Virginia Cavalry," http://www.14thvirginiacavalry.org/regiment_history.htm.

22. MacMaster, *Augusta County History*, 28–30.

23. MacMaster, *Augusta County History*, 28.

24. Some of the schools that the Freedmen's Bureau constructed in outlying communities doubled as churches.

25. John T. O'Brien, "From Bondage to Citizenship: The Richmond Black Community, 1865–1867" (PhD dissertation, University of Rochester, New York, 1974), 67–68, quoted in Peter Rachleff, *Black Labor in Richmond, 1865–1890* (Chicago: University of Illinois Press, 1989), 11.

26. MacMaster, *Augusta County History*, 30.

27. Mal Goode, "All God's Children," in Stanton L. Wormley and Lewis H. Fenderson, *Many Shades of Black* (New York: William Morrow, 1969), 41.

28. Bright Hope shared members and services with Cochran's Chapel Free Will Baptist Church, also built on land that the Cochrans made available. The churches were intertwined, with Sunday school classes staggered so that members could attend both sessions, one in the morning, the other in the afternoon. They held services on alternate Sundays for the same reason.

29. Douglas Cochran, email, June 24, 2016.

30. MG and Ramey, "Notes for an autobiography."

31. Laten Ervin Bechtel with Susie Brent King, *"That's Just The Way It Was": A Chronological and Documentary History of African-American Schools in Staunton and Augusta County* (Staunton, VA: Lot's Wife Publishing, 2010), 186–91. There is no clear record that identifies where Mary Ellen Hunter studied to become a teacher. Although Mal Goode thought that his mother attended the West Virginia Colored Institute (later West Virginia State University), and her obituary stated the same, the school could find no record of her enrollment. Neither did Hampton University and Virginia Union University. It is possible that she attended one of these schools, but no records survived. "Last Rites for Mrs. Mary Goode Set for Friday in Homestead," *Pittsburgh Courier*, July 21, 1956, p. 1.

32. Robert Heinrich and Deborah Harding, *From Slave to Statesman: The Life of Edu-*

cator, Editor, and Civil Rights Activist Willis M. Carter of Virginia (Baton Rouge: Louisiana State University Press, 2016), 7, 43.

33. Heinrich and Harding, *From Slave to Statesman*, 69–72.

34. Washington quoted from https://www.loc.gov/exhibits/civil-rights-act/multimedia/booker-t-washington.html.

35. *Staunton Spectator* 58, no. 31 (April 19, 1881), http://virginiachronicle.com/cgi-bin/virginia.

36. Douglas Cochran, emails, June 24, July 14, 2016. The imbalance of power between white and Black people in the area might have affected how people discussed and remembered these times.

37. "The family story is that James Cochran freed some of the slaves at Folly about 1860," Douglas Cochran said. "We don't know if that's true, and if it was done for ethical or financial reasons. But those slaves continued to work for the family through the war and for many years thereafter. They were almost members of the family and seemed to stay on for life." Cochran, email, July 14, 2016.

38. *Staunton Spectator and Vindicator*, no. 49 (December 9, 1897), http://virginiachronicle.com/cgi-bin/virginia.

39. MacMaster, *Augusta County History*, 99–107.

40. Writers' Program of the WPA, *Negro in Virginia*, 238–40.

41. Heinrich and Harding, *From Slave to Statesman*, 59–82.

42. Neale, *Brunswick County, Virginia*, 208.

43. The family pronounced the name as "Guud."

44. Tracing their backgrounds and determining where they lived and to whom they were enslaved remains elusive, barring the emergence of a list on which they appear.

45. George Brown Goode, *Virginia Cousins: A Study of the Ancestry and Posterity of John Goode of Whitby* (repr., Heritage Books, 2013), 27–32, https://heritagebooks.com.

46. US Census, 1860, http://www2.census.gov/library/publications/decennial/1860/population/1860a-36.pdf; Neale, *Brunswick County, Virginia*, 500–508, 192.

47. Brown Goode, *Virginia Cousins*, xxv.

48. Those culturally conservative ways persisted. When we visited in June 2016, Trump yard signs could be found in Lawrenceville and White Plains. The Southside sits in the Piedmont, which runs from southeastern Pennsylvania and Maryland to the North Carolina border, between Virginia's coastal plain and the Blue Ridge Mountains.

49. There are no records indicating whether Thomas and Margaret lost family or friends to the internal slave trade.

50. Other members of the Goode clan owned plantations on the western side of the county, but for the Southside's African Americans, historian John Caknipe observed, that geographical divide endured long after slavery. John Caknipe, email correspondence, July 18, 19, 20, 2016.

51. Goode had sold his Lombardy Grove Manor to William Baskervill, a friend (the white Baskervills spelled their name without an "e" at the end) with whom he had bought and sold slaves. But no manifest confirms that Thomas Goode was ever John C. Goode's property.

52. Plantations "policed themselves, punished their own, promoted their own, took care of their own, and mandated religious practice." Caknipe, email, July 20, 2016.

53. Caknipe, emails, July 18, 19, 20, 2016.

54. Neale, *Brunswick County, Virginia*, 193–95, 200–208; http://freepages.genealogy. rootsweb.ancestry.com/~ajax/vs mecklenburg.htm. There was also a substantially larger free African American population. When fighting began, the Confederacy conscripted free Black people to fortify positions in nearby Richmond and Petersburg and forced slaves into work gangs that built earthen ramparts around these cities.

55. As a result, the authors of a WPA history of African Americans in Virginia wrote: "Where slaves were the only occupants on farms, Union troops considered possession as sufficient basis for ownership." Writers' Program of the WPA, *Negro in Virginia*, 217.

56. Writers' Program of the WPA, *Negro in Virginia*, 218.

57. Edith Rathbun Bell and William Lightfoot Heartwell Jr., *Brunswick Story* (Lawrenceville, VA: *Brunswick Times-Gazette*, 1957), 55.

58. Mal Goode, interview with Rob Ruck, February 23, 1991, at Duquesne University, Pittsburgh, Pennsylvania, conducted for *Kings on the Hill: Baseball's Forgotten Men*, which aired on PBS in October 1993 and on NBC on July 25, 1995. See also Ida B. Wells-Barnett, *On Lynchings*, 1892 (ebook, Dover Publications, 2014); Philip Dray, *At the Hands of Persons Unknown: The Lynching of Black America* (New York: Modern Library, 2003); Stewart E. Tolnay and E. M. Beck, *A Festival of Violence: An Analysis of Southern Lynching, 1882–1930* (Champaign: University of Illinois Press, 1995); W. Fitzhugh Brundage, *Lynching in the New South: Georgia and Virginia, 1880–1930* (Champaign: University of Illinois Press, 1993); Amy Louise Wood, *Lynching and Spectacle: Witnessing Racial Violence in America, 1890–1940*, New Directions in Southern Studies (Chapel Hill: University of North Carolina Press, 2011).

59. Ida B. Wells-Barnett, *On Lynchings*; http://wtkr.com/2016/05/13/lynchings-a-shameful-chapter-in-virginia-history.

60. James Weldon Johnson, *Along This Way: The Autobiography of James Weldon Johnson* (New York: Viking Press, 1933), 331, also 12–23.

61. Caknipe, email, July 20, 2016.

62. Neale, *Brunswick County, Virginia*, 208.

63. Leon Litwack, *Been in the Storm So Long: The Aftermath of Slavery* (New York: Knopf, 1979), quoted in John Hope Franklin, *Reconstruction after the Civil War*, 2nd ed. (Chicago: University of Chicago Press, 1994), 6.

64. http://www.virginiaplaces.org/agriculture/tobacco.html.

65. Edith Rathbun Bell and William Lightfoot Heartwell Jr., *Brunswick Story* (Lawrenceville, VA: *Brunswick Times-Gazette*, 1957), 58–59.

66. Brunswick County Deed Books, bk. 45, May 29, 1889, 260, and bk. 46, January 1, 1891, 84, Circuit Court, 216 North Main Street, Lawrenceville, VA 23868.

67. MG and Ramey, "Notes for an autobiography."

68. MG and Ramey, "Notes for an autobiography." On the Southside, John Caknipe observed, masters often studied blacksmithing and other trades and taught or hired someone to teach these skills to slaves. Slaves who only worked in the fields usually lacked these skills, which was problematic for them in making the transition to freedom. Caknipe, email, July 31, 2016.

69. Neale, *Brunswick County, Virginia*, 214. James Solomon Russell arrived in Lawrenceville, a few miles from where the Goodes lived, and established Saint Paul's Nor-

mal and Industrial School in 1882. Like Thomas Goode, Russell was born in slavery in Mecklenburg County; unlike Goode, he attended the Hampton Normal and Industrial Institute. Russell built what became a college on the hill where a Freedmen's Bureau school once stood, overlooking Lawrenceville. Stressing industrial and teacher training as well as basic education, Saint Paul's was a beacon to Brunswick's Black community, but we can only speculate about its impact on the Goodes.

70. Patty Buford, "A Hospital for Negroes," *Christian Union* 42 (November 27, 1890): 704. Fern K. Buford Walker, "BUFORD, Martha 'Pattie' Hicks," http://www.buford-families.com/bufordpattiehicks.htm (no longer available; last accessed July 14, 2016).

71. Buford, "Hospital for Negroes," 704.

72. Buford, "Hospital for Negroes," 704. The Freedmen's Bureau intervened in the Southside after the war, sending trainloads of food and clothing, which were quickly exhausted by homeless and hungry African Americans, and monitoring contracts governing sharecropping, tenancy, and hiring out. The bureau's most significant local accomplishment was building schools, but William Goode never got much of a chance to attend one of them.

73. MG, speech to the Conference of Black Mayors, 1988, Philadelphia, PA.

74. Neale, *Brunswick County, Virginia*, 221.

75. MG, speech to the Conference of Black Mayors; Russell Goode, phone interview, September 12, 2019. All our interviews in the research for this book were conducted in person, by telephone, and via email; all notes and transcripts are in the authors' possession.

76. Rachleff, *Black Labor in Richmond*, 4–14, 24–33.

77. Mal Goode, interview, "Teen Summit," February 22, 1992, VC (video cassette) in MG Papers.

78. Brunswick County Deed Books, May 28, 1904, Brunswick County Circuit Court, 216 North Main Street, Lawrenceville, Virginia.

79. There's some question about their birthplaces. Sharon Goode said that her father, William, told her he was born in Staughton, Virginia, at Folly Farm. It seems likely that Mary went to her mother or mother-in-law's to give birth. Sharon Goode, interview with authors, July 25, 2016, Pittsburgh. Transcript in authors' possession.

80. It's also possible that Mary and her sons spent some of those years at Folly Farm, which was closer to Pittsburgh. Her parents were better-off than William's and able to provide more support.

81. MG and Ramey, "Notes for an autobiography."

82. Richard Wright, *Black Boy* (1945; repr., New York: Harper and Row, 1966), 284.

CHAPTER 2: HOMESTEAD

1. Bethune quoted from MG and Ramey, "Notes for an autobiography."

2. John A. Fitch, *The Steel Workers* (1910; repr., Pittsburgh, PA: University of Pittsburgh Press, 1989), 4–6.

3. Dennis C. Dickerson, in *Out of the Crucible: Black Steelworkers in Western Pennsylvania, 1875–1980* (Albany: State University of New York Press, 1986), focuses on the experiences of African Americans working in the steel industry.

4. Peter Gottlieb, *Making Their Own Way: Southern Blacks' Migration to Pittsburgh, 1916–30* (Urbana: University of Illinois Press, 1987), 70–73.

5. Gottlieb, *Making Their Own Way*, 70–73. "William H. Goode Buried Wednesday," *Pittsburgh Courier*, May 28, 1960, 3.

6. Laurence A. Glasco, "High Culture and Black America: Pittsburgh, Pennsylvania, 1900–1920" (unpublished paper, May 28, 1997), 41.

7. MG and Ramey, "Notes for an autobiography." Unless otherwise noted, all quotes from MG in this chapter are from this manuscript.

8. It's doubtful that William Goode or many of his Black neighbors on Hilltop were union men. After the 1892 shoot-out, the steel companies stamped out the remnants of the Amalgamated Association of Iron, Steel, and Tin Workers. When half a million men walked off the job in 1919 in one of the biggest strikes in American labor history, few skilled men joined them. The strike for union recognition, which the companies and the press characterized as the "Hunky strike," involved more recent immigrants who held unskilled jobs but received little support from either Black or native-born white workers in Homestead. In 1919 only one single Black worker (of the eight who belonged to the union) struck, while the other 1,736 African Americans stayed on the job. Dickerson, *Out of the Crucible*, 88; Laurence Glasco, ed., *The WPA History of the Negro in Pittsburgh* (Pittsburgh, PA: University of Pittsburgh Press, 2004), 222. See also Dickerson, *Out of the Crucible*, 12–15.

9. David Montgomery, *Workers' Control in America: Studies in the History of Work, Technology, and Labor Struggles* (Cambridge: Cambridge University Press, 1979), 9–31.

10. Margaret Byington, *Homestead: The Households of a Mill Town* (1910, Russell Sage Foundation; repr., Pittsburgh, PA: University Center for International Studies, 1974), 175.

11. Gottlieb, *Making Their Own Way*, 90–91.

12. "William H. Goode Buried Wednesday."

13. Mal Goode, Letter to the Editor, "Documentary's Omission of Blacks Obscene," *Pittsburgh Courier*, August 16, 1989, A7.

14. Fitch, *Steel Workers*, 163.

15. "William H. Goode Buried Wednesday."

16. Toki Schalk Johnson, "The Golden Years," *Pittsburgh Courier*, October 9, 1954, 11; "William H. Goode Buried Wednesday."

17. The plot was on land laid out by the Homestead Bank and Life Insurance Company. Katie and Jacob Steinberg had deeded this plot to their daughter Sara in September 1904.

18. Rob Ruck, "The Origins of the Seniority System in Steel" (master's thesis, University of Pittsburgh, 1977). See references to the *Rogers and Turner vs. U.S. Steel* for long-term consequences of the LOPs and general hiring practices.

19. Gottlieb, *Making Their Own Way*, 89. The obituary "James Goode, Former Owner of Realty Firm," posted on Find a Grave, does not list a newspaper or a date. James Goode died on February 29, 1988. https://www.findagrave.com/memorial/233919916/james-t-goode.

20. English iron- and steelworkers then sustained a 37 percent higher mortality rate than men otherwise employed. Fitch, *Steel Workers*, 62–63; Oliver Thomas, *Dangerous Trades*(London: J. Murray, 1902), 141.

21. The phrase "in the shadow of the mill" comes from S. J. Kleinberg, *The Shadow of the Mills; Working-Class Families in Pittsburgh, 1870–1907* (Pittsburgh, PA: University of Pittsburgh Press, 1989).

22. Curtis Miner, *Homestead: The Story of a Steel Town* (Pittsburgh: Historical Society of Western Pennsylvania, 1989), 33. Black workers at the Homestead Works accounted for 2 percent of the workforce. Dickerson, *Out of the Crucible*, 39.

23. Byington, *Homestead*, 27–28, 92, 145.

24. Byington, *Homestead*, 14. When her colleague John Fitch spoke of the "race problem" in Homestead, he was referring to Slavs and other recent European émigrés, not African Americans, whom he hardly mentioned. Fitch, *Steel Workers*, 147–49.

25. Byington, *Homestead*, 14.

26. Byington, *Homestead*, 14, 14, 35.

27. Richard R. Wright Jr. "One Hundred Negro Steel Workers," in *Wage-Earning Pittsburgh: The Pittsburgh Survey*, ed. Paul Kellogg (New York: Survey Associates, 1914), 102.

28. Byington, *Homestead*, 102.

29. Glasco, "High Culture and Black America," 13, see also 3–15.

30. *Pittsburgh Courier*, September 12, 1925, 3.

31. Byington, *Homestead*, 57.

32. Byington, *Homestead*, 41.

33. Five dollars in 1918 would be worth $101.22 in 2023.

34. MG and Ramey, "Notes for an autobiography"; Robert Goode, interview, May 12, 2017, Pittsburgh, PA.

35. Robert Goode, interview, May 12, 2017, Pittsburgh.

36. MG and Ramey, "Notes for an autobiography"; Russell Goode, telephone interview, April 27, 2016.

37. Mal Goode, "All God's Children," in *Many Shades of Black*, ed. Stanton L. Wormley and Lewis H. Fenderson (New York: William Morrow, 1969), 262. See also Russell Goode, email, December 31, 2018.

38. See also Dickerson, *Out of the Crucible*, 64.

39. Gottlieb, *Making Their Own Way*, 198–201.

40. William H. Goode Buried Wednesday"; "Last Rites for Mrs. Mary Goode," *Pittsburgh Courier*, July 21, 1956, 1; Schalk Johnson, "Golden Years."

41. Gottlieb, *Making Their Own Way*, 198–201. See also *Pittsburgh Courier*, January 10, 1923, 3.

42. MG and Ramey, "Notes for an autobiography"; Rob Ruck, *Sandlot Seasons: Sport in Black Pittsburgh* (Urbana: University of Illinois Press, 1987), 13.

CHAPTER 3: THE EDUCATION OF MALVIN GOODE

1. The Office of Education counted 16.8 percent of the population aged seventeen and older as high school graduates in 1919–1920. Kenneth A. Simon and W. Vance Grant, *Digest of Educational Statistics*, Office of Education, bulletin no. 4 (Washington, DC: US Government Printing Office, 1965), 56.

2. MG and Ramey, "Notes for an autobiography." Unless otherwise noted, all MG quotes in this chapter are from these notes.

3. "Last Rites for Mrs. Mary Goode Set for Friday in Homestead," *Pittsburgh Courier*, July 21, 1956, 1.

4. Mal Goode, interview, February 23, 1991, Pittsburgh, conducted for *Kings on the Hill: Baseball's Forgotten Men* (PBS, October 1993; NBC, July 25, 1995).

5. Rob Ruck, *Sandlot Seasons: Sport in Black Pittsburgh* (Chicago: University of Illinois Press, 1987), 125–29.

6. Mal Goode, interview, February 23, 1991.

7. Wendell Smith, *Pittsburgh Courier*, January 20, 1934, sec. 2, p. 4.

8. Mal Goode, interview, February 23, 1991.

9. "Blue and Gold," *The Homesteader*, Homestead High School Yearbook, 1926.

10. See Debran Rowland, "Mal Goode to Keynote Homestead Lecture Series," *Pittsburgh Courier*, October 22, 1988, A4.

11. "Young Homestead Physician Slain in Kansas: Claim Motive for Slaying Was Jealousy," *Pittsburgh Courier (1911–1950)*, August 3, 1935, City Edition.

12. Ruck, *Sandlot Seasons*, 23.

13. The Interchurch World Movement, Commission of Inquiry, *Report on the Steel Strike of 1919* (New York: Harcourt, Brace and Howe, 1920), 81.

14. W. E. B. Du Bois, "The Talented Tenth," in *The Negro Problem: A Series of Articles by Representative Negroes of Today* (New York: James Potts and Co. 1903), 31–75.

15. By 1900, 2,000 African Americans had earned college degrees, 390 conferred by predominantly white institutions. *Journal of Blacks in Higher Education,* https://www.jbhe.com/chronology; *Western University Courant* 31 (May 1906): 11.

16. Andrew Buni, *Robert L. Vann of the* Pittsburgh Courier (Pittsburgh, PA: University of Pittsburgh Press, 1974), 29, 36.

17. Buni, *Robert L. Vann*, 34, 40.

18. Philip Jenkins, "The Ku Klux Klan in Pennsylvania, 1920–1940," *Western Pennsylvania Historical Magazine* 69, no. 2 (April 1986): 121–37.

19. Curtis Miner, *Homestead: The Story of a Steel Town* (Pittsburgh, PA: Historical Society of Western Pennsylvania, 1985), 46.

20. Alpha Phi Alpha Fraternity, https://apa1906.net/our-history.

21. "Alpha Kappa Alpha Celebrates Centennial," *Pitt Chronicle*, February 25, 2008.

22. Robert C. Alberts, *Pitt: The Story of the University of Pittsburgh, 1787–1987* (Pittsburgh, PA: University of Pittsburgh Press, 1986), 19.

23. "Student Princes Honor Graduate Members," *Pittsburgh Courier*, February 19, 1927, 7.

24. *The Mathematicians of the African Diaspora,* math.buffalo.edu; Vivian O. Sammons, *Blacks in Science and Education* (Washington, DC: Hemisphere Publishers, 1989), 167.

25. *Chicago Defender,* July 11, 1936.

26. Everett Utterback, interview, May 28, 1980, Pittsburgh.

27. Ruck, *Sandlot Seasons*, 140–52.

28. MG Diary, 1929, in the possession of his family.

29. "Mary Lavelle Is Lovely Bride of Malvin Goode," *Pittsburgh Courier,* October 3, 1936.

30. "The Trend's toward Curls," *Pittsburgh Courier,* July 26, 1930.

31. "New Yorker Feted at Surprise Reception," *Pittsburgh Courier,* July 19, 1932.

32. "Letter from Mal to Mary," 1931 (undated), Correspondence 1911–1931, folder 1, MG Papers.

33. "Alpha's Party," *Pittsburgh Courier,* January 28, 1933.

34. Mal Goode, interview, February 23, 1991.

35. Ruck, *Sandlot Seasons*, 13.

36. "Mary Lavelle Is Lovely Bride of Malvin Goode."

37. "Talk of the Town," *Pittsburgh Courier*, October 3, 1936.

38. Randy Wilburn, interview, December 15, 2018, Pittsburgh.

CHAPTER 4: GETTING REAL, 1936–1948

1. Peter Gottlieb, *Making Their Own Way: Southern Blacks' Migration to Pittsburgh 1916–30* (Urbana: University of Illinois Press, 1987), 65; John Bodnar, Roger Simon, and Michael Weber, *Lives of Their Own: Blacks, Italians, and Poles in Pittsburgh, 1900–1960* (Champaign-Urbana: University of Illinois Press, 1983), 187.

2. Laurence Glasco, "Double Burden: The Black Experience in Pittsburgh," in *The City at the Point: Essays on the Social History of Pittsburgh*, ed. Samuel P. Hays (Pittsburgh, PA: University of Pittsburgh Press, 1989), 79–80.

3. Glasco, "Double Burden," 76.

4. For "crossroads of the world," see Ishmael Reed, "In Search of August Wilson," *Connoisseur* (March 1987): 95, who cites Glasco, "Double Burden," 76.

5. Constance A. Cunningham, "Homer S. Brown: First Black Political Leader in Pittsburgh," *Journal of Negro History* 66, no. 4 (Winter, 1981–1982): 304–17.

6. Edna McKenzie, "Daisy Lampkin: A Life of Love and Service," *Pennsylvania Heritage* (Summer 1983); Steve Levin, "Daisy Lampkin Was a Dynamo for Change," *Pittsburgh Post-Gazette*, February 2, 1998; Earl Childs, interview, March 23, 2023, Pittsburgh.

7. Colter Harper, "'The Crossroads of the World': A Social and Cultural History of Jazz in Pittsburgh's Hill District, 1920–1970" (PhD dissertation, University of Pittsburgh, 2011).

8. MG and Ramey, "Notes for an autobiography."

9. MG and Ramey, "Notes for an autobiography."

10. Glasco, "Double Burden," 179; Bodnar, Simon, and Weber, *Lives of Their Own*, 13; Dennis C. Dickerson, *Out of the Crucible: Black Steelworkers in Western Pennsylvania, 1875–1980* (Albany: State University of New York Press, 1986), 8–9, 20, 24.

11. Glasco, "Double Burden," 69–70; Bodnar, Simon, and Weber, *Lives of Their Own*, 185–86.

12. MG, "Mal Goode's First Jobs," recording, March 24, 1987.

13. MG, "Mal Goode's First Jobs."

14. MG, "Mal Goode's First Jobs."

15. Schramm founded the National Council of Juvenile and Family Court Judges, the oldest such judicial council in the United States, in 1937, soon after Mal began working for him. Mal Goode, "All God's Children," in *Many Shades of Black*, ed. Stanton L. Wormley and Lewis H. Fenderson (New York: William Morrow, 1969), 263–64.

16. Leon Haley, telephone interview, October 3, 2016.

17. MG, "Mal Goode's First Jobs."

18. MG and Ramey, "Notes for an autobiography."

19. MG, "Mal Goode's First Jobs."

20. Haley, telephone interview, October 3, 2016.

21. Death notice for Walter E. Goode, January 1, 1942, Office of the Coroner, family collection.

22. MG, "Mal Goode's First Jobs."

23. Haley, telephone interview, October 3, 2016.

24. MG, "Mal Goode's First Jobs"; Robert Goode, interview, May 12, 2017, Pittsburgh. See also MG, "All God's Children," 261–70.

25. Leon Haley, *A Citadel of Hope: The Centre Avenue YMCA, a History* (Pittsburgh: Leon L. Haley, 2012), 10–18.

26. Haley, *Citadel of Hope*, 7–11; Nina Mjagkij and Margaret Spratt, *Light in the Darkness: African Americans and the YMCA, 1852–1946* (Lexington: University of Kentucky Press, 1994), 142.

27. Haley, *Citadel of Hope*, 18, see also 31–32.

28. Haley, *Citadel of Hope*, 1–12, 19–24.

29. Haley, *Citadel of Hope*, 35–36.

30. Glasco, "Double Burden," 88; Bodnar, Simon, and Weber, *Lives of Their Own*, 35–36. Mal had always been in coeducational settings and witnessed girls achieve academically, his work as a probation officer and at the YMCA focused on boys.

31. Haley, telephone interview, October 3, 2016. See also Haley, *Citadel of Hope*, 58.

32. Malvin R. Goode, "Let's Build a Monument to Two Giants," *New Pittsburgh Courier*, December 10, 1983.

33. Haley, *Citadel of Hope*, 40. See also MG, "Let's Build a Monument to Two Giants."

34. MG and Ramey, "Notes for an autobiography."

35. MG and Ramey, "Notes for an autobiography."

36. MG and Ramey, "Notes for an autobiography."

37. MG and Ramey, "Notes for an autobiography."

38. MG and Ramey, "Notes for an autobiography."

39. MG and Ramey, "Notes for an autobiography."

40. MG, "All God's Children," 264. MG, "Mal Goode's First Jobs."

41. MG, "Mal Goode's First Jobs."

42. *Pittsburgh Courier*, August 22, 1936.

43. MG and Ramey, "Notes for an autobiography."

44. MG and Ramey, "Notes for an autobiography."

CHAPTER 5: SPEAKING TRUTH TO POWER

1. Roy Wilkins quoted from Howard Ball, *A Defiant Life: Thurgood Marshall and the Persistence of Racism in America* (New York: Crown Publishers, 1998), 134.

2. Robert Goode, interview, July 28, 2017, Pittsburgh.

3. Ralph Koger, "Deaths of Heagy and Spalding Call for More Investigations," editorial, *Pittsburgh Courier*, April 3, 1954, 1.

4. Ralph Koger, "Heagy, Partner Were 'Good Joes' . . . There Are Others," *Pittsburgh Courier*, April 3, 1954, 1.

5. Frank Bolden, "Patrolman Bill Heagy, Blood Donor, Friend of Stork, Slain in Gun Fight," *Pittsburgh Courier*, April 3, 1954, 23.

6. MG and Ramey, "Notes for an autobiography."

7. MG, "Mal Goode's First Jobs," recording, March 24, 1987.

8. Buck Leonard quoted from John Holway, "Washington's 'Other' Baseball Team Was a Winner," *Washington Post*, July 10, 1988.

9. Laurence Glasco, "Double Burden: The Black Experience in Pittsburgh," in *The City at the Point: Essays on the Social History of Pittsburgh*, ed. Samuel P. Hays (Pittsburgh: University of Pittsburgh Press, 1989), 82.

10. Andrew Buni, *Robert L. Vann of the Pittsburgh Courier: Politics and Black Journalism* (Pittsburgh, PA: University of Pittsburgh Press, 1974), 54.

11. Buni, *Robert L. Vann*, 3, 30–33, 44–47, 53, 54. Buni's book is the best account of Vann and the *Courier*.

12. MG, "Mal Goode's First Jobs."

13. MG and Ramey, "Notes for an autobiography."

14. MG, "Mal Goode's First Jobs."

15. William Barlow, *Voice Over: The Making of Black Radio* (Philadelphia: Temple University, 1998), 53–54.

16. Martha Jean Steinberg quoted from Bill Barlow, "Talks on . . . Black DJs in the Community," https://legacy.npr.org/programs/lnfsound/talkon/barlow.html#style.

17. W. H. Tymous quoted from J. Fred MacDonald, *Don't Touch That Dial! Radio Programming in American Life from 1920 to 1960* (Chicago: Nelson-Hall, 1979), 327.

18. *Pittsburgh Courier* May 31, 1947, 15.

19. Gilbert A. Williams, *Legendary Pioneers of Black Radio* (Westport, CT: Praeger, 1998), 12, cites MacDonald, *Don't Touch That Dial!*, 327–70.

20. MacDonald, *Don't Touch That Dial!*, 333, 327–29, 339–41, 357–77.

21. MG and Ramey, "Notes for an autobiography."

22. Laurence A. Glasco, "Black Radio in Pittsburgh . . . Search for Identity and Profits," part 1, *New Pittsburgh Courier*, June 17, 2009, 1.

23. Patrick Cloonan, "Goode Tells Family's Story to McKeesport Audience," *TRIB LIVE*, August 19, 2013, https://triblive.com/neighborhoods/yourmckeesport/yourmckeesportmore/4547050-74/goode-mal-mary.

24. Williams, *Legendary Pioneers of Black Radio*, 7–15.

25. "Station WHOD Put Democracy to Work, It Paid Off in Cash," *Pittsburgh Courier*, August 1, 1953, 34.

26. "Station WHOD Put Democracy to Work."

27. Albert Abarbanel and Alex Haley, "A New Audience for Radio," *Harper's Magazine*. (February 1956).

28. "Station WHOD Put Democracy to Work."

29. There was crossover between radio and the press. Mal worked for both WHOD and the *Courier*, whose correspondents Toki Schalk Johnson and Hazel Garland addressed community and women's issues on Mary Dee's show. See "Station WHOD Put Democracy to Work"; Glasco, "Black Radio in Pittsburgh," part 1.

30. MG and Ramey, "Notes for an autobiography."

31. Frank Bolden, "Patrolman Bill Heavy, Blood Donor, Friend of Stork, Slain," *Pittsburgh Courier*, April 3, 1954, 23.

32. Bolden, "Patrolman Bill Heagy," 23.

33. MG, "Notes for WHOD commentaries" (unfortunately, there are no dates on these commentaries), MG Papers.

34. MG, "Notes for WHOD commentaries."

35. MG, "Notes for WHOD commentaries."

36. Editorial, *Pittsburgh Courier*, April 1, 1954, 1.

37. "Cop Killed in Effort to Nab Hill Gunman," *Pittsburgh Post-Gazette*, March 26, 1954, 1.

38. Koger, "Deaths of Heagy and Spalding Call for More Investigations."

39. MG, "Notes for WHOD commentaries."

40. MG, "Notes for WHOD commentaries"; Editorial, *Pittsburgh Courier*, April 3, 1954, 1.

41. Hop Kendrick, interview, July 27, 2017, Pittsburgh. All quotes from Hop Kendrick in the following paragraphs are from this interview.

42. Robert Goode, interview, July 28, 2017, Pittsburgh; MG, "Mal Goode's First Jobs."

43. MG, "The Making of a Journalist," draft chapter included in MG and Ramey, "Notes for an autobiography," folder 306, MG Papers.

44. MG, "Making of a Journalist."

45. MG, "Making of a Journalist."

46. "Mayor Asks Civic Unity Council to Probe Police Brutality Charge," *Pittsburgh Courier*, April 17, 1954, 1.

47. MG, "Making of a Journalist"; "Mayor Asks Civic Unity Council."

48. *Pittsburgh Press*, April 13, 1954.

49. Frank Bolden quoted from Matthew P. Smith, "Rights Activist, Pioneer Journalist," *Pittsburgh Post-Gazette*, September 14, 1995, B-4.

50. George E. Barbour, "Testify Spalding Beaten," *Pittsburgh Courier*, May 1, 1954. Until further notice, all quotes are from this source.

51. *Pittsburgh Press*, May 27, 1954.

52. Letters, April 1954–November 1955, in MG Correspondence, folder 3, MG Papers.

53. Letters, April 1954–November 1955, in MG Correspondence, folder 3, MG Papers.

54. Toki Schalk Johnson, "Mal Goode Testimonial," *Pittsburgh Courier,* July 3, 1954; Robert Carter, "Civil Rights Champion to Be Lauded by Citizens," *Pittsburgh Courier*, June 26, 1954, 11.

55. Hop Kendrick, interview, July 27, 2017, Pittsburgh.

56. Sandy Hamm, "Civil Rights Crusader Mal Goode: Pioneer Journalist, Activist Dead at 87," *Pittsburgh Courier*, September 30, 1995, 1.

57. Mal Goode, interview, February 23, 1991, Pittsburgh, conducted for *Kings on the Hill: Baseball's Forgotten Men* (PBS, October 1993; NBC, July 25, 1995).

58. Robert Goode, interview, July 28, 2017, Pittsburgh.

59. Mal Goode, interview, February 23, 1991.

60. Mal Goode quoted from Rob Ruck, *Raceball: How the Major Leagues Colonized the Black and Latin Game* (Boston: Beacon Press, 2011), 100.

61. MG, "Mal Goode's First Jobs."

62. Mal Goode, "All God's Children," in *Many Shades of Black*, ed. Stanton L. Wormley and Lewis H. Fenderson (New York: William Morrow, 1969), 268.

63. Diana Nelson Jones, "Pittsburgh's Cooperatives Are a Little-Known Sweet Deal," *Pittsburgh Post Gazette*, December 20, 2018.

64. MG and Ramey, "Notes for an autobiography"; Henry Aaron, telephone interview, August 13, 2020.

65. Henry Aaron, telephone interview, August 13, 2020.

66. Robert Goode, interview, May 12, 2017, Pittsburgh.

67. Rosalia Parker, interview, May 15, 2023, Pittsburgh.

68. Roberta Goode Wilburn, interview, May 15, 2023, Pittsburgh; Rosalia Parker, interview, May 15, 2023, Pittsburgh

69. Rosalia Parker, interview, May 15, 2023, Pittsburgh.

70. Mal Goode interview, February 23, 1991, Duquesne University, Pittsburgh.

71. Mal Goode interview, February 23, 1991.

72. Randy Wilburn, interview, December 15, 2018, Pittsburgh.

73. Randy Wilburn, interview.

74. Robert Goode, interview, May 12, 2017, Pittsburgh.

75. "Mal Goode Answers Dan Lapp as Homestead Citizens Press Demand for Negro Teachers," *Pittsburgh Courier*, November 1, 1958.

76. Mal quoted from Phyl Garland, "McKeesport's Little Tigers Getting Raw Deal, Says Coach," *Pittsburgh Courier*, January 20, 1962, 3.

77. Ronald Goode, Roberta Wilburn, and Rosalia Parker, interviews, June 9, 2023, Pittsburgh.

78. Laurence A. Glasco, "Black Radio in Pittsburgh . . . Search for Identity and Profits," part 2, *New Pittsburgh Courier*, June 24, 2009, 1.

79. MG and Ramey, "Notes for an autobiography."

80. Glasco, "Black Radio in Pittsburgh," part 1.

81. Brakkton Booker, "Juanita Abernathy, 'Cornerstone' of Montgomery Bus Boycott, Dies at 87," NPR.org, September 13, 2019, https://www.npr.org/2019/09/13/760527109/juanita-abernathy-cornerstone-of-montgomery-bus-boycott-dies-at-87; "Juanita Abernathy, Long at the Forefront of the Civil Rights Movement Dies at 89," *Washington Post*, September 13, 2019; Rosalind Bentley and Ernie Suggs, "Atlanta Remembers: Juanita Abernathy," *Atlanta Journal-Constitution*, September 13, 2019; Jo Ann Robinson, *Montgomery Bus Boycott and the Women Who Started It: The Memoir of JoAnn Gibson Robinson* (Knoxville: University of Tennessee Press, 1987).

82. The Martin Luther King, Jr. Research and Education Institute, https://kinginstitute.stanford.edu/encyclopedia/southern-christian-leadership-conference-sclc.

83. William H. Chafe, *The Unfinished Journey: America since World War II* (New York: Oxford University Press, 1986), 165–71.

84. Phyl Garland, "Freedom Lovers of All Races Expected to Attend Sunday's Forbes Field Rally," *Pittsburgh Courier*, June 18, 1960, 5.

85. "Remembering MLK's Impact in Pittsburgh," *Pittsburgh Post-Gazette*, January 21, 2019, https://newsinteractive.post-gazette.com/thedigs/2019/01/21/mlk-martin-luther-king-jr-legacy-in-pittsburgh.

86. MG and Ramey, "Notes for an autobiography."

87. Martin Luther King quoted from Julia Moore, "'U.S. Cannot Remain a First-Class Nation and Have Second-Class Citizens,' Dr. King," *Pittsburgh Courier*, July 15, 1961, 3.

88. Moore, "U.S. Cannot Remain a First-Class Nation."

89. "Remembering MLK's Impact in Pittsburgh."

90. Chafe, *Unfinished Journey*, 206–13.

91. MG and Ramey, "Notes for an autobiography."

92. MG and Ramey, "Notes for an autobiography."

CHAPTER 6: OCTOBER 1962

1. MG, "The Time Is Ripe," unpublished manuscript, folder 309, MG Papers.

2. MG, "The Time Is Ripe."

3. Jackie Robinson to MG, July 23, 1956, folder 4, MG Papers.

4. These comments are from a column by Bill Keefe "Viewing the News by Bill Keefe," that ran in the *Times-Picayune*. The *Courier* reprinted the column alongside a response that Robinson wrote Keefe. They both were on the front page of the *Courier* on August 4, 1956.

5. Jackie Robinson to MG, July 23, 1956, folder 4, MG Papers.

6. Jackie Robinson, letter to Bill Keefe, *Pittsburgh Courier*, August 4, 1956, 1.

7. Jackie Robinson to MG, July 23, 1956, folder 4, MG Papers.

8. Pauline Frederick's early career was transformed when she stepped in at the last moment to broadcast a meeting of the Council of Foreign Ministers in New York. Subsequently, she specialized in international affairs and politics. "Pauline Frederick Is Dead at 84; Was News Analyst for 3 Networks," *New York Times*, May 11, 1990.

9. Tim Brooks and Earle Marsh, *The Complete Directory to Prime Time Network and Cable TV Shows 1946–Present*, 9th ed. (New York: Ballantine Books, 2007), 1683.

10. Martin Weil, "James Hagerty Dies at 71 in N.Y.," *Washington Post*, April 12, 1981.

11. MG, "The Time Is Ripe."

12. Rick Shrum, "McKeesport Little Tigers a Big Success Story," *Pittsburgh Post-Gazette*, October 21, 2006.

13. Phyl Garland, "Who's Pestering 'Puddin'? McKeesport's Little Tigers Getting Raw Deal, Says Coach," *Pittsburgh Courier*, January 20, 1962, 3. See also "Faces in the Crowd, *Sports Illustrated*, November 27, 1961.

14. Over the years, the team attracted players from the town and environs who went on the NFL, including Hall of Fame running back Curtis Martin, who attended the University of Pittsburgh.

15. Gerald "Puddin'" Grayson, telephone interview, June 17, 2019. Grayson played at Boise State University and returned to McKeesport where he taught and coached. One of his players was Swin Cash, who won several NCAA basketball championships with the University of Connecticut and starred in the Women's National Basketball Association. Both Curtis Martin and Swin Cash became Hall of Famers, Martin in the Pro Football Hall of Fame, Cash in the Naismith Basketball Hall of Fame.

16. MG to Jim Hagerty, March 1962, folder 6, MG Papers.

17. MG to Hagerty, March 1962.

18. Mal Goode, "The Time Ripened," folder 309, MG Papers. Mal wrote multiple drafts of chapters or sections of chapters about his hiring. "The Time Ripened" and "The Time is Ripe" are substantially the same but not identical.

19. "We're With You, Mal!" *Pittsburgh Courier*, August 11, 1962, 1.

20. MG, "The Time Is Ripe."

21. MG, "The Time Is Ripe."

22. MG, "The Time Is Ripe."

23. MG, "The Time Ripened."

24. MG, "Mal Goode's First Jobs," recording, March 24, 1987.

25. *Pittsburgh Courier*, September 8, 1962; "'Mal' Goode Swamped by Community's Best Wishes," *Pittsburgh Courier (1955–1966)*, September 15, 1962, City Edition.

26. Mrs. A. M. Sharp (formerly Miss Gibbs of Homestead faculty) to MG (no date), folder 309, MG Papers.

27. MG and Ramey, "Notes for an autobiography."

28. Herb Wilkerson, Western Union telegram to MG (no date), MG Correspondence, folder 7, MG Papers.

29. "'Mal' Goode Swamped by Community's Best Wishes."

30. "Mal Goode Raps Pitt Image," *Pittsburgh Courier (1955–1966),* March 17, 1962, City Edition.

31. "'Mal' Goode Swamped by Community's Best Wishes."

32. Various letters and telegrams in MG Correspondence, folder 7, MG Papers.

33. MG to Evelyn Brooks, September 17, 1962, MG Correspondence, folder 7, MG Papers.

34. Mary Ellen Butler, *Heart and Soul: The Remarkable Courtship and Marriage of Josh and Virginia Craft Rose* (Pittsburgh: Senator John Heinz History Center, 2018), 9; Robert Hill, email, March 31, April 10, 2019; "Henry Craft Dies; Y.M.C.A. Official, 90," *New York Times,* September 2, 1974.

35. Hazel Garland, "Lt. Malvin R. Goode Takes Lovely German for Bride," *Pittsburgh Courier (1955–1966),* September 22, 1962, City Edition.

36. Marty Mulé, "A Time for Change: Bobby Grier and the 1956 Sugar Bowl," December 27, 2005; http://Blackathlete.net/2005/12/a-time-for-change-bobby-grier-and-the-1956-sugar-bowl.

37. Benjamin E. Mays, "My View: Bobby Grier," *Pittsburgh Courier,* December 31, 1955, A8.

38. MG and Ramey, "Notes for an autobiography."

39. Tom Schuster and Andy Vettel, eds., *Portal to the Past: Senior History Project 95–96* (State College: Josten's, 1996), 117, based on a Ruth Goode White interview with Ed Egan in Pittsburgh (no date for interview). The book is a compilation of over one hundred short pieces about the history of Homestead.

40. Don Munton and David Welch, *The Cuban Missile Crisis: A Concise History* (New York: Oxford University Press, 2007), 10.

41. Munton and Welch, *Cuban Missile Crisis,* 31–48.

42. Munton and Welch, *Cuban Missile Crisis,* 52–54.

43. Munton and Welch, *Cuban Missile Crisis,* 57–58.

44. Munton and Welch, Cuban Missile Crisis, 63.

45. Munton and Welch, *Cuban Missile Crisis,* 64. See also James A. Nathan, *Anatomy of the Cuban Missile Crisis* (Westport, CT: Greenwood Press, 2001), 171–75.

46. Munton and Welch, *Cuban Missile Crisis,* 66.

47. Munton and Welch, *Cuban Missile Crisis,* 71.

48. Zorin is quoted in James M. Lindsay, "Blog Post," *Council on Foreign Relations,* October 25, 2012, https://www.cfr.org/blog/twe-remembers-adlai-stevenson-dresses-down-soviet-ambassador-un-cuban-missile-crisis-day-ten.

49. Adlai Stevenson, "UN Security Council Address on Soviet Missiles in Cuba," American Rhetoric On Line Speech Bank, https://www.americanrhetoric.com/speeches/adlaistevensonunitednationscuba.html.

50. Munton and Welch, *Cuban Missile Crisis,* 62–70.

51. "75 Milestones in International Cooperation," *Why It Matters, An Annual Series* 1 (United Nations, 2020), 36, http://research.un.org/en/UN70/1956-1965.

52. Munton and Welch, *Cuban Missile Crisis*, 76.

53. Mark J. White, *The Cuban Missile Crisis* (London: Macmillan Press, 1996), 210–11.

54. Peter Jennings, "The Missiles of October: What the World Didn't Know" (ABC 1992), https://www.youtube.com/watch?v=ZEZB7eHmcoY.

55. McNamara quoted from Episode 10: Cuba, Interview with Robert McNamara, https://nsarchive2.gwu.edu/coldwar/interviews/episode-10/mcnamara3.htmlhttps:// nsarchive2.gwu.edu/coldwar/interviews/episode-10/mcnamara3.html. See also Martin J. Sherwin, "'One Step from Nuclear War,' the Cuban Missile Crisis at 50: In Search of Historical Perspective," *Prologue Magazine* 44, no. 2 (Fall 2012).

56. Robert F. Kennedy, *Thirteen Days: A Memoir of the Cuban Missile Crisis* (New York: W. W. Norton, 1969), 212–13.

57. "John MacVane Dies; Radio Correspondent," *New York Times,* February 24, 1984, B-16; also https://www.revolvy.com/page/John-MacVane.

58. MG, "The Time Is Ripe."

59. MG, "The Time Is Ripe."

60. Robert Goode, email, December 29, 2018.

61. MG, "The Time Is Ripe."

62. David Salinger, "Broadcast Pioneer: Mal Goode Recalls Mon-Yough News Career," *Daily News (McKeesport, PA)*, March 14, 1980 (copy in the MG Papers).

63. MG, "The Time Is Ripe."

64. Don Munton and P. William J. Midland, *The Cuban Missile Crisis of 1962: Needless or Necessary* (New York: Praeger, 1988), 28.

65. The deal was implemented in a herky-jerky fashion, and Castro blocked UN inspections. The United States would later dismantle its Jupiter missiles in Turkey, removing the warheads and scrapping the missiles.

66. Mark Kramer, "Review: New Perspectives on the Cuban Missile Crisis," *Public Historian* 16, no. 3 (Summer 1994): 101–6; Jennings, "Missiles of October."

67. Mal quoted from Paul Weingarten, "And Now, the Minority View . . .," *Chicago Tribune,* July 13, 1986.

68. Russell Goode, email, December 31, 2018; Robert Goode, email, December 29, 2018.

69. Linda Dudley, "Black Reporter Recalls Start of TV Career," *San Diego Tribune,* February 2, 1985.

CHAPTER 7: AFRICA, 1963

1. David Snell, Interview, October 31, 2019, Atlanta.

2. "Inaugural address of Governor George Wallace," January 14, 1963, Alabama Department of Archives and History, https://digital.archives.alabama.gov/digital/collection/voices/id/2952/.

3. Adam Fairclough, *To Redeem the Soul of America* (Atlanta: University of Georgia Press, 2001), 138.

4. Bobby M. Wilson, *America's Johannesburg: Industrialization and Racial Transformation in Birmingham* (Athens: University of Georgia Press, 2019).

5. "The Nation: Races, Freedom—Now," *Time* 20 (May 17, 1963): 1.

6. MG and Ramey, "Notes for an autobiography."

7. MG and Ramey, "Notes for an autobiography."

8. Andrew Young, interview, October 31, 2019, Atlanta, Georgia.

9. *New York Times*, May 4, 1963, 1.

10. JFK quoted in Fairclough, *To Redeem the Soul of America*, 138.

11. Claude Sitton, "Birmingham Blasts: 50 Hurt in Birmingham," *New York Times*, May 13, 1963, 1; Fairclough, *To Redeem the Soul of America*, 138.

12. Sade Tukuru did substantial research for this section as a First Experience in Research undergraduate at the University of Pittsburgh.

13. Paul Hoffman, "Bunche says '60 Is Year of Africa," *New York Times*, February 17, 1960. See also Adom Getachew, "It Was the Year of Africa," in "A Special Section: A Continent Remade" *New York Times*, February 9, 2020, 7.

14. "Declaration on the Granting of Independence to Colonial Countries and Peoples," General Assembly resolution 1514 (XV) of December 14, 1960, UN Human Rights, Office of the High Commissioner, https://www.ohchr.org/EN/ProfessionalInterest/Pages/Independence.aspx.

15. Julien Engel, "The African-American Institute," *African Studies Bulletin* 6, no. 3 (October 1963): 15. Recognizing that Africa was the least favored region of the world when it came to US assistance, the AAI raised funds from the US Agency for International Development and the State Department as well as private donors.

16. Final Report to the Department of State on Grant NO. SCC-30046, African-American Institute Regional Workshops for African Journalist, 1963, November 21, 1963.

17. MG, "The Time Is Ripe," folder 309, MG Papers. Unless otherwise noted, all MG quotes describing the Africa trip are from this manuscript.

18. Christopher H. Sterling, Claude-Jean Bertrand, Douglas Boyd, Donald R. Browne, Susan Tyler Eastman, and Kenneth Harwood, "Sydney W. Head (1913–1991): Remembering the Founder of Modern Broadcasting Studies," *Journal of Broadcasting & Electronic Media* 50, no. 3 (September 2006), https://worldradiohistory.com/Archive-Journal-of-Broadcasting/60s/Journal-of-Broadcasting-BEA-1966-09.pdf.

19. Nelson Mandela Foundation website, March 4, 2008, https://www. nelsonmandela.org/news/entry/passports-tell-a-story#search-form.

20. The last quotation in this paragraph is from Final Report to the Department of State on Grant NO. SCC-30046, African-American Institute Regional Workshops for African Journalist, November 21, 1963, 3.

21. Paul Bjerk, "Postcolonial Realism: Tanganyika's Foreign Policy under Nyerere, 1960–1963," *International Journal of African Historical Studies* 44, no. 2 (2011): 215–47.

22. Final Report to the Department of State on Grant NO. SCC-30046, African-American Institute Regional Workshops for African Journalists, 1963, African-American Institute, New York City, November 21, 1963, 14.

23. Final Report to the Department of State, November 21, 1963, 3.

24. Mal Goode, "The Making of a Journalist," folder 306, MG Papers.

CHAPTER 8: THE LONG HOT SUMMER

1. "Martin Luther King's 'I Have a Dream' speech, *Talk of the Town*, NPR, January 16, 2023, https://www.npr.org/2010/01/18/122701268/i-have-a-dream-speech-in-its-entirety.

2. MG and Ramey, "Notes for an autobiography."

3. Reginald G. Damerell, *Triumph in a White Suburb* (New York: William Morrow, 1968); Aaron Morrison, "Fifty Years Ago, Teaneck Took a Bold Step Forward," *Record Digital Edition*, May 15, 2014, https://drive.google.com/file/d/1wrDg58QNDCcmMf8l-gUyYZzToGdMDjhB8/view?pli=1.

4. Mal Goode to Elston Howard, November 8, 1963, folder 11–19, MG Papers. See also Clifton Cox, "Interview with Mal Goode," October 24, 1984, Archive Collection of the Teaneck Public Library, https://archive.teanecklibrary.org/OralHistory2/goode3.html.

5. MG, memo titled "A Look at the Negro Vote for November 6, 1962," folder 280, MG Papers.

6. ABC production sheets re: rent strikes, Jersey City, August 4, 1963, and the Tennessee program, December 1963–August 1964, folder 283, MG Papers.

7. "The Winds of Change," undated memo, folder 307, MG Papers.

8. David Snell, telephone interview, July 25, 2019.

9. John F. Kennedy, "Televised Address to the Nation on Civil Rights," June 11, 1963, https://www.jfklibrary.org/learn/about-jfk/historic-speeches/televised-address-to-the-nation-on-civil-rights.

10. John Kennedy, "Statement by the President on the Sunday Bombing in Birmingham," September 16, 1963, https://www.presidency.ucsb.edu/documents/state-ment-the-president-the-sunday-bombing-birmingham.

11. Martin Luther King Jr., "Eulogy for the Martyred Children," September 18, 1963, https://kinginstitute.stanford.edu/eulogy-martyred-children; "1963 Birmingham Church Bombing Fast Facts," CNN Library, October 7, 2019, https://www.cnn.com/2013/06/13/us/1963-birmingham-church-bombing-fast-facts/index.html.

12. *Afro-American*, December 14, 1963 (the Philos); Stanton L. Wormley and Lewis H. Fenderson, *Many Shades of Black* (New York: William Morrow, 1969), 267.

13. Doris Kearns, *Lyndon Johnson and the American Dream* (New York: St. Martin's Griffin, 1991), 178.

14. William H. Chafe, *The Unfinished Journey: America since World War II* (New York: Oxford University Press, 1986), 229–31.

15. In 1975 the number of votes required for cloture was dropped to sixty.

16. Adah Lavelle, interview, January 26, 2016, Pittsburgh.

17. Robert M. Lavelle, Columbus, MS, to MG, June 30, 1964, folder 23, MG Papers.

18. Bob Lavelle to MG, June 30, 1964.

19. Bob Lavelle to MG, June 30, 1964; Adah Lavelle, interview, January 26, 2016, Pittsburgh.

20. Editorial, "'Hot Summer': Race Riots in North," *New York Times*, July 26, 1964, E:1.

21. "Harlem Riots of 1964," NYC data, Baruch College Zicklin School of Business, https://www.Baruch.cuny.edu/nycdata/disasters/riots-harlem_1964.html; Editorial, "Hot Summer."

22. Michael W. Flamm, *In the Heat of the Summer: The New York Riots of 1964 and the War on Crime* (Philadelphia: University of Pennsylvania Press, 2016), 2.

23. Radio commentary, 1984, and ABC memo dated July 13, 1964, 12:45pm, commentary folder 296, memo folder 282, MG Papers.

24. Bob Teague, *Live and Off-Color: News Biz* (New York: A&W Publishers, 1982), 33.

25. Douglas Martin, "Bob Teague, WNBC Reporter Who Helped Integrate TV News, Is Dead at 84," *New York Times*, March 28, 2013, A23.

26. Flamm, *In the Heat of the Summer*, 12.

27. Flamm, *In the Heat of the Summer*, 53. This book is the best resource for analysis and context of the New York riots.

28. Flamm, *In the Heat of the Summer*, 84, 102.

29. Malcolm X, *The Autobiography of Malcolm X, as Told to Alex Haley* (New York: Ballantine Books, 1965), 362. See also MG, memo "Malcolm X Returns to Country," May 19, 1964, folder 281–282, MG Papers; Russell Goode, telephone interview, September 12, 2019.

30. MG's undated transcripts of his WABC News broadcasts during the disturbances can be found in folder 281–282, MG Papers. The "Cool It Baby" leaflet is in the same folder.

31. MG, WABC News, undated transcripts in folder 281–282, MG Papers.

32. Malcolm X, "The Black Revolution Is Part of World-Wide Struggle, Malcolm X, 1964," April 8, 1964, https://www.icit-digital.org/articles/malcolm-x-on-the-black-revolution-april-8-1964.

33. Flamm, *In the Heat of the Summer*, 102.

34. LBJ quoted from Michael Oreskes, "Civil Rights Act Leaves Deep Mark on the American Political Landscape," *New York Times*, July 2, 1989.

35. Barry Goldwater quoted from Flamm, *In the Heat of the Summer*, 127, see also 8, 11–20.

36. MG, WABC News, undated transcripts, folder 281–282, MG Papers.

37. MG, WABC News, undated transcripts, folder 281–282, MG Papers.

38. Martin, "Bob Teague, WNBC Reporter," *New York Times*, March 28, 2013.

39. Flamm, *In the Heat of the Summer*, 94–96.

40. MG, WABC News, transcripts, folder 283, MG Papers.

41. MG, WABC News, transcripts, folder 283, MG Papers.

42. Bill Beutel and MG quoted from Leonard Reed, "Goode: Changes," *The Record*, January 3, 1988.

43. MG, WABC News, transcripts, folder 283, MG Papers.

44. Dr. Martin Luther King Jr. speaking about race riots in Rochester and New York City, New York, July 27, 1964, Civil Rights Digital Library, WSB-TV film clip, http://crdl.usg.edu/do:ugabma_wsbn_wsbn46951.

45. Editorial, "Hot Summer," *New York Times*, July 26, 1964.

46. ABC production sheets on Jersey City, August 4, 1964, folder 283, MG Papers.

47. Martin Luther King Jr., Acceptance speech at Nobel Peace Prize Awards, The Martin Luther King, Jr. Research Institute, Stanford University, https://kinginstitute.stanford.edu/encyclopedia/nobel-peace-prize.

CHAPTER 9: "OUR OWN BLACK SHINING PRINCE"

1. Russell Goode, telephone interview, July 26, 2019.

2. Robert Goode, interview, May 12, 2017, Pittsburgh.

3. Manning Marable, *Malcolm X: A Life of Reinvention* (New York: Viking, 2011), 31–32.

4. Randy Roberts and Johnny Smith, *Blood Brothers: The Fatal Friendship between Muhammad Ali and Malcolm X* (New York: Basic Books, 2016), 195–201.

5. Roberts and Smith, *Blood Brothers*, 157.

6. Dan Pompei, "NFL 100: At No. 2, Unstoppable Force Jim Brown Was 'Fast as the Fastest, Hard as the Hardest,'" September 7, 2021, theathletic.com, https://theathletic.com/2796576/2021/09/07/nfl-100-at-no-2-unstoppable-force-jim-brown-was-fast-as-the-fastest-hard-as-the-hardest. See also a movie that dramatized their exchanges: Regina King, director, *One Night in Miami . . .* (2020).

7. Cassius Clay and MG from https://www.instagram.com/p/BvzcRMOnc2x; "Clay, on a 2-hour Tour of U.N., Tells of Plans to Visit Mecca," *New York Times*, March 5, 1964.

8. Roberts and Smith, Blood Brothers, 217.

9. Cassius Clay and MG from https://www.instagram.com/p/BvzcRMOnc2x. See also Roberts and Smith, *Blood Brothers*, 215–17.

10. "Malcolm interviewed by Mal Goode at the United Nations in New York City on March," https://www.facebook.com/LuckyLoves8/videos/114246706579153.

11. All quotes are from folder 254, MG Papers.

12. https://www.youtube.com/watch?v=W1bt9F0BmPg&feature=share. (This video is no longer available, last accessed March 19, 2020.)

13. "Malcolm X Splits with Muhammad: Suspended Muslim Leader Plans Black Nationalist Political Movement," *New York Times*, March 9, 1964.

14. "Malcolm X Splits with Muhammad."

15. "Malcolm X Splits with Muhammad."

16. "Malcolm X: Program against Injustices," https://www.youtube.com/watch?v=-juFkTGtV5GM (at 0.42).

17. Malcolm X, "The Ballot or the Bullet," King Solomon Baptist Church, Detroit Michigan, April 12, 1964, https://americanradioworks.publicradio.org/features/blackspeech/mx.html.

18. Malcolm X, "The Ballot or the Bullet."

19. Malcolm X, "The Ballot or the Bullet."

20. "God in America, People and Ideas: The Civil Rights Movement," PBS.org, https://www.pbs.org/wgbh/americanexperience/features/godinamerica-civil-rights.

21. Malcolm X, *The Autobiography of Malcolm X, as Told to Alex Haley* (New York: Ballantine Books, 1964), 321.

22. Robert Goode, December 29, 2018, interview in Pittsburgh.

23. Hans J. Massaquoi, "Mystery of Malcolm X," *Ebony* (September 1964): 40.

24. "Malcolm X Pleased by Whites' Attitude on Trip to Mecca," *New York Times*, May 8, 1964.

25. Robert Goode, interview, July 28, 2017, Pittsburgh.

26. Malcolm X, Speech at the founding of the OAAU, June 28, 1964, https://www.blackpast.org/african-american-history/speeches-african-american-history/1964-malcolm-x-s-speech-founding-rally-organization-afro-american-unity.

27. FBI Records: The Vault, https://vault.fbi.gov/cointel-pro; "COINTELPRO and the History of Domestic Spying," January 18, 2006, NPR, https://www.npr.org/templates/story/story. php?storyId=5161811.

28. *Who Killed Malcolm X?*, episode 2, directed by Rachel Dretzin and Phil Bertelsen for Fusion, Netflix, February 2020.

29. Scripts, ABC, 1964, 23 December–1965, February, folder 283, MG Papers.

30. MG with Bernie Robertson crew, February 1965, folder 283, MG Papers.

31. ABC Scripts, December 23, 1964–February 1965, folder 283, MG Papers.

32. ABC Scripts, March–September 1965, folder 284, MG Papers.

33. ABC Scripts, December 23, 1964–February 1965, folder 283, MG Papers.

34. Ossie Davis, "Faith Temple Church of God," February 27, 1965, https://www.malcolmx.com/eulogy.

35. Davis, "Faith Temple Church of God."

36. MG, memo to Walter Porges, June 9, 1966, regarding Walk Against Fear, Missouri, folder 285, MG Papers.

37. MG, memos to Walter Porges, June 16, 17, 1966, regarding Walk Against Fear, folder 285, MG Papers.

38. DVD of newsclips and footage from Mal's time at ABC, courtesy of Roberta Goode.

39. DVD of newsclips and footage from Mal's time at ABC, courtesy of Roberta Goode.

40. DVD of newsclips and footage from his time at ABC, courtesy of Roberta Goode. Mal would also report on a second march that Meredith organized through Mississippi in July 1967. Mal went from small town to small town, interviewing marchers and spectators, mindful of the police and those carrying Confederate flags. By then, he knew people in most of those towns. While in Mississippi, Mal filed several television stories and radio reports each day. It's difficult to know just how many of his television spots were aired or how often he was on the radio. Few television stories and virtually no radio spots were archived at that time.

41. "Turn This Town Out": Stokely Carmichael, Black Power, and the March against Fear, Tina Ligon, National Archives, June 7, 2016, https://rediscovering-black-history.blogs.archives. gov/2016/06/07/turn-this-town-out-stokely-carmichael-black-power-and-the-march-against-fear.

42. Marian Wright Edelman, "Revisiting Marks, Mississippi," Child Watch Column, March 25, 2011, https://www.childrensdefense.org/child-watch-columns/health/2011/revisiting-marks-mississippi.

43. Debbie Elliott, "How A Mule Train from Marks, Miss., Kicked Off MLK's Poor People Campaign, NPR Weekend Edition, May 13, 2018, https://www.npr.org/2018/05/13/610097454/how-a-mule-train-from-marks-miss-kicked-off-mlks-poor-people-campaign.

44. Folder 287, MG Papers.

Chapter 10: On the Front Lines

1. Kerner Commission, *Report of the National Advisory Committee on Civil Disorders* (Washington, DC: US GPO, 1967), 1, 219.

2. Kerner Commission, *Report*, 201.

3. Kerner Commission, *Report*, 206.

4. Kerner Commission, *Report*, 202.

5. Kerner Commission, *Report*, 207.

6. Kerner Commission, *Report*, 211.

7. Elmer W. Lower to MG, ABC Interdepartmental Correspondence, August 18, 1967, folder 288, MG Papers.

8. James McGrath Morris, *Eye on the Struggle: Ethel Payne, the First Lady of the Black Press* (New York: Harper Collins, 2015), 3.

9. Daina Beth Solomon and Dexter Thomas, "Urban Legend about *Times* Reporting during Watts Riots Conceals a Sadder Tale," *Los Angeles Times*, August 14, 2015.

10. Earl Caldwell interview, *Frontline*, July 6, 2006, https://www.pbs.org/wgbh/pages/frontline/newswar/interviews/caldwell.html.

11. Ansi Vallens, "The World of the Multiracial Woman," *Cosmopolitan* (October 1986): 260–63, 271.

12. Carla Hall, "The Rise, and Dizzying Fall, of Max Robinson," *Washington Post*, May 26, 1988.

13. George Wallace quoted from his 1963 inauguration speech, https://media.al.com/spotnews/other/George%20Wallace%201963%20Inauguration%20Speech.pdf. See also Dennis Hevesi, "Richmond Flowers Is Dead at 88; Challenged Segregation and Klan," *New York Times*, August 11, 2007.

14. Information for this paragraph comes from notes in folder 280, MG Papers.

15. MG to Governor George Wallace, November 13, 1965, MG Correspondence, folder 29, MG Papers.

16. George Wallace to MG, January 6, 1966, folder 40, MG Papers.

17. MG, memo to Jack O'Grady, December 1965, and Jack O'Grady, memo to Nick Archer, December 22, 1965, both in folder 30, MG Papers.

18. MG, memo to Jack O'Grady, January 6, 1966, folder 288, MG Papers.

19. Mal Goode, "A Piece of the Rock," undated speech, folder 339, MG Papers.

20. Memo, folder 288, MG Papers.

21. ABC scripts, December 1966–July 1967, folder 287, MG Papers.

22. MG, stand-upper on weekend TV news, July 22, 1967, folder 287, MG Papers.

23. MG, memo to Jack O'Grady, January 6, 1966; Ev Aspinwall, memo to MG, August 25, 1967; Syd Byrnes, memo to MG, July 24, 1967, all in folder 288, MG Papers. Van Deerlin letter to MG, folder 47, MG Papers.

24. Elmer W. Lower to MG, August 18, 1967, ABC Interdepartmental Correspondence, folder 288, MG Papers.

25. Dennis Hevesi, "Elmer Lower, Former President of ABC News, Dies at 98," *New York Times*, July 31, 2011.

26. Thomas J. Hrach, "Media Are Blamed for Causing Riots," https://muse.jhu.edu/chapter/1900972/pdf. See also Thomas J. Hrach, *The Riot Report and the News: How the Kerner Commission Changed Media Coverage of Black America* (Amherst: University of Massachusetts Press, 2016); Kathleen Weldon, "The Long Hot Summer: Riots in 1967," The Roper Center, August 28, 2017, https://ropercenter.cornell.edu/blog/long-hot-summer-riots-1967.

27. Elmer W. Lower, memo to Mal Goode, August 1967, ABC Interdepartmental Correspondence, folder 288, MG Papers.

28. MG, memo to Elmer W. Lower, August 1967, ABC Interdepartmental Correspondence, folder 288, MG Papers. Quotes in the following paragraphs are from this memo.

29. MG memo to Elmer W. Lower, August 18, 1967, ABC Interdepartmental Correspondence, folder 288, MG Papers; Dennis Hevesi, "Elmer Lower, Former President of ABC News, Dies at 98," *New York Times*, July 31, 2011.

30. Elmer Lower, "Racial Stress and the Mass Media: Reflections on a Long Hot Summer," address to Sigma Chi, Buffalo, New York, September 21, 1967, *Congressional*

Record: Proceedings and Debates of the US Senate, vol. 113, pt. 21, US Congress, entered in the *Congressional Record*, October 11, 1967. Quotations will be from this source.

31. MG, memo to James Hagerty, December 30, 1962, folder 280, MG Papers.

32. MG, memo to James Hagerty, December 30, 1962, folder 280, MG Papers.

33. MG to Leonard Goldenson, chairman of the board, ABC, May 21, 1973, folder 290, MG Papers; Robert Goode, interview, October 18, 2019, Pittsburgh.

34. Thelma Sanders to MG, folder 49, MG Papers.

35. MG to President Lyndon B. Johnson, October 13, 1965, folder 26, MG Papers.

36. Lyndon Johnson to MG, March 29, 1965, folder 26, MG Papers. See also LeRoy Collins to MG, May 16, 1966; MG to LeRoy Collins, September 16, 1966; LeRoy Collins to MG, September 22, 1966; MG to Lyndon B. Johnson, October 13, 1965; all in folder 26, MG Papers.

37. MG quoted from Janice Perkins, "NAACP Hears ABC-TV Newsman: Gains of Negro in South Held Surpassing Efforts in North," *Evansville Courier*, September 24, 1965, 17.

38. Perkins, "NAACP Hears ABC-TV Newsman," 17.

39. Perkins, "NAACP Hears ABC-TV Newsman," 17.

40. Perkins, "NAACP Hears ABC-TV Newsman," 17.

41. Mal Goode, "A Place to Stand," Hill District Community Council, Wesley Center AME Zion Church, Pittsburgh, PA, January 28, 1965, folder 340, MG Papers.

42. MG, "A Place to Stand."

43. MG, "A Place to Stand."

44. MG, "A Place to Stand"; John F. Kennedy, Civil Rights Address, June 11, 1963, White House, Washington, DC, https://www.americanrhetoric com/speeches/jfkcivilrights.htm.

45. MG, "A Place to Stand."

46. LBJ quoted in William Chafe, *The Unfinished Journey: America since World War II* (New York: Oxford University Press, 1995), 233.

47. MG, "A Place to Stand."

48. Donn Clendenon to MG, December 3, 1963, folder 19, MG Papers.

49. Henry Aaron with Lonnie Wheeler, *I Had A Hammer: The Hank Aaron Story* (New York: HarperCollins, 1991), 322.

50. Joe Browne, "Making It, the Goode Way," *Pittsburgh Post-Gazette*, May 30, 1985; Henry Aaron, telephone interview, August 13, 2020.

51. Henry Aaron, telephone interview, August 13, 2020; Robert Goode, email to Rob Ruck, April 27, 2020.

52. MG to Henry Aaron, November 11, 1966, folder 40, MG Papers.

53. MG to Willie Mays, June 14, 1966, folder 36, MG Papers. See also MG to Jackie Robinson, December 29, 1966; Gus Heninburg to Robinson, December 29, 1966, folder 40, MG Papers; Louis Moore, *We Will Win the Day: The Civil Rights Movement, the Black Athlete* (Santa Barbara, CA: Praeger, 2017), xiv.

54. Neil Faulkner, "The Guerrilla of Arabia," *Independent*, September 17, 2010, quoting T. E. Lawrence from *Seven Pillars of Wisdom*.

55. *Roots of a War Episode: Vietnam, a Television History* (PBS 1981).

56. Paul A. Schuette, "King Preaches on Non-Violence at Police-Guarded Howard Hall," *Washington Post*, March 3, 1965.

57. Russell Goode, telephone interview, September 12, 2019; Robert Goode, interview, October 18, 2019, Pittsburgh.

58. "Remembering MLK's Impact in Pittsburgh," *Pittsburgh Post-Gazette*, January 21, 2019.

59. "Remembering MLK's Impact in Pittsburgh," January 21, 2019.

60. "The Rev. Dr. Martin Luther King in Pittsburgh," *Pittsburgh Post-Gazette*, January 21, 2013.

61. Russell Goode, telephone interview, September 12, 2019.

62. "Dr. King Leads Chicago Peace Rally," *New York Times*, March 26, 1967.

63. Taylor Branch, *At Canaan's Edge: America in the King Years, 1965–1968* (New York: Simon and Schuster, 2006), 588–90.

64. Transcript of "Beyond Vietnam," April 4, 1967, Martin Luther King, Jr. Research and Education Institute, Stanford University, California, https://kinginstitute.stanford.edu/encyclopedia/beyond-vietnam.

65. "A Tragedy," *Washington Post*, April 6, 1967.

66. Branch, *At Canaan's Edge*, 595; *New York Times*, April 11, 1967, 1, and April 13, 1967, 1.

67. "Beyond Vietnam"; Robert Goode, interview, October 18, 2019, Pittsburgh.

68. "To Establish a National Commission on Negro History and Culture," Hearing before the Select Subcommittee on Labor of the Committee on Education and Labor, House of Representatives 90th Congress, 2nd sess., on HR 12962, Hearing held in New York, March 18, 1968 (Washington DC: USPGO, 1968), 54, 52, 52, 53.

69. "To Establish a National Commission on Negro History and Culture," 64.

70. "Action against Apartheid: What YOU Can Do about Racial Discrimination in SOUTH AFRICA," http://africanactivist. msu.edu/document_metadata.php?objectid=32-130-B67; Statement Protesting South Africa's Possible Readmission to the Olympics, American Committee on Africa with Jackie Robinson, K. C. Jones, February 8, 1968, http://african activist.msu.edu/document_metadata.php?objectid=32-130-FEB.

71. Gordon K. Mantler, *Power to the Poor* (Chapel Hill: University of North Carolina Press, 2015), 19. The 1960 census, Bureau of Labor Statistics, US Commerce Department, and the Federal Reserve estimated anywhere from 40 to 60 million Americans—or 22 to 33 percent—lived below the poverty line.

72. Mark Engler, "Dr. Martin Luther King's Economics: Through Jobs, Freedom," *The Nation*, January 15, 2010.

73. MG and Ramey, "Notes for an autobiography."

74. "Newark Man Remembers Inviting MLK Jr. to School 50 Years Ago," http://new jersey.news12.com/story/37873961/newark-man-remembers-inviting-mlk-jr-to-school -50-years-ago, April 3, 2018; "Newark Reflects on Dr. King's Last Visit 50 Years Ago," Barry Carter, NJ Advance Media, https://www.nj.com/essex/2018/04/newark_reflects_on_dr _kings_visit_50_years_ago_car.html, posted April 1, 2018. Mal quoted from MG and Ramey, "Notes for an autobiography."

75. "Vietnam War," The Martin Luther King, Jr. Research and Education Institute, Stanford University, https://kinginstitute.stanford.edu/encyclopedia/vietnam-war. See also "Dr. Martin Luther King: Beyond Vietnam and Remaining Awake through a Great Revolution," 90th Cong., 2nd sess., *Congressional Record* 114 (April 9, 1968): 9391–97; Branch, *At Canaan's Edge*, 745–46; Martin Luther King Jr., "Showdown for Non-Violence," *Look*, April 16, 1968, 23–25.

76. MG, "There Can Be Peace," speech to the Foreign Affairs Council of Reading and Berks County, Reading, PA, 1968, folder 344, MG Papers.

77. Branch, *At Canaan's Edge*, 666.

78. "Final Words: Cronkite's Vietnam Commentary," NPR, July 18, 2009, https://www.npr.org/2009/07/18/106775685/final-words-cronkites-vietnam-commentary.

79. Branch, *At Canaan's Edge*, 704–5.

80. Lyndon Johnson, March 31, 1968, audio of nationally televised remarks, The Miller Center, University of Virginia; https://millercenter.org/the-presidency/presidential-speeches/march-31-1968-remarks-decision-not-seek-re-election; Branch, *At Canaan's Edge*, 748–49.

81. Dr. Martin Luther King Jr., "I've Been to the Mountaintop," https://www.afscme.org/union/history/mlk/ive-been-to-the-mountaintop-by-dr-martin-luther-king-jr; Branch, *At Canaan's Edge*, 756–58.

CHAPTER 11: AND THEN MARTIN

1. MG and Ramey, "Notes for an autobiography." Unless otherwise noted, all MG quotes telling this story are from this manuscript.

2. See also "Remembering MLK's Impact in Pittsburgh," *Pittsburgh Post-Gazette*, January 21, 2019; "The Rev. Dr. Martin Luther King in Pittsburgh," January 21, 2013.

3. Hunter Street was renamed Martin Luther King Jr. Drive after his death.

4. William Grimes, "Marlene Sanders, Pathbreaking TV Journalist, Dies at 84," *New York Times*, July 15, 2015.

5. Marlene Sanders to Jannette L. Dates and Lee Thompson, May 23, 1984, family collection.

6. DVD of Mal Goode stories, courtesy of Roberta Goode.

7. DVD of Mal Goode stories, courtesy of Roberta Goode.

8. Douglas Martin, "Bob Teague, WNBC Reporter Who Helped Integrate TV News, Is Dead at 84," *New York Times*, March 28, 2013.

9. Notes from "Mal Goode at Atlanta, Georgia, April 9, 1968," in folder 253, MG Papers.

10. "Mal Goode at Atlanta, Georgia."

11. "Mal Goode at Atlanta, Georgia."

12. "Mal Goode at Atlanta, Georgia."

13. "Mal Goode at Atlanta, Georgia." See also "Mays, Benjamin Elijah," the Martin Luther King Jr. Research and Education Institute, Stanford University, https://kinginstitute.stanford.edu/encyclopedia/mays-benjamin-elijah.

14. "Mal Goode at Atlanta, Georgia."

15. "Mal Goode at Atlanta, Georgia."

16. "Mal Goode at Atlanta, Georgia."

17. Andrew Young, interview, October 31, 2019, Atlanta, Georgia (hereafter cited as Young, interview).

18. Jules Tygiel, *Baseball's Great Experiment: Jackie Robinson and His Legacy* (New York: Vintage Books, 1973), 66.

19. Rosalia Parker, interview, December 11, 2022. See also MG to Leonard Goldenson, chairman of board, ABC, May 21, 1973, folder 290, MG Papers.

20. MG to Leonard Goldenson, Chairman of Board, May 21, 1973.

21. Andrew Young, *An Easy Burden: The Civil Rights Movement and the Transformation of America* (New York: HarperCollins, 1996), 479–80, 443.

22. Young, interview. Her name was then Marian Wright. In 1968, after marrying Peter Edelman, then a legislative assistant to Senator Robert Kennedy, she became Marian Wright Edelman.

23. William Chafe, *The Unfinished Journey: America since World War II* (New York: Oxford University Press, 1995), 242.

24. Young, interview.

25. Young, *Easy Burden*, 443. See also Marian Wright Edelman, "Revisiting Marks, Mississippi," Child Watch Column, March 25, 2011, https://www.childrensdefense.org/child-watch-columns/health/2011/revisiting-marks-mississippi.

26. Erik Ortiz, "Fifty Years after the Poor People's Campaign," June 22, 2018, https://www.nbcnews.com/news/nbcblk/fifty-years-after-poor-people-s-campaign-america-s-once-n885451. See also Debbie Elliott, "How a Mule Train from Marks, Miss., Kicked Off MLK's Poor People Campaign," May 13, 2018, https://www.npr.org/2018/05/13/610097454/how-a-mule-train-from-marks-miss-kicked-off-mlks-poor-people-campaign; Jerry Mitchell, "MLK's Poor People's Campaign Continues 50 Years Later," *Clarion Ledger*, February 12, 2018; Adam Gabbatt, "Fifty Years On, the Mississippi Town that Sparked Dr King's Poverty Fight," https://www.theguardian.com/us-news/2018/jun/23/poor-peoples-campaign-washington-dr-king-mississippi.

27. Young, *Easy Burden*, 480.

28. King quoted from "Poverty," National Civil Rights Museum, https://www.civilrightsmuseum.org/poverty.

29. Reverend Ralph Abernathy from notes in folder 288, MG Papers.

30. Young, interview.

31. Roy Reed, "Alabama Police Use Gas and Clubs to Rout Negroes," *New York Times*, March 8, 1965.

32. Colleen Shogan, "'We Shall Overcome': Lyndon Johnson and the 1965 Voting Rights Act," https://www.whitehousehistory.org/we-shall-overcome-lbj-voting-rights.

33. Martin Luther King Jr., "Our God Is Marching On," March 25, 1965, Montgomery, Alabama, Address at the Conclusion of the Selma to Montgomery March, https://kinginstitute.stanford.edu/our-god-marching.

34. Lyndon B. Johnson, "Remarks in the Capitol Rotunda at the Signing of the Voting Rights Act," August 6, 1966, *Public Papers of the Presidents: Lyndon B. Johnson, 1965*, bk. 2, 1966; Lyndon B. Johnson, "Special Remarks to the Congress: The American Promise," March 15, 1965, in *Public Papers of the Presidents: Lyndon B. Johnson, 1965*, bk. 1, 1966; Lyndon B. Johnson, "Statement by the President on the Situation in Selma, Alabama," March 9, 1965, in *Public Papers of the Presidents: Lyndon B. Johnson, 1965*, bk. 1, 1966; cited in "Selma to Montgomery March," The Martin Luther King Jr. Research and Education Institute, Stanford University; https://kinginstitute.stanford.edu/encyclopedia/selma-montgomery-march.

35. MG to Joe L. Brown, May 22, 1968, folder 77, MG Papers.

36. DVD of newsclips and footage from his time at ABC, courtesy of Roberta Goode.

37. DVD of newsclips and footage from his time at ABC, courtesy of Roberta Goode.

38. DVD of newsclips and footage from his time at ABC, courtesy of Roberta Goode.

39. DVD of newsclips and footage from his time at ABC, courtesy of Roberta Goode.

40. Young, interview. See also Gerald McKnight, *The Last Crusade: Martin Luther King, Jr., the FBI, and the Poor People's Campaign* (Boulder, CO: Westview Press, 1998), 122–23.

41. Young, interview.

42. Young, *Easy Burden*, 485–86; Young, interview.

43. Nick Kirkpatrick and Katie Mettler, "Reflecting on RFK's 200-Mile Funeral Train," *Washington Post*, June 1, 2108; Louis Menand, "Robert Kennedy's Funeral Train Fifty Years Later, *New Yorker*, April 3, 2018.

44. Helen Wright to MG, June 7, 1968, folder 57, MG Papers.

45. Dr. B. K. Jackson to MG, June 7, 1968, Walter Pfister to Ruth White, May 14, 1968, folder 57, MG Papers.

46. Young, interview; Young, *Easy Burden*, 480.

47. Young, *Easy Burden*, 483.

48. Young, interview.

49. DVD of newsclips and footage from his time at ABC, courtesy of Roberta Goode.

50. MG and Ramey, "Notes for an autobiography."

51. Edelman quoted from Elliot, "Mule Train from Marks, Miss." In 1973 Edelman, the catalyst to the Poor People's Campaign, founded the Children's Defense Fund to advocate for poor children.

52. MG quoted from notes in folder 288, MG Papers; last quote from DVD of newsclips and footage from his time at ABC, courtesy of Roberta Goode.

53. Harry Edwards, *The Revolt of the Black Athlete: 50th Anniversary Edition* (Melton: University of Illinois Press, 2017), Appendix E,153.

54. Jackie Robinson quoted from Henry Aaron with Lonnie Wheeler, *I Had A Hammer: The Hank Aaron Story* (New York: HarperCollins, 1991), 194.

55. Andrew Maraniss, "The Mexico City Olympics and the Media," *The Undefeated*, October 15, 2018.

56. These ABC news clips from October 17 and 18, 1968, can be accessed on Youtube, https://www.youtube.com/watch?v=1ZttN9hPvx4, and https://www.youtube.com/watch?v=fEg3uNqsTYQ.

57. ABC reports of news stories, including the meeting of the Loyal Democrats of Mississippi, Jackson, on August 12, 1968, and events in October 1968, folder 288, MG Papers.

Chapter 12: Telling It Like It Is

1. Mal Goode, "A Perspective on 1969," ABC Radio Commentary (n.d.), folder 288, MG Papers.

2. MG quoted from Hazel Garland, "Video Vignettes," *Pittsburgh Courier*, December 14, 1968, 13.

3. "Mal Goode Speech," *Valley Dispatch News*, October 5, 1970, marking the fortieth anniversary of the Alle-Kiski NAACP chapter.

4. "Mal Goode Speech," *Valley Dispatch News*, October 5, 1970.

5. MG quoted from *Akron Beacon Journal*, May 26, 1969.

6. Millicent Massey and Doris McMillan, *Pioneer of Color: A Conversation with Mal Goode*, WHMM-TV, Howard University Public Television, prod. Millicent Massey, dir. Mary Lawrence, 1992.

7. Massey and Doris McMillan, *Pioneer of Color.*

8. Ronald Bayor, "Ivan Allen Jr. Biography: Mayor William B. Hartsfield," Ivan Allen Jr. Digital Collection, Georgia Tech, https://ivanallen.iac.gatech.edu/biography/mayor-william-hartsfield. See also International Civil Rights Walk of Fame, Martin Luther King Jr. National Historic Site, https://www.nps.gov/features/malu/feat0002/wof/Ivan_Allen.htm.

9. MG, *It Can Be Done*, documentary film in the *Time for Americans* series, by Stephen Fleischman, Arthur Holch, Mal Goode (host, reporter), ABC News, ABC Television Network, Peabody Collection African-American History and Culture Programs, ABC News, New York, July 3, 1969. (Unless otherwise noted, all quotes in the following section are taken from this documentary.)

10. Robert Thomas Jr., "Calvin F. Craig, 64, Enigma In Klan and Civil Rights Work," *New York Times*, April 24, 1998. Craig did an about-face a few years later and sought to revive the KKK in Georgia, before later resigning a second time.

11. MG, *It Can Be Done*, documentary.

12. Maria Saporta, "Civil Rights Icon Xernona Clayton's Unlikely Friendship with a KKK Grand Dragon," *Atlanta Magazine*, May 1, 2011.

13. MG, *It Can Be Done*, documentary. (Again all quotes in this section are from here unless noted otherwise.)

14. Angela Tuck and Ernie Suggs, "Lonnie King and Atlanta Student Movement Changed Atlanta and U. S.," *AJC*, March 5, 2019.

15. MG, *It Can Be Done*, documentary.

16. MG, *It Can Be Done*, documentary.

17. ABC press release, June 19, 1969 re: July 3, 10–11 PM EST, showing of *It Can Be Done*, ABC News.

18. MG in Doris McMillon, *Pioneer of Color: A Conversation with Mal Goode* (1991), VHS tape, authors' possession. Henry Ford to MG, July 16, 1969, folder 251, MG Papers. MG, "Notes for an Autobiography."

19. MG to Ernest Pharr, July 1969, folder 251, MG Papers.

20. MG, *It Can Be Done*, documentary. See also "Network Touts Racial Gains in Atlanta," newspaper clipping, document 54, folder 17, box 3, Ivan Allen Mayoral Records, Georgia Tech, http://allenarchive-dev.iac.gatech.edu/items/show/1501.

21. Mary Frances Perry to MG (no date), and MG to Perry, folder 61, MG Papers.

22. A. H. Galloway, RJ Reynolds president, to MG, April 2, 1970, folder 71, MG Papers.

23. MG to Mr. Marshall Bass at RJR, May 13, 1970, folder 73, MG Papers.

24. Lisbeth Iglesias-Rios and Mark Parascandola, "A Historical Review of R. J. Reynolds' Strategies for Marketing Tobacco to Hispanics in the United States," *American Journal of Public Health* 103, no. 5 (May 2013): e15–e27, published online, May 2013, doi:10.2105/AJPH.2013.301256, also https://www.ncbi.nlm.nih.gov/pmc/articles/PMC3698830; Vernellia R. Randall, "Targetting of African Americans," on the website Race, Health Care and the Law: Speaking Truth to Power, https://academic.udayton.edu/health/01status/smoking/tobacco6.htm.

25. "The Black Manifesto at The Riverside Church," https://www.trcnyc.org/black-manifesto; "Jim Forman Delivers Black Manifesto at Riverside Church," Digital SNCC

Gateway, https://snccdigital.org/events/jim-forman-delivers-black-manifesto-at-riverside-church.

26. "Elfreda" to MG, May 31, 1969, folder 61, MG Papers.

27. MG, memo to Syd Byrnes, "The Racial Crisis in Erie," February 25, 1970, folder 288, MG Papers. See also *Emergency School Aid Act of 1970: Hearings on H.R. 17846 and Related Bills, Before the General Subcomm. on Education and Labor*, 91st Cong. (1970). SPONGE was also referred to as "Students for the Prevention of Niggers Getting Everything."

28. Rob Ruck, Maggie Jones Patterson, and Michael P. Weber, *Rooney: A Sporting Life* (Lincoln: University of Nebraska Press, 2010), 374–75.

29. ABC News script, October 23, 1969, folder 288, MG Papers. See also Chris Barton, "The Power of the panther," nzherald.co.nz, August 21, 2009, https://www.nzherald.co.nz/entertainment/the-power-of-the-panther.

30. MG quoted from *Columbus Dispatch*, March 19, 1971.

31. MG quoted from Steve Crosby, *Savannah Morning News*, May 11, 1973.

32. MG to Governor Linwood Holton, Virginia, January 27, 1970, folder 69, MG Papers.

33. Robert B. Semple Jr., "The New U.S. Ambassador to Sweden," *New York Times*, January 13, 1970; Joan Cook, "Jerome Holland, Former U.S. Envoy," *New York Times*, January 14, 1975.

34. Jerome Holland to MG, January 14, 1972, folder 87, MG Papers.

35. MG to Holland, January 20, 1972, folder 87, MG Papers.

36. MG to Holland, January 20, 1972.

37. John Guthrie, US Information Service Field, message dated March 14, 1972, folder 88, MG Papers.

38. Guthrie, USIS memo, March 14, 1972.

39. Guthrie, USIS memo, March 14, 1972.

40. Guthrie, USIS memo, March 14, 1972.

41. Guthrie, USIS memo, March 14, 1972. There is a USIS memo (field message 84), signed by Patrick E. Nieburg, undated, that includes the entire text of the student resolution.

42. MG to Per-Ake Walton, March 28, 1972, folder 88, MG Papers.

43. Patrick Nieburg, public affairs officer, USIS, field message, subject: The Goode Incident, March 24, 1972, folder 88, MG Papers.

44. Erin Wright, "Reviving 'Lost Southern Voices' at Georgia State University," March 21, 2018, https://www.wabe.org/reviving-lost-southern-voices-georgia-state-university.

45. Sherman Adams to Tom O'Brien at ABC, October 1972, folder 89, MG Papers.

46. Jerome Holland to Leonard Goldenson, president of ABC, March 23, 1972, folder 88, MG Papers.

47. MG to Sherman Adams, October 1972, folder 89, MG Papers. See also Sherman Adams, "The Case of Mr. Goode and Ambassador Holland," *Gothenburg Post*, March 3, 1972, in which he calls MG "a black bourgeois propergandist [*sic*]" and the *Courier* a very conservative Negro Newspaper; copy in folder 89, MG Papers.

48. DVD of Mal Goode's retirement affair, 1973, audio tape 66 in MG Papers. (All following quotes are taken from this DVD.)

CHAPTER 13: THE LION IN WINTER

1. David Snell telephone interview, July 29, 2019.

2. Gerald D. Jaynes, ed., *Encyclopedia of African American Society* (Thousand Oaks, CA: Sage Publications, 2005), 581–82.

3. MG quoted from "Grandson of Slaves Heads UN. Correspondents," *World Peace* 3, no. 2 (February 1972), folder 291, MG Papers.

4. Mal stayed at NBN until it was acquired by the Pittsburgh-based Sheridan Broadcasting Network (SBN) and the two merged to become the American Urban Radio Networks in 1991.

5. Leonard Reed, "Goode: Changes," *The Record*, January 3, 1988.

6. Reed, "Goode: Changes."

7. "Opposition to Apartheid," https://www.britannica.com/topic/apartheid/Opposition-to-apartheid.

8. "Opposition to Apartheid."

9. MG to Charles Mathias, May 30, 1985, folder 152, MG Papers. See also Terry Atlas, "Senators Act to Pinch South Africa's Economy," *Chicago Tribune*, June 5, 1985.

10. MG to Jeremiah Denton, September 17, 1985, folder 154, MG Papers. Jerry Falwell, a Baptist pastor and conservative activist, founded Liberty University and cofounded the right-wing evangelical organization The Moral Majority.

11. Reginald G. Damerell, *Triumph in a White Suburb: The Dramatic Story of Teaneck, N.J., the First Town in the Nation to Vote for Integrated Schools* (New York: W. Morrow, 1968).

12. Hazel Garland, "Pioneer Broadcaster Mary 'Dee' Leaves a Legacy," *Pittsburgh Courier*, April 4, 1964.

13. Garland, "Pioneer Broadcaster Mary 'Dee'."

14. Rosalia Parker, interview, June 9, 2021. See also Roberta Wilburn and Ronald Goode, interviews, June 9, 2021, Pittsburgh.

15. Rosalia Parker, interview, January 23, 2023; Rosalia Parker, email correspondence, March 1, 2023. "Brenda Becton, Karen Bethea-Shields, and Evelyn Omega Cannon are the first Black women to attend Duke Law School," September 1974, https://spotlight.duke.edu/50years/timeline-2.

16. "Teaneck, N.J., Called Model of Democracy," *N.Y. Herald Tribune*, 1961 (exact date unknown).

17. Rachel Mark, "Reputation and Reality in America's Model Town: Remembering Racial Integration in Teaneck, New Jersey, 1949–1968" (senior thesis, Columbia University, April 4, 2011), 16, 63.

18. Ronald Goode, interview, January 20, 2023, Pittsburgh; see also Rosalia Parker, Roberta Wilburn, interviews, January 20, 2023, Pittsburgh.

19. Rosalia Parker, telephone interview, February 16, 2023.

20. Rosalia Parker, Roberta Wilburn, interviews, January 20, 2023, Pittsburgh.

21. Ronald Goode, Rosalia Parker, and Roberta Goode Wilburn interview, June 9, 2021, Pittsburgh.

22. Snell interview, July 25, 2019.

23. Snell interview, July 25, 2019.

24. Snell interview, July 25, 2019.

25. Snell interview, July 25, 2019.

26. Tim Grant, "Obituary: Robert R. Lavelle," *Pittsburgh Post-Gazette*, July 6, 2010.

27. Adah Lavelle, interview, January 26, 2016, Pittsburgh.

28. Christee Goode Laster, telephone interview, January 25, 2023.

29. Randy Wilburn, interview, December 15, 2018, Pittsburgh.

30. Troy Goode, telephone interview, January 26, 2023.

31. Christee Goode Laster, telephone interview, Troy Goode, telephone interview, January 26, 2023.

32. Douglas Martin, "James E. Cheek, Forceful University President Dies at 77," *New York Times*, January 21, 2010.

33. MG speech, "A Place to Stand," folder 340, MG Papers; MG, interview with Clifton B. Cox, October 24, 1984, transcribed by Jackie Kinney (hereafter cited as MG interview), https://archive.teanecklibrary.org/OralHistory2/goode.html.

34. Theodora Lacey, Zoom interview, July 12, 2021. See also Melanie Eversley, "For King's Good Friend, 'The Struggle Continues,'" *USA Today*, August 19, 2013; Monsy Alvarado, "Recalling the Fight for Civil Rights, a Pioneer Reflects on Progress in North Jersey," NorthJersey.com, https://www.northjersey.com/story/archive/2020/02/03/theodora-smiley-lacey-civil-rights-pioneer-weighs-nj-progress/4610580002.

35. Lacey, Zoom interview, July 12, 2021.

36. Lacey, Zoom interview, July 12, 2021

37. Tom Doran, "A Potential Was Tapped," *Miami Herald*, May 27, 1973.

38. MG quoted in "Goode Sees Little Progress in Pittsburgh," *Pittsburgh Courier*, July 12, 1975.

39. MG quoted from "Goode Sees Little Progress in Pittsburgh," *Pittsburgh Courier*, July 12, 1975.

40. MG quoted from Eileen Peterson, *Register-Star, Rockford, IL*, November 16, 1975.

41. MG interview.

42. MG interview.

43. MG interview.

44. MG interview.

45. MG interview.

46. MG interview. See also Tricia Duffy, "Malvin R. Goode: Soldier for Equality," *Bergen Record*, March 31, 1981.

47. MG interview.

48. MG to Jimmy Carter, July 19, 1979, folder 213, MG Papers.

49. MG to George Bush, November 5, 1980, folder 213, MG Papers.

50. Undated radio commentary script, folder 300, MG Papers.

51. MG quoted from Leonard Reed, "Goode: Changes," *The Record*, January 3, 1988.

52. MG, undated speeches, "Here We Go Again" and "I Knew MLK, Jr.," MG Papers.

53. MG quoted from Tom Doran, "A Potential Was Tapped," *Miami Herald*, May 27, 1973.

54. MG to Daniel Moynihan, no specific date, 1984, folder 147, and MG to Arlen Spector, January 7, 1985, folder 154, MG Papers.

55. MG to George Will, June 14, 1985, folder 153, MG Papers.

56. MG to Clarence Thomas, March 14, 1985, folder 176, MG Papers.

57. MG to Thomas, March 14, 1985.

58. MG to Thomas, May 15, 1985, MG Papers.

59. Susan Baer, "Carl Rowan's New Reality," *Baltimore Sun*, February 14, 1991.

60. Paul Hendrickson, "Carl Rowan, Roaring Back," *Washington Post*, January 9, 1991.

61. MG to Carl Rowan, March 18, 1991, folder 95, MG Papers. In 1961, Rowan became the highest-ranking Black American in the State Department. He later served as ambassador to Finland and the director of the US Information Agency.

62. Violet Anderson to MG, May 7, 1980, and MG to Violet Anderson, May 16, 1980, folder 135, MG Papers.

63. MG to Mickey Rivers, July 31, 1979, folder 128, MG Papers.

64. MG to OJ Simpson September 27, 1984, folder 148, MG Papers.

65. MG to Pete Rozelle, January 25, 1980, folder 132, MG Papers.

66. MG to Roone Arledge, January 14, 1980, folder 132, MG Papers.

67. MG to Leonard Goldenson, 1980, MG Papers.

68. MG quoted from Starla Vaughns, "Interview with Mal Goode," *Miami Times*, February 20, 1986, 2.

Aftermath

1. RTDNA was renamed the Radio-Television Digital News Association in 2010.

2. CPAN video, Panel on newswriting, September 3, 1987, https://www.c-span.org/video/?151081-1/newswriting.

3. CPAN video, Panel on newswriting.

4. CPAN video, Panel on newswriting. See also Leonard Reed, "A Portrait: Mal Goode," *Bergen Record*, January 3, 1988.

5. Desk Diary, 1990, in possession of Goode family. Unless otherwise noted, following quotes are from this diary.

6. Robert Hanley, "Officer Kills Teen-Age Boy in Teaneck," *New York Times*, April 11, 1990.

7. Ronald Goode, Rosalia Parker, and Roberta Goode Wilburn, interview, June 9, 2021, Pittsburgh.

8. Sharon Goode, interview, July 25, 2016, Pittsburgh.

9. Bolden quoted from Sandy Hamm, "Pioneer Journalist, Activist Dead at 87," *Pittsburgh Courier*, September 16, 1995.

10. Jennings quoted from Dennis Hevesi, "Malvin R. Goode, 87, Reporter Who Broke a TV Color Barrier," *New York Times*, September 15, 1995.

11. George Strait quoted from Hevesi, "Malvin R. Goode, 87."

12. Bernard Shaw quoted from Matthew Smith, "Malvin Goode: Rights Activist, Pioneer Journalist," *Pittsburgh Post-Gazette*, September 14, 1995.

13. Lou Cioffi and Aaron quoted from Smith, "Malvin Goode."

14. David Snell, telephone interview, July 25, 2019.

15. Rosalia Parker, telephone conversations, February 5, 2023.

16. Mary Louise Lavelle Goode funeral program, folder 408, MG Papers.

INDEX

Note: Page references in *italics* refer to figures.

Fenderson, Louis, 75, 80, 97
Fitch, John, 430n24
Fix, Lester, 92
Fletcher, John, 312
Flowers, Richard, 274
Folly Mills, 26
Ford, Henry, 349
Forman, James, 352
Frazier, E. Franklin, 296
Frederick, Pauline, 177, 341, 437n8
Freedmen's Bureau, 30, 39, 53, 428n72
Freedom Jubilee, 158, 159, 161
Freedom Riders, 11, 159–60
Freeland, Wendell, 150
Frick, Henry Clay, 70
Friendly Rivalry Often Generates Success (FROGS), 51
FROGS. *See* Friendly Rivalry Often Generates Success

Galloway, A. H., 351
Garland, Hazel, 372, 434n29
Garland, Phyl, 159
Garrow, David, 390–91
Garvey, Marcus, 213–14, 249
Gettysburg battle (1863), 29
Giancana, Sam, 201
Gibson, Josh, 108, 121
Gillespie, Dizzy, 115
Gilliam, Dorothy Butler, 14
Glasco, Laurence, 61, 109, 129, 156
Glass, Carter, 35
Gloster, Hugh, 317
Godwin, Kimberly, 19
Goldenson, Leonard, 319, 361, 393
Goldston, James, 18
Goldwater, Barry, 234, 235, 239, 242
Gone with the Wind, 296, 343
Goode, Bill Jr. *See* Goode, William Jr.
Goode, Bob. *See* Goode, Robert
Goode, Christee, 379, 380
Goode, Elizabeth, 37
Goode, James, 85
Goode, John C., 36–38
Goode, Malvin Russell, Jr. *See* Goode, Russell
Goode, Mary Dee, 8, 69, 135–37, 156, *168*, 372–73

Goode, Mary Hunter, 6, 9, 10, 21–22, 47, 57, 69, 425n31; Baptist affiliation in Homestead, 30; empowerment from slavery, 31–33; experiencing slavery in Shenandoah Valley, 23; teaching in Homestead and Pittsburgh classrooms, 63; expectations of children, 75–76
Goode, Mary Lavelle, 7–8, 74, 79, 93–97, 100–101, 113, 122, 144, 154–55, *163*, *166*, 182, 223–25, 371–72, 409; jobs, 378; death of, 414–15; family life in Teaneck and Pittsburgh, 374–77, 379–80; high school portrait, *165*; legacy of, 415–16; living at Folly Farm, 428n80; with Malvin Goode, *166*, *402*; photograph on wedding day, *167*; photograph with family members, *172*
Goode, Richard, 113, 122, 154, *172*, 182, 224, *308*, *308*, 412, 413–14, *414*
Goode, Robert, 51, 113, 122, 144, 150, *172*, 192, 199, 224, 249, 295, *304*, *308*, 401
Goode, Roberta, 113, 122, 144, 153, *172*, 182, 224, *308*, 374, 379, 412, 414
Goode, Ronald, 113, *172*, 224, *308*, 373
Goode, Ronnie. *See* Goode, Ronald
Goode, Rosalia, 113, 153, *171*, *172*, 224, 247, *308*, 373, 374, 411
Goode, Russell, 113, 122, *172*, 185–86, 192, 199, 224, 247, 285, *308*, 293, 2
Goode, Troy, 381
Goode, Walter Emory James, 113
Goode, Ruth, 69, 93, 411, 412
Goode, Sara Jane, 409
Goode, Sharon, 412, 428n79
Goode, Thomas, 36, 37–38, 41, 43–47
Goode, Troy, 380–81
Goode, William, 6, 21–22, 23–24, 36, 40, 42, 44, 62–63, 74, 85, 91–92, 100, 122, 412; accident in steelwork, 58–59; characteristics, 66–67; family history, 57–58; migration, 47; expectations of children, 75–76; religious beliefs, 68–72; steelwork in Homestead, 52–57; in Tredegar Iron Works, 45–46; work in tobacco factory, 45
Graber, Elmer, 91
gradualism, 160
Grant, Ulysses, 28

www.ingramcontent.com/pod-product-compliance
Lightning Source LLC
Chambersburg PA
CBHW020329030425
24532CB00002B/49